ADMINISTERING DISTRICT PLANS IN INDIA

By the same author

Quit India Movement in Bengal, 1994
Indian Politics at the Crossroads (ed.), 1998

About the Author

Anil Kumar Jana, an M.A, LL.B., M.Phil. and Ph.D., currently heads the Department of Political Science with Rural Administration, Vidyasagar University, West Bengal. He is also the editor of *Samaj Jijnasa*, a journal of social sciences in Bengali, and Founder Secretary and Director of the Vidyasagar Centre for Social Sciences, Midnapore.

Dr. Jana has authored a book titled *Quit India Movement in Bengal*. He has also edited *Indian Politics at the Crossroads*. He has published many research papers in national and international journals of repute.

ADMINISTERING DISTRICT PLANS IN INDIA

Issues, Constraints and Choices

ANIL KUMAR JANA

Department of Political Science with Rural Administration
Vidyasagar University, West Bengal

CONCEPT PUBLISHING COMPANY, NEW DELHI-110059

ISBN-81-8069-081-4

First Published 2004

Published and Printed by
Ashok Kumar Mittal
Concept Publishing Company
A/15-16, Commercial Block, Mohan Garden
NEW DELHI-110059 (India)

Phones : 25351460, 25351794
Fax : 0091-11-25357103
E-mail : publishing@conceptpub.com

Dedicated to the

Friends at the University

who taught me to view things differently

PREFACE AND ACKNOWLEDGEMENTS

The constitutional recognition of the multi-level character of planning in a federal polity like ours is a major step wherein all of us have become planners. Quite obviously, now the issue is no longer whether to plan, but how to plan. Hence the sharp detachment between formulation and implementation of plans, hitherto followed in India, ceases to exist in the changed scenario. Planning of plan implementation has become an inescapable step in a meaningful endeavour of planning practices. The objective of this book is to highlight both the issues in an organized manner within an integrated social science perspective.

With this objective in the backdrop, this book attempts a critical review of the state of decentralized district planning in India with its major focus on the administrative arrangements for district planning. The issues discussed in this volume are of crucial importance and must be addressed once we are committed to the policy of decentralization in development and planning. The analysis in this book is quite simple and non-technical; a clutch of issues involved in planning have been raised and examined in a readily understandable language in order to reach a wider readership than that of the economists, administrators and specialists. It is expected that the book will reach those involved in formulation and implementation of policies at the field level.

The idea of taking up such an area of academic interest emerged sometime in the middle of eighties when I was personally involved as an activist in the formulation and implementation of village plans in a southern most block of West Bengal. Prior to that I had the rare opportunity to exchange views on the issues of rural development and planning with late Binoy Krishna Choudhury (Minister of Land, Land Reforms and Panchayats, WB) and late Satyabrata Sen (Chairman of the State Finance Commission, WB, afterwards), the two celebrities of the alternative development model, who helped me to develop an objective framework for understanding the issues of development. Subsequently, I had the occasions to interact over the issues of planning with Shri Ajit Narayan Bose, a formerly Professor of IIT, Kharagpur, and an activist who had been championing the cause of people's planning since the eighties. In fact, I have been benefited a lot through my interactions with the three in demystifying the concept of planning without which, I apprehend, I could miss the relish in research. My teacher Professor Mohit Bhattacharya, Centenary Professor of Public Administration at the University of Calcutta and formerly Vice-Chancellor of the University of Burdwan (West Bengal), who has been a constant source of inspiration and motivation for me since the eighties, has supervised my studies in spite of his busy schedule. His kindness and support were indispensable for completion of the work. I find no words to express my feeling of gratitude and respect for these kind and noted personalities.

The support of a good number of academics and institutions has been vital in the preparation of this book. Professor Asok Kumar Mukhopadhyay, Professor Keshab Chaudhuri, Professor Rakhahari Chatterjee and Professor Prabhat Datt of the Department of Political Science, University of Calcutta encouraged the work from the very beginning and suggested various improvements for its enrichment for which they deserve the most special thanks. I am also heavily indebted to some of my esteemed colleagues, friends and former students at the university and friends outside without whose encouragement, help and assistance the publication of this book would not have materialized. Though they had no hand in the shortcomings, the final shape is better for their help. But I dare not record formal thanks of mine obviously for two reasons: conveying mere thanks may belittle their contributions and, I am afraid, there may be exclusions since the list may be a long one.

The library, the librarians and the members of the staff of the Central Libraries of the University of Calcutta, Vidyasagar University, National Library (Calcutta), Indian Institute of Public Administration Library (New Delhi), West Bengal Assembly Library, State Library (West Bengal) proved extremely helpful for the work. Thanks are also due to the persons interviewed, the authors acknowledged in Notes and References, the officials and functionaries of the District Administration, Zilla Parishad, District Planning Cell, different panchayat bodies, the State Secretariats (Karnataka, Kerala and West Bengal) for extending all sorts of help and information in the related field. I am grateful to the authorities of the University of Calcutta for awarding the degree of Doctor of Philosophy to me for the original work. I also wish to acknowledge the helpful support of the university authorities and the UGC for funding the research project.

I also wish to acknowledge the helpful support and interest of Mr. Ashok Mittal of the Concept Publishing Company, New Delhi and also of Mr. S.P. Sinha, who worked with this book from the initial review process to its publication.

The love and affection of the members of my family has always been a sustaining force in my efforts. They deserve my sincere thanks. During the entire period of my research, our only son Anindya was deprived of my affection and company, which pains me a lot. My wife Krishna has been all along with me providing encouragement and support ever since the days when this book was no more than a gleam in the eye. Her warmth and caring always ring in my heart.

Vidyasagar University ANIL KUMAR JANA

CONTENTS

LIST OF TABLES

LIST OF FIGURES

ABBREVIATIONS

ADM	Additional District Magistrate
AEP	Additional Employment Programme
ARC	Administrative Reforms Commission
BDO	Block Development Officer
BLCC	Block Level Co-ordination Committee
BMS	Basic Minimum Services
BPC	Block Planning Committee
BPCC	Block Planning Co-ordination Committee
CAARD	Committee to review the existing Administrative Arrangements for Rural Development and Poverty Alleviation Programmes
CADA	Comprehensive Area Development Authority
CADC	Comprehensive Area Development Corporation
CPI(M)	Communist Party of India (Marxist)
CSS	Centrally Sponsored Schemes
DDCC	District Development Consultation Council
DISNIC	District Information System under National Information Collection
DLCC	District Level Co-ordination Committee
DPAP	Drought Prone Areas Programme
DPCC	District Planning and Co-ordination Council
DPDC	District Planning and Development Council
DPF	District Plan (Schemes) Fund
DRDA	District Rural Development Agency
DUDA	District Urban Development Agency
EO	Executive Officer
GP	Gram Panchayat
HUDCO	Housing Urban Development Corporation
IRD	Integrated Rural Development
IRDP	Integrated Rural Development Programme
JRY	Jawahar Rozgar Yojana
KPR Act	Karnataka Panchayati Raj Act
MLA	Member of Legislative Assembly
MP	Member of Parliament
MT	Metric Tones
MWS	Million Wells Scheme
NDC	National Development Council
NGO	Non-Government Organization
NICNET	National Information Collection Network
NRDMS	National Resource Data Management System
PLC	Post-Literacy Centre
PRI	Panchayati Raj Institutions
PS	Panchayat Samiti
RDC	Rural Development Centre
SAE	Sub-Assistant Engineer
SC	Scheduled Caste
SCP	Special Component Plan
SPB	State Planning Board
ST	Scheduled Tribe
TLC	Total Literacy Campaign
UBSP	Urban Basic Services for the Poor
VLW	Village Level Worker
ZP	Zilla Parishad

GLOSSARY

Abedan	Appeal
Abhijnata	Experience
Abong	And
Achiracharit	Non-conventional
Adhiniyam	Act
Adhyaksha	Chairman of the Zilla Parishad
Agradhikar	Priority
Anchal	Gram Panchayat (Previously)
Andolan	Movement
Aprachalita	Non-traditional
Arhar	A kind of pulse
Artha	Finance
Bon	Forest
Barga	Share
Bargadar	Share-cropper
Bhabana	Thoughts
Bhumi	Land
Bibartan	Evolution
Bidi	Country made cigerette
Bidyut	Electricity
Bikendribhuta	Decentralized
Boro	Winter paddy
Bundh	Small embankment
Chatal	Platform
Chuar	Uncivilized
Chetana	Consciousness
Chowkidar	Village watchman
Chllah	Woven
Dafadar	Village Police Personnel
Dwara	By
Galda	Prawn
Gram	Village
Grambasi	Villagers
Gram-bhittik	Village-based
Gramonnayan	Village-development
Gram-star	Village-level
Itihas	History
Jana	Masses
Janagan	People
Jijnasa	Enquiry
Janasasthya	Public health
Kachhe	Near
Kalyan	Welfare
Karmadhyaksha	Chairman of the Standing Committee
Karya	Work
Kayekti	A few

Kendra	Centre
Khadya	Food
Krira	Sports
Krisak	Peasant
Krishi	Agriculture
Kshetmajoor	Agricultural Labour
Kshetra	Sector
Kshudra	Small
Mandal	A tier in the PRI
Magur	A kind of local fish
Matsya	Fish
Medinipur	Midnapore
Nagar Unnayan	Urban Development
Nirdeshabali	Guidelines
Nirdeshika	Guidelines
Niyamabali	Regulations
Paddhati	Method
Paddhatigata	Methodological
Paik	Guards
Panchayat	Village Council
Panchayat Samiti	Block level tier of the PRIs
Para	A cluster of households
Paribahan	Transport
Paribesh	Environment
Parichalana	Management
Parichayika	Introductory
Parikalpana	Planning
Parishad	Council
Pashupalan	Animal keeping
Patta	Record
Pradhan	Chairman of the Gram Panchayat
Prakalpa	Project
Prani	Animal
Prasange	About
Pratichhabi	Reflection
Prayog	Application
Puran	Filling up
Purta	Public Works
Rachana	Formulation
Ruparekha	Outline
Sabha	Assembly
Sabhadhipati	Chairman of the Zilla Parishad
Sabhapati	Chairman of the Panchayat Samiti
Sadharan	General
Sahakari-Sabhapati	Vice-Chairman of the Panchayat Samiti
Sakti	Energy
Samaj	Society
Samannaya	Coordination

Samay Suchi	Time Schedule
Sambandhiya	Regarding
Samiksha	Survey
Samiti	Society/Assembly
Sansad	Council
Sanskar	Reform
Sanskriti	Culture
Sarbarah	Supplies
Sasthya	Health
Sech	Irrigation
Siksha	Education
Silpa	Industry
Sthayee	Standing
Tairi	Preparation
Talika	Schedule
Taluk	A tier in the PRI at block level
Tathyabali	Information
Theke	From
Tran	Relief
Unnayan	Development
Upadhyaksha	Vice Chairman of the Zilla Parishad
Upapradhan	Vice Chairman of the Gram Panchayat
Zamindar	Land Lord
Zela / Zella / Zilla	District
Zilla Parishad	The highest tier in the PRIs

1

INTRODUCTION

While there is much discussion on planning methods and the economics of planning, the administrative dimensions including decision-making process, choice of appropriate planning agencies for planning and implementation, monitoring and evaluation do not generally receive serious attention from the planners. Additionally people's participation in different stages of planning is considered axiomatic in contemporary planning thought. People did not figure very prominently in development planning in the past. But now planners have begun to think differently. 'Putting people first' in development programmes is now acknowledged as a major concern of the planners.[1] Guy Gran prefers to assign the role of an actor, not of a subject, to the individual 'who defines the goals, controls the resources and directs the processes affecting his or her life.'[2] The main objective of the people-centred approach is to locate 'people at the centre of power so that they may become the basic engine of the development process and not, as hitherto, merely its beneficiaries.'[3] Though the experiences in decentralization in most of the countries of the Third World do not exhibit a healthy trend and in most cases have 'fallen short of the expectations of the policy makers'[4] yet people's participation is now considered as a means of reinterpretation and reinforcement of democratic ethics.[5] A high degree of people's participation in the development programmes helps both the task of plan formulation and implementation. Moreover, it helps in developing a congenial socio-psychological environment that in turn strengthen the institutional base for launching and actualisation of development programmes. No plan can take off the ground without deciding about agencies, institutions, policies and their inter-connections. Programme formulation and mechanisms of programme implementation are separate steps in the process of planning. From the administrative point of view, a plan becomes ready for implementation when the selection of goals, programmes and agencies are decided, and resources are allocated to programmes and projects. Conceptually, it may be said that where the process of plan formulation ends, the process of plan implementation begins. This, of course, does not mean a division of these two aspects in water-tight compartments. There has to be a continuous interaction between the two. Planning is always a multi-actor activity, and as Professor Sukhamoy Chakravarty, the noted economist, has pointed out, "It is possible that plans did not work because the desired coordination of activities among different actors was faulty…."[6]

The process of economic development in India commenced with the launching of the First Five-Year Plan in 1952. Over the years, planning in India has lost a good deal of credibility and effectiveness because of, among other factors, the unsatisfactory performance of centralist planning.

There is a general agreement now that much of the failure in planning can be attributed to the gaps in the sphere of implementation, lack of cohesion among multiple actors and the constraints imposed by political, social and administrative factors. All these have led to a change in the strategy of planning from a highly centralized system to a decentralized one with emphasis on planning at the district level. One can identify three distinct phases of Indian planning: *one,* the first plan with its basic orientation towards 'national' development, *two,* the fourth plan with an orientation towards a search for a decentralized level, ultimately settling down at the District Level (this can be called the first step towards decentralized planning) *three,* the Constitutional Amendment in 1992 (73rd and 74th) further decentralizing the process treating the *gram sabha sansads* in panchayat areas and *wards* in municipal towns as micro-planning units with people's active participation.

At present the planning process in India involves a protracted decision-making process of interactions among a number of levels. Within the framework of a national perspective, plans are formulated at the central level over which the Central Government exercises control. Subsequently plans are formulated and implemented by the states and Union territories. Now there are the District Planning Committees in many states and the Panchayati Raj Institutions which are also engaged in the formulation and implementation of plans at their respective levels. Thus in course of evolution a new tier of planning at the district level has come into existence.

Prior to the Constitutional Amendments of 1992 and the enactment of subsequent state legislations, attempts towards district planning were backed by certain weak and loosely defined policy framework in terms of which district planning below the state level was sought to be regulated. The policy setting and the administrative arrangement were too weak to be able to deal with the inter-sectoral and inter-regional issues in a decentralized context in the absence of micro-macro interactions. The institutional innovation of the District Planning Committee to deal with (consolidation of plans prepared by the panchayats and municipalities and preparation of draft) development plans for the district has imposed some additional responsibilities for the policy makers. The constitutionally backed local self-governing institutions like the panchayats and municipalities (73rd and 74th Amendments) have marked a step in the direction of people's empowerment. The institution of *Gram Sabha Sansads* in the panchayats and *Ward Committees* in the municipalities which ensures people's participation is an arrangement that has yet to take full and active form. This study, besides examining the administrative infrastructure of district planning, attempts to analyse and understand the issues centred around the formulation, implementation and monitoring of district planning.

District Planning and Decentralized Planning

'Decentralization', in the context of planning, refers to the transfer of decision-making in respect of planning and administrative functions to the local and area level organizations. It involves the process of conferring powers and authority to the formally created area and local authorities. In this sense decentralization involves both the processes of decentralization and devolution.[7]

District planning is a type of area-planning below the state level where the district is identified as the unit or meeting point between the 'top-down' and 'bottom-up' processes.[8] At the district level, the grassroots or micro plans merge with the national plans and *vice versa.* District is the point below which centralist planning becomes irrelevant and above which micro plans become meaningless. Thus decentralized planning is a two-way process which starts both at the macro level (centre and state) and at the grassroots levels simultaneously. When these two processes converge at the district level, the decentralized district planning emerges.

Thus decentralized planning is not antithetic to national planning; rather it is complementary to it. The macro and the micro plans are mutually supportive of each other with clear demarcation of areas for attaining the wider goals and broader objectives set forth by the policy makers. The macro plan provides the broad outlines within which micro plans are formulated and implemented. On the contrary, micro plans supply the necessary inputs for setting up of objectives, priorities and strategies for macro plans. In fact decentralized plan is not locationally fixed at a particular level of planning. It takes a whole hierarchy of both central and local levels as its locus. For all practical purposes, district planning is not to be considered as synonymous with decentralized planning. Decentralized planning stands for a broader conceptual rubric within which district planning occupies a position of centrality. It may be noted that after the Constitutional Amendments (1992), the scheme of decentralized district planning has been institutionalised in India and now the concept of district planning is conceived in the context of decentralized planning carried out at different levels, symbolising an integrating focus of a family of sub-state planning units. In fact, there are now four distinct levels of planning in a district under the decentralized planning system : (a) Village or *Gram Sabha Sansad* level at the bottom; (b) Gram Panchayat level; (c) Block/Municipality level; and (d) District level. Each of the four tiers are provided with required autonomy and authority in its own domain of decision-making. It will be, therefore, contrary to the principles of decentralization if the decisions needed to be taken at the village level, is taken at the Gram Panchayat or Block level. Similarly, integration in the process will be jeopardised if the issues relating to the district level functioning are settled at the block or at the level below the block. Thus the planning process visualised through these Amendments is both diffused and well integrated.

Politics of Planning

Planning as discussed in this research is basically focused on the administrative infrastructure and institutional disposition at the sub-state level, considered as the locus of decentralized planning. It is not being suggested that the planning process is a depoliticised, mechanical and technical exercise. Planning involves conflicts at different levels and stages among the different actors participating in it. The centre, being in a hegemonic position in India, seeks to 'impose' planning from above, while the states have been clamouring for more resources and need-based planning, keeping in view their own order of regional priorities. Hence planning in India has been a conflict-prone platform where the two levels have often collided only to be resolved through some patchwork at the National Development Council level. Within the states, the politics of planning has been manifested in resource-competition among the different regions within the state. Also, the sub-state level local institutions compete for power and resources to bend 'planning' to their need-fulfilment. Again, there is an area of passive politics where the state's departments silently but decisively strive for resources with people's representative institutions. With the passage of Constitutional Amendments (1992), grassroots planning under the aegis of local self-governing bodies is now being legitimised. The new voices being raised by the people at the micro level are going to be, many a time, discordant and cacophonous. It will need a valiant and tactful effort to orchestrate all these forces, factors and actors. Planning will, thus, have to be more accommodating in nature rather than a cool, calculated, economic exercise.[9] Politics of planning has been discussed at some length in three seminal papers by Terence J. Byres, Partha Chatterjee and Deepak Nayyar.[10]

The other dimension of politics of planning is subsumed in the structuring of people's participation, so often advocated as a precondition and an objective of planning. The traditional literature in planning-thought occasionally refers to the needs of decentralization and people's participation in the process of planning. But the contemporary approach lays emphasis on the people as the critical centre in the total process. In this sense people's participation is not to be viewed as an instrument of administrative efficiency but as a preferred political objective for the development of the democratic system. People's participation is, in a vital sense, a political issue.[11] Participation aims at reducing power differences and ensuring power equalisation. Hence an attempt to achieve a meaningful level of participation may be problematic since the exercise may become the focus of power struggle.[12] Planning requires the intervention by the state through some institutional mechanisms. The structure of decision-making is shaped by the socio-political environment which also supplies the values, preferences and contents for it. The traditional approach considers planning as a neutral and value-free economic exercise engineered by the government. But planning is a tool of development, which can be used by both individuals and groups as well as by the state. Hence it is necessarily value-laden when it is in actual operation. It is guided by political considerations, apart from obvious economic and administrative considerations.

Political considerations become prominent in decentralized planning. Decentralization in essence is a political choice and hence policies of decentralization are essentially political strategies. Since decentralization itself is political in nature, decision-making in decentralized planning exercises obviously becomes a political issue.[13]

Review of Literature

There is a plethora of literature available on different aspects of planning in India. However, given the scope of the study, there is the need to confine oneself to the review of those literatures which directly deal with decentralized planning and more particularly with district planning. In addition to numerous public documents, reports and recommendations of various committees and commissions on decentralized planning, some major works in this field may be cited. Possibly, the pioneering analytical work on Indian Planning was by Hanson[14] which, even if dated (1966), contains considerable insights into the structure and process of planning in India.

Misra (1969)[15] in an edited volume covering different aspects of regional planning has highlighted the various dimensions of the subject. The work under review, perhaps the first of its kind, is divided into five parts including a variety of areas like concepts, techniques, policies and case studies. The collection is based on the assumption that regional planning cannot be reduced to partial and sectoral solutions and approaches based on allocative model of planning. The main thread which runs through the whole work is that regional planning could be used as a tool for creating a better environment for human development. As the title suggests, the study focuses on the conceptual and methodological issues in regional planning and does not specifically deal with the administrative problems. However, the volume contains some studies with particular reference to West Bengal which are helpful in the understanding of decentralized planning in macro perspectives.

Misra and Sundaram (1980)[16] carry over the arguments raised previously by Misra in favour of decentralized planning in the greater interest of fulfilling the local needs and attainment of local autonomy. The objectives set forth by Misra motivate the authors to outline the framework of planning for integrated rural development. To the authors, multi-level planning is an integrated area-based approach eminently suited to the decentralization of the planning process. The multi-level system represents a system approach to planning. An important dimension of the work relates to the highlighting of issues pertaining to administrative decentralization for rural development. While examining the administrative machinery for planning, they propose the creation of planning machinery at the local levels corresponding to the spatial levels of planning: district, block, *mandal* and village panchayats. The idea behind the proposed set-up is to enable the decision-making process to be pragmatic and quick and to have the planning personnel at the grassroots. The whole scheme in the work is intended to bring down the development efforts to the lowest levels of hierarchy for the optimum benefits of the people.

Inamdar and Kshire (1986)[17] in a study of two Panchayat Samitis in the district of Pune have examined the practice of district planning in Maharashtra from the points of view of popular participation, initiative and coordination among different agencies in the process of formulation, implementation and modification of district plans. In the study they have identified the weaknesses of the planning machinery at the district level and particularly in the urban areas. It is found that the role of the Panchayati Raj Institutions was negligible in the formulation of plans and was mainly confined to suggesting schemes and proposals for inclusion in the district plan. The study points out the weaknesses of the DPDC. The scope of popular participation, as they could observe, was confined to the process of implementation of plans only. The authors have also suggested policy formulations in some respects including the identification of the role of the Panchayati Raj Institutions specifically in plan formulation rather than in plan implementation. They have also stressed the need for improvements in the functioning of the DPDC, regular flow of funds, improvements in the scope of popular participation and the devolution of decision-making power to the district level to make the district planning exercise a real success.

The contribution made by Kamta Prasad (1988)[18] to the conceptual, methodological and organizational aspects of planning at the grassroots deserves special mention. The author while examining the slow progress in India's planning has put special emphasis on planning institutions and their functions at different micro levels below the state. The author also makes some policy recommendations for qualitative improvements in the decentralized planning process.

Arun Ghosh's writings (1989)[19] in the form of a travel diary throws light on the decentralised rural development planning activities in West Bengal in the wake of the launching of decentralised planning. The book is particularly useful for understanding planning below the district level. Moreover, it has got some direct relevance to Midnapore situation. The author has given a more concrete shape to his ideas in another contribution (1992)[20] in which he has developed a new approach to the problems of economic planning and development in India. With his firm belief in planning as the best way for achieving the objectives through utilisation of scarce resources, he proposes decentralization and debureaucratization of both the polity and the economic decision-making through financial and administrative devolution from the centre to the states and then from the states to the locally elected bodies. After scrutinising the causes of failure of the planning experiments in the past, the author has suggested basic structural changes in the polity: in the style of governance, ordering of priorities in development programmes and the functioning of the economy.

R.P. Misra's edited volume (1990)[21] consists of two parts of which the first part is concentrated on the theory and practice of district planning, while the second part contains an empirical study on district planning in the district of Chitradurga (Karnataka), with the focus on issues and methodology. The first part contains materials dealing with the foundations of district planning process in India. The book seeks to highlight the intervening role of the district planning between grassroots level and the national level through empowerment of the people. The stages of district planning together with a brief review of decentralized planning set-up in some states have been examined in the volume. It also includes the *guidelines* for preparation of district planning (issued by the Planning Commission in 1969) which helps a lot to understand the methodological and administrative aspects of the problem. The experiences of different states in district planning are also reported in the book with a clear message for integrating the development administration of the district with the Panchayati raj and empowering the district panchayat with 'reviewing, approving and authenticating' the district plan. The book helps understand both the theoretical and conceptual aspects of district planning and their applications in practice.

Amitava Mukherjee, the former adviser to the District Planning Unit of the National Academy of Administration, Mussorrie, has tried to synthesize the whole theoretical underpinning of decentralized planning. In a series of publications (1990)[22] Mukherjee has dealt with different aspects of district planning such as major methodologies of decentralized planning including those of Gadgil and K.N. Raj, different approaches to district planning, village-based and Land Reforms-based district planning (including West Bengal's model) and the experiences of various states in respect of district planning. After a synthesis of the models presented in the volume, an attempt has been made to reconstruct a general methodology of district planning. Two series of major publications (1991 & 1992)[23] edited by Amitava Mukherjee and B.N. Yugandhar have made lasting contribution to the literature of decentralized planning. These two volumes include a good number of articles relating to decentralized planning with particular reference to district planning, contributed by the academics, planners and administrators from all over the country and abroad.

Hooja and Mathur (1991)[24] in an edited volume, make an attempt to introduce the issues and problems of decentralized district planning with the premise that the methodology of decentralized planning is quite different from that of the macro level planning. The book identifies the issues like non-availability of data, inadequate flow of fund, lack of technical skill, absence of functional linkages and coordinations among different agencies as major constraints, which hamper the process of decentralized planning. Similarly the volume covers issues such as the question of appropriateness of the district as the level of decentralized planning, agro-climatic regional planning and the revival of Panchayati Raj Institutions for effective implementation of decentralized planning. There are also detailed discussions on the state of decentralized planning in three states, namely Gujarat, Maharashtra and West Bengal which have been directly relevant to the present study. The volume moreover presents an overview of decentralized planning experiences and their prospects for the country as a whole.

Mukarji and Bandyopadhyay (1993)[25] in their report submitted to the Government of West Bengal have presented a serious and thought provoking analysis of the process of decentralization in administration and planning. In their 'Status

Paper on Decentralized Planning', included in the report, they have dealt with the decentralized planning methodology adopted in the state. The report contains a critical review of the decentralizing process highlighting both the positive achievements in some respects and failures in others. Some of the observations in the report have been subsequently modified by Mukarji in his writings elsewhere.[26]

There are similar studies on the development policies and issues followed in West Bengal over the years. Ross Mallick (1993)[27] has come out with such a study in the long chain of related studies. But the major limitation of the study lies in the fact that most of his conclusions are guided more by subjective considerations than by objective facts. A reference may also be made to an earlier work edited by Bhaduri and Rahman (1982).[28] The contributors have highlighted the role and importance of the people as the focal point in the process of development and planning. In their papers, the contributors have documented the role of popular participation in regional planning.

There is another notable contribution from Arora and Hooja (1994)[29] which deals with administration of rural development in a comparative perspective. Besides providing a conceptual overview, the volume attempts an examination of rural development administration of some Asian and African countries including India and Bangladesh. In the Indian context, the focus on Panchayati raj and development administration is of particular importance for understanding the administrative dimension of decentralized planning in India.

Meenakshisundaram (1994)[30] in his comparative study on the patterns of decentralization in some developing countries including India has given a theoretical understanding of the concept of decentralization and its importance in a plural society, which strengthens the rationale for decentralized planning in India as a logical consequence. Apart from highlighting the experiments in decentralization carried out in Nigeria and China, the author has concentrated on the process of decentralized planning in Karnataka where the *Gram Sabha* played a vital role in organizing people's participation in local level planning. The author, while attributing the failure in decentralized planning to the weak machinery, has made some suggestions for strengthening the planning system based on people's participation. In course of examining the factors behind the success of Chinese experiments in decentralization, the author has identified four important elements: strong political commitments, autonomy of the local level bodies in decision-making and implementation of schemes, popular participation in village meetings and the mobilization of local resources. These are of special relevance in the Indian context.

Lieten (1996)[31] in his study on the development process in West Bengal in the larger context of political situation has highlighted the perspectives and conditions for introduction of decentralized development planning in the state. It is in continuation of his previous investigation on the theme (1992).[32] Though the earlier study is not directly concerned with decentralized planning process yet it helps understand both the objective and subjective conditions of the state, which provided inputs for the introduction of decentralized planning. After a detailed analysis the author has drawn the conclusion that the measures undertaken by the State Government have brought about a radical change thereby setting in motion a viable transition in rural power structure. His recent contribution (1996) is based on field works in two blocks belonging to two different districts of West Bengal including the district of Midnapore. The researcher has tried to explore the linkages among political mobilization, panchayat functioning and people's participation in the context of devolution of decision-making process to the lower levels and the changing role of the administration. The author has also identified the major policy initiatives undertaken by the government, which have extended the horizons of democracy and decentralization. Side by side, the author has pointed out the serious drawbacks and lapses that have followed the process of decentralization and empowerment in the state. These two studies provide the background for investigations into the state of actual operations of decentralized planning in West Bengal.

Kuldeep Mathur (1996)[33] in an edited volume brings together a series of articles that seek to go beyond the traditional approach and emphasize the importance of a broader context in development administration. The papers contain a wide range of discourses but most of them have a common point: the formulation and implementation of development planning in India. Some of the papers provide a critical survey of the philosophy and practice of planning in India with the suggestion for revitalization of the planning system under conditions of decentralization even below the state level. There is also a critical review of the strength and weaknesses in policy formulations and of the absence of appropriate institutions. The volume attributes the failure of institutions of development to the wrong designing of state intervention. A large section of the volume is devoted to the experiences in West Bengal. The contributors have traced the shift towards decentralization and assessed the functioning of grassroots institutions at the local level. The central emphasis of the section is placed on effective decentralization even through structural changes. Though the volume does not deal with district planning directly, yet the contributions are of much help in terms of planning of plan implementation. The specific mention of politics-administration nexus in course of implementation of redistributive policies, as emphasized by Professor Mathur, is worth our quotation:

> "What this means is that administration needs to be seen as part of the political process itself. Social and political forces have to be included as determinants of administrative performance. Economic constraints and social pressures cannot be relegated to the background. When administration is involved in the implementation of redistributive policies, the operational process cannot be free of conflicts and of the nature of policy design. The way conflicts are resolved also influences the fortunes of the administrators who seek to resolve them. Their interests are also at stake and they come as interested parties in the political arena itself. In this sense, it is difficult to regard administration as insulated from politics."[34]

Critical aspects of policy debates around development planning from both theoretical and operational perspectives are to be found in K.N. Kabra's recent publication (1997)[35] on development planning in India. Besides the issues of general concern and debate (like Plan *versus* market debate, mode of production in post-independence India, Planning and liberalization), specific problems of district planning, planning of plan implementation, planning strategy, Social Science approach to Planning constitute central focus of the volume. Deviating from the 'productionist and economy-centred' view, the author emphasizes the holistic and logical implications of planning and recommends planning of plan implementation to reduce the gap between objectives and achievements. Examining the experience of decentralized planning the author argues forcefully for financial autonomy at the district level through adequate financial allocations to the districts.

The *Indian Journal of Public Administration* has been providing scope for continuous interactions among the policy-makers, academics and administrators on different issues and aspects of decentralized planning. Apart from the regular issues, special issues exclusively devoted to this subject have been published. One of the issues (July-September, 1973)[36] deals with the administrative machinery of district planning. A section of the said issue is entirely devoted to the organizations and processes of planning in different States and Union Territories, presenting a detailed picture of the machinery of planning in the seventies. Other concerns like the rationale of district planning, its methodology and location, monitoring and information system, urban plans, gaps in the planning system have also been discussed.

Another special issue on planning system (July-September, 1984)[37] has thrown light on methodology, implementation, organization in planning in different parts of Asia including India. Some of the articles included in this volume seek to provide a logic for inclusion of political and administrative factors as determinants of planning performance.

Apart from the major literatures reviewed above, there are other publications which deal with the methodology and implementation of decentralized district planning in India to some extent. Most of these works are related to the experiments in different states. Nevertheless, they present a synoptic picture of district planning exercise in India as a whole. *District Planning in India* (Mundle, 1977), *Manual for Block Level*

Planning (Roy and Patil, 1977), *Grass without Roots* (Jain, 1985), *The Myth of Planned Development* (Sarkar *et al*., 1989), *Planning for Millions* (Anand Sarup and Brahme, 1990), *District Planning and Economic Development* (Degaonkar, 1990), *Decentralizing for Participatory Planning?* (Valk and Wekwete eds., 1990), *Development Administration in India* (Inamdar, 1992), *Panchayati Raj and Decentralization of Development Planning in West Bengal* (Webster, 1992), *Planning and Economic Policy in India* (Chattopadhyay *et al*., 1996), *Governance, Administration and Development* (Turner and Hulme, 1997) are some of the titles which attempt to bind together the issues of decentralized planning, development administration and Panchayati raj with a common thread of decentralization.

Research Gap

One of the major findings that emerges from this hurried review of the relevant literature on the subject is that none of the studies has taken an integrated and comprehensive view of the administrative and organizational issues involved in the formulation and implementation of decentralized district planning. The administrative and organizational aspects of district planning form the crux of the problem of management. But it has not received adequate attention in the literature of decentralized planning. There are very few studies which have made attempts to examine the administrative aspects of the problem in the context of functioning of the Panchayati Raj Institutions. The importance of analytical and empirical studies on the machinery of decentralized district planning in respect of personnel problems and plan implementation has never been adequately appreciated. In fact very few studies have focused on individual case studies of planning at the district, block and village levels. Moreover, the horizon of decentralized planning has been extended by 73rd and 74th Constitutional Amendments, particularly the 74th, which have accorded legitimacy to the concept of decentralized planning within the overall framework of decentralization. Consequent upon these amendments almost all the states have enacted either separate legislations or have brought about changes in their respective state acts incorporating detailed provisions for the organization and functioning of District Planning Committees. Prior to these changes, the District Planning Committees were in existence under government decisions in some of the states including West Bengal and these bodies used to look after the activities of district planning. The Constitutional Amendments have opened up new possibilities of grassroots planning which need to be compared with the conventional district planning so far practised. The emergence of decentralized planning has to be matched and merged with the planning process of the local institutions of self-government.

Realising the need for filling up this gap, and to present a more rounded and analytical study of the realities of decentralised planning, the present study is designed to make an appraisal of the role of the planning machinery and development administration at the district level at different stages of plan formulation and implementation. It seeks to highlight the administrative problems of the PRIs and to link those problems with the decentralized planning process in the present context. The study is focused on the district of Midnapore in West Bengal, which has become one of the pioneers in district planning in India. Though it is difficult to generalize the findings and conclusions from this investigation which is based on the experiences of a particular district and of a state in the light of experiences in a few others, it is expected that this study would succeed in exploring the general status of decentralized planning in India and motivate further investigation in this field.

Objectives of the Study

More pointedly, the basic objectives of the present study have been identified as follows:

- to look into the state of district planning operative in the district in the context of multi-level planning;
- to study the appropriateness and effectiveness of organizational infrastructure available at the district for

district planning in the light of recommendations of various committees and commissions;
- to identify the various issues like popular participation, resource allocations and mobilization, involvement of statutory bodies, Panchayati Raj Institutions and district development administration; and
- to draw appropriate conclusions out of the analysis which might be useful in improving organizational infrastructure and methodology of district planning as a whole.

Research Questions

The major research questions can be derived from the main objective of the study. The following are the key research questions:

The introduction of district planning has substantially affected the planning process and has evoked initiative at different levels. The research has to probe into the extent of real autonomy that the district planning has been able to achieve.

Planning requires active participation of the people in both plan formulation and implementation. Participation is channelled through certain institutions, both informal and formal, created for this purpose. Hence it is important to study the nature and extent of people's participation.

The District Planning Committee is composed of both the official and non-official representatives. The effectiveness of such a body largely depends on the mutual relationship between the official and non-official representatives as well as on the linkages and coordination between the different departments and Panchayati raj bodies. The study seeks to explore the role and effectiveness of the DPC, and the panchayats in this respect. Attempt is also made to unravel the intra-institutional linkages and network at different levels of planning.

District planning is implemented in a certain political environment. Hence, the study seeks to enquire the role of political parties and organizations in course of the planning process. Since the role of development administration is important in decentralized planning, the involvement of the bureaucracy deserves consideration in our context.

Timely formulation and effective implementation of district plan depend much on the coordination, control, supervision and monitoring of the process. Identification of constraints and shortcomings and their timely removal is a precondition for effective planning. Those questions are examined in the context of functioning of the District Planning Committee and other planning agencies.

Methodology of Study

This study is partly historical and mostly empirical. The historical part has been sought to be analyzed with the help of desk research. The data and information have been collected from published literature, both primary and secondary. Relevant documents like Constitutional Amendments Legislative Acts, rules, guidelines, reports, documents of Five-Year and Annual Plans, Government Orders, Instructions, Reports and Recommendations of the Planning Commission, Governments and Committees and Commissions appointed from time to time have been carefully studied and analyzed. For a clear understanding of the process of formulation and implementation of district plans, primary sources of information have been tapped through examination of the district plan documents, proceedings of the District Planning Committee and District Planning and Co-ordination Council, Working Groups and Sub-Committees of the DPC and DPCC, Zilla Parishad and Panchayats, circulars of the DPC and the district development administration. Reports of the statutory bodies and government departments have been meticulously examined in course of the investigation.

The investigation has been supplemented by making personal visits to some panchayats. After the collection of information and preparation of the preliminary draft, the findings have been checked and cross-checked, wherever possible by personal interviews with the members of the DPC, the leading district level functionaries (both official and non-official) and panchayat representatives at different levels. The methods employed for obtaining supplementary information and cross-verification have been the interviews based on detailed discussions and the technique of participant observation.

Interactions with the bureaucrats, the leading panchayat office-bearers and selected members of the Village Committees have helped the researcher to understand the role of development administration in decentralized planning. The data and information so collected have been arranged and analysed to chart out the process of work-flow, the administrative infrastructure, the methodology of planning and implementation and the issues and constraints of planning at the district level.

Plan of the Study

The present book has been organized into eight chapters to cover the entire gamut of decentralized district planning. The *introductory chapter* discusses the theoretical framework and the relevance of the study. Besides stating the problem in the context of the changing perspectives, this chapter undertakes a review of the existing literature to find out the gaps and to outline the broad objectives of the study. The research questions are followed by the methodology pursued in the investigation. The organization of the work is also devised briefly to present the study in an orderly manner.

The *second chapter* deals with the transition in the planning process in India from a centralist to a decentralized strategy, covering a period of almost a half-century, and the rationale of decentralization in planning. In this chapter, an attempt has been made to present an overview of the planning process in India together with the dilemma in choosing the appropriate level for decentralization. It has been divided into a number of sections and sub-sections in a logical sequence to trace the evolution of decentralized planning.

The *third chapter* is concentrated on the status of decentralized planning in the states. The experiments carried out in some states, which are considered to be pioneers, have been taken up and classified into three models to examine the actual state of development in decentralized planning. In the case of West Bengal, the perspectives of planning have been dealt in brief to understand the background in which decentralized planning has been introduced in the state. Similarly, the strategy adopted to ensure popular participation in Kerala in the Ninth Plan has been discussed.

The contents of the *fourth chapter* have been organized to cover the methodology and introduction of decentralized planning in the district under study. Before introducing the methodology, an attempt has been made to present the profile of the district. The chapter has been planned in such a way as to underline the basic elements that constitute the planning methodology in this district. The chapter includes the essential components like planning design, data base, prioritization of schemes and projects. projections and time-table, plan formulation, route chart, resource mobilization and credit planning. Attempts are also made to examine the process of plan formulation at different levels in the district.

Timely formulation and effective implementation of decentralized district planning necessitates an integrated and well designed planning organization at the district level. *Chapter five* of the study is devoted to chart out the planning machinery at different levels in the district. After a brief reference to the planning organization at the national and state levels, the organizational scheme of the district has been classified into two phases: one created in the eighties, and the other created after the enactment of the District Planning Committee Act in the state. The planning machinery including its supporting organizations and establishments at different levels in the district have been outlined to present a total view of the administrative infrastructure for decentralized district planning. Similarly, the planning organization at the block level in the district has been detailed out. In addition to the planning machinery, the role of the panchayats, municipalities, government departments and other agencies in the formulation and implementation of plans has been discussed in this chapter.

The *next chapter six* of the study is concerned with the implementation of planning in the district. The chapter is divided into two broad sections, one, relating to the planning of implementation and, the other, actual implementation by different bodies and agencies at various levels. Since the operation of decentralized planning has been in existence in the district from the middle of the eighties, a brief review of the implementation strategy over these years has been outlined.

Chapter seven of the study deals with the issues, constraints and choices. It is organized into two sections: issues and constraints, and the choices. In the first section, some important issues have been discussed together with the major constraints that have cropped up in course of implementation of the district plan. The core issues like people's participation, flow of funds, time-schedule, prioritization, linkage and coordination, monitoring and data collection together with the scope and extent of autonomy of the local level bodies in planning have been identified in general terms as well as in the concrete situation in the district. In the following section, certain policy formulations have been suggested for actualisation of decentralized district planning in an effective manner.

The *concluding chapter* of the study contains the major highlights and findings. Together the chapters constitute an integrated whole, the purpose being to delineate the processes, institutions and interactions centred on the phenomenon of 'decentralized district planning'.

Notes and References

1. Cemea, Michael M. (ed.) 1985, *Putting People First; Sociological Variables in Rural Development Projects,* New York : Oxford University Press.
2. David, C. Korten. 1984, 'People Centred Development : Toward a Framework,' in Korten and Rudiklaus (eds.), 1984, *People Centred Development : Contribution Toward Theory and Planning Framework, Connecticut : Kumarian Press, p. 300.*
3. Kothari, Rajni. 1999, 'Issues in Decentralized Governance' in Jha, S.N. and Mathur, P.C. (eds.), *Decentralization and Local Politics,* New Delhi : Sage, p. 48.
4. Smith, B.C. 1985, *Decentralization– The Territorial Dimension of the State,* London: George Allen & Unwin, p.188.
5. Fagence, Michael. 1977, *Citizens' Participation in Planning*, Oxford : Paragon Press, p.11.
6. Chakravarty, Sukhamoy. 1987, *Development Planning,* Oxford: Clarendon Press, p.47.
7. Maddick, Henry. 1963, *Democracy, Decentralization and Development,* Bombay: Asia Publishing Co., p.23.

8. Aziz, Abdul. 1993, *Decentralized Planning– The Karnataka Experience*, New Delhi: Sage Publications, p.19.
9. Grindle, Merilee. 1980 'Policy Content and Context in Implementation' in Grindle (ed.), *Politics and Policy Implementation in the Third World*, New Jersey: Princeton University Press, pp.17-18.
10. Byres, Terence J. 1994, 'State, Class and Development Planning in India' in T.J. Byres (ed.), *The State and Development Planning in India*, Oxford: Oxford University Press, pp.5-50.
    – Chatterjee, Partha. 1994, 'Development Planning and the Indian State' in T.J. Byres (ed.), *op.cit*. pp.51-72.
    – Nayyar, Deepak. 1998, 'Economic Development and Political Democracy – Interaction of Economics and Politics in Independent India', *Economic and Political Weekly*, Vol.XXXIII, No.49 (December 5-11), pp.3121-31.
11. Cohen, John and Uphoff, Norman. 1978, *Rural Development Participation*, Washington, D.C.: AID, p.11.
12. Fagence, 1977, *op.cit.*, p.6.
13. Parker, R.S. 1972, 'Planning and Politics' in Parker and P.N. Troy (eds.), *The Politics of Urban Growth*, Canberra: ANU Press, pp.34-35.
    Wekwete, K.H. 1990, 'Constraints to Planning for Socialism in Zimbabwe' in P. De. Valk and K.H. Wekwete (eds.), *Decentralizing for Participatory Planning?* USA: Aldershot, p.38.
    Also, Turner, Mark and Hulme, David. 1997, *Governance, Administration and Development*, London: Macmillan Press Ltd., p.77.
14. Hanson, A.H. 1966, *The Process of Planning: A Study of India's Five Year Plans 1950-1964*, London: Oxford University Press.
15. Misra, R.P. 1969, *Regional Planning– Concepts, Techniques, Policies and Case Studies*, New Delhi: Concept Publishing Company, (Revised edn., 1992).
16. ——— and Sundaram, K.V. 1980, *Multi-Level Planning for Integrated Rural Development in India*, New Delhi: Heritage Publishers.
17. Inamdar, N.R. and Kshire, V.K. 1986, *District Planning in India*, New Delhi: Oxford & IBH Publishing Company.
18. Prasad, Kamta. 1988, *Planning at the Grassroots*, New Delhi: Sterling Publishers.
19. Ghosh, Arun. 1989, *West Bengal Landscape*, Calcutta: K.P. Bagchi & Company.
20. ———, 1992, *Planning in India– the Challenges for the Nineties*, New Delhi: Sage Publications.
21. Misra, R.P. (ed.) 1990, *District Planning – A Handbook*, New Delhi: Concept Publishing Company.
22. Mukherjee, Amitava. 1990, *Researches in Decentralization*, New Delhi: Heritage Publishers.
    ———, 1990, *Foundations of Decentralization*, *op.cit.*
23. Yugandhar, B.N. and Mukherjee, Amitava. 1991, *Readings in Decentralized Planning*, Vol. I & II, New Delhi: Heritage Publishers.
    ———, *Methodology and Database in Decentralized Planning*, Part-A (1991), Part-B (1991), Part-C (1992), *op.cit.*

24. Hooja, Rakesh and Mathur, P.C. 1991, *District and Decentralized Planning*, Jaipur: Rawat Publications.
25. Mukarji, Nirmal and Bandyopadhyay, D. 1993, *New Horizons for West Bengal Panchayats*, Government of West Bengal, Calcutta.
26. Mukarji, 1993 (June), 'Making third stratum vibrant, dynamic' *Kurukshetra*, pp.13-17 and 21. And
———, 'The Third Stratum', *Economic and Political Weekly*, Vol. XXVIII, (1993) No. 28, pp.859-62.
27. Mallick, Ross. 1993, *Development Policy of a Communist Government : West Bengal since 1977*, New Delhi : Cambridge University Press.
28. Bhaduri, A. and Rahman, M.D. (eds.), 1982, *Studies in Rural Participation*, Delhi: Oxford & IBH Publishing Company.
29. Arora, Ramesh K. and Hooja, Rakesh. (eds.), 1994, *Administration and Rural Development: Indian and Comparative Perspectives*, New Delhi: Arihant Publishing House.
30. Meenakshisundaram, S.S. 1994, *Decentralization in Developing Countries*, New Delhi: Concept Publishing Company.
31. Lieten, G.K. 1996, *Development, Devolution and Democracy – Village Discourse in West Bengal*, New Delhi : Sage Publications.
32. ———, 1992, *Continuity and Change in Rural West Bengal*, New Delhi: Sage Publications.
33. Mathur, Kuldeep. (ed.), 1996, *Development Policy and Administration*, New Delhi: Sage Publications.
34. ———, *op.cit.*, p.15.
35. Kabra, K.N. 1997, *Development Planning in India*, New Delhi : Sage Publications.
36. *The Indian Journal of Public Administration*, 1973 (July-September), Vol. XIX, No.3.
37. *The Indian Journal of Public Administration*, 1984 (July-September), Special Number on Planning Systems, Vol.XXX, No.3.

2

DECENTRALIZED PLANNING IN INDIA
An Overview

The importance of decentralized planning in India is not at all a debatable issue today. Certainly it was an issue among the experts and bureaucrats in the sixties and early seventies. Now it is recognized both politically and constitutionally that decentralized planning may provide an alternative and appropriate approach to effective and sustainable development. After the enactment of the 73rd and 74th Amendment Acts decentralized district planning has made a permanent imprint on the national scene. Both the planners and politicians have realised the stern reality that decentralized planning has no substitute for a vast and a heterogeneous country like India having multiple units of administration ranging from the national to the village level. The doubt about the capacity of the common people in understanding their problems and in suggesting solutions thereof is a thing of the past. Viewed from this angle, regional or decentralized planning should not be understood as a miniature of national planning or simply a carbon copy of national plan in a smaller area. It involves the introduction of additional tiers of planning in a multi-level planning system linking the micro to the macro.[1]

The story of India's planning experiments since the inception of the Five-Year Plans is not at all encouraging. The planning as introduced was technocratic in character based on a 'satellite imagery view' of the society having no popular involvement.[2] At the beginning, the planners adopted the view of understanding the problems of the people from the top. They did not come to the ground and had only a photographic view of the society that helped in creating a data-based image, not the picture of the society. On the contrary, the planning from below organizes and ensures all comprehensive developments of human as well as material resources by taking into consideration the felt needs and requirements of the people at the grassroots. This understanding of the need of decentralized planning is not the product of a day. It had to encounter a long journey before it has been able to establish its credibility and feasibility.

THE CASE FOR DECENTRALIZED PLANNING

India's planning experiments began with a complete centralized process. The objectives, goals, strategies and priorities were set out at the national level by the Planning Commission, an apex body created under a Cabinet decision. Centralized planning was considered essential to control and augment national economy and to gear up national development in India after her emergence from the long period of colonial exploitation. The process thus continued to be characterized grossly by a 'top-down', bureaucratic-technocratic approach rather than a grassroots-participative one, in which predetermined targets were imposed from the top. Such an approach in the Indian context contains in itself a demand for redirection of both the scope and the process of planning. In order to promote speedy rate of growth and development in the fields of production, employment and income a new strategy is required, which would mean a different type of planning system for which nobody seems to be eager. It is a tragedy of India's planning system that neither the bureaucrats nor the politicians are prepared to decentralize the power that has been concentrated on the state over the years.[3] The new strategy required for the decentralization of planning should be based on the devolution of decision-making powers from the centre to the below by way of abandoning the central level macro-planning. It is quite natural, therefore, that the new strategy is not easily acceptable to the huge planning machinery built up over the years. But decentralization in planning is essential for the proper formulation and implementation of projects. It is very much common that secondary and less useful projects are sometimes given priority in some departments while important schemes are either neglected or set aside following the norms of 'first come, first served basis'.[4] Formulation of a good project planning depends largely on collection of complete data, investigation of alternatives, analysis of costs and benefits and the assessment of possible impacts on the people. Such an assessment calls for a complete knowledge of the situation and perspectives, which is possible only when there is a sound planning machinery both at the national and the local levels. Moreover, problems like duplication and contradiction in the formulation of plans and projects may be avoided through planning at the regional levels.

Decentralized planning or planning from below helps the planners to decide on objectives and priorities in the light of specific requirements of a locality *vis-a-vis* the availability of resources.[5] Planning means the setting up of objectives and priorities and to transform those into concrete actions in the context of local-level economics.[6] Further, a well organized planning body at the grassroots-level is capable of comprehending the situation so as to identify specifically the bottlenecks standing on the way of growth and development. It also helps to adopt suitable and effective remedial measures through institutional arrangements for removing such bottlenecks. Objective formulation and successful implementation of planning demand adequate understanding of the nature of the problems, proper identification of the target-groups, examination of their socio-economic constraints and sorting out of the factors retarding the process of growth and development. Decentralized planning lays greater emphasis on a systematic assessment of local needs and priorities as well as the scope of utilising local resources to the fullest possible extent even through the adoption of innovative approaches by way of designing and grafting innovative practices relevant to the endogeneous development. Decentralized planning can also check the abuses and leakages and may also reduce the cost involved in the administrative arrangements. It helps to fill up the gaps in the process of implementation and takes note of various leakages that prevent the impacts of plan programmes being felt. The plan programmes under decentralized process are more sensitive in containing proposals for strengthening the administrative organizations and management which could prevent such leakages.[7]

One of the basic objectives of planning is to balance the disparities among different parts of the country. Usually the planners adopt both short-term and long-term policies from time to time with a view to reducing the uneven space of development among the regions and to forging a balanced and integrated growth.[8] It was a common belief in the past that the poor regions were poor due to the scarcity of natural resources. Such a belief is untenable today since it is well-known now that many of the poor regions are otherwise rich in resources, both natural and human. Hence the planners would have to find out the ways and means to reduce the inter-regional disparities and to break the vicious circle of poverty and backwardness with determined and deliberate choice of suitable measures. The weakness of macro planning in dealing with the inter-sectoral and inter-regional problems in the context of the growing role of informal sectors cannot be bypassed due to inadequate interactions between micro and macro planning. Decentralized planning through its thrust on area specific development programme within a multi-level framework may help to solve the problems of regional imbalances and intra-regional differences.[9]

Decentralization in planning is necessary in order to integrate and coordinate the activities and programmes undertaken by different departments of the government. Under the centralized planning system the usual practice is that the district officials, even when district planning is undertaken, continue to compile information and prepare proposals in departmental isolation with little appreciation of the comprehensive nature of planning and the need for proper integration and coordination of sectoral or departmental plans. Most of the projects of the government have failed in the past due to lack of this coordination and interlinkages. The execution of programmes becomes difficult when there exist multiple developmental agencies like the Panchayati raj, co-operatives, banks and other public sector bodies. In such a situation district planning is considered to be an effective instrument in dovetailing the various resources for different schemes and projects in an integrated way.[10]

Planning has become an integrated and the most important part of India's economic life. The continuity of the planning process, with its thrusts and checks, has helped the government to create and renew national assets and to take up programmes for economic and social development together with the upliftment of the backward regions.[11] Nevertheless, there is a big gap between expectations and achievements.[12] Apart from its failure in attaining the main objectives of planning – eradication of poverty, unemployment and illiteracy, the successive five-year plans have failed miserably in redistributing incomes and assets.[13] Among others, wrong planning process, inappropriate strategy, poor project formulation and inadequate planning for plan implementation are considered to be important factors responsible for these failures. In most cases, the failure of the programmes is attributed to the absence of an 'integrated planning of related facilities and coordination among different agencies involved.'[14]

Thus the need for integration and coordination in different development programmes and the urgency in ensuring cooperation among the various departments of the government necessitates the planning from below. The usual practice followed so far was to confine the planning exercise to the Central and the State Governments which led to the formulation of diverse departmental plans some of which appeared to be at variance and even in contradictions with one another occasionally.[15] Planning is a collective effort. It involves a good number of actors and various institutions. The Panchayati raj bodies are important institutions involved in rural development and planning. Now they have been accorded constitutional responsibility in the preparation of schemes and proposals for development and in providing infrastructural support and financial assistance for formulation and execution of schemes and projects. Hence there is the need for ensuring proper coordination between the government departments and Panchayati raj bodies, which may be possible only below the state level. Developmental programmes would be more rational if both the Government departments and panchayat authorities adopt policies supplementing each other. This coordination is all the more important when resources are scarce and the felt needs are greater.

Closely related to this aspect of integration and coordination in planning, there is the need to ensure the involvement of people in the planning exercise. Previously plannings were exclusively conceived at the national and state levels and implementations were done at the local levels. Even when implementation was designed at the local level, people's involvement in the execution of plans and schemes was absent. If there were a mechanism to air the priorities and preferences of the people at least, the commoners' needs were known to the government. Now the panchayats provide the mechanism, though limited in scope, through which the choices and priorities of the people may be reflected. But the problem is that there is seldom any arrangement through which such priorities and preferences are transmitted to those who make projects and schemes for the people. Decentralized Planning apparatus may act as an effective instrument in that direction. Active participation of the people can only be expected when the people know and feel that the planning is being done for them. This sense of complete attachment to the process can only be attained through the process of people's planning, by associating people at both the stages of formulation and implementation of plans. In the remote areas, people know each other, they know the problems in their surroundings. Besides the ideological and political considerations, efficiency, economic and technical viability of a project demand participation of the beneficiaries. The entire process of development in the Third World is now perceived as dependent on people's participation. The logic of technical complexities and expertise involved in planning is untenable today. The whole philosophy of decentralized planning is concentrated on the concept of community partici-pation as an integral part of the development process throughout the world. The successful experiments of people's participation in rural development programmes conducted in different Asian countries have proved the fallacy of opposition to decentralized development model factually incorrect.[16] Decentralized planning provides the scope for bringing the planning closer to the people since it seeks to negate the possibilities of becoming the exclusive preserve of the bureaucracy or in effect the bureaucracy's plan for the district.[17]

Thus the need for people's participation in developmental process is not at all a debatable issue. Today the question veers round the choice of an appropriate machinery to ensure effective popular participation. The Committee to Review the existing Administrative Arrangements for Rural Development and Poverty Alleviation Programme, popularly known as the CAARD (1985), pointed out the lack of involvement of the people in rural development programmes and traced the exploitation and deprivation of the people to their alienation from the process of planning and development over the centuries. The Committee recommended participation of the target groups, i.e. the poor in developmental schemes for their successful implementation. It recommended that the rural poor for whom all these programmes are intended, should be directly and actively associated with both the formulation and the implementation of development programmes 'so that the programme contents may take into account the social factors, the aspirations of the local people, their capabilities and requirements'.[18] Thus a broad consensus exists among experts, policy makers and planners that effective participation of the people is possible only when policy planning, project formulation and implementation take place at the grassroots. There can be no doubt in the hypothesis — the more the decentralization, the more will be the participation.

Viewed from another angle, decentralized planning is of utmost importance. Formulation of goals, objectives and strategies is not the whole thing of a planning process, timely implementation is also vital. It is now well recognized that if the schemes of allocation included in the five-year plans are not implemented on the lines proposed in the plan documents, the desired state of affairs cannot be ensured. The major weakness in the planning experiments arises at the implementation stage. Again, approval of new proposals and schemes takes a long time for finalization due to procedural delays, lack of sufficient details and incomplete formulation. Further, some schemes are required to be approved each year after the budget is approved by the state legislature. The preparation of detailed schemes becomes necessary for the achievement of targets. Today the concept of development has undergone a sea-change. Now it is viewed as target-oriented, goal-oriented and participatory. In absence of clear-cut provisions relating to targets, goals and priorities, the diversification and dechannelization may take place. It is a common experience that the schemes and programmes meant for a particular section of the society have actually benefited others than the target groups since necessary checks and balances were not spelt out in the plan proposal.[19] Greater devolution of power and decentralization of decision-making authority are preconditions for effective implementation of plans and programmes and these may provide for the necessary checks and balances against such deviation. Continuous and participatory supervision at the time of execution of plans may act as a safety-valve against the pitfalls. Effective supervision and continuous monitoring are possible only when the formulation and implementation of plans are decentralized to the possible micro-level.

Decentralized planning may also act as a cost minimizer. The experiences of decentralized planning introduced in a few states reveal that the estimated cost of projects has been reduced significantly when executed through the Panchayati raj bodies. This is because the scope of corruption is minimal in a decentralized system when the people and their local institutions are involved in the administration, and the implementation of schemes and projects is done under the supervision and vigilance of the people directly. The experience from Karnataka in the eighties suggests that the involvement of the people reduces the project costs by utilising local resources more efficiently than a bureaucratic apparatus does. It is revealed that a project originally estimated to cost Rs. 24 crore could be completed only at Rs.4 crore when the *Mandal Panchayat* undertook the job. Not only in the sphere of minimising the costs, decentralized planning has also helped the increasing of revenues substantially. For instance, when the Fishery Department in Karnataka used to lease out a particular pond for fishing, the amount of revenues never exceeded Rs.5000. But when the *Gram Sabha* took over, the amount went up to Rs.75000.[20]

Decentralization in planning and execution opens up the scope for voluntary participation and contributions from the local people. A study conducted by the Sociological Research Unit of the ISI, West Bengal reveals that the repairing of a primary school building at Beloa in Birbhum district (West Bengal) would cost an amount of Rs.1,25,000 but an assistance of Rs.80,000 was provided by the local Panchayat Samiti for this purpose. The villagers, mostly mason and peasants, came out to contribute the balance through their own labour and the building was repaired in less than a year. The active participation of the village people has a remarkable impact on the locality when the villagers started to send their wards regularly to the school which they themselves constructed so successfully.[21] The experience gathered from Kerala is more interesting and stimula-ting at the same time. The Thathavely Bridge over the Moova-thupuzha river in Kottayam has not only reduced the distance by road between Kottayam and Ernakulam but has brought down the cost substantially.The bridge has been constructed at a cost of Rs. 1.1 crore while the State Public Works Department had reportedly estimated its cost around Rs. 5 crore. More significant is that the bridge has been built with men and materials from the two panchayats having opposite political affiliations. Thus the construction of the bridge, besides linking the inhabitants across the river, seems to bridge the political divide in a southern state in India.[22]

There is another instance from Midnapore which is both exciting and exemplary at the same time since it demonstrates how a massive development work could be done successfully with mobilisation of people's active support and resources. People belonging to two Gram Panchayats—Amlagora and Benachapra of Garbeta Block I — were deprived of steady communication and transportation since there was no bridge on the river *Silabati*. The villagers belonging to these Gram Panchayats under the leadership of the local Panchayat Samiti decided to construct a wooden bridge on their own and accordingly, a beneficiary committee was formed with the Pradhans of the two Gram Panchayats, seven members of Garbeta I Panchayat Samiti, and representatives of the local farmers and residents. The Gram Panchayats issued an appeal to the villagers for raising funds for construction of the bridge. Within a short span of time, an amount of Rupees one lakh and eighty-nine thousand was collected as contribution and loan. Necessary wood was also collected from the social forestry schemes of the panchayats. The bridge, 140 feet long and 15 feet wide, with an approach road of 400 feet was completed in March 1991. The committee was aware of the need for maintenance of the community asset created and accordingly, made arrangement for collection of *toll taxes* from the users of trucks, motor cars, bullock-carts and bicycles by engaging daily wagers for collection. The money collected for construction of the bridge was deposited in a local bank in the name of the committee which together with the collection of *toll taxes* accumulated to Rs. Three lakh eighty-nine thousand two hundred fifty by August 1993. After repayment of loan and incurring expendidure on maintenance and payment of wages to the employees, there was a balance of Rs. Forty-eight thousand which was kept for future maintenance. The collection of *toll taxes* has been continuing since then with a view to meeting the costs of maintenance in future.[23]

Hence, it is a common experience that when the local people are involved in the execution of a project, they 'keep a tighter lid' on expenditure and try to ensure efficiency. The lessons from Philippines confirm that the schools which 'rely more heavily on local funding are more efficient and operate with lower unit costs than comparable schools financed centrally.'[24]

Thus it appears that the large size of the country with heterogeneous characteristics and agro-climatic variations increases the possibilities of decentralized planning to neutralize the forces promoting uneven development amongst the regions and to harness the local resources to meet the felt needs and priorities of the people. A system of decentralized planning offers maximum possibilities in considering the felt needs and aspirations of the local people and making an attempt with people's participation to solve local problems like poverty, unemployment and under-utilization of locally available resources. Besides the compulsions of economics and efficiency, the logic of democratic governance and the process of 'learning by doing' call for decentralization in approaches and methodology although it may not be without a cost.

PLANNING IN INDIA : THE CHANGING PROFILE

Over the last few decades planning in India has been sectoral rather than spatial. Decentralized or area planning has never been introduced; only piecemeal attempts in the name of district planning were made in different parts of the country. It did not take off the ground in most states. However, different states envisaged progressive steps towards district planning.[25] But in actual practice planning below the national level – State, District, Block or Village – were nothing but the break-ups of the sectoral and departmental programmes undertaken by the various administrative units. The first two decades of India's planning are better considered as the periods of 'revolution from the top'. The results of this so-called revolution did not reach the vast majority of the Indian people. When the planning was introduced, the country's development prospects were rated high. It had a very stable government with a strong commitment to planned development based on Nehru's vision of a mixed economy moving towards a socialistic pattern of society.[26] Political parties, their leaders and the bureaucracy – all were pushed in the background as long as Nehru was at the helm of affairs. But with the passage of time, the people were not satisfied with the plan achievements and got frustrated and cynical. India got both the best and the worst of this 'revolution from the top'. Though planning in India cannot be described on the whole a total failure, it has failed to ensure full employment and creation of an equitable order which are considered to be the major objectives of planning. It has ignored the important issues involved in the phasing of investment outlays and has bypassed the question of effective land reforms leaving the agrarian transition incomplete. Moreover the pattern of income distribution has remained largely unchanged and those especially at the lowest strata of the society have gained very little from the five-year plans in reality.[27]

Thrust on National Development

In India planning was introduced following the Soviet model first on the 'top down' model. There was almost a national consensus on socio-economic objectives of the country and the approach to national development was determined along the socialistic lines in the context of a mixed economy.[28] The Central Government developed its own methodology and infrastructure for formulation of plans and development schemes and the states were required to follow and to execute the central programmes. They had no independent authority to decide their objectives and to draw their schemes according to their needs and priorities. Naturally the states did not feel the urge for resource mobilization. Their main purpose was to secure the largest amount of grants from the Centre and they became gradually more dependent on Central assistance and less interested in the mobilization of their own revenues and resources.[29]

In a federal set-up like ours it is expected that both the union and the units should have equal rights and responsibilities in the spheres of planning, but the situation is quite different and the states were given little role in regulating the economic behaviour of the country. Again, since the late seventies and early eighties the role of the states in the spheres of planning and development gradually eroded through the introduction of a good number of Centrally Sponsored Schemes (CSS). This has added insult to injury of the states which were crippled due to a variety of economic factors. Further, below the state-level no serious attempt was made to develop decentralized planning machinery though occasional references were made for district planning since 1969. Even the Planning Boards created at the states were not serious about decentralized planning. Very often the Boards at the state-level were constituted with persons close to the power that be, regardless of their expertise or knowledge in the fields of planning and development.[30]

Though there were occasional comments on the importance of decentralized planning since the commencement of five-year plans[31] the formulation of plans were done entirely at the national and state levels. The First Five-Year Plan emphasised the importance of the decentralized planning but nothing was done to put the process into practice. With a view to reducing poverty in rural India and introducing people's participation in the developmental programmes, Community Development Programme was launched in 1952 by creating 55 development blocks throughout the country which increased to 1075 at the end of the First Five-Year Plan.[32] The Community Development Programme was a method of rural development based on people's participation which sought to initiate the process of democratic decentralization for the transformation of the social and economic life of the villages in a coordinated and planned way.[33] Right from the beginning of the programme participation of the people, not only in the execution of the programmes but also in the formulation of schemes, was stressed, and accordingly, provisions for the setting up of a Project Advisory Committee as the representative of all the non-official elements within the project areas was visualised. But people's participation in the developmental process was sought to be achieved through an agent engaged in rural work, customarily described as the Village Level Worker (VLW).[34]

The First Five-Year Plan itself accepted the principle of democratic planning in which the people's cooperation was solicited in the implementation of the plan programmes. The plan document emphasised not only the vital role of the State Governments, but also of the Local self-governing bodies in the field of development. Different local, regional and functional bodies were required to be involved actively in the preparation of plans and the role of the Central planning authority was visualised to be the preparation of a general framework of the plan.[35] Thus the concept of decentralized planning became an important aspect of the successive five-year plans.[36]

As pointed out, the preparation of the First Five-Year Plan in the states was mainly done at the state headquarters. Subsequently, attempts were made to divide the state plans into district plans. The need for execution of local development works in cooperation with the people compelled the bureaucracy to realise the urgency to introduce schemes of development through a process of comprehensive village planning taking into account the requirements and priorities of the community. It was also realised that without a representative agency of the people in the villages all the people could not be brought together under the umbrella of rural development. The review of progress followed during the Community Development era opened the eyes of the planners and politicians who understood the need for creating an active organization at the village level that could involve all the people into the common programmes. These considerations were taken into account in the formulation of the Second Five-Year Plan. Early in 1954, the State Governments were advised to ensure local initiatives in formulating plans and development schemes so as to attain a close relation between the local needs and priorities based on public participation and voluntary efforts. Thus the methods adopted for the preparation of the Second Five-Year Plan have provided valuable linkages between the village people and rural officials.

In spite of contradictions in the ideology of the Second Five-Year Plan,[37] it emphasised the need for inclusion of local varieties into national and state plans. It pointed out the main programmes and activities for the formulation of district plans and suggested the establishment of District Development Council for coordinating the developmental activities of different agencies at the district level. The Second Five-Year Plan stressed the need for creating effective administrative and developmental institutions at the base-level for decentralized planning and rural development: "Unless there is a comprehensive village planning which takes into account the needs of the entire community; weaker sections like tenants, cultivators, landless workers and village artisans may not benefit sufficiently from assistance provided by the government. Secondly, rural progress depends entirely upon the existence of an active organization in the villages which can approach each family and bring all the people including the weaker sections of the community into productions and other programmes to be carried out with the help of administration".[38] The Second Five-Year Plan emphasised the need of district planning including the planning for blocks, and groups of village and municipal areas. The need for creating a well-organized structure of administration at district level and below was also felt. But no concrete progress in this direction could be traced during the Second Plan period. The practice followed hitherto in planning and development remained almost the same during this period although the Second Five-Year Plan discussed the concept and the scope of decentralized horizontal plans in great details.[39]

Phase of Development Administration

During the initial period of the Second Five-Year Plan an important event took place having a far reaching implication in the fields of decentralization in administration and development planning. During this period, the Balwantrai Mehta Study Team was appointed to evaluate the plan projects under the Community Development Programme. The recommendations of the Committee led to the genesis of Panchayati Raj Institutions. The Committee stressed the need for placing rural development administration fairly at the hands of the local representatives of the people to ensure people's participation in the developmental works at the local levels. It recommended the establishment of a single representative and vigorously democratic institution to take charge of all developmental works in the rural areas. It was suggested that the body would be statutory, elected and comprehensive in its duties and functions, equipped with the necessary executive machinery with adequate resources in its possession. In the ultimate analysis, the body was visualized to be an instrument of expression of the local people's will with regard to local development.[40]

Thus the main objective was to place the task of rural development on the local democratic institutions. With the creation of Panchayati Raj Institutions in the early sixties the idea of planning from below became popular.[41]

The introduction of the Panchayati raj system by the end of the Second Five-Year Plan added a new dimension to the concept of development administration. It created an agency at the grassroots level which could easily be utilised for strengthening the process of decentralized planning below the state level.

Though limited in functioning, the establishment of Panchayati raj was no doubt a bold experiment in the spheres of democratic decentralization.[42] It became a representative body at the local level which could very well play an important role in rural development and planning.

The Second Five-Year Plan put much emphasis on district development administration especially on the models on which District Development Councils were proposed to be built up in future. Thus the district development administration was considered as 'an agency of change towards a new social order... to respond to the needs and aspirations of the people.'[43] In the context of this new addition to the field of rural administrative machinery the Third Five-Year Plan was launched. The Third Plan attached considerable importance to decentralized planning and identified district level programmes similar to the lines contained in the Second Five-Year Plan. The success of the ambitious Second Plan already created a sense of confidence in the planners and they could now draw up the village production plan. During the Third Plan, attempts were made to formulate state plans taking the district plants into account. Though the Plan expounded a methodology for decentralized planning, practically no tangible result could be achieved.[44]

Search for a Decentralized Level

During the sixties, the economic atmosphere changed drastic-cally. The successive droughts caused by hostile monsoon, the declaration of 'plan holidays' and large-scale imports of food-grains aggravated the crisis and uncertainty.[45] There was also a speedy change in the political scenario after the Fourth General Elections (1967). This changed political situation coupled with the economic uncertainty necessitated rethinking and reorienta-tions of the development and planning policies. Certain progre-ssive measures like the Abolition of Privy Purses and the Nationalization of fourteen commercial banks were undertaken by the government. Pursuant to this attitude of the Government at the Centre, the Fourth Five-Year Plan laid more emphasis on social justice and equity as well as on the solutions of the problems of the weaker sections of the society. At the time of the formulation of the Plan the idea of the multi-level planning impressed the planners. It was recognized that planning was not something that came from without or from the above but what each state, district or even cluster of villages would develop according to its own resources and potentialities. Realization had its genesis in the failure of the Third Plan and brought home the point that state plans to be successful must be based on district plans.

The real breakthrough in the sphere of planning process was made during the Fourth Plan period when some concrete steps were taken by the Planning Commission to decentralize the planning system. Credit for this shift in outlook goes mainly to D.R. Gadgil, the then Deputy Chairman of the Planning Commission, who popularised the concept of district plan. Prior to the launching of the Fourth Five-Year Plan, India's planning was highly centralized in both concept and content. Planning Commission, being primarily concerned with planning techniques, was the sole authority in the formulation of an integrated plan of development. It used to prepare plans on the basis of discussions on desirable strategy and decisions regarding allocations and priorities were made accordingly. Thus the five-year plans were the products of different recommendations arrived at by various working groups, task forces and committees concerned with some specific subjects and departments. "They were all more or less mechanically combined to form the plan and when, as a result of decisions regarding allocations, adjustments have to be made upwards and downwards they are made independently for each separate set of programmes."[46] The situation at the lower levels was more deplorable. Preparation of plans at the state level was used to be done by the secretaries. In most of the states there was no planning machinery and the objectives and strategies of planning were rarely considered. For all practical purposes, the five-year plans became mere extensions of annual budgets with some modifications in the sense that the departmental proposals formulated by various sections of the government were put together by the secretariat. There was no scope for public discussions or consultations of general or specific nature except for the debates in the legislatures and no information was available outside in these regards.[47] Thus planning below the national level continued to be a compilation of different schemes and proposals of various departments of the Government. The schemes and proposals were prepared in such a manner as to attract the Planning Commission with a view to inducing it to release handsome assistance from the Central pool.[48]

In spite of the prevalent practice in the matter of plan formulation, there was little difference among the politicians and planners on the desirability and need for changing the existing system of centralized and sectoral planning. But very little thought was given to concretize the idea of decentralized planning. Gadgil developed his own ideas. Guided by a Puritan ethic and inspired by the Japanese success, he wanted to make the planning to fulfil its role effectively.[49] His methodology of district planning was based on two primary requirements: the *first* being the knowledge regarding local conditions, and the *second* was the participation of the local people in the formulation and implementation of plans. Together with these twin requirements, Gadgil advocated the integration of 'mandi areas' (market, sale and supply centre) as the homogeneous lower units of planning for carrying out at least some aspects of district planning.

District as the Unit of Planning

In 1969, the Planning Commission finally decided to settle down at the district level and recommended district as the unit of both plan formulation and execution and issued 'Guidelines for the formulation of District Plans.' The Commission advised the states to adopt district as the unit of planning below the state level and to put emphasis on 'the integration of the plans of local self-government bodies, Panchayati Raj Institutions, cooperative organizations and government departments.'[50] The 'Guidelines' also recommended continuous consultations not only after the preparation of plans but also before and during the formulation of plans. It is needless to point out that such a change emerged in the minds of planners from the utter disillusionment with the results of the highly centralized planning and development process followed in the fifties and sixties.

At this stage one interesting fact deserves special mention. During all these years both the planners and politicians had reduced the size of the unit of planning – from the national and state levels to the district and block levels, but the real question remained unsettled. In all these plans, 'people' were missing. The planners were perhaps confused. They could not settle the vital question: planning for whom? The whole concept of decentralized planning appeared to be confused in a perception of getting the plans formulated for the people instead of planning by the people. But "a decentralized plan is not produced by administrative decentralization only (for instance, by making state, district or even village level of administration responsible for implementing or even drawing the plans related to the geographical territory covered by them). In the absence of involving primary units of production in all aspects of planning, there is no decentralized planning."[51]

The failure of the Indian planning to attain the self-sustained economic growth based on an equitable distribution of income and improved standard of living is mostly attributed to its heavy reliance on bureaucracy. Indian planners believed that with the help of the state-bureaucracy they would be able to achieve the targets. But the state-apparatus modelled on the heritage and tradition inherited from the British raj was not well suited for the task of rural reconstruction and development in a country so vast and heterogeneous like India. Indian bureaucracy developed and nourished under the highly centralized steel-frame of the British administration was turned into a distinct class which preferred to live in a narrow, circumscribed world of its own. The bureaucracy with its narrow horizon and exclusiveness fails to reach the masses, not to talk of influencing the way of life of the rural people. Moreover, it lacks the social attitude necessary to perform the huge task of nation building. Virtually a different kind of development machinery was required which could be entrusted with the responsibilities of planning and development.

A close review of the operation of the five-year plans in India amply substantiates the hypothesis that there was a lack of eagerness in implementing the process of decentralized planning. The elite associated with the formulation and implementation of plans believed that increase in productivity, capital formation, utilization and appropriation of national resources, regulation of trade and commerce, management of financial resources and control over price mechanism required the intervention by the Central Government as well as planning at the top. Such a theory gained considerable support in a comment of D.T. Lakdawala, a former Vice Chairman of the Planning Commission: "There are problems of national concern which cannot be left to states because of their inter-state implications like population planning, inter-state power transmission lines, etc." Highlighting the role and importance of the Centrally Sponsored Schemes (CSS) he went further that "there are other plan priorities where the states should be interested but because of their power structure or because of limited vision or lack of resources they have to be specially spurred and induced. Many of the interesting experiments in agricultural planning like SFDA, MFAL and CDA etc. have come through Centrally Sponsored Schemes." [52]

Thus it is clear that during the first two Plans there was no specific programme, but only statements and declarations regarding regional planning and development. Only the Third Five-Year Plan made some headway in this direction. But it was the Fourth Five-Year Plan which spelt out for the first time concrete steps in the direction of multi-level planning with the district as the main focus in the process and thereby it marked a watershed in the history of Indian Planning. From the Fourth Plan onwards necessary steps were proposed to actualise decentralized planning.[53] Later on, the Central Government initiated a scheme for financial assistance to the states for meeting additional expenditure for strengthening and reorganizing the state planning machinery. It strengthened the awareness already developed in favour of decentralized planning in the states, and the states, taking cue from it, strengthened their state-level planning organization and some states even set-up planning organizations below the state-level.[54] Now the concept of decentralized district planning became a development strategy which necessitated the creation of an infrastructure and an effective change in the attitudes of the bureaucrats and politicians for the success of decentralized planning. Though both the Fourth and Fifth Five-Year Plans were directed towards decentralization taking district and the block as the micro-levels of planning to speed up the work of planned rural development, no adequate concrete steps were taken to materialize the idea. An attempt was made for the first time to treat the village as the lowest unit of decentralized planning by adopting the scheme '*Antyodaya*' (whole village development programme) in 1977 in order to bring about the integrated development of the village as a whole.[55] Real thrust on decentralized planning was given in the late seventies when the surplus production in wheat induced the Central Government to undertake new programmes like 'Food For Work' to combat rural poverty. It is interesting to note that the 32nd National Sample Survey showed that in 1977-78, the proportion of the population in rural areas living below the poverty line was 51.2 per cent.[56] Thus the renewed urge for concrete steps emerged from utter disillusionment with the results of India's planning practices followed for almost three decades.

REVIVAL OF THE DEBATE ON DECENTRALIZATION

The establishment of the Janata Government at the Centre (1977) paved the way for real experiments in decentralization in the spheres of both administration and planning. Special mention may be made about the constitution of the two important committees viz., the Working Group on Block Level Planning headed by M.L. Dantwala and the Committee on Panchayati Raj popularly known as the Asoka Mehta Committee in 1977. The Dantwala Committee was required to address the question of appropriateness of a block as a unit of planning and it recommended 'the case for selecting a small area for planning.'[57] However, in view of infrastructural difficulties at the block level, the committee assigned the responsibility of block planning to the district-level organization and suggested slow movement towards introduction of effective block planning.[58] The committee proposed the integration of block plans with the district plan and thus the committee viewed the preparation of both block and district plans to be a part of the same exercise.

The recommendations of the Asoka Mehta Committee opened a new era in local-government and decentralized planning in India. Besides identifying the district as the first point of decentralization below the state-level under popular supervision, it recommended the formulation of plans at the district level on the lines suggested by the Dantwala Committee. It also stressed the need for accommodating the views articulated about the Mandal Panchayats and the questions of rural-urban continuum from time to time.[59]

The national debate on decentralization in planning was thus revived after the submission of the reports of the Asoka Mehta Committee and the Dantwala Committee. These two reports opened a new chapter where the decentralized district planning and the role of people's representatives in local bodies were considered basic to strengthen the process of development planning and democracy. A few state governments took these recommendations seriously and started experiments in planning and decentralization in their own way.[60] But there were certain inadequacies and even confusions in these recommendations. The Working Group on Block Level Planning, though it recommended 'the placement of planning team at the district headquarters' to meet the imperatives of vertical and horizontal linkages, could not take into account the necessary complexities involved in decentralized planning under a unitary planning infrastructure. Moreover, the group while emphasizing the importance of popular participation in planning could not take a definite stand on this vital issue.[61]

However, the Sixth Five-Year Plan sought to accommodate the recommendations of these committees and adopted the strategy 'to strengthen the process of democratic decentralization.'[62] But there was no perceptible change in the process of planning and the bureaucracy at the district level controlled the whole process under a more or less concentrated arrangement.[63] Different poverty alleviation programmes like the Food-For-Work, the National Rural Employment Programme, Drought

Prone Area Projects, Integrated Rural Development and the Rural Landless Employment Guarantee Programme etc. were introduced in the Central budget and a beginning in effective decentralization was made. With the launching of large scale multi-sectoral, country-wide programmes of rural development the need for developing an appropriate infrastructural machinery to ensure their planning and implementation in an effective and integrated manner was felt.[64] The Planning Commission appointed a Working Group on District Planning in 1982 under the Chairmanship of C.H. Hanumantha Rao and the recommendation of this Group formed the basis for evolving the district planning and the approach was outlined in the Seventh Plan. The Seventh Plan incorporated the main ideas outlined in the recommendations of the Working Group and stated to pursue 'the decentralization of the planning process' for development. It was also realized that planning activities at the district level would vest in a single district planning body which would determine the strategies and priorities and allocate funds for various departments taking into account the planning and other capabilities available at the grassroots-level.[65]

Both the expert groups, the Working Group on Block Level Planning and the Working Group on District Planning, have thoroughly studied various aspects of decentralized planning at the district and block levels and have arrived at a number of recommendations which are, by and large, identical in substance. The important point of convergence is that both the expert groups have assigned the basic functions of decentralized planning to the district level.[66]

The idea of decentralized planning got a further fillip in the recommendations of the Commission on Centre-State Relations popularly known as the Sarkaria Commission and the Committee to Review the Existing Administrative Arrangements for Rural Development and Poverty Alleviation Programmes (CAARD) headed by G.K.V. Rao. The Sarkaria Commission appointed mainly to examine and review the arrangements between the Centre and the States provided a scope for strengthening the idea of regional planning in its recommendations on issues like greater role for the State Planning Committees and the reorganization of

National Development Council.[67] The G.K.V. Rao Committee (CAARD) while dealing with the issue of decentralized planning endorsed the major recommendations of the Working Group on District Planning in respect of setting up of district planning bodies and the decentralization and devolution of administrative and financial powers.[68] But the findings of the CAARD were somewhat different from those of the Working Group report on district planning so far as the CAARD emphasized representative leadership of the Panchayati Raj Institutions at different levels.[69] Highlighting the planning operation as a single holistic one, the committee, in broad agreement with the approach to decentralization indicated by the Working Group, suggested the total accommodation of local needs and aspirations in the district plan. The Committee stress-sed the need for 'establishing a sound planning and implemen-ting machinery' for effective integration and coordina-tion of all the rural development activities under the 'umbrella of district planning.'[70] It also recommended the rationalization in the activities of different institutions of development activities at the district level under the effective leadership of democratic bodies of local governance.[71] These recommendations together with those of the two Working Groups provided the ideological and operational foundations of district planning in India.

In the ultimate analysis, the way in which planning has been administered has left the people as mere spectators rather than active participants in the entire process. Hence the need for institutionalization of the process of decentralization to check the process of alienation of the people was felt. Accordingly, the Eighth Five-Year Plan laid down the emphasis on institution building to make the people's initiative and participation a key element in the process of development. In this sense, the Eighth Plan may be considered as 'more a manager's plan than an abstract economist's plan of cliches and pious wishes.'[72]

The Eighth Plan stressed the role of the government to facilitate the process of people's participation through the creation of necessary institutional infrastructure particularly in the rural areas. But the progress was slow 'due to the fact that the other tiers of the government were not fully integrated into the development strategy.'[73] A review of the planning process provides enough indication that the Eighth Plan itself was involved in an experiment in distric planning though the importance of decentralization was widely established.[74]

CONSTITUTIONALIZATION OF DISTRICT PLANNING

Besides this neglected state of affairs in the process of decentralized planning, the over-all progress in effective decentralization through Panchayati raj was not at all satisfactory excepting in a few states. Rather the signs of instability and concentration of power became more visible in the process. There was a growing realization that the ineffectiveness and non-functioning of rural local self-governing bodies were the result of the absence of constitutional sanctions for these institutions. The idea of according constitutional recognition to the Panchayati Raj Institutions articulated by the Asoka Mehta Committee gained ground in the reports of the Thungon Committee which recommended constitutional status for these bodies.[75]

The 73rd and 74th Constitution Amendment Acts (1992) are considered as milestones in the field of decentralization in administration and planning. These amendments seek to initiate a genuine process of decentralized planning with the total involvement of local self-governing institutions together with the District Planning and Metropolitan Planning Committees.[76] Now it has become mandatory on the part of the states to constitute 'District Planning Committee to consolidate the plans prepared by the panchayats and the municipalities in the district and to prepare a draft development plan for the district as a whole.'[77]

These twin amendments contain larger implications for decentralized planning process since they attempt to elevate the status of the panchayats and the municipalities as effective institutions of self-governance by making the Panchayati raj, District Planning Committee and the Metropolitan Planning Committee as necessary parts of the basic structure of the Constitution itself. The amendments also seek to ensure periodical elections and assign active and enhanced roles to them in the planning process. In this way, the amendments may be considered as the culmination of the long debate that was revived in the aftermath of Asoka Mehta and Dantwala Committee reports. These amendments are viewed by some scholars rightly as attempts towards real decentralization in an evolving 'federal nation' based on participatory democracy and popular base.[78]

The 73rd and the 74th Amendments have paved the way for multi-level planning in India. The constitutional stipulations for establishment of *District Planning Committee* at the district level, *Gram Sabha* at the village level (Art.243-A) and *Ward Committees* within the municipalities (Art. 243-S) as the structural means for devolution of decision-making powers from the centre to the grassroots-level together with other constitutional provisions[79] give new meaning and content to multi-level decision-making process in which Panchayats, Municipalities and District Planning Committees become institutions of self-governance throughout the country.

Moreover, the 73rd Amendment Act provides for devolution of powers and responsibilities upon the panchayats at the appropriate levels for preparation of plans for economic development and social justice.[80] An elaborate list of 29 items has been included in the Eleventh Schedule which adds a new dimension to the devolution of powers outlined in the 73rd Amendment. Similar provisions have also been made to include 18 items in the Twelfth Schedule under the 74th Amendment. The inclusion of the items in Eleventh Schedule is intended to permit the State Governments to 'endow the panchayats with such powers and authority as may be necessary to enable them to function as institutions of self-government.'[81]

But the interesting point is that there are some items which cannot be transferred by the state legislatures, without the approval of the Centre. Again, the provision seems to be optional in nature and the states are not under compulsions to comply with the purposes of the Act. Such a view is strengthened by the fact that some of the states are even reluctant to hold elections to the local bodies on time,[82] not to speak of their willingness to transfer power to the sub-state-level.

Thus the Panchayati Raj Institutions in collaboration with the District Planning Committee have now become constitutionalized institutions for planning and development below the state level. In fact, one more layer has been added to the existing two-level planning system by these amendments. These amendments, viewed critically, not only constitutionalize three strata in planning — national, state and district, but also propose to create a five-storied pyramid of planning starting from the village panchayats at the grassroots level. Again, given the structure based on land ownerslip, caste and power and the reality of rural life and the experiences of the working of the institutions of local governance, it is doubtful whether the vast majority of people living in the peripheral areas of power would be able to share the gains and benefits of development.[83]

The concept of decentralized district planning has been accepted by almost all the states excepting Goa, Sikkim and Tripura. Sikkim and Goa are small states and hence they preferred to strengthen their planning machinery at the state level which could look into the problems of integrated development plan effectively while Tripura proposed decentralized planning at the block level. Although the need for decentralized planning has been recognized and several measures have been taken to effectively decentralize the planning process, the progress has not really got off the ground in most states.[84] Moreover, the pattern and level of decentralization attained in various states have also not been uniform. While some states like Karnataka, Gujarat, Maharashtra, Jammu & Kashmir and West Bengal have made appreciable progress, other states have made a beginning or are still in the process of completing some necessary preliminarics.[85] Thus it is evident that planning in India over the last four decades has not moved far beyond the experiment stage in bringing about real decentralization in planning.[86]

The Ninth Plan Scenario

The Ninth Plan gave due emphasis on decentralized district planning but the final outcome is yet to be assessed. It envisaged a people-oriented planning process in which not only the involvement of the Central and the State Governments but also of the people at large designed.[87] It emphasized the transfer of adequate powers and authority to the panchayats so as to enable them to function as institutions of self-governance as visualised in the Constitution. The recommendations of the National Development Council for devolution of 41 per cent of plan allocations to decentralized district planning were accepted but the extent of actual devolution of resources is yet to be ascertained. Though the plan sought to realize people's involvement in the decentralized planning through their elected representatives in order to evolve 'shared vision' of development towards common purpose[88] it is widely viewed that 'Ninth Plan failed to dovetail multi-level planning with multi-level public finance'.[89]

The significance of this multi-level planning process is not yet understood in its entirety. The introduction of decentralized district planning calls for a new ecological setting and a new culture in planning and decentralization radically different from the one the country has been following up to the Eighth Five-Year Plan. However, the new experiments have already been started. All the states have passed the State Conformity Acts and have incorporated the constitutional changes in their respective state laws. In most of the states, District Planning Committees have been constituted for undertaking decentralized district planning. But these changes necessitate a determined and sustained effort for introducing multi-level federalism in administration and planning with greater autonomy and people's initiative under less bureaucratic control. Constitutional amendments have created the necessary structure for decentralized planning and now conditions are required for implementing the schemes and strengthening the process of decentralized district planning in its actual practice. A brief review of the planning processes followed in different states in India may give us a synoptic picture of the state of decentralized district planning in its actuality.

Notes and References

1. Rao, V.M. 1988, 'Decentralized Planning : Priority Economic Issues'. *Conference volume, Indian Economic Association*, Calcutta. p.1.

2. Misra, R.P. 1991, 'On the task of District Planning', in B.N. Yugandhar and A. Mukherjee (eds.), *Readings in Decentralized Planning,* Vol. I, New Delhi: Concept Publishing Company, p.3.
   Also, Johnston, B.F. and Clark, W.C. 1982, *Redesigning Rural Development: A Strategic Perspective*, Baltimore: Johns Hopkins University Press, p.24.
3. Report of the *Commission on Panchayati Raj Institutions,* 1978, 'Note from E.M.S. Namboodiripad', Government of India, New Delhi, p.160.
4. Report of the *Commission on Power,* 1980, Government of India, New Delhi, p.18.
5. Misra, R.P. and Sundaram, K.V. 1988 in Moonis Raza (ed.), *Regional Development,* New Delhi : Heritage Publications, p.68.
6. Rao, 1988, *op. cit.,* pp.1-3.
7. Report of the *Working Group on District Planning,* 1984, Government of India, New Delhi, Vol. I, p.55, par. 6.31.
8. *Fourth Five-Year Plan,* 1970, Government of India, New Delhi, p.11.
9. *Sixth Five-Year Plan,* 1980, Government of India, New Delhi, p.93.
10. Report of the *Working Group on District Planning, op. cit.,* p.56, par. 6.39.
11. *Sixth Five-Year Plan*, 1980, *op. cit.*, p. (iii).
12. *Draft of the Sixth Five-Year Plan,* 1978, *ibid.* p.2.
13. *Ibid.*, pp. 2-9.
14. Report of the *National Committee on the Development of Backward Areas* (NCDBA), 1981, Government of India, New Delhi, p.32.
15. Ghosh, Arun. 1985, Decentralized Planning, Paper presented at a Seminar, Calcutta: Indian Institute of Public Administration, West Bengal Regional Branch, *News Letter*, July-September, 1985.
16. Uphoff, N.T. 1979, *Feasibility and Application of Rural Development Participation*, U.K.: Cornell University Press, p.3.
17. Kabra, K.N. 1977, *Development Planning in India*, New Delhi: Sage, p.184.
18. Report of the *Committee to Review the Existing Administrative Arrangements for Rural Development and Poverty Alleviation Programme*, 1985, (hereafter referred to as CAARD), Government of India, New Delhi: p.54, par. 7.34.
19. Report of the *National Commission on Agriculture*, 1976, Government of India, New Delhi, Part XIV, p.17.
20. Hegde, Ramkrishna. 1992, *Seminar paper*, reproduced in the *Nation*, New Delhi: Vol.3, No.26, October 16, 1992.
21. Dasgupta, Atis. 1998, *Seminar Paper* presented to the State Level Seminar *on 'Decentralization: Devolution and Participation'*, organized by the State Planning Board, West Bengal at Calcutta, 20-22 November, 1998.
22. *The Hindustan Times,* 1 June, 2000.
23. *Records of the Gram Panchayats. Also, interview, with the Pradhans,* Amlagora and Benachapra Gram Panchayats, Garbeta – I.

24. *Human Development Report,* 1993, United Nations Development Programme (UNDP), Delhi: Oxford University Press, p.75.
25. Turner, Mark and Hulme, David. 1997, *Governance Administration and Development*, London: Macmillan Press Limited, pp. 136-37. Also, *Report* of the *Working Group on District Planning,* 1984, *op.cit.*, p.37., par. 4.49.
26. Chakravarty, Sukhamoy.1987, *Development Planning – The Indian Experience,* Oxford: Oxford University Press, p.81.
27. *Ibid.*, p.8. Also Raj, K.N. 1965, *Indian Economic Growth : Performance and Prospects,* Bombay: Allied Publishers, p.27.
28. Minhas, B.S. 1974, *Planning and the Poor,* New Delhi: S. Chand and Company, p.120.

    _____, Mozoomdar, Ajit. 1996, 'The Rise and Decline of Development Planning in India' in Kuldeep Mathur (ed.), *Development Policy and Administration,* New Delhi: Sage Publications, p.49.

    _____, Kurien, C.T. 1978, *Poverty, Planning and Social Transformation,* New Delhi: Allied Publishers Pvt. Ltd., p.105.

    _____, Sengupta, Ramprasad. 1996, 'Planning, Institutions and Technical Change : A Review of Development Planning in India' in Manabendu Chattopadhyay, *et al. Planning Economic Policy in India,* New Delhi: Sage Publications, pp. 60-63.
29. Misra, R.P. 1991, *op.cit.*, p.1.
30. Jha, D.N. 1988, 'Regional Disparities have widened' in V.S. Mahajan (ed.), *Studies in Indian Planning*, New Delhi: Deep and Deep Publications, pp. 90-91.
31. *First Five-Year Plan,* 1952, Government of India, New Delhi, p.140.
32. Jain, L.C. *et al.* 1985, *Grass without Roots — Rural Development Under Government Auspices,* New Delhi : Sage, p. 28.
33. *Second Five-Year Plan*, 1956, Government of India, New Delhi, pp.235-45.

    Also, Minhas, B.S. 1974, *op.cit.* p.3.
34. *First Five-Year Plan*, 1952, Government of India, New Delhi, p.223.
35. *Ibid.*, p.10.
36. Mehta, Balraj. 1988 (May), *The Tribune.*
37. Bandyopadhyay, N. 1988, 'The Story of Land Reforms in Indian Planning' in Amiya Kumar Bagchi (ed.), *Economy, Society and Polity,* Calcutta: Oxford University Press, p.16.
38. *Second Five-Year Plan,* 1956, Summary, Government of India, New Delhi, Chap. VII, p.53.
39. Report of the *Working Group on District Planning,* 1984, *op.cit.*, p.21, par. 3.2.
40. Dubashi, P.R. 1984, 'The Federal Principle in Indian Polity' in R.S. Rajput and D.R. Megha (eds.), *Panchayati Raj in India,* New Delhi: Deep & Deep Publications, pp.18-19.
41. Report of the *Working Group,* 1984, *op. cit.*, p.21, par. 3.2.

42. Mukherji, R. 1988, 'Indian Planning leading to maldistribution of Income: an appraisal' in V.S. Mahajan (ed.), *op.cit.*, p.80.
43. *Second Five-Year Plan*, 1956, *op.cit.*, p.164.
44. Ghosh, Arun. 1985, *op.cit.*
45. Chakravarty, Sukhamoy. 1987, *op.cit.*, p.85.
    Also, Frankel, Francine R. 1978, *India's Political Economy*, 1947-77, London: Oxford University Press, p.314.
46. Gadgil, D.R. 1966, *R.R. Kale Memorial Lecture*, Bombay: Asia Publishing House, pp.9-10.
47. *Ibid.*, p.10.
48. *Ibid.*, p.13.
49. Kamat, A.R. 1974, 'D.R. Gadgil : The Last Phase', *Economic and Political Weekly*, Vol. IX, No.26, p.1029.
50. 'Guidelines of the Planning Commission' 1969, reproduced in R.P. Misra (ed.), *District Planning : A Handbook*, New Delhi: Concept Publishing Company, p.166.
51. Kurian, C.T. 1978, *op. cit.*, p.142.
52. Lakdawala, D.T. 1979, 'Dr. V.S. Krishna Endowment Lecture' quoted in M.L. Dantwala *et al.* (eds.) 1986, *Asian Seminar on Rural Development*, New Delhi: Oxford & IBH, p.197.
53. Kabra, K.N.1997, *op.cit.*, p.14.
54. Nair, K.R.G.1982, *Regional Experience in a Developing Economy*, New Delhi: Wiley Eastern Limited, p.132.
55. Report of the *Department of Rural Development*, 1978-79, Government of India, New Delhi, pp.15-19.
56. Chakravarty, Sukhamoy. 1987, *op.cit.*, p.85.
57. Report of the *Working Group on Block Level Planning*, 1978, Government of India, New Delhi, Vol. II, Chap.10, pp.133-49, par.3.
    Also, Mukarji, Nirmal. 1996, 'Decentralization below the State Level : Need for a New System of Governance' in Mathur *op. cit.*, p. 268.
58. *Ibid.*, par(s). 4 & 5.
59. Report of *the Commission on Panchayati Raj Institutions*, 1978, *op.cit.*, Chap., 6 (hereinafter referred to as *Asoka Mehta Committee*, 1978).
60. Report of *the CAARD*, 1985, p.24, par. 4.3.
61. Report of *the Working Group on Block Level Planning*, 1978, *op.cit.*, pp.133-49, par(s). 3, 4, 11 & 13.
62. *Sixth Five-Year Plan*, 1980, Government of India, New Delhi, p.176.
63. Ranga Rao, S.P. 1997, 'Decentralized Planning – the emerging scenario' in *Kurukshetra*, Vol. XLV, No.9, (June), p.3.
64. Lieten, G.K. 1992, *Continuity and Change in Rural West Bengal*, New Delhi: Sage, p.213.
    Also, *Seventh Five-Year Plan*, 1986, Government of India, New Delhi, p.63.
65. Report of the *Working Group on District Planning*, 1985, *op.cit.*, p.23, par(s). 3.14 & 3.15.

66. *Proceedings of the National Workshop held at NIRD,* 1985, 'Administrative Arrangements for Rural Development', Hyderabad, p.62.
67. Report of the *Commission on Centre-State Relations,* 1988, Government of India, New Delhi, Part-I, pp.382-84.
68. Report of the *CAARD,* 1985, p.30, par.4.21.
69. *Ibid.,* p.45, par(s). 6.24 & 6.26.
70. *Ibid.,* pp.27-28, par. 4.11.
71. *Ibid.,* par. 4.21.
72. Sengupta, Nitish. 1992, *Yojana,* Vol.36, No.14 & 15, pp.33-34.
73. *Approach Paper to Ninth Five-Year Plan,* 1997, Government of India, New Delhi: Planning Commission, p.14.
74. Kabra, K.N. 1997, *op.cit.,* p.176.
75. *Note*: A sub-committee of the Consultative Committee of Parliament was appointed under the Chairmanship of P.K. Thungan in 1988, which recommended that Panchayati Raj Institutions should be constitutionally recognized.
76. *The Constitution of India, Articles,* 243ZD and 243ZE.
77. *Ibid.,* Article 243ZD.
78. Khan, Rasheeduddin. 1992, *Federal India: A Design for change,* New Delhi: Vikas Publishing House, pp.29-30.
79. *Note*: Fifth and Sixth Schedules of the Constitution provide for the creation of units of decentralization in the Tribal areas of the North East through the creation of district autonomous councils and the creation of advisory councils in other states, (Art. 244). Moreover, Article 371(2) provides for the establishment of sub-state structure in Maharashtra and Gujarat.
80. *The Constitution of India,* Article, 243G.
81. *Articles 243G and 243W* of the Constitution of India.
82. Observation *of the Minister-in-Charge* of Rural Development, *Government of India, Panchayati Raj Update,* 2000, (October) Vol. VII, No. 8, p. 3.
83. Hirway, Indira. 1986, *Abolition of Poverty in India,* New Delhi : Vikas Publishing House, pp. 57-58.
84. Sarkar, Goutam K. 1995, *Agriculture and Rural Transformation in India,* Delhi: Oxford University Press, p.95.
85. Misra, R.P. (ed.), 1990, *op.cit.,* p.84.
    Also, *Report of the CAARD,* p.25, par. 4.5.
86. Kabra, K.N. 1997, *op.cit.,* p.176.
87. Dandavate, Madhu. 1997, 'Ethos of Planning and Plan Implementation in India', *Indian Journal of Public Administration,* Vol. XLIII, No.4, p.870.
88. *Approach Paper to the Ninth Five-Year Plan,* 1997, *op.cit.*
89. Oommen, T.K. 2002 (September), 'Rationalizing fiscal federalism *vis-à-vis* rural local governments,' *Panchayati Raj Update*, vol. IX, No. 9, p.6.

3

DECENTRALIZED PLANNING EXPERIMENTS IN THE STATES

Various states in India have made attempts to decentralize the planning process up to the district level, though as *ad hoc* exercise in many cases. Again, some states have made efforts to undertake planning even below the district level. But in most cases the machinery, framework and methodology of decentralized planning could not be moved below the district level. District as the unit of planning may not be an appropriate stage from the viewpoint of economic considerations, yet it is being recognized as the most convenient in many respects. The districts are the advantageous territorial levels where the people can meet and exchange their views. Moreover, at the district level there is an integrated administrative structure built over the centuries, which can be well utilised for spearheading decentralized planning. Naturally, most of the states have considered it wise to decentralize their planning processes up to the district level at the initial stage.

The appointment of the Balwantrai Mehta Committee was a landmark in the process of decentralization in India. Following the recommendations of the Mehta Committee, Panchayati Raj Institutions were established in different states almost within a span of two years. But in most of the states, the decentralized practice was more or less a ceremonial affair excepting the experiments carried out in a few states. The 73rd and 74th Constitution Amendment Acts (1992) have triggered off new attempts on the part of the states to proceed in the direction of decentralized planning and development with the help and involvement of the 'institutions of self-government.'[1]

THE LEADING MODELS IN DECENTRALIZED PLANNING

The organizational structure and the methodology of planning at the district level varies from state to state, though a certain degree of similarities may be traced in the structure and process adopted in different states. This brings us to the diversified experiences of the states in decentralized planning and the involvement of the people and their representatives. For a clear understanding of the typology, the experiments in decentralized planning, carried out in different states, may be classified into three major models:[2] (a) the traditional Maharashtra-Gujarat model which has been in operation since the seventies, (b) the innovative Karnataka model of the late eighties, and (c) the land reforms-based West Bengal model of decentralized planning developed in the post-Asoka Mehta report. The Kerala methodology of decentralized planning is more or less modelled on the design developed in West Bengal with emphasis on actual operation of decentralized district planning.[3] The organizational framework and methodology followed in other states may be fitted into either of these models with minor differences.

MAHARASHTRA-GUJARAT MODEL

The two states of Maharashtra and Gujarat are the forerunners in the field of district planning and have continued their experiments for a long time.[4] Both the states introduced decentralized planning at the district level in the late sixties to provide an alternative method of development and planning in the aftermath of introduction of Panchayati Raj Institutions, though the Government of Maharashtra had its own organizational scheme with regard to decentralization and development.

District Planning in Maharashtra

After the creation of the state of Maharashtra, the State Government appointed a committee headed by V.P. Naik, the then Revenue Minister, in 1961 to study the recommendations of Balwantrai Mehta Committee and recommend steps for decentralizing the rural development administration in the state. Following the recommendations of the Naik Committee, Panchayati raj was inaugurated in Maharashtra in 1962 *inter alia* 'to plan and implement all schemes of a local nature with efficiency, speed and economy'.[5]

The decentralized planning exercises attempted in Maharashtra before the Fifth Five-Year Plan concentrated on the preparation of production plan and public consumption plan in respect of the districts other than Greater Bombay.[6] Maharashtra actually made serious attempts towards decentralized planning in the Fifth Plan and considered the district as a unit of planning below the state level since 1972. The State Government also prepared indices of development for districts and tehsils and also village-wise index cards.

Planning Machinery at the District

With a view to giving the idea of district planning a concrete shape, the Government of Maharashtra constituted the Planning Department at the state level and subsequently set up the State Planning Board. In conformity with this, the State Government formed the District Planning Boards in early 1972 as the machinery for planning at the district level and assigned the following functions to them: (i) co-ordination of the activities of the various implementing agencies, (ii) formulation of guidelines for the preparation and implementation of district plans and (iii) approval of the five-year plan and annual plans of the district. The composition of the District Planning Board was heavily biased in favour of the government and bank officials. The constitution of the Board evoked strong criticism since it did not include representatives of Parliament and State Legislature, not to speak of the Panchayati Raj Institutions. Accordingly, the elected representatives and persons of other interests like trade and commerce, industry, universities and social welfare organizations were associated with the district planning process and District Development Consultative Councils were created for the districts (except for Greater Bombay) by the Government.[7] The District Development Consultative Council (DDCC) functioned as a reviewing mechanism of the district plans from time to time and was merely an advisory body. Naturally, the need for creating an appropriate planning body at the district level to look after all the aspects of district planning was felt to be severe and accordingly District Planning and Development Councils (DPDC) were constituted in each of the district of the state in 1974.

The formation of District Planning and Development Councils (DPDC) by way of amalgamation of the District Planning Board and the District Development Consultative Council marked the culmination of a trend. With wider functions and increasing strength, the DPDC has become dynamic and useful, particularly keen in acting as a watchdog over the implementation of various schemes and in providing a positive check on the pitfalls and misuses. The District Planning and Development Council is headed by a minister-designate for the district known as the '*Palak Mantri*' and includes the members of Parliament and State Legislature belonging to the district, President and Chief Executive Officer of the Zilla Parishad, Mayor of Municipal Corporation, Municipal Commissioner, representatives of Municipal Councils and Co-operative Banks among others.[8] The conversion of the post of the Chief Executive Officer to that of Member-Secretary of the DPDC and the appointment of the District Collector to the redesignated post of Member-Secretary from December 1975 onwards, have strengthened the position of the District Planning and Development Council. Likewise, changes have been introduced in the composition of the Executive Committee of the DPDC with the inclusion of the legislators of all categories within it. Again, in the organizational framework of decentralized planning, voluntary organizations have been fruitfully associated with the process in Maharashtra.[9] The day-to-day functions of the Council are vested in the Executive Committee which meets as often as necessary, but is required to meet at least once in a month.[10] In any case, the replacement of the Chief Executive Officer of the Zilla Parishad by the District Collector as the Member-Secretary of the DPDC has an adverse effect on the functioning of the decentralized administration at the district level. The action has eroded the autonomy and the role of the Panchayati Raj Institutions in the area of district Planning.[11]

Moreover, under the Maharashtra Panchayat Act, 1994 the Collector is empowered to call for any information from the Zilla Parishad and enjoys emergency powers in respect of health and safety of the people. The whole concept of decentralization is given a secondary role when the local bodies close to the people are denied powers in emergency situations even when safety and health of the people are endangered.[12] It is amusing that although the 74th Constitution Amendment Act provides for the constitution of District Planning Committee, in the context of changed circumstances in each state, the Maharashtra Panchayat Act, 1994 did not provide for the creation of District Planning Committee and dwelt on the existing arrangements incorporated in the State Municipal Act. Thus in Maharashtra the District Planning and Development Councils discharged the planning functions at the district level and the Panchayati Raj Institutions were associated with these bodies.[13]

Now the District Planning Committee has been constituted. The State Planning Board has recently recommended the empowerment of the *Gram Sabhas* in prioritisation of projects for the villages and also in respect of monitoring their implementation in its approach paper for the Tenth Plan.[14]

Fund Allocations

The Planning process that was in existence at the districts in Maharashtra continues to be operative at present. The process is very simple though the basis on which funds are distributed among the districts raises the question of autonomy in decentralized planning.[15] The allocations for the districts are fixed by the State Government and the District Planning Committees formulate the district plans within the limits of such allocations. The allocation is based on 'Guidelines' issued by the State Government as per the time schedule. The district plan consists of two parts: State Sector Schemes and District Level Schemes and, accordingly, the plan outlay is divided.[16] The schemes having the benefits confined to a single district are included in the district sector. From the mid-seventies, there has been an important development that deserves special considerations. A component named 'State Pool' of the district level schemes has come into existence according to which the expenditure that is incurred for such schemes as are considered relevant from the view point of National and State importance by the State Government, is later debited to the district.[17] The very concept of 'State Pool' amounts to centralization and thereby negates the autonomy and the principles of decentralized planning. Again, the directives issued by the State Government in the form of 'Guidelines' is considered to be an encroachment on the liberty of the state and 'frustrates efforts to put substance into planning from below despite district sector allocation.'[18] Thus to make the district planning real, there is the urgent need to reduce the number of items as well as the amount involved in 'State pool' schemes and to include those schemes in the respective district plan, if required. Similarly, no one can doubt the necessity of providing guidelines for the districts so as to make district plans relevant in the context of National and State plans but attempts are to be made to enhance the scope of autonomy of the district planning bodies in the formulation, prioritization and implementation of plans.

For quite sometime, decentralized planning has been sought to be extended to the block level on the identical lines of the district planning but there is no block plan. Recently, the State Government has prepared a formula for the allocation of funds for the blocks. This is certainly a big leap towards decentraliza-tion. But the problem lies elsewhere. Originally it was decided to allot about 60 per cent of the total State Plan outlay to the district sector schemes and remaining 40 per cent to the state sector schemes but subsequently the tentative ratio of expenditure on plan schemes between the state and the district came down from 40 : 60 to 60 : 40. This is not an encouraging development. Again, the main plank of decentralized planning is the participation of the people in both plan formulation and implementation. But in Maharashtra, in spite of high sounding talks, no significant role has been provided for the Panchayati Raj Institutions.[19] One of the most essential preconditions for the success of decentralized planning is land reforms. But the situation in Maharashtra with regard to land reforms is extremely disappointing. A recent study, conducted in eight villages of the state, has highlighted the cases of benami transfer of lands, the connivance of village level and Taluka level functionaries with the landlords and the weakness in implementation of ceiling laws.[20]

District Planning in Gujarat

Gujarat is another pioneering state that introduced decentralized planning at the district level. Gujarat's experiments with district planning have many similarities with those of the district planning in Maharashtra, in the sense that provisions for dividing the state budget in 'State Sector' and 'District Sector' have been made with a view to transferring a definite portion of states' financial resources to the District Panchayats. Rational allocation of funds to the different levels of planning is an essential precondition for the successful implementation of decentralized planning. Under our constitutional arrangements provisions have been made for the division of resources between the Centre and States. There is also provision for a 'divisible pool' for distribution of incomes between them but such a provision earmarking the division of funds below the state-level is absent.

Planning Organization

In the initial years of decentralized planning in Gujarat, District Planning Boards were created at the districts which looked after the planning functions below the state level.[21] The Gujarat Panchayat Act, passed in 1993 to conform to the requirements of the provisions of the Amendment Act of 1992, does not provide for the District Planning Committee while other states, excepting Maharashtra of course, have made provisions in their Acts.[22] Following the practice of other states, Gujarat has also made provisions for the accommodation of the members of the Legislature in the planning boards. The District Planning Board in Gujarat is more broad-based and participatory than its counterpart in Maharashtra in a way that the former includes the Presidents of panchayats and representatives of municipalities as members.[23] The District Planning Board is headed by a State Minister and works with a handful of government staff under the administrative guidance of the District Planning Officer. Thus Gujarat follows the Minister-Chairman model of Maharashtra together with Uttar Pradesh and Bihar.[24] But the overall attitude of the political leadership in Gujarat is not congenial towards the growth and development of an effective decentralized system. After postponing the elections to the gram panchayats twice in recent past, the Government has now launched a *Samras Gram* (harmonious village) Scheme under which cash awards up to Rs. One lakh will be given to such Gram Panchayats as are formed unanimously. The Scheme has been defended on the ground that 'the government wants that people must live in amity and brotherhood and not let the petty politics obstruct development works.'[25] It may be noted that in 1997 panchayat elections were held in the state when 27 per cent of the candidates won the elections without any contest.

Planning Methodology and Devolution of Funds

The process of plan formulation in Gujarat is akin to that of Maharashtra model. The State Government prepares a time schedule and transmits it to the District Planning Boards along with a 'Guideline' to streamline the operation of the programme for normal district plan and for discretionary outlay. The District Planning Board collects proposals for district level schemes from different district level officers and District Panchayats. The district level officers submit proposals for sectoral schemes while the District Panchayat prepares panchayat sector schemes. The district plans are required to be submitted to the State Planning Department for finalisation. In contrast with the practice followed in Maharashtra, the State Planning Department is not actively associated with the District Planning Board in Gujarat. Again, the autonomy of the District Planning Boards is restrained compared to the methodology followed in Maharashtra. The District Planning and Development Council in Maharashtra is vested with the authority for reallocation of plan funds depending on the monthly review of district development programmes for effective utilization within the district.[26] This provision for reallocation of plan funds based on periodical review gives essence to decentralized planning. But the serious weakness in the Gujarat model lies in the fact that out of the funds available for district development schemes, approximately eighty per cent of the plan allocation is withheld by the State Planning Department and proposals relating to it are prepared by the sectoral departments, almost without any consultation with the District Planning Boards. The remaining twenty per cent which is placed at the disposal of the District Planning Board is divided into two parts: (i) fifteen per cent Discretionary Outlay for district level schemes to be formulated by the DPB, and (ii) five per cent Incentive Outlay to be matched by the state, the ratio of contribution depends upon the backwardness.[27] Thus, in effect "there are three district plans, one each for the eighty per cent, fifteen per cent and five per cent sectors with no underlined unity among them."[28] Such a situation leads to the problem of integration and coordination which are the essential aspects of decentralized planning. The approach is 'truncated' and basically goes against 'the logic of development planning.'[29]

The District Planning Body in Gujarat is authorised to sanction development schemes within a certain limit fixed by the government. The body has been assigned the duties of selecting schemes relating to Minimum Needs Programmes, with a view to creating durable assets and providing basic amenities for the people of the district according to the 'Guidelines' which is issued periodically by the State Planning Department. In this regard, the authority of the District Planning Board is limited to the extent that allocation should not be made on non-development items.

In the initial phase of planning in Gujarat, there were anomalies in the sphere of selecting schemes but subsequently the situation was reviewed and a list of admissible and non-admissible schemes was prepared in 1984 for the guidance of the District Planning Boards. The list consists of three parts: (i) Schemes admissible under discretionary and incentive outlays, (ii) Schemes admissible only under incentive-outlay and (iii) Schemes inadmissible under discretionary and incentive outlay.[30] This was a minor problem the solution of which has been worked out. But the major problem relates to the pinching of the heart, the flow of funds for district planning. It was expected that with the passing of time decentralized planning would be strengthened or would pass from Stage I to Stage II and then to Stage III so that the states including Gujarat might reach the final phase of complete decentralization within this century. It was also expected that the first two stages of 'Initiation' and 'Limited Decentralization' could be attained by the end of the Seventh Plan period. The expectations are belied.[31] A review of the outlay provided for district level schemes in Gujarat out of the State Plan Outlay for Seventh Five-Year Plan (1985-90) and Annual Plans 1986-87 to 1989-90 shows a gradual decline in the flow of funds towards district level schemes from the State Plan Outlay.[32] Similar conclusions are drawn by the Study Group on Planning Process and Rural Labour (1991) when it concludes that "the actual district planning was confined exclusively to the twenty per cent discretionary and incentive funds available to the district."[33] Moreover, under the methodology of fund allocations 'only a small fraction of the district plan is formulated in the light of local needs'[34] in Gujarat which frustrates the objective of decentralized planning.

However, there has been a perceptible change in the attitude of the policy-makers since the submission of the report by the Tenth Finance Commission. The Commission recommended an *untied fund* of Rs. 192 crore to the PRIs in Gujarat for the period from 1996 to 2002 at the rate of Rs. 48 crore a year. The panchayats have started receiving this money from 1999-2000 due to the delay in submission of the recommendation of the State Finance Commission.[35]

Thus the review of decentralized district planning exercises in Maharashtra and Gujarat suggests that the planning in these states came to be decentralized only in name but not in substance. Moreover, the people and their representatives in panchayats have not been assigned the desired place in the whole mechanism of district planning.[36] In spite of the inadequacies and pitfalls, the Maharashtra and Gujarat experiments were a good beginning in the process of decentralized planning 'for they evoked questioning attention from the State Governments which felt threatened by the emergence of a rival centre of power and authority.'[37]

KARNATAKA MODEL OF DISTRICT PLANNING

The Karnataka model of decentralized planning produced certain encouraging trends in the field of decentralization and planning in the eighties and 'remains perhaps the most sophisticated effort made by any state'[38] prior to that period. The Karnataka experiment is different from that of Maharashtra and Gujarat. At least in two respects, the Karnataka model can claim its superiority to those which are being practised in other states: (i) the decentralized planning machinery is fully representative in character and it enjoys autonomy, within certain limits, in the spheres of selecting priorities, locations and parameters of implementation at the district level. (ii) Unlike in Maharashtra and Gujarat, there is the provision for 'lump sum allocation' of plan funds for the districts in Karnataka. In fact, the Government of Karnataka has carried out a good number of experiments in the past in respect of allotment of plan funds for the districts. Planning at the district level in Karnataka is as old as that in Gujarat and Maharashtra and as such the planning process in Karnataka has gained a colourful experience.

The Beginning

District Planning in Karnataka was first introduced in the sixties and it was in the form of disaggregation of the State Plans.[39] The role of the district agency was mainly advisory in character and supervisory in functions. The district plans were formulated at the state headquarter by the planners and were implemented by the official machinery of the district. The funds at the disposal of the district planning bodies were meagre and were not 'free funds'. Following the 'Guidelines', issued by the Planning Commission in 1969, Karnataka introduced District Plans in an organized way under the Fifth Five-Year Plan, as was the case with most of the states. A District and Regional Planning Division was set-up in the State Planning Department and District Planning Officers were appointed at the district levels. A District Planning Committee headed by a Deputy Commissioner was also constituted. The District Planning Officer was appointed to act as the Member-Secretary. This body was responsible for preparation of the draft plan, which was subsequently placed before the District Development Council for approval. The Council was a larger body having both the bureaucratic and representative components.

The district plan in Karnataka thus turned out to be a mere aggregation of departmental schemes. This process in decentralized planning continued with minor modifications, as and when required. However, in the absence of an effective and regularly elected local level people's bodies, the opportunity for meaningful decentralization in planning was rather limited. Moreover, a mere desegregation of the State Plan into district plans, without any regard to the local needs, priorities and resources, could not be considered as decentralized planning. For formulation and implementation of local development plans based on local conditions and resources, the local representative bodies should have the autonomy to determine their objectives and priorities.[40]

Developments in the Eighties

The prospects of decentralized district planning brightened in Karnataka in 1987 with the setting up of Zilla Parishads at the district level and the Mandal Panchayats for a cluster of villages. The establishment of panchayat raj system in Karnataka is considered as an important effort in the direction of democratic decentralization, the objective of which was to carve out a tier of government at the district level. The introduction of the two-tier[41] system of rural local self-government headed by the Zilla Parishad marked a watershed in the evolution of decentralized planning and development in Karnataka in the sense that Zilla Parishad inherited all the functions of the state in respect of rural development and planning. Under the Karnataka Panchayat Act of 1983 the Zilla Parishad was required to exercise overall supervision, co-ordination and integration of development works within the district and to prepare, administer and monitor plans for the district since there was no separate planning body at the district level in Karnataka in the eighties.[42]

The methodology of decentralized planning developed in Karnataka in the eighties continues to exist though there have been some changes in the organizational set-up in district planning. The scheme of devolution of funds under the methodology is simple and more decentralized than the Maharashtra model where the provision for 'State Pool' retards the process of decentralization. In Karnataka, all schemes with a mandal orientation were transferred to the Mandal Panchayats; schemes with an inter-mandal, inter-taluk or district orientations were placed under the Zilla Parishad while the schemes involving more than one districts or World Bank or external assistance were left for the State Sectors. The entire Special-component Plan and the Tribal Sub-plan were made over to the Zilla Parishad for implementation.[43] Thus Karnataka had a three-level planning process in the eighties and early nineties: (i) State Planning administered from the state headquarters; (ii) Zilla Parishad Planning at the district level and (iii) Mandal Panchayat Planning, below the district level.

Resource is an important factor in the formulation and implementation of integrated decentralized planning and for that purpose 'untied or free funds with no tie ups' are required. Karnataka Government considered various alternatives like lump sum allocation, sector-wise allocation and minor head-wise allocation under each sector from the beginning of the eighties for this purpose. The main reason behind such experiments in the pattern of fund allocations lies in the urge for effecting parity between the district priorities and the state priorities. It was a dominant practice in almost all the states during the earlier plans to give the highest consideration to the scheme-wise outlays, decided at the state-level, while finalising the district plans. In this process, the District Planning exercises turned to be the plans imposed from the state level. The situation in Karnataka prior to 1987 was not different. Subsequently the Government decided to work out a provision for a free outlay in the form of a lump sum allocation for district planning. This allocation includes not only outlay from State Planning Schemes, but also the outlay from Centrally Sponsored Schemes and Central Sector Schemes. But scheme-wise allocation of funds is available only when the state level schemes do not come under the purview of either district or the panchayats. The Zilla Parishad (Panchayat) formulates its plans against the 'lump sum allocations' indicated to the district and the panchayats based on the functions assigned to them. Thus the planning function of the state is confined to the formulation of state level schemes, integration of district and panchayat level schemes with the state level schemes and ensuring priorities in the district and panchayat level schemes.

To remove regional disparities and imbalances through decentralized planning, the government has developed a weightage schedule on the lines of 'Gadgil formula' for the distribution of plan allocations among the districts. As per this criterion, backward regions or areas enjoy preferential treatment in the allocation of funds.[44] The mode of allocation of plan funds for the district is again strengthened by the provision of per capita grants to the district of which seventy-five per cent goes to the panchayats below the district level and the balance to the district.[45]

Implementation is an important aspect of planning. Implementation depends largely on the monitoring and information systems. Along with the introduction of 'planning calendar', the Karnataka model has made considerable innovations in this regard. Two types of progress monitoring systems have been worked out from the beginning : (i) Monthly Multi-Level Review (MMR) and (ii) Karnataka Development Programme Review (KDPR). Though the Zilla Parishad, now the District Planning Committee, enjoys full autonomy in the formulation and implementation of development schemes and the government interference is minimal, nevertheless, there is a continuous monitoring of performance at all levels. The government has drawn a time schedule consisting of respective dates together with the levels and the concerned authority for such review. A particular date of the month for review is fixed by each authority in such a way as the review reports are available to the next level in time. Each department also carries a detailed, scheme by scheme review at corresponding levels, which gets related to the Karnataka Development Project Review.[46] Thus the Karnataka model is unique in its monitoring system. In fact Karnataka is the first state in India where the monitoring arrangements for decentralized planning are so systematically and consistently organized.

The above review suggests that the decentralized planning process introduced in Karnataka within the overall framework of Panchayati raj system in the eighties was a worthwhile exercise but the outcome is depressing. The position for the first year of decentralized planning is illustrative. Out of the State Plan of Rs.920 crores, Rs.239.78 crores was earmarked for the districts. Of this 86 per cent amounting to Rs.205.88 went to five items under 'Committed Expenditure' over which the Zilla Parishad had no control and its autonomy was squeezed into the balance of only 14 per cent. Such a situation could be encountered 'if these levels (Local levels) raise their own resources sufficiently to feel autonomous.'[47] Moreover, a recent trend in expenditure schedule is visible that the ratio of non-developmental and developmental expenditure is increasing in favour of the former. It is an all-India phenomenon and Karnataka is not the odd man.[48] It has been observed that in Karnataka, in a period of ten years ending in 1988-89, non-developmental expenditure increased at the rate of 19 per cent while developmental expenditure has grown at the rate of 15 per cent.[49]

In a multi-level planning system, objective formulation and effective implementation of plans depend upon a high degree of coordination, consultation, interaction and resolution of conflicts at different stages and tiers and hence a state level agency is preferred to discharge these important functions. The Govern-ment of Karnataka has decided to retain the Planning Depart-ment as a nodal department for the guidance of the Zilla Parishad and Mandal Panchayats in matters relating to planning for development.[50] The Karnataka model of the eighties provided such an administrative structure as was almost like a state within the state. The Zilla Parishad appeared to be an assembly presided over by the *Adhyaksha* and assisted by the *Upadhyaksha*, enjoying the rank, pay and status of a Minister-of-State and a Deputy Minister respectively. The experts, planners, field officers, educationists, health officers and other functionaries associated with rural development of the district were placed under the Zilla Parishad. Moreover, the Zilla Parishad had a Chief Executive Officer called the 'Chief Secretary.'[51]

Recent Changes

The Zilla Parishads created in the eighties were entrusted with the sole responsibility in decentralized district planning in Karnataka. Under the Act of 1993[52] the Zilla Parishad has been changed to Zilla Panchayat and the overall planning functions of the district have been taken over by the District Planning Committee though the three-tier panchayats and the municipalities have been assigned the role of preparing their annual plans within the limits prescribed by the Act. The District Planning Committee is composed of the Members of Parliament and the State Assembly representing the district or registered as electors in the district, *Adhyakshas* of the Zilla Panchayat and Municipal Corporation, President of the Municipal Council and such other members, not less than four-fifth of the total members of the committee, as elected from amongst the members of the Zilla Panchayat, Nagara Panchayat and Councillors of the Municipal Corporation and the Municipal Councils in the district. The Chairmanship of the District Planning Committee is left to be decided by the government while the Act designates the Chief Executive Officer of the Zilla Parishad as the Secretary of the DPC.[53] The District Planning Committee consolidates the plan prepared by the Zilla Panchayat, Taluk Panchayats, Municipal Councils and Municipal Corporations in the district and prepares a draft development plan for the district as a whole.[54] It is interesting to note that there is no scope for representation of the Taluk Panchayats, which constitute the middle-tier in the Panchayati raj hierarchy in Karnataka. Viewed from this aspect, the District Planning Committee lacks organic linkages in its composition.

The whole arrangement for decentralized development and Planning in Karnataka is worth-emulating for other states. Karnataka has done a lot of things: it has set up three-tier Panchayati Raj Institutions on the lines suggested by the Asoka Mehta Committee and has constituted *Gram Sabha* at the village levels even prior to the 73rd Constitution Amendment Act (1992). It has laid down the scheme for decentralized planning and has strengthened the planning machinery at both the state and district levels. It has made provisions for the constitution of District Planning Committee for the districts subsequently in conformity with the stipulations of the 74th Amendment Act. The constitution of a State Development Council on the model of National Development Council with the Chief Minister as its Chairman to review and supervise the works in the state, apart from planning schemes, is being considered by the Government of Karnataka.[55] It has also made provisions for the constitution of State Election Commission and the State Finance Commission in the Panchayat Raj Act of 1993.[56] These institutional arrangements have strengthened the decentralized planning framework created in Karnataka. Moreover, the decentralized planning experiences in Karnataka have established the hypothesis that both cost and corruption in the implementation of schemes are reduced to a remarkable extent when the people and their representatives are involved in the preparation and implementation of plan projects.[57]

The Retarding Features

In spite of these achievements attained in the eighties and early nineties, the decentralized planning and the process of decentralization as a whole is now reversed considerably. It is an established fact that decentralized planning cannot be strengthened when the local self-governing bodies, the Panchayati Raj Institutions are weakened. It may be mentioned that Karnataka is the first state to pass a new piece of legislation in 1993 in conformity with the Constitutional Amendments.[58] While according statutory recognition to the decentralized district planning, the Act has strengthened the bureaucratic control over the Panchayati raj bodies. The State Act has put the panchayats under the control of the government and its officials, the Commissioner and the Deputy Commissioner.[59] The concept of decentralization suffers a severe jolt by the provisions of the Act itself which authorises the government to take back or add to 1the functions of the Panchayati raj bodies.[60] It is a sad ex-perience in Karnataka that some important functions of the panchayats like Public Distribution System, Co-operatives, Drinking Water Schemes, distribution of house-sites etc. have been withdrawn. The State Development Council formed in the eighties was made defunct subsequently.[61] Now there is no provision for such a council in the Act.

The present act strengthens the position of the Chief Executive Officer of the Zilla Panchyat. The designation of

Chief Secretary accorded to the Chief Executive Officer of the Zilla Parishad under the Act of 1983 has now been withdrawn and the power to transfer officials previously enjoyed by the Zilla Parishad is at present vested fully with the government. Moreover, the new Act is silent on the status of the *Adhyaksha* of the Zilla Panchayat.[62] The provisions for appointment of administrators at the Panchayats and the authority of the government to specify the role and functions of these bodies raise doubts about the future of the Panchayati raj in Karnataka.[63] Serious challenge is posed by the statutory provision for the dissolution of panchayats by the State Government. The mandatory provision for reconstitution of Panchayati raj bodies within six months through election[64] is not guaranteed, at least in Karnataka. A very interesting but disappointing fact will expose the intention of the powers that be. Elections to the Panchayati raj bodies in Karnataka, due to be held in January 1992, were postponed by the government. A Division Bench of the Karnataka High Court issued a writ asking the state to conduct the said elections before December 1992, which the State Government challenged in the Supreme Court. The Supreme Court granted an extension up to 30 June, 1993 but the government preferred an appeal to the Supreme Court again pleading for further extension to 31 December 1993, which was granted. Yet the government did not hold the election as directed, but the climax as it were, instead postponed the elections to Zilla Panchayat and Taluk Panchayat indefinitely. Now the hope that pinned on Karnataka model was belied with the indefinite postponement and delay in elections. However, the elections for the constitution of Gram Panchayats and two other tiers were held in 1993 and 1995 respectively after a prolonged delay.[65] Hence, the major problem that threatens the nourishment, if not the survival, of the experiments in decentralization in Karnataka is the unwilling and callous attitude of the politicians and bureaucrats to share power with the local representatives. This was one of the reasons why the first generation Panchayats failed. In West Bengal, this problem has been minimised to a certain extent through a combination of strong ideological commitments and organizationnal discipline in the State Government, which is absent in Karnataka.[66]

Thus Karnataka which had once become a model for decentralized planning has entered itself into a phase of reversal and is struggling to attain complete decentralization in planning though the mechanism and process are yet to be worked out finally and in details. The government is now contemplating for a comprehensive legislation to actualise real decentralization in planning and local administration. In fact Karnataka follows the step of moving forward and backward in introducing decentralized plans in the state. Recently, the Government appointed a working group on decentralization, which has sub-mitted its report, and accordingly it has introduced a bill (August 2, 2002) to amend the existing Panchayat Act of the state. Though the draft bill includes some encouraging features in it, it does not seek to amend the provisions relating to 'Inspection and Control'. The 1993 Act was much retrogressive in many respects especially in empowering the bureaucracy with the power of inspection and control of elected local bodies. In the spheres of decentralized planning the bill contains 'a lot of verbiage without much substance'. Thus in reality the bill seeks to bypass the main thrust of the Constitutional Amendments that aim at ensuring 'maximum democracy and maximum devolu-tion', both at the same time.[67] It is too early to comment on the future, but the experience gathered in Karnataka raises a basic question: given the harsh grassroots reality of poverty and illiteracy of the populace, what are the preconditions necessary for successful decentralized planning under a regime of central planning? The answer to this question may be sought for in another experiment, initiated in West Bengal.

ALTERNATIVE MODEL OF WEST BENGAL

District Planning of a sort has been in existence in West Bengal since the early seventies. But it was merely a disaggregation of the state plans based on sectoral allocation of funds. The planning activities remained centred around the state though the District Planning Boards were created to organize the preparation of plans for the districts. In fact district planning was yet to take roots in West Bengal when the Left Front Government came to power in 1977. For adequate understanding of the revitalized district planning in West Bengal, it is necessary to comprehend the perspectives and background in which district planning was launched. The entire edifice of decentralized district planning was developed on the axis of land reforms and panchayats which constitute the core of the alternative approach to rural development and planning in West Bengal.

Perspectives of Decentralized Planning in West Bengal

Two major characteristics of planning pursued up to the later part of the 1970s, however, have been apparent over the years: *first,* contrary to the objectives and priorities, benefits of the process of development planning did not reach the poorer sections of the society; *secondly,* as a related matter, people in general and the poor in particular, were not involved in the process of decision-making and implementation of the development projects. The Left Front Government after assuming office in June, 1977 realised that the tardy implementation in planning was mainly due to the lack of popular involvement in the formulation, implementation and monitoring of plan projects.[68] Naturally, it decided to reverse both these trends at the state level within the limitations imposed on it by the existing socio-economic structure. Rural Development and Planning, the government stressed, should come primarily through the rural poor by involving them in an organized manner. The Panchayati Raj Institutions, which were considered to be a platform for organizing people's participation in rural development works, prior to 1978 failed to give shape to the people's aspirations as they were not formed with elected representatives of the people.

Revitalization of Panchayats

The State Government decided to reactivate the 'moribund' Panchayati raj system with the aim of ensuring people's participation in decentralized planning and development. The politicised Panchayat in West Bengal is an institutional innovation of the Left Front Government led by the CPI(M) to consolidate its power base at the grassroots.[69] The decision of the

State Government to revitalize the panchayats through elections and allow the political parties to set their own candidates in 1978 was a total break with the previous practices. The leadership was convinced that if Panchayats failed, the decentralizing experiment to empower people would fail.[70] Hence, it would be difficult to understand the dynamics of development strategy in West Bengal without analyzing the total context in which this 'institutional innovation' was pursued. The three tiers Panchayat system comprising Zilla Parishad, Panchayat Samiti and Gram Panchayat came into existence on 4 June, 1978. Fifty-six thousand representatives directly elected to different tiers contested the Panchayat elections with their respective party symbols.[71] Subsequently, the Second, Third, Fourth and Fifth General Panchayat elections were held in 1983, 1988, 1993 and 1998 respectively. Interestingly in all these elections, the ruling Front established its political supremacy over the rural polity in West Bengal.

The State Government viewed rural development as a process of assisting primarily the rural poor with a view to increasing production in agriculture and allied activities and in rural industry and to maintaining a certain balance between agricultural and industrial development. It was convinced from different studies on Farm Management and Agricultural Census of different districts as well as from several other states that agricultural production, in terms of per acre yield and cropping-intensity taken together, is higher for the small and marginal farmers in comparison to those of the rich farmers. The lack in resources and other non-labour inputs are compensated by them (small and marginal farmers) through intensive application of their labour which increases yield per unit.[72] Naturally such a perception led to the development of an 'Alternative Approach' to rural development and planning, the basis of which was land-reforms. For more than two decades, Land Reforms Acts were in practice in West Bengal, though there was a gulf of difference between the provisions of the law and its application.[73] Immediately after being voted to power, the Left Front Government resolved to change the scenario by enforcing those laws and in each area of land reforms programme, cooperation of the peasant organizations and active participation of the newly elected panchayats were sought for and encouraged. Moreover, the State Government led by the CPI(M) 'successfully pushed the local panchayats into playing a vital role in local conflict resolution and in establishing a rule of law at the local level that (has) clearly benefited the poor and marginal groups.'[74] This was for the first time in West Bengal that direct participation of the people and their representatives were ensured in development programmes.[75]

Implementation of Land Reforms

In any comprehensive planning for rural development, the importance of land reforms cannot be overlooked. The main target of land reforms is to abolish intermediary rights and to establish legal rights of the actual peasants on land. Through the imposition of land ceiling provisions, arrangements were made to vest surplus land in government and distribute the same among the cultivators. The State's achievement was much spectacular in comparison to all India figures. So far as the present position is concerned, approximately 52.99 lakh acres of agricultural land have been vested throughout the country while 13.81 lakh acres of agricultural land has been vested in the state,[76] of which 10.55 lakh acres of land have been distributed to about 25.30 lakh beneficiaries. Thus total area of land distributed is not only the highest in the country but also accounts for about one-fifth of the total area of the surplus land distributed in all the states taken together.[77] Another important point that needs to be mentioned here is that the poorest section of the poor, i.e. the scheduled castes and the scheduled tribes constitute more than 37% and 19% respectively of the total beneficiaries. The percentage is much more than the percentage of this population in the state.[78]

The following table 3.1 reflects the pattern of distribution of land in West Bengal in comparison to the all-India position.

Alongside the land reform measures directed towards vesting and distribution of surplus land beyond the ceiling, the Government launched the scheme of *Operation Barga* after the formation of panchayats in 1978. The underlined objective of the scheme was to record immediately the names of *bargadars* (share-croppers) in the field in order to protect their rights against forceful eviction by the landlords. Most of the share-cropping arrangements hitherto prevalent were of oral nature without any record of documentary evidence at the hands of *bargadars* and as such the system was completely at the mercy of the landowners so far as the continuance of the *bargadars* were concerned. The remedies available under the traditional system of revenue courts were negligible and were not easily available to the common people. Very often their lawyers at the revenue courts represented the landowners and thus they were always placed in advantageous positions. In most cases, the *bargadars* were implicated in false cases and were harassed by the police.[79]

Table 3.1 : Pattern of Land-ownership : India and West Bengal – 1972, 1982 and 1992

Categories of Peasantry		1972		1982		1992	
		Percentage of families	Percentage of land	Percentage of families	Percentage of land	Percentage of families	Percentage of land
All India	Small	78.11	24.44	81.35	28.72	85.30	35.52
	Medium	19.77	52.65	17.23	53.21	13.82	50.65
	Rich	2.12	22.91	1.42	18.07	0.88	13.83
Total		100.00	100.00	100.00	100.00	100.00	100.00
West Bengal	Small	90.26	52.97	93.10	59.11	95.35	69.40
	Medium	9.69	46.33	6.82	39.35	4.65	30.60
	Rich	0.05	0.70	0.08	1.54	0.00	0.00
Total		100.00	100.00	100.00	100.00	100.00	100.00

Source : Government of India, NSS - 48th Round (1992).

The State Government was keen on effecting a change in land system and it considered land reforms as the basis of rural development strategy in West Bengal. Therefore, it decided to supplement the bureaucratic apparatus of land reforms developed over the years by establishing functional linkages among bureaucracy, panchayats and peasant organizations. It also brought about a vital change in the statute book : the onus of proving that a person is lawfully cultivating the land in question lies on the landowner and not on the *bargadars* cultivating the land. This simple amendment incorporated in the Land Reforms Act changed the entire situation and restored a sense of confidence against the owner-bureaucracy combine. Related to this statutory change, the Revenue Officials were directed to move to the localities inhabited by a large number of unrecorded *bargadars* in the evenings to organize joint-sittings, with the active help of the panchayat members and peasant workers, to explain the need and method of *Barga-recording* to the *bargadars.* This change in the *modus operandi* of recording the names of share-croppers, besides instilling a sense of confidence, led them to organize collective actions against the onslaught of the landlords and zamindars, whenever necessary. After the publication of the provisional list of share-croppers for display at public places with a view to inviting objections, if any, 'certificates of *barga*' (share-cropping recordings) were issued to the share-croppers. As a result of *operation barga,* till December, 1996, the names of more than 14.98 lakh *bargadars* could be recorded out of which 4.48 lakh belonged to scheduled castes, 1.70 lakh to scheduled tribes. Of the cultivable land coming under the purview of *Operation barga*, 32 per cent belonged to the scheduled castes and 14 per cent to scheduled tribes. Apparently not much revolutionary but reformist in nature, West Bengal has at least recorded the names of the share-croppers and has ensured their access to the land revenue administration of the state.[80]

Other Pro-people Measures

To ensure participation of the poorer section of the society in rural development process, the government took measures for allotment of homestead plots to the agricultural workers and share-croppers alongside the distribution of surplus land and the recording of the names of the share-croppers through *operation barga.* It is a fact that a large number of *bargadars* and *Kshetmajoors* (agricultural workers) used to live on the lands owned by others as permissive occupiers. They were allowed to live on the implied condition of rendering services at the beck and call of the owners. Whenever *bargadars* recorded their names or the *Kshetmajoor* demanded higher wages they faced the fear of eviction which affected their position adversely and put them in immense difficulties. To obviate this situation the government undertook the programme of conferring titles on such permissive possessors in rural area up to 0·08 acres of land. Till 1997, 2.80 lakh persons were provided with the title of their homestead plots.[81]

All these changes in land reforms, introduced in the spheres of both distribution of surplus lands to the landless and recording the names of share-croppers, raised a very pertinent question: the problem related to the economic viability of the schemes of distribution and recording among the landless poor people from the point of view of increasing production.[82] The Government was conscious of such a problem. In order to make the land reforms viable, it introduced programmes of assistance for the poor in the forms of institutional credits and non-land inputs, such as irrigation facilities, implements, manure and fertilisers. The arrangement for institutional credit support system was an important element, which helped to protect the share-croppers and the poor peasants from their subjection to 'distress sale' of their paddy. The government organized the Co-operatives, Regional Rural Banks and Commercial Banks to provide short-term loans to the *patta*-holders (allottee of vested lands) and *bargadars* directly through the Rural Agricultural Co-operative Credit Societies. Apart from preparing credit plan, the government provided huge subsidies for the small and marginal farmers.[83] The number of beneficiaries under the category of share-croppers and *patta-holders* so financed increased from 59,114 in 1979-80 to 3,74,538 in 1982-83. Along with land reforms, a special emphasis was given to the extension of irrigation facilities. As a result, it has been possible to increase the proportion of cropped areas under irrigation from less than thirty per cent in the first half of the seventies to nearly fifty per cent in 1995-96, and this proportion has further increased to 62.5 per cent in 2000-2001.[84]

Apart from this development aspect, a good beginning in the process of participatory planning can be traced in the management of minor irrigation projects. The government has already undertaken a scheme to transfer the operation and maintenance of the tube-well command area to the local people through the formation of beneficiary committees under the supervision of panchayats. Experience has shown that in such cases, not only have the operation and maintenance costs been fully recovered, but enough surplus has also been generated which the farmers have ploughed back for installing new tube-wells. In coordination with overall plan priority and organization, this experiment is an example of efficient and accountable decentralization.

Table 3.2 : Production of major crops in the state during Ninth Plan

Crops	Ninth Plan Target (Terminal Year 2001-02)	1997-98 (Actual)	1998-99 (Actual)	1999-2000 (Actual)	2000-01 (Actual)	2001-02 (Estimated)
Rice	14240.00	13236.59	13316.44	13759.68	12428.03	14319.00
Wheat	900.00	810.48	778.09	850.78	1058.61	1075.00
Pulses	200.00	152.67	126.46	141.58	219.58	240.00
Total Foodgrains	15444.00	14354.27	14367.48	14845.55	13815.23	15734.00
Total Oilseeds	540.00	386.57	379.13	405.70	570.66	580.00
Potato	7600.00	5949.30	6689.63	7482.31	7673.13	7500.00
Jute (000' bales)	7700.00	7549.70	7373.63	7593.68	7428.40	7500.00

Source : *Review of the Ninth Plan,* 2002, Department of Development and Planning, Government of West Bengal, p. (xix).

Because of these steps taken on the basis of land reforms, extension of irrigation facilities and provisions for other inputs like improved seeds, fertilisers etc., the curve of agricultural production in the state has become noticeably upward-rising. It has been possible for West Bengal to attain, over a period of ten years from 1980-83 to 1990-93, an annual rate of growth of food grains production amounting to 5.9 per cent against the all-India average annual rate of growth of 2.8 per cent.[85] During the Seventh Plan period, all the previous records in production were surpassed and a new height of 115 lakh tonnes was reached, thus already significantly exceeding the Seventh Plan target of a 105 lakh tonnes.[86] The trend in production of food grains continued to be on the increasing side in different years of the Ninth Plan in the state. It is evident from the table produced below that the state was expected to surpass the production targets set for the terminal year of the Ninth Plan for all the major crops excepting jute and potato. From Table 3.2, it also appears that the state has been able to sustain agricultural production even in the face of hostile weather (droughts in four districts and floods in nine districts in 2000-2001) and register significant growth. Thus, in spite of decline in production of food grains in 2000-01, the average annual growth of production in the Ninth Plan was 3 per cent in food grains and 2.9 per cent in case of rice.

It should, however, be admitted that the achievements in land reforms cannot be judged solely in terms of increase in production. The land reforms measures aided by other pro-people policies of the government 'raised the social standing of formerly low-ranking groups' in the state[87] and may be viewed from the angles of psycho-social rehabilitation and political mobilization of the peasantry for bringing about a change in the correlation of class forces in favour of the poor and working people by involving them, in an organized manner, in the process of planning and development. Thus the land reforms measures have not only generated a sense of confidence and participation among the beneficiaries, who constitute the majority of the rural population, but also brought about a change in the rural power structure.

Generation of employment opportunities under different programmes with the twin objectives of providing employment to agricultural workers and other rural poor especially during the slack season and creation of assets for infrastructure develop-ment in rural areas was viewed as an important area of activity by the State Government. Different rural development programmes and Centrally Sponsored Schemes were launched through which the poor were provided employment by involving them in the construction of social assets like dug wells, irrigation schemes, rural roads, sanitation, construction of *Anganwadi* houses and repairing of primary school buildings. The two major employment generation programmes in the rural areas, Jawahar Rozgar Yojana (JRY) and Employment Assurance Scheme[88] launched by the Central Government in 1989-90 and 1993-94 respectively to provide employment for the rural poor in the lean seasons were immediately introduced in the state. JRY was introduced in all the blocks simultaneously while EAS was extended to all the blocks in a phased manner and ultimately covered all the 341 blocks of the state by 1997-98. The implementation of both these Centrally sponsored programmes was entrusted to the panchayats in West

Bengal since their commencement. Compared with other states, in the context of the performance of broad range of economic and social indicators, viz., agricultural production, rural poverty, child mortality rate, illiteracy etc. between 1977-78 and 1987-88 as well as between 1980-81 and 1989-90 in rural West Bengal, the state has vastly improved its relative position. Due to application of improved techniques and multiple cropping, the dry and lean seasons have disappeared and now there is no idle labour in the districts to overcrowd the streets in Kolkata. Again, effective implementation of various wage employment programmes at the initiative of the government and the panchayats led to a progressive increase in the wage rate of the male agricultural field labourers (major component of prospective migrants) in the state. Table 3.3, it is evident that the rate of growth of daily wage rate

Table 3.3 : Agricultural Wage Rate for male field labourers, West Bengal 1993-94 to 1998-99 (in Rupees)

Sl. No.	Districts	1993-94	1994-95	1995-96	1996-97	1997-98	1998-99
1.	Burdwan	35.58	36.22	38.14	41.12	44.11	51.79
2.	Birbhum	21.68	24.3	25.66	34.09	38.69	44.96
3.	Bankura	27.05	28.31	30.32	37.33	40.68	48.50
4.	Midnapore	27.55	28.64	30.92	36.79	41.68	49.43
5.	Howrah	31.00	32.92	34.89	43.77	46.16	54.80
6.	Hooghly	32.51	34.25	–	39.55	43.43	50.99
7.	24 Parganas (N)	30.07	30.84	32.92	38.68	43.96	49.99
8.	24 Parganas (S)	38.13	40.56	42.65	48.43	51.84	59.93
9.	Calcutta	–	–	–	–	–	–
10.	Nadia	25.72	27.46	31.04	38.92	42.5	48.71
11.	Murshidabad	25.42	27.18	29.25	39.58	42.00	48.06
12.	Uttar & Dakshin Dinajpur	24.28	24.37	26.44	37.22	40.82	47.09
13.	Malda	24.18	25.93	27.78	36.32	38.4	46.01
14.	Jalpaiguri	28.33	29.00	–	45.66	46.1	51.69
15.	Darjeeling	36.67	37.75	39.59	48.07	49.27	62.75
16.	Coochbehar	24.40	26.47	28.12	36.22	39.21	46.16
17.	Purulia	22.00	22.17	23.37	31.50	32.69	39.08

Source : Department of Agriculture, Government of West Bengal. Also, Chatterjee, B. and Ghosh, D.K. 2001, in *Search of District Development Index,* State Institute of Panchayats and Rural Development, West Bengal, p. 20.

over a period of five years since 1993-94 in the state is 12.69 per annum. Performance evaluation has also been made in terms of achievements in creating employment opportunities or mandays and infrastructure assets but the crucial significance lies in developing a sense of active participation, motivation and confidence in the larger section which consolidates the base of democracy.[89]

Thus the reconstitution of the Panchayati raj bodies, effective land reforms measures and the alternative approach to rural development planning aiming at changing the existing pattern of distributions and inequalities in land and resources constituted the basis of decentralized planning in West Bengal. The ideological regimentation coupled with strict discipline at the organizational level of the leading partners of the State Government provided the new ecological settings for the implementation of such decentralized policies. The Government at the first instance decided to restructure the Panchayat organizations in the state in order to devolve power to the rural poor. It took a realistic view of bringing about a genuine reform in decentralized democracy and the political leadership was convinced that it could enhance its possibilities in coming to the centre of politics in other states if it could bring about an effective and meaningful reform at the local levels in West Bengal through restructuring the Panchayat system in the state.[90] The ruling Marxists participate in the State Government to use it as an instrument of class-struggle against the bourgeois-landlord combine for the cause of people's democracy apart from providing relief to the poor.[91] Thus, to the Marxists, the government is viewed as an agency of people's mobilization and struggles and not capable of solving the basic problems.[92] The main objective of such a mobilization is to help the people to learn, from their day-to-day experience of organized participa-tion in planning and implementation of schemes and projects, about the constraints imposed by the state apparatuses and the need to organize people's democratic revolution to overcome these limitations.[93]

Functioning of the Panchayats

As a first step towards decentralization in planning, the panchayat bodies were given the task of implementing the Food for Work Programmes. National Rural Employment Programme took its place later on. The Zilla Parishads and Gram Panchayats prepared the schemes on receipt of district-wise allocations of funds and implemented them. The Gram Panchayat undertook the small schemes and the Zilla Parishad executed the bigger ones, so that infrastructure could be created for the total development of the village. The Project Evaluation Committee set up by the Planning Commission appreciated the intensive participation of the panchayats in the implementation of rural development schemes. It is appropriate, in this connection, to mention that the 'Second generation panchayats' are more pro-people in their attitudes and represent the poorer segments of the society. After the first general panchayat elections (1978), a survey of a representative sample of 100 Gram Panchayats was conducted by the Economic Planning Stream of the State Development and Planning Department in 1978-79, which revealed that the members of the Panchayats, by a significant majority, represented the poorer sections in villages. Of the following tables given below, the *first* shows that over eighty per cent of the elected panchayat members came from the occupational groups like owner-cultivators, teachers, unemployed, landless labourers, *bargadars* and artisans and the *second* exhibits that more than 70 per cent of them originated from the small and marginal farmers with land holdings below five acres.

Table 3.4 : Distribution of Gram Panchayat Members according to Occupational Groups (1978-79)

Occupation	Percentage
Owner-Cultivators	50.7
Teachers	14.0
Unemployed	07.5
Landless Labourers	04.8
Bargadars	01.8
Artisans	01.6
Shop owners	01.4
Doctors	01.1
Technical Workers	01.3
Tailors	00.6
Students	00.6
Fishermen	00.4
Others	14.0

Sources : Department of Development and Planning, Government of West Bengal, 1981.

Table 3.5 : Distribution of Land holdings of Gram Panchayat Members (1978-79)

Area (in acres)	Percentage
Below – 02	42.9
02 – 05	28.2
05 – 08	13.0
08 – 10	08.1
Over – 10	07.8

Source : ibid.

Subsequent studies, both macro and micro, on the social background of panchayat leaders elected in 1983 and 1988 also confirm the presence of poor and small farmers in these rural bodies. An empirical study conducted by Lieten has shown that poor peasants, agricultural labourers and the scheduled castes have come to the forefront of development politics in rural West Bengal.[94] A similar study was conducted in 19 Gram Panchayats involving 246 members of 6 blocks in Coochbehar district from which it has been established that 34 members representing 14 per cent of the Gram Panchayat members were landless, 53 members (21.54 %) owned land below two acres each, while 62 members (25.20 %) were small and marginal farmers. Only 12 members possessed ten acres above each.[95] A comprehensive survey of the socio-economic conditions of the panchayat members of the state was conducted by the State Institute of Panchayat and Rural Development after the Panchayat Elections of 1993 which reiterated the earliar position in composition of the panchayat bodies. It is revealed from the above survey that in spite of negligible variations in individual components, the over all picture in class and social composition of the members of panchayat raj bodies has confirmed the attachment of the main socio-economic actors—the landless, the share-croppers and the small and marginal farmers—to the left in West Bengal. From a review of the position in six districts, three from the North and another three from the South Bengal (Burdwan, North 24 Parganas, South 24 Parganas from the South and Jalpiguri, North Dinajpur, South Dinajpur from the North) of the state, it appears that around 95 per cent of the panchayat members belong to the categories of landless, *bargadars*, small and marginal peasants.

Table 3.6 : Socio-economic Status of Panchayat Members (1993)

Status / Category	Percentage
Landless Labourers	30.53
Bargadars (Share-Croppers)	02.32
Below 05 acres	62.54
Scheduled Castes	33.29
Scheduled Tribes	05.36
Women	34.37

Note : Elections were held before the 73rd Amendment Act came into force in the state.

Source : State Institute of Panchayat and Rural Development, Government of West Bengal.

Thus the panchayats in West Bengal represent a total break from the past political pattern and have never been so free from the controls of landlords and rich peasants as found in contemporary West Bengal.[96] In fact West Bengal stands to be a class by itself in comparison to other states in India, excepting one or two, 'where political organization of disadvantaged classes have significantly altered the balance of political power, especially in rural areas,' and "this change in the balance of power has made it possible to implement a number of far-reaching social programmes that are often considered 'politically infeasible' in many other states."[97]

Introduction of Decentralized Planning

With this experience and perspective in the background and a highly organized and politicized panchayat system, the State Government undertook decentralized district planning formally in 1985-86, the first year of the Seventh Five-Year Plan. Prior to that, almost two years were spent in revamping the planning machinery so as to enable it to shoulder the responsibility of decentralized planning.[98] Institutional devices in the form of committees and conferences were organized for the formulation and implementation of decentralized planning. In spite of a laudable beginning with the involvement of common people through the revitalized panchayat bodies in the formulation and implementation of development schemes and plan projects, it was noticed that the implementation of important programmes in major departments like Agriculture, Irrigation and Public Works were still being done through the vertical hierarchy of the respective departments at the district level. Sectoral implementation of schemes led to the lack of coordination between the panchayat run and the departmentally executed programmes and also among the departmental programmes themselves. Hence the government decided to establish a three-tier organizational structure below the state level for decentralized planning. At the beginning the government did not dwell on the question of separate machinery at the Gram Panchayat level, though the involvement of the Gram Panchayats was sought for in actual implementation of schemes and projects. Thus the West Bengal model exhibited a sharp contrast to the Karnataka System, where the responsibilities for sub-plan relating to local works, such as water supply, sanitation, rural communications, etc. have been assigned to the Mandal Panchayats (redesignated as Taluk Panchayats).[99]

Planning Organization

The scheme for organizational structure at the district level, prior to the Act of 1994, was composed of two bodies: one larger body with the functions of deliberations and approval named the District Planning and Co-ordination Council (DPCC). A minister of the State Government hailing from the same district and the *Sabhadhipati* of the Zilla Parishad were designated as the Chairman and Vice-Chairman respectively of the DPCC. The MLAs and MPs of the district and the Chairmen (*Sabhapatis*) of the Panchayat Samitis, Municipalities and the Notified Areas, besides all the district level officers, were included in this larger body. Thus a scheme of functional linkage between the lower bodies and higher authorities was established through the DPCC. The District Planning Committee headed by the *Sabhadhipati* of the Zilla Parishad as the Chairman and the District Magistrate as the Member-Secretary was the actual planning body. The *Karmadhyaksha* of the *Sthayee Samitis* (Standing Committees) of the Zilla Parishad, the *Sabhapatis* of the Panchayat Samitis, the Chairmen of the Municipalities under the concerned district, representatives of the statutory or other authorities functioning within the district (like the Sundarban Development Board in 24 Parganas), the head of all district level line departments of the State Government were included in the District Planning Committee.[100]

The District Planning Committee thus formed was solely responsible for the formulation of the Draft District Plan, which was required to be placed before the DPCC for approval. After final approval by the DPCC and concurrence from the State Government, the implementation of the plan proposals was entrusted with the Zilla Parishad, Panchayat Samitis, Municipalities, Gram Panchayats and the line departments of the government as the case may be. It was expected that with the passage of time, all the schemes of various line departments of the government would be subjected to the approval of the District Planning and Co-ordination Council.

The District Planning Committee constituted in the Seventh Plan period and continuing to function during the Eighth Plan (1992-97)[101] had to work under the overall supervision of the DPCC. In this arrangement, the State Government ensured total representation of the people in the district planning bodies. Inclusion of a minister, all MLAs and MPs of the district in the DPCC was found to be advantageous as this established effective linkage between the district and the state. The inclusion of the members of the State Legislature and Parliament paved the way for the representation of different shades of opinion and for the integration of all planning and developmental activities within the state. Apart from this, the composition of the District Planning and Co-ordination Council accommodated the national and the state level politicians in a local politico-administrative framework. The majority of the states, where decentralized district planning has gained some footings have created separate organizations for planning and development at the district level and have made attempts for the accommodation of these politicians through the creation of separate organizations at the district level, like the District Level Vigilance and Monitoring Committee in addition to the DPC in West Bengal.[102] In other states, similar attempts were made through the establishment of the District Planning and Development Council as in Maharashtra or the District Planning Board in Gujarat.[103]

The State Government resolution also constituted the Block Planning Committee (BPC) at the same time since the government decided to introduce decentralized planning at the block level simultaneously with the district planning since the beginning of the Seventh Plan. The Block Planning Committee was formed with the *Sabhapati* of the Panchayat Samiti as the Chairman and the Block Development Officer as the Member-Secretary. The members of the Block Planning Committee were the *Gram Pradhans* (head of the Gram Panchayats), the *Karmadhyakshas* under the Panchayat Samiti and the block level officers in the line departments of the State Government and other agencies functioning in the block, in the same manner as in the DPC. Both the District Planning Committee and the Block Planning Committees were assisted by a team of technical experts with supports from administrative staff.[104] In these committees, the elected representatives of the panchayats and municipalities at the relevant levels and the government officials of various departments at the corresponding levels were tied together organizationally.

The district planning machinery which existed in West Bengal was different from that of Karnataka prior to the constitution of the District Planning Committee under the new Act.[105] In the Karnataka district planning set-up, the role of the District Magistrate was minimal. Practically, the District Magistrate had no functions relating to district planning which was assigned to the Chief Secretary of the Zilla Parishads in Karnataka, (the designation 'Chief Secretary' has been dropped under the Act of 1993). The involvement of the District Magistrate in district planning process has at least one advantage. The District Magistrate is the head of the law and order affairs of the district, proper maintenance of the law and order creates an atmosphere for effective implementation of district plans. In fact there can be no watertight compartment between law and order functions and planning functions. For better coordination, it is desirable that either the District Magistrate is designated as the Member-Secretary of the District Planning Authority or the law and order functions are brought under the purview of the Zilla Parishad. However, there was a strong opinion in favour of West Bengal structure of district planning.[106] But the provision for holding the executive body responsible to the people's body by integrating the sectoral departments under the aegis of the Zilla Parishad in Karnataka was a step forward towards effective decentralization.

Planning Methodology

Planning is not a unidimensional process; decentralized planning is never so. It involves a variety of factors and a number of stages. The involvement and interaction of these elements requires a clear demarcation or task-boundaries among the different agencies at different levels. There can be no rigid principle of sorting out the tasks and the agencies to be assigned with these tasks. It depends upon a number of variables ranging from circumstances, experiences, capabilities and political supports. Given this organizational structure, district planning was introduced in West Bengal quite successfully. Decentralized planning in West Bengal starts with the Gram Panchayats that prepare statements of priorities based on the immediate needs of the locality. Again, at the intermediary level, the Panchayat Samiti prepares schemes of urgent concern to the Gram Panchayats, keeping in view the state's priorities. The line departments of the State Government are required to furnish the district and block-wise distribution on these schemes to the District Planning Committee at the district level and the Block Planning Committee at the block, after disaggregating the plan budgets. The district and block level beneficiary-oriented special programmes are also integrated within the district plan.

In this context, a minor reference to the process of plan formulation at the state level is considered relevant. Under the changed scenario of decentralized planning, the plan budget of each of the concerned departments of the State Government is divided into two parts; one relating to the *State Level Schemes* and the other to the *District Level (or below) Schemes,* on the basis of general criterion adopted for decentralized planning. If a scheme has a command area encompassing more than one district, then it is not settled at the level of any district and is treated as a State Level Scheme. But if the scheme is confined to the command area of a single district or is restricted within one district, it is regarded as a District Level Scheme.[107]

Thus it appears that the schemes of essentially non-divisible and capital-intensive characters having wider beneficial implications throughout the state or in a number of districts are treated as State Sector Schemes. Schemes of divisible and operationally restricted characters conferring benefits on the people of a particular district are considered as District Sector Schemes. While the administrative departments of the State Government implementing plans continue to draw up State Sector Schemes as usual, certain sectoral programmes may have district level overtones.[108] To cite an example, the Teesta Barrage Project is a State-Sector Scheme but the programmes of rural electrification with its different ramifications or the canal net-works under the Teesta Project in the irrigation sector flowing through different districts would come under the District Plan as a departmental scheme. During the initial days of the launching of district plan, there was confusion as to what constituted a District Sector Scheme or what should be taken up at the state level. This caused serious handicap in the formulation of district plan. But after a year of decentralized planning practice, the district authorities and the government departments were able to set the confusion at rest. The State Government has been publishing the 'White Book' indicating therein the breakdown of the plan schemes of the departments and the departments have been cataloguing the schemes designating these as State Level and District Level schemes concerning their departments since 1986-87.[109]

After careful consideration of different aspects, the government decided to transfer the responsibilities of implementation of schemes to the lower authorities and to keep the tasks of coordination and approval reserved for the district level organization.[110] At the outset, the procedure initiated may appear to be akin to the previous one, but in actuality it differs from the centralized practice in the sense that under this methodology plans are formulated with specific reference to the needs of the people by the local people themselves and are subsequently approved by them through their representatives at a higher level.

Flow of Funds

The decentralized district planning passed through the stage of initiation in West Bengal during the Seventh Plan and Eighth Plan periods. In this period, a further innovation was introduced. Under the changed methodology, budgetary provisions of the various departments for district level schemes are communicated to the District Planning Committee and a significant part of the allocations are transferred to the block level planning bodies. Within the budgetary allocations, the Block Planning Committee formulates the block plan taking into consideration the plan proposals submitted by different Gram Panchayats. The block plans are sent to the district authorities and are integrated into the district plan which constitutes an integral part of the state plan. The plans thus formulated are placed with the District Planning Committee and Block Plan Committee for implementation and monitoring. Through this process of decentralized district planning, funds are dovetailed from the state to the districts. The trend in this respect is encouraging and shows gradual improvements. Started with a meagre 25.62 per cent component of the approved state plan outlay in 1986-87, the share of the district plans in the state increased to 39.75 per cent in 1988-89 and then to 47.52 per cent at the end of the Seventh Plan.[111] Thus there was a gradual increase in the percentage of disintegrated outlay during the Seventh Plan period. Through this process, it has been possible now to devolve around fifty per cent of the entire plan budget of the state to the command of the District and Block Planning Committees.[112]

Apart from disintegration of plan funds to meet the critical gaps between their percentage of outlay from the budgetary provisions of the concerned departments, a separate budget head is being operated since the beginning of the Seventh Plan, namely 'District Plan Schemes Fund' (DPF) and funds from this budget head are entirely placed at the disposal of the District Planning Committees. The District Planning Committee has been advised to utilise these funds to meet the critical gap between their fund requirements (according to the district plan) and the available funds from diverse sources. The year-wise allotment and expenditure on account of District Plan Scheme indicates a healthy trend. The scheme of district plan fund was introduced in 1985, incurred an actual expenditure of Rs.64.04 crore in 1994-95 as against Rs.17.75 crore in 1985-86.[113]

The experience gathered in the decentralized district planning during the Seventh Five-Year Plan period induced the State Government to extend it below the district level. Under the existing methodology, along with the formulation of block plans and district plans, attempts are made to integrate the plans with the credit plans of the blocks and the districts. Moreover, to ensure flow of funds from banks and other financial institutions, the representatives of the banks are involved in the process through meetings at the district levels. The involvement of banks under 'Lead Bank Scheme' is a good design in the direction of formulating a comprehensive credit plan for the districts to remove the dissension among the states.[114]

Resource Mobilization

Success of decentralized rural development and planning depends very much on the effective resource mobilization at the lower levels. Apart from the statutory arrangements for resource mobilizations at the Zilla Parishad, Panchayat Samiti and Gram Panchayat levels[115] continuous efforts have been made since the beginning of the Seventh Plan for gradual increase in resource mobilization. As for example, in 1988-89, the targets of small savings collections were fixed for the blocks and municipalities and the panchayats and municipalities were involved in the process. As a result, in the first year of the introduction of the scheme, the total collection of small savings in the state was nearly doubled in 1988-89 in comparison to the previous year.[116] In keeping with this spirit of decentralization and also having regard to weightage to the item of resource mobilization in the Mukherjee Formula of plan assistance, the State Government has launched the scheme of Decentralized Resource Mobilization in the districts in the Eighth Plan.[117] This collaborative programme was designed in such a way as to enhance the revenue collection of four specific items, namely (a) Stamp duty and Registration fee, (b) Amusement Tax, (c) Motor Vehicles Tax, (d) Royalty / Cess from Major/Minor Minerals which, in turn, benefit both the state and the individual district. The individual district is benefited in that if the collection of the district at anytime exceeds the stipulated target, then 50 per cent of the additional collection would be shared by the district for purposes of development expenditure, to be decided by the District Planning Committee. Moreover, with a view to mobilizing additional resources for significant industrial projects, a new Infrastructure Development Finance Corporation has been set up, which in coordination with the State Planning Board (SPB), concerned departments and District Planning Committees (DPC) provides funds to the districts for major schemes of infrastructure development.[118]

Institutional Mechanism for Decentralization

All these are of peripheral importance. The ultimate success of decentralized development planning depends on the people. A responsive administrative system must have an in-built arrangement for the fulfilment of public needs and for being sensitive to public grievances. In West Bengal, the government has made certain structural changes in planning and development administration network through the introduction and implementation of some effective measures like: (i) delegation of some functions of the government departments to the local bodies, (ii) arrangement for ensuring timely and regular elections to the local self-governing institutions and the provisions for establishment of State Election Commission,[119] (iii) the establishment of the State Finance Commission along with clear provisions outlining the subjects to be dealt with below the state level and the constitution of the District Planning Committee,[120] and (iv) statutory mechanism for involvement and participation of the people at the lowest levels even at the villages through the creation of *Gram Sansads* and *Gram Sabhas.*[121]

Statutory provisions of mandatory accountability of the Panchayats to the people have made the Panchayati Raj Institutions the agencies of responsive and democratic administration. Through the successive Amendments of 1992 and 1994 in the Panchayat Act, the State Government has made elaborate provisions for annual and half-yearly meetings of the *Gram*

Sansads. Under the statutory initiative of the Gram Panchayat these are required to have public deliberations, interactions and recommendations on different development issues of local nature and to ensure accountability of the representatives.[122] Under the amended provisions, the Gram Panchayat is required to place its budgets, a report on the works done during the previous year, a proposal of activities to be performed and the latest reports on audit of the accounts of the Gram Panchayat for deliberation, recommendation and suggestion at the meeting.[123] Similar provisions have also been inserted in the Act requiring the Gram Panchayats to hold within the local limits of the *Gram*, an annual meeting of the *Gram Sabha* for consideration of the above issues.[124] The Act also includes a time-schedule for such meetings.

Apart from these routine works, the *Gram Sansad* and the *Gram Sabha* are authorised to guide and advise the Gram Panchayat in the identification of schemes, constitution of beneficiary committees, identification of beneficiaries and the mobilization of people's participation in development and planning activities.[125] It is insisted that the accounts and the list of works executed by the Gram Panchayat are notified in public places. In addition to this open publication of accounts, verbal direct communications with the people in an open meeting is considered essential. Thus the process of people's participation and organized monitoring has been introduced through the revitalization of Panchayati Raj Institutions, which has added a new dimension to the perspectives of planning and development. Now almost all the states have amended the provisions of their Panchayat Acts in conformity with the 73rd Amendment to create and establish *Gram Sabhas* within the area of Gram Panchayat. In West Bengal the system has been working fairly well since it was introduced in 1992.[126]

The process of democratic decentralization has further been strengthened in the state after the enactment of 73rd and 74th Constitution Amendment Acts in 1993. The state well placed to be in the first rank with some other states, again took the initiative to accelerate the process further. Both the Panchayat (Amendment) Act, 1994 and the District Planning Committee Act, 1994 were passed by the State in succession during the first half of 1994. Subsequently, the State Government formulated the District Planning Committee Rules and constituted District Planning Committees at the districts. Through these statutory provisions, detailed schemes have been outlined for composition and functions of the District Planning Committee, the *Gram Sansad* and the *Gram Sabha* in West Bengal. These changes introduced in the statutes have strengthened the already stable grassroots political institutions in the state.

West Bengal :The Experience and the Change in Approach

The decentralized district planning in West Bengal has gathered a lot of momentum over the years and has since been revamped to overcome the problems, mainly in the spheres of maintaining linkages and time schedule. There were inordinate delays in receiving communications from the departments. Again most of the departments, which submitted the necessary information, depended more on guesswork and failed to furnish any authentic figure. The district level officers of various departments, however, did not have communication from their respective departments, as a result of which some of the departments failed to furnish details of district-wise and block-wise schemes to the District Planning Committee to enable the DPC to give its recommendations on the location and priority of the schemes proposed by various departments.[127] To remove these difficulties the government decided to work out time schedule in 1986-87 and in conformity with the schedule the planning exercise begins from the very beginning of each financial year. The preparation of a time schedule and the decision to comply with the same by all the departments help the completion of the process of consultation with District Planning Committee by September each year. The government prepared the schedule in such a way so as to enable the State Planning Department to submit the State Plan Document to the Planning Commission by the first week of December.[128]

For the last few years, formulation of development plans at the Gram Panchayat levels and below has been indeed the preparation of the lists of priorities and demands and the lists of action plans or shelf of schemes based on expected allocations. Such practice followed by most of the panchayat bodies shattered the objectives and the spirit of decentralized planning. Hence the primary goal of development through effective decentralization remained mostly unfulfilled. Learning from the experiences of implementation of decentralized planning in the district of Midnapore (West Bengal) and Kerala, the State Government has worked out an action plan for effective formulation of development plans at the Gram Panchayats based on the plans of the villages from the very beginning of the Tenth Plan to reverse the prevalent trend. The government has also decided to shift the leadership in the field of socio-economic development from the representatives of the people in the panchayats to the people themselves. After the growth and sustenance of the local government in the panchayats and municipalities, the government now seeks to assume the role of the facilitator in the functioning of the local bodies and the implementation of development plans.[129]

In this way, the State Government in West Bengal through its development policy has been able to pursue these important tasks: '*first*, penetration of the country-side without being captured by the landed classes; and *second*, controlled mobilization and incorporation of the lower classes to buttress state power as a tool of social reform.'[130] The district planning in West Bengal and for that matter in other states has become an integral part of a multi-level planning system linking the micro to the macro. This is done to activate the trickle-down and percolation processes helping the growth of impulses and to spread out widely and evenly reaching all areas and categories including the peripheries.

KERALA : A NEW APPROACH FOR PLANNING

Like other states in India, Kerala also started the experiment in decentralized planning in the background of successful land reforms and organized political mobilization in the state in the late fifties. Previously it had a system of panchayats, though slightly different from the all-India pattern, before the enactment of the Kerala Panchayat Raj Act, 1994 and Kerala Municipalities Act, 1994, introduced in pursuance with the requirements of the Constitution Amendment Acts of 1992. The two-tier experiments in rural local-governments in Kerala came to an end with the introduction of the new three-tier Panchayati raj system under the State Conformity Act.

In the period prior to the new Act, though several attempts were made towards decentralization at the district and lower levels, the efforts did not produce any result and the forces of centralization were in command. Even the Kerala Panchayat Raj Act, 1994 contained the seeds of 'contradictions and the yearning for decentralization'.[131] The Act failed to establish the panchayats as institutions of self-government since there were various sections which empower the state bureaucracy to interfere and hinder the functioning of panchayats.[132] The chapter relating to government control over Panchayati raj was 'obnoxious in nature' and betrays the spirit of decentralization.[133]

In spite of all these difficulties, the Left Democratic Front Government in Kerala while elected to office in May 1996, decided to pursue the process of decentralized planning setting aside the initial 'phase of confusion'.[134] The State Government appointed a committee headed by Satyabrata Sen, a former Vice Chairman of West Bengal State Planning Board and the Chairman of First State Finance Commission of West Bengal, to review the State Panchayat Act in order to make decentralization real and effective. However, the State Government preferred not to wait but to introduce decentralized planning in the state.[135]

People's Campaign for Ninth Plan

As a prelude to the effective decentralized planning, the State Planning Board launched *People's Campaign for the Ninth Plan* in Kerala in July 1996 to enable the panchayats and the municipalities to draw up Ninth Plan schemes within their respective areas. The main objective of the campaign was 'to ensure maximum people's participation at every stage of the planning process from proposals to implementation.'[136] The State Planning Board also decided to transfer 35 to 40 per cent allocations of the Ninth Plan towards the projects and schemes to be formulated and implemented at the decentralized levels below the state.[137] The background of the People's Campaign was developed in Kerala on the success of land reforms achieved between the period from 1958 to early 1970s, the mass literacy programmes at all the levels, people's mobilizations through grassroots organizations (GROs) and a vibrant civic society that exists in Kerala. But the objective condition for launching the campaign for people's planning was expedited in view of the continued economic crisis in the state and the political commitment of the Left Government for decentralization. The campaign also assumed importance from the point of view of the existing crisis in Kerala's widely acclaimed development model in the context of having a highly unproductive production sector in the state.

The campaign was a time-bound programme completed within a period of five months spreading over five interrelated stages. Since the programme is a novel experiment and has attracted nation-wide attention,[138] a brief summary of the campaign strategy would not be out of place here. To carry out the extensive campaign for the programme, the State Planning Board provided training for the resource persons. The state faculty comprising experts from different academic institutions, voluntary organizations, State Planning Board and government departments trained Key Resource Persons (KRPs). District Level Resource Persons (DRPs) were trained by the KRPs at the district level and the Local Level Resource Persons (LRPs) by the DRPs at the block level. The number of persons trained at the state level was 400 and 15000 at the district level and at the local level it was estimated around one lakh. Thus People's movement for decentralized planning in Kerala struck to the roots which has never been attempted in any state in such a massive way.[139]

A High Level Council of Guidance (HLCG) comprising eminent personalities in the state has been constituted at the state level to ensure the widest possible consensus on the proposed campaign. Apart from the leaders of different political parties, the HLCG includes the Vice Chancellors of the universities, eminent academics, cultural leaders and representatives of mass organizations. The Chief Minister is the patron and the Local Administration Minister is the convenor of the council.[140]

The campaign was originally designed in five phases but subsequently additional phases have been added to ensure techno-financial appraisal and implementation of projects.[141] The *first phase* starts with the special *Gram Sabha* in the form of convention to identify the felt needs of the people, development problems, resource inventory and suggestive measures and solutions. This phase is confined to the creating and developing awareness of the programmes of decentralization, establishing the basic organisational structure and coming up with innovation. Large size of Gram Panchayats in Kerala creates problems in holding meetings of the *gram sabhas* effectively and hence small groups have been set up to consider sectoral matters and to make recommendations. The *second phase* has two stages: preparation of development reports and development seminars. At this stage comprehansive survey is conducted of all development sectors of the local bodies for preparation of local data-base and resource mapping through PRA methods. The geography, history and major problems of the area as also the local resources are recorded in details followed by development seminars linking resources to the needs. After the preparation of panchayat and municipal development reports and development seminars, the organisation of a task force comprising experts is formed to prepare development plans. The task force prepares the panchayat and municipal development plans in simple formats translating the aspirations of the people as expressed in the conventions and the issues brought out by the development seminars. This is what is precisely done at the *third phase* of the campaign. For this purpose, 8 to 12 task forces on different sectors have been constituted by each of the local bodies. In *phase four*, the plans prepared at the Gram Panchayats and municipalities are integrated with the block plan along with Block Panchayat's plan emerging from block seminars. The *fifth phase* is meant for the preparation of the district plans within the areas assigned to it under the Panchayat Act. At this phase, the District Planning Committee integrates the plans of the panchayats and municipalities and the task forces are formed to prepare plans as per guidelines issued by the State Planning Board.[142]

The *sixth phase* is mainly concerned with the examination of the technical soundness and making rectifications, wherever necessary, in the projects before their implementation.

Accordingly, *Voluntary Technical Corps* (VTC) has been raised at the block and district levels. The *seventh phase* is related to the implementation of the projects which are implemented through beneficiary committees. The government has also introduced a transparent process in the identification and selection of beneficiaries under plan schemes including the Centrally Sponsored and State Sponsored Schemes. To ensure transparency in functioning, all documents like application forms, verification reports, enquiry reports and decision minutes are declared as public documents to which everybody has access and copies of which everyone can procure.[143]

An integral part of the methodology of decentralized planning in Kerala has been the attempt to use natural resources of the micro area in an effective and sustainable manner for growth and development. Resource appraisal survey was undertaken throughout the state before the commencement of people's plan. After attainment of total literacy in the state 'Land Literacy Drive' was launched in Kerala with the objective of preparing resource maps at the village level by mobilizing direct and active participation of the villagers. The programme entitled 'Participatory Resource Mapping' (PPM) was introduced by the government under the joint auspices of the *Kerala Shastra Sahitya Parishad* (KSSP) and the *Centre of Earth Science Studies* (CESS) with the help of the *Kerala Panchayat Mandali* and financial assistance from the Government of India. The task of selecting the village volunteers, their training and involving them in the preparation of village resource maps was taken up by the KSSP and the CESS with all seriousness. On the basis of available data, resource maps of the villages were prepared and subsequently village plans were formulated in the state. It would be worthwhile in this context to point out that the experimentation with survery and mapping of land and water resource has now been taken up in some other states for the purpose of micro level development planning. This programme launched initially in four different states (Bhanjnagar of Ganjam in Orissa, Palamau in Bihar, Purulia in West Bengal and Ramanathapuram in Tamil Nadu) with financial assistance from the Government of India and the UNICEF, has now been in operation in other states (Himachal Pradesh, Madhya Pradesh, Maharashtra, Orissa,

Tamil Nadu, Tripura and Rajasthan) for preparation of resounce maps for effective implementation of Watershed Development Programmes.[144]

The Experience in Kerala

The Campaign has been completed to some extent successfully. During the campaign, a perceptible change was noticed in the attitudes of different political leaders, people and their representatives towards planning and development. Designed after the total literacy movement, the campaign was able to bring together different categories of people in the preparation of the Ninth Plan: the elected representatives, the officials, the non-official experts, the people and their mass organizations. The experience of Kerala is highly emulating in the sense that it was successful in motivating a quite large number of people including retired technical and professional experts and the mass of people, usually considered to be the passive objects of development process, to come out of their circles to participate in the democratic project for improving the conditions of life.[145]

The methodology adopted in Kerala is innovative and at the same time flexible based on a system of feedback. Once a hurdle was developed in appraisal of the plans during the sixth phase when assessment of about one lakh projects and plans generated at the lowest levels during the campaign was pending due to want of adequate number of technical personnel of the government. To overcome this problem, formation of *Voluntary Technical Corps* consisting of retired professionals and volunteers having expertise in different fields was contemplated and implemented, which proved to be seccessful in formation of expert committees at all the levels of planning. Thanks to innovative skill, now there are *Block Level Expert Committees* (BLEC) at the blocks, *District Level Expert Committees* (DLEC) at the districts, *MLEC* at the municipalities, *CLEC* at the corporation levels and there is the *State Level Expert Committee* (SLEC) at the state level. Each expert committee is composed of three categaries of personnel : (i) members of the VCTs, (ii) other volunteers, and (iii) officers. The expert committees assist in preparation of plan documents and in appraisal of the project reports.

The issue of autonomy of the local level bodies in preparation of development plans is at the very core of the decentralized planning. It is a welcome feature in the state that this aspect of local autonomy has been recognized. The usual practice of giving guidelines by the State Planning Board to the districts has been gradually discontinued. The District Planning Committees now formulate their own guidelines for preparation of plans and accordingly, development perspectives are being developed. Moreover, perspective plans are now prepared at the local levels to provide linkages, both forward and backward. Preparation of perspective plans has now become a regular feature in the decentralized planning process in Kerala though it could not be done in the first year of the planning campaign.[146]

An important feature of the scheme of decentralization in Kerala is the devolution of funds for decentralized planning, which is reflected in the budget-document and forms a part of the finance bill. The fund is allocated to the local bodies on the basis of certain transparent formula and is free from government discretion and delay. In the Budget-Estimates of 1997-98, provisions for schemes transferred to local bodies were introduced as grants against separate sub-heads of accounts below the minor head. In addition, plan funds have been earmarked to be given to the local bodies for the plans prepared by them. Besides, a certain portion of stamp duty, vehicles tax etc. is released to the local bodies as grants. Subsequently, detailed guidelines have been prepared by the government outlining the flow of funds and utilisation of budgetary provisions.[147] In 1998-99, out of a total outlay of Rs. 3500 crore, an amount of Rs. 1100 crore was devolved to the local bodies of which Rs. 1024 crore were untied. The fund released under Centrally Sponsored Schemes like *Jawahar Gram Samriddhi Yojana* (JGSY) and *Swarnajayanti Gram Swarozgar Yojana* (SGSY) was not included in this category. It may be noted here that the schemes under these programmes are not turned into some kind of parallel activities but are treated as anti-poverty sub-plans of the block panchayats.[148] Recently, the State

Government has allocated one-third of the outlays for the Tenth Plan (2002-07) and Annual Plan (2002-03) in the draft for the local bodies.[149]

Another outstanding feature underlying the Kerala model of decentralized planning is that the issue of urban-rural continuum has been ensured in the state. There has been a criticism that the 74th Amendment recognizes 'an artificial dichotomy between rural and urban' in an attempt to serve 'the Panchayat dish with Municipal sauce'.[150] The organizational network developed in Kerala seeks to rectify the problem of rural-urban dichotomy through making the entire local self-government as a single developmental entity and bringing both the rural and urban local self-governments under the control of the Local Self-government Department, a one-umbrella system. There is no basic difference between the facilities available and in the basic features of a municipality and a panchayat. Both the institutions are non-hierarchical in structure having complete autonomy at all the levels. In the case of municipalities and corporations, the procedure prescribed for the PRIs are applied *mutatis mutandis*. In place of *Gram Sabhas*, Ward Committees are required to perform the functions.[151]

The uniqueness of the Kerala model of decentralized development planning is that the system has been completely institutionalized and an elaborate arrangement of laws and structure has been developed afresh to translate the political will into administrative actions. The roles and functions of the local bodies under the existing scheme of decentralization modelled by the Left Government are supposed to cover the entire range of administrative functions that an institution is required to perform. Accordingly, administration of a good number of service institutions such as hospitals, schools, veterinary institutions, agricultural offices etc. has been transferred to the local bodies. Simultaneously, the functional jurisdiction and role performance of different bodies have also been worked out by Acts, Government Orders and Rules. The personnel attached to different development departments have been placed under the local bodies at various levels and these bodies are empowered to exercise control and impose punishment on them. This has given rise to the problem of dual control : the professional control continues to lie with the departmental authorities while the minimum administrative control is vested with the local bodies.[152]

After the launching of People's Campaign programme, a meeting of the secretaries to the government and the heads of the departments was organised in the second week of August, 1996 to identify the steps to be taken for organising campaign for formulation of the Ninth Five-Year Plan and related issues. At that meeting it was reiterated that the officers at all the levels should play a critical role for the smooth and effective conduct of the campaign. Accordingly, the government issued orders outlining the roles to be played by the officers in the campaign and implementation of schemes falling under the area of responsibilities of the panchayats, municipalities and municipal corporations.[153]

The first year of the planning exercise was devoted primarily to the experimentation while the second year was confined mainly to the identification and rectification of the shortcomings and pitfalls. Now the process of institutionalization of the whole system is on the way of its completion. During this period, the process has moved from *ad hoc* arrangements to a formal structural framework through trial and errors. At the beginning of the Ninth Plan, decentratized planning in Kerala was at the phase of campaign in the form of sensitization, and at the close of the same it has become almost a system through the process of institutionalization and internalization. A long standing achievement in the campaign process is the growth of capacity building at all levels. More than one lakh of resource persons have been trained in the state which means that each panchayat body will now have about 100 trained persons under its disposal.

The progress outlined above does not mean that there has been absolutely smooth sailing in all the spheres of decentralized planning in Kerala. The issue of personal ego, the question of equation between the officials and the politicians, difference in perceptions about the roles and responsibilities of the panchayat members, presidents and vice-presidents, chairmen of the standing committees have been the recurrent phenomena even in an egalitarian state like Kerala. But such types of problems could not create major bottlenecks in the process of decentralized planning. Moreover, to overcome the problems, conscious procedural and institutional steps were taken as and when necessary. *Empowered Committees* were constituted at different levels and stages besides a *Coordination Committee* chaired by the Minister-in-Charge of Local Self-government at the state level to ensure coordination in planning and implementation. Moreover, State Development Council in the lines of National Development Council consisting of all Cabinet Ministers, District Panchayat Presidents, all heads of associations of panchayat bodies, Vice-chairman of State Planning Board and the Chief Secretary has been set up to decide policy issues in development and planning. Further, there has been a practice of holding interactive sessions by the Minister-in-Charge and the Secretary with all the presidents of panchayat bodies at least once in four months for review of the planning process and clarification of different Government Orders and Circulars. Networking with committed individuals and personalities is a process which has been continuing since the commencement of decentralized planning in Kerala.[154]

In spite of certain other limitations, like inadequate linkages between rural and urban plans below the district level[155] or insignificant involvement of the people, especially the weaker sections of the community and women and also the low level of participation in municipal area,[156] the methodology adopted in Kerala for decentralization of decision-making process in planning has been quite successful in achieving transparency in administration, ensuring people's involvement in planning and development, mobilizing resources from the people in the form of money, materials and labour and strengthening the local level institutions for participatory governance.[157]

The operation of decentralized district planning had made a good start in Kerala in the Ninth Plan period. The experience gathered so far reveals that the state has come out of the traditional method of sectoral planning consciously and in an organized manner. The time is not ripe for an appraisal but the direction is clear. The idea of people's campaign to ensure mass participation and mobilisation of people in the process of development planning of the state is an organizational innovation designed for social development that demands a fair trial in other states. Moreover, from the viewpoint of depeening democracy, the experience of Kerala is stimulating. Different studies have established that in Kerala 'interests and social resources have been mobilised along class lines, a democratically accountable state and a mobilized society have become organizationally and functionally linked in a manner conducive to the transformative projects broadly associated with development, particularly those of redistributive character'.[158] Thus the movement for decentralization in Kerala has taken a new dimension, which may help, if materialized, in giving a new direction to the practice of decentralized planning in India.

The above review of the progress in decentralized planning in different states excepting Kerala suggests that the phase of *initiation* is yet to be crossed while in West Bengal the phase of *limited decentralization*[159] representing the 'Stage-II' is likely to take off. The failure in financial decentralization is a major problem and is more prominent than decentralization in administration of economic programmes. The general hesitancy on the part of the state governments to delegate powers and functions to the local level institutions has adversely affected the process of decentralization in planning in the states.

There is no dispute about the fact that decentralized development planning cannot be ensured in a vacuum. It takes place within stable political conditions, and the political atmosphere must fulfil at least four necessary *preconditions* for augmenting sustainable development: *first*, there must be the constitutional and statutory provisions for local governments below the state level with adequate devolution of both financial and administrative powers; *second*, organized political mobilization of the weak and the disadvantaged to countervail the dominating influence of the propertied class and the elite; *third*, related to the second, effective land reforms; and *fourth*, organization of a suitable and responsive administrative machinery for effective implementation and proper coordination of decentralized plans both vertically and horizontally. It also appears that the decentralization of decision-making is a comprehensive and major political strategy that can only be implemented as a part of the political agenda of the government.[160] In the foregoing discussion, we have seen that the first three preconditions are, more or less, satisfied in West Bengal and Kerala; the fourth one needs a closer scrutiny in the subsequent chapters.

Notes and References

1. Mishra, Sweta. 1997 (June), 'Decentralized Planning: Retrospect and Prospect', *Kurukshetra,* p.24.
2. Meenakshisundaram, S.S. 1994, *Decentralization in Developing Countries,* New Delhi : Concept Publishing Co., p.61.
3. *Note*: The Kerala Government appointed a Committee headed by S.B. Sen, a former Vice-Chairman of West Bengal State Planning Board and the First Chairman of the West Bengal State Finance Commission to examine and suggest effective measures for genuine decentralization in Kerala.
4. Sinha, Arun. 1990, 'Decentralized District Planning – The Indian Experience' in R.P. Misra (ed.), *District Planning – A Handbook.* New Delhi: Concept Publishing Company, p.19.
5. Meenakshisundaram, 1994, *op.cit.,* p.62.
6. Inamdar, N.R. and Kshire, V.K. 1986, *District Planning in India,* New Delhi: Oxford & IBH Publishing Company, p.18.
7. *Ibid.,* pp. 22-23.
8. Mukherjee, Amitava. 1992, *Methodology and Database for Decentralized Planning,* Vol. III, Part-C, New Delhi: Heritage Publishers, pp.54-55.
   Also, Kshire, V.K. 1991, 'Legislative Behaviour and the Reversal of Democratic Decentralization in Maharashtra' in Rakesh Hooja and P.C. Mathur (eds.), *District and Decentralized Planning,* Jaipur: Rawat Publications, pp.181-83.
9. Sarkar, Goutam. 1995, *Agriculture and Rural Transformation in India,* Calcutta: Oxford University Press, p.100.
10. Inamdar and Kshire, *op.cit.* 1986, p.23.
11. Jain, L.C. *et al.* 1985, *Grass Without Roots,* New Delhi: Sage Publications, p.75.
12. Voluntary Action Network India, 1995, *State Panchayat Acts – A Critical Review,* New Delhi: VANI, p.97.
13. *Ibid.,* 1995, p.97.
14. *Panchayati Raj, Update,* 2002 (March), p. 4.
15. Sarkar, Goutam K. 1995, *ibid.* p.93.
16. Inamdar and Kshire, 1986, *op.cit.,* pp.28-32, 113.
17. *Ibid.,* p.61.
18. Jain, L.C. *et al.,* 1985, *op.cit.,* p.76.
19. Inamdar and Kshire, 1986, *op.cit.,* p.252.

20. Iyer, K.Gopal, *The Findings of the Empirical Study on Land Reforms in India,* 1989-90, Summary Report, Land Reforms Unit, L.B.S. National Academy of Administration, Mussoorie, p.15.
21. Mishra, Sweta. 1997, *op.cit.*, p.25.
22. Voluntary Action Network India (VANI), 1995, *op.cit.*, p.45.
23. Report of *the Government of Gujarat,* 1988, abridged in Mukherjee, 1992, *op.cit.*, p.14.
24. Mishra, Sweta. 1997, *op.cit.*, p.25.
25. *Comments of the State Election Commissioner*, quoted in *Panchayati Raj Update*, 2001 (November), Vol. VIII, No.11, p.3.
26. Jain *et al.*, 1985, *op.cit.*, p.74.
27. Patel, Himmat. 1991, 'Decentralized District Planning in Gujarat' in Rakesh Hooja and P.C. Mathur (eds.), *op.cit.* pp.158-59.
    Mukherjee, 1992, *op.cit.*, Vol. III, Part-B, pp. 380-82.
28. *Planning Commission,* quoted in Jain *et al.*, 1985, *op.cit.*, p.75.
29. Kabra, K.N. 1997, *Development Planning in India,* New Delhi: Sage Publications, p.175.
30. Mukherjee, 1991, *op.cit.*, Vol. III, Part-B, p.379.
31. Report of the *Working Group on District Planning,* 1984, Government of India, New Delhi, Vol. I, p.92, par., 10.3.
32. Mukherjee, 1992, *op.cit.*, Vol. III, Part-C, p.15.
33. Quoted in Kabra, 1997, *op.cit.*, p.175.
34. *Ibid.*
35. *Panchayat Raj Update,* 2000 (March), Vol. VII, No. 3, p.7.
36. Sarkar, 1995, *op.cit.*, p.93.
37. Ghosh, Arun, 1989 August, 'Lessons for the Future', *Seminar,* No.360, pp.20-21.
38. Mukarji, Nirmal, 1993, 'Plan From Below', *The Statesman,* Calcutta, September 29.
39. Government of Karnataka, 1988, *District Governments and Decentralized Planning,* Bangalore, p.48.
40. *Government of Karnataka,* 1986, Order No. PD-3, PRN, *ibid., p.47.*
41. *Note:* Taluk Panchayat Samithi was purely a nominated body in Karnataka entrusted with advisory, supervisory, review and inter-mandal coordination functions.
42. *Government of Karnataka*, 1988, *op.cit.*, pp.7-9 & 41-46.
43. *Ibid.*, p.9.
44. *Ibid.*, pp.47-49.
45. *Ibid.*, pp.9-11.
46. Mukherjee, Amitava. 1991, *Methodology and Database for Decentralized Planning, op.cit.*, Vol. III, Part-B, pp.363-68.
47. Mukarji, Nirmal. 1993, *op.cit.*
48. *The Adminstrator,* 1995 (April-June), Vol. XL, No.2, p.262.
49. Hanovar, R.M. 1989, August, 'Sharing the resource pie', *Seminar* 360, *op.cit.*, p.27. Also, *The Administrator, op.cit., p.263.*
50. *Government of Karnataka,* Order dated December 19, 1980, par., 17, *op.cit,*
51. Hanovar, 1989, *op.cit.*, p.26.

52. *Note:* The Karnataka Panchayat Raj Act (KPR Act), 1993 was passed in 1993 in conformity with the Constitution 73rd & 74th Amendment Acts, 1992.
53. *Section* 310 of the KPR Act, 1993.
54. *Section* 310(6) of the KPR Act, 1993.
55. *Panchayat Raj Update,* 1997, February, Institute of Social Sciences, New Delhi, p.4.
56. *Sections 267 and 308* of the KPR Act, 1993.
57. Hegde, Ramkrishna. 1992, *Seminar Paper* reproduced in *Nation,* Vol. III, No.26, October 16, p.21.
58. *Note:* The Karnataka Panchayat Raj Act, 1993 received the assent of the Governor on April 13, 1993 and published in the Karnataka Gazette (Extraordinary) on the same day. *Notification No.* Law 26, LGN. 93, Bangalore, dated May 18, 1993.
59. Voluntary Action Network India (VANI), 1995, *op.cit.,* p.74.
60. *Section* 182 of the Karnataka Zilla Parishads, Taluk Panchayat Samitis, Mandal Panchayats and Nyaya Panchayats Acts of 1983.
61. *Panchayati Raj Update,* 1997, February, No.38, p.4.
62. Chandran, T.R. 1995 in George Mathew (ed.), *Status of Panchayati Raj in the States of India,* New Delhi: Concept Publishing Company, p.102.
63. Sections 268 and 240 of the KPR Act, 1993.
64. *Ibid.,* Section 268(5).
65. Bhargava, B.S. and Samal, Avinash, 1998 April, 'Institutional Mechanism for Decentralised Planning', *Kurukshetra,* Vol. XLVI, No.7, p.36.
66. Mukarji, Nirmal. 1989, 'Panchayat Governments', *Seminar, op.cit.* pp. 29-32.
67. Bhargava and Samal, 1998, *op.cit.,* p.36.
    Also, Bandyopadhyay, D. 2002, 'Panchayats in Karnataka–Two Steps Back' in *Economic and Political Weekly,* Vol.xxxvii, No. 35, August 31- September 6, pp. 3572-73.
68. Mukherjee, Amitava. 1992, *op.cit.,* p.114.
69. Kohli, Atul. 1987, *The State and Poverty in India,* Bombay: Orient Longman, p.108.
70. Mitra Ashok. *Quoted in ibid.* p.109.
71. *Left Front Government in West Bengal– Nine Years.* 1986, Government of West Bengal, Calcutta, p.132.
    Jana, Anil Kumar. 1998, 'Participatory Governance : In Search of an Effective Model for Rural India' in Anil Kumar Jana (ed.), *Indian Politics at the Crossroads,* New Delhi: Commonwealth Publishers, pp. 308-11.
72. *Rural Development Planning Under the Left Front Government in West Bengal.* 1981, Government of West Bengal, Calcutta, p.7.
73. *The Zamindari Abolition Act.,* 1953 and *The Land Reforms Act.* 1955.
74. Webster, Neil. 1999, 'Institutions, Actors and Strategies in West Bengal's Rural Development – A Study on Irrigation', in Rogaly, B., Harriss-White, B., and Bose, Sugata. (eds.), 1999, *Sonar Bangla?*

Agricultural Growth and Agrarian change in West Bengal and Bangladesh, New Delhi : Sage, p. 330.

75. Kohli, Atul. 1991, *Democracy and Discontent*, Cambridge, U.K. : Cambridge University Press, Indian edn., (Reprint, 1995) pp. 281-82. Also, *Left Front Government in West Bengal: Nine Years, op.cit.*, pp.132-39.
76. Tenth Five-Year Plan (2002-2007),Vol. I, Government of West Bengal, Kolkata, p. xxi.
77. *Ibid.*
    Summary of the Findings of the Study of Land Reforms in India, 1989-90, Mussoori : LBS National Academy of Administration.
    The Ganashakti. Special Issue. 1997. Calcutta, June 20, p.16.
78. *Annual Plan.* 1997-98, *op.cit.*, p.77.
79. *Left Front Government and Some Aspects of Activities in Rural Areas: A Study by an Observer.* 1978. Government of West Bengal, Calcutta, p.9.
    Bagchi, Amiya Kumar. 1998 (December), 'Studies on the Economy of West Bengal since Independence', *Economic and Political Weekly,* Vol.XXXIII, Nos.47 and 48 (December 4), pp.2974-77.
80. *Annual Plan, 2002-2003, Government of West Bengal,* Kolkata, p. 68.
    Webster, Neil. 1992, *Panchayati Raj and the Decentralization of Development Planning in West Bengal*, Calcutta: K.P. Bagchi & Co., pp. 50, 119 & 127. Also, Satyamurthy, T.V. 1985. *India Since Independence– Centre-State Relations: The Case of Kerala,* Vol. I, Delhi: Ajanta Publications, p.290.
    Baruah, Sanjib. 1990, 'The End of the Road in Land Reform? Limits to Redistribution in West Bengal', *Development and Change,*. p.140.
    Mishra, S.K. 1991. *An Alternative Approach to Development: Land Reforms and Panchayats,* Government of West Bengal, Calcutta, p.12.
    The Ganashakti. op. cit., p.15.
81. *Annual Plan,* 1997-98, *op.cit.*, p.77.
82. Ghosh, Arun. 1989. *West Bengal Landscape.* Calcutta : K.P. Bagchi & Co. pp.84-85.
    Sanyal, Manoj Kumar *et al.* 1998 (December), 'Institutional Change and Output Growth in West Bengal Agriculture — End of Impasse', *Economic and Political Weekly,* pp. 2983-86.
83. Webster, 1992, *op.cit.,* p.49.
84. Tenth Five-Year Plan (2002-2003),Vol. I, Government of West Bengal, Kolkata, p. xxi.
85. Banerjee, Sarmila and Ray, Samik. 1998 (December), 'On Construction of District Development Index in West Bengal', *Economic and Political Weekly, op.cit.,* pp.3024-25.
    Annual Plan 1997-98, *op.cit.,* Vol. I. p.viii.
    Also, Bhalla, G.S. and Singh, G. 1997 'Recent Development in Indian Agriculture — A State Level Analysis', *Economic and Political Weekly,* March 29, pp.A-2-6 and Saha, Anamitra, and Swaminathan, Madhura. 1994, 'Agricultural Growth in West Bengal in the 1980s', *Economic and Political Weekly,* March 26, p.A-9.
86. Source: *Department of Planning and Development. op.cit.*

Also, Lieten, G.K. 1996, *Development, Devolution and Democracy,* New Delhi: Sage, pp. 34-35.

87. Ruud, Arild Engelsen. 1999, 'From Untouchable to Communist : Wealth, Power and Status among supporters of the Communist Party (Marxist) in Rural West Bengal', in Rogaly, B., Harriss-White, B. and Bose, Sugata. (eds.), 1999, *op. cit.,* p. 275.

88. *Note : Jawahar Rozgar Yojana* was originally launched by the Central Government in 1989-90 as a major poverty alleviation programme of the country by merging the NREP and RLEGP into it. Since then the contents of the programme have remained almost unaltered though the scheme has been modified and restructured to ensure better implementation. The scheme was first modified in 1993-94 when it was restructured into three streams. Again, the Government of India decided to streamline and restructure the JRY into *Jawahar Gram Samriddhi Yojana* (JGSY) in April, 1999 for the development of rural infrastructure in a planned manner. Similarly, *EAS*, introduced in 1993, was revised in 1999 but its basic parameters were retained as the single wage employment scheme.

Now both the programmes (JGSY and EAS) have been merged into *Sampoorna Grameen Rozgar Yojana* (SGRY) from this financial year (2002-03) onwards. The new pragramme will be implemented in *two streams* : the *first stream* will be implemented at the district and intermediate panchayat levels; 50% of the funds is earmarked out of the total funds available under SGRY and distributed between the zilla Parishad (20%) and Panchayat Samiti (30%). The *second stream* will be inplemented at the village panchayat levels, 50% of the funds available under the SGRY is earmarked for the village panchayats and distributed among the Gram Panchayats through Zilla Parishads. Thus the programmes, in spite of integration and modifications, have retained the essential feature-implementation at the ground level. In conformity with the spirit of democratic decentralization, the panchayats have been designated as the implementing authority under the programme. They enjoy sole jurisdiction in preparation of Annual Action Plans and their implementation.

DO. No. V – 24011/34/2001/SGRY, dated 12 October, 2001, Department of Rural Development, *Government of India*, New Delhi : addressed to the Chief Secretary, Government of West Bengal.

89. Dasgupta, B. 1995, 'Institutional Reforms and Poverty Alleviation in West Bengal', *Economic and Political Weekly,* October 14 & 21, p.2691.

Lieten, 1996, *op.cit.*, p.35.

Westergaard, Kristen. 1987, 'Marxist Government and People's Participation: The Case of West Bengal', *Social Studies,* Bangladesh, No.38, pp.110-13.

Also, Mishra, S.K. 1991. *op.cit.*, pp.9, 23-26.

90. Marcus Franda. 1979, *India's Rural Development.* USA: Indiana University Press. pp.142-43.

91. *Programme of the CPI(M)*. 1964, 7th Congress, Calcutta, par. 112 and, Webster, 1992, *op.cit.* p.110.

92. Dass, Ram. 1984, *The Marxist.* Vol. II. No.2. pp.12-13. Also, Lieten, G.K. 1992, *Continuity and Change in Rural West Bengal,* New Delhi: Sage, p.279.
93. Mishra, S.K. 1991, *op.cit.,* p.10.
94. Lieten, G.K. 1992. *Continuity and Change in Rural West Bengal.* New Delhi: Sage, pp. 110-18.
95. Bhaumik, Swapan. 1991, *Samaj Samiksha,* Vol., No.4, Calcutta: Indian School of Social Sciences, pp.48-49.
96. Kohli, Atul. 1987, *op.cit.,* p.113.
97. Dreze, Jean and Sen, Amartya. 2002, *India : Development and Participation*, New Delhi : Oxford University Press, pp. 94-95.
98. Ghosh, Arun. 1989, *op.cit.,* p.1.
99. *District Government and Decentralized Planning.* 1988, Government of Karnataka, Bangalore, p.43.
100. Ghosh, Arun. 1988, Decentralized Planning: West Bengal Experiment. *Economic and Political Weekly.* March 26.
101. Statutory recognition was given to DPC under the *West Bengal District Planning Committee Act,* 1994.
102. *Government of West Bengal, Memorandum No.* 838(73)-RD/0/13C-1/95 dated 3-2-1997. Calcutta.
103. George Mathew. 1994, *Status of Panchayati Raj in the States of India.* New Delhi: Concept Publishing Company. p.131 *and Gujarat Panchayat Act,* 1994.
104. Ghosh, Arun. 1988, *op. cit.*
105. Section 310 of the Karnataka Panchayat Raj Act, 1993.
106. Yugandhar and Mukherjee (eds.), 1990, *Readings in Decentralized Planning.* Vol. II. New Delhi : Concept Publishing Company. p.79.
107. Government of West Bengal, 1989, *12 Years of Left Front Government in West Bengal,* Department of Information and Culture, Calcutta, p.19.
108. Government of West Bengal, *G.O.No. 6299(30). Development and Planning* dated 23-8-1995.
109. Government of West Bengal, *G.O. No.2237 (12) DP-2C-2/86.* dated 31-3-1986.
110. Ghosh, Arun. 1989, Lessons for the Future. *Seminar. op.cit.,* pp.20-24.
111. *Source: Department of Development and Planning,* Government of West Bengal, Calcutta, January, 1990.
112. *Annual Plan,* 1995-96, Vol. I. Government of West Bengal, Calcutta, p.14.
113. *Ibid., p.15.*
114. Chakravarty, Sukhamoy. 1987, *Development Planning: The Indian Experience.* London : Clarendon Press, Oxford. P.59.
115. *The West Bengal Panchayat Act.* 1973 and subsequent Amendments.
116. *Department of Development and Planning.* 1990, *op.cit.,* p.9.
117. Introduced by the Government since 1-11-1992.
Note : According to Mukherjee Formula of Plan Assistance, fifty per cent of additional collection in respect of certain specified items of revenue will be paid back to the districts concerned. The specified items include

Registration Fee, Stamp Duty, Motor Vehicles Tax, Amusement Tax, and Royalty and Cess on major or minor minerals in some states.

118. *Annual Plan.* 1997-98. Vol. I. Calcutta: *op.cit.*, p.X.
119. Sec.203, as amended by the *West Bengal Panchayat Amendment Act, 1994.*
120. *Note: The West Bengal District Planning Committee Act,* 1994 was passed and subsequently the *West Bengal District Planning Committee Rules,* 1994 were framed in conformity with the WB. DPC Act, 1994.
121. Sections 16A and 16B of *The West Bengal Panchayat Act, 1973.* *Note: Gram Sabha* means a body consisting of persons registered in the electoral rolls pertaining to a village and *Gram Sansad* means a body consisting of persons registered at anytime in the electoral rolls pertaining to a constituency of a Gram Panchayat delimited for the purpose of last preceding general election to the *Gram Panchayat.*
122. Section 16A of *the West Bengal Panchayat Act, 1994.*
123. *Ibid.*, Section 17A.
124. *Ibid.*, Section 16B.
125. *Ibid.*, Section 16A.
126. *The Telegraph.* 10 July 1997, Calcutta.
127. *Government of West Bengal, Department of Development and Planning,* G.O. No. 2720(45)/DP/1S-21/86, dated 19-4-1986.
128. *Ibid.*, G.O. No. 3328(46)/DP/1S-21/86, dated 19-5-1986.
129. *No. 1 / PA / JS (DG) / P & P.D. / 5 M — 19 / 99* dated, 2 January, 2002, *Government of West Bengal*, Panchayat and Rural Development Department, Kolkata. *Also, Tenth Five-year Plan*, West Bengal (2002 – 2007), *Government of West Bengal*, Development and Planning Department, *Vol. I, Chap. II*, p.61.
130. Kohli, Atul. 1987, *op.cit.*, p.96.
131. Ramchandran, V. 1995, in George Mathew (ed.), *Status of Panchayati Raj in the States of India,* New Delhi: Concept Publishing Company, pp.112-14.
132. Pal, Mahi. 1996, 'Participatory Planning, Decentralized Governance and the Kerala Panchayat Act', *Seminar Paper,* Institute of Social Sciences, New Delhi, December 9-11.
133. Bhargava and Samal, 1998, *op.cit.*, p.37.
134. Chathukulam. Jose and Thomas, Jose T. 1997 June, 'Power to the People: People's campaign for Ninth Plan in Kerala', *Kurukshetra,* p.35.
135. Bhargava and Samal, 1998, *op.cit.*, p.36.
136. *People's Campaign for Ninth Plan – An Approach Paper,* 1996, Kerala State Planning Board, Government of Kerala, Thiruvanthapuram, p.1.
137. Gulati, I.S., 1996, *Ibid.*, preface. Also, *A New Beginning*, Keral State Planning Board, People's Plan Campaign Cell, Government of Kerala.
138. Namboodiripad, E.M.S. 1996 October, 'A Kerala Experiment: Planning from the Below and Above', *Frontline,* p.91.
139. Leelakumari, P. 1997, 'Functioning of Gram Sabhas Through 73rd Amendment', *Seminar Paper,* Institute of Social Sciences, New Delhi, October 21. Also, Namboodiripad, 1996, 'From Land Reforms to People's Planning', *People's Democracy,* September 21, p.5.

140. *People's Campaign for Ninth Plan. op.cit.*, p.12, par.31.
Also, *G.O.(MS)No.10/96/Plg.*, dated, 30-7-1996 and *G.O.(MS) No. 12/96/Plg.*, dated, 8th August,1996.*Government of Kerala.*,Planning and Economic Affairs(A) Department.
141. Sheela Varghese and Rejimon, P.M. 2001, 'People's Campaign for Decentralised Planning : An Assessment', *Mainstream*, 12 May, p.13.
142. Pal, Mahi. 1997, 'People's Campaign for Decentralized Planning', *Mainstream*, June.
143. *G.O. (P) No. : 220/97/LAD., dated 2 October*, 1997, *Government of Kerala*, Local Administration (P) Department.
144. *Village Based Planning and Development*, 2001, Government of *West Bengal*, State Institute of Panchayats and Rural Development, p. 20.
145. Isaac, T.M. Thomas and Harilal, K.N. 1997, 'Planning for Empowerment-People's Campaign for Decentralized Planning in Kerala,' *Economic and Political Weekly*, January 4-11, pp. 53-58.
Also, Leelakumari, 1997, *op.cit.*, pp.8-9.
146. Gangadharan, T. 1999, 'People's Plan : Methodology, Execution and the Strategy for enlisting People's participation', *Workshop on 'People's Participation in Development'*, Calcutta 15-16 December, organised by the Department of Panchayats and Rural Development, Government of West Bengal and UNICEF.
Note : Mr. Gangadharan is an activist and associated with *Kerala Shastra Sahitya Parishad (KSSP)*, a voluntary organisation which played a leading role in people's Campaign Programme. Mr. Gangadharan's experiment in Kalliessary Gram Panchayat in Kunnur district of Kerala is considered as a model of participatory planning.
147. *G.O., (P) No. 676/97/Fin., dated 6 August, 1997, Government of Kerala*, Department of Finance (BWJ).
148. Vijayanand, S. 1999, 'Administrative Innovations for Participatory Planning-sustainability of the Kerala Model : Problems and Prospects' workshop on 'People's Participation in Development', Calcutta, 15-16 December, *loc cit.*
149. *Panchayati Raj Update*, 2002, March, p.3.
150. Mukarji, Nirmal. 1993, 'Making third stratum vibrant, dynamic', *Kurukshetra*, June (Special Number), p.14.
151. G.O. (P) No. 220/97/LAD., dated 2 October, 1997 Government of Kerala. Also, Mishra Sweta, 1997 (June), *Kurukshetra*, p. 23.
152. *G.O. (Rt.) No. 350/96 Plg., dated 10 September, 1996 and G.O. (Ms) 10 / 96 / Plg.*, dated 30 July, 1996, *Government of Kerala*, Department of Planning. Also, Vijayanand, S. 1999, 'Administrative Innovations for Participatory Planning-Sustainability of the Kerala Model : Problems and Prospects', *Workshop, loc cit.*
153. *G.O., dated 10 September, 1996, op cit.*
154. Vijayanand, *op. cit.*
155. Pal, Mahi. 1996, *Seminar Paper, op cit.*
156. Leelakumari, 1997, *op.cit.*, pp.10-13.
157. *Ibid.*, Table No.3, p.12.

158. Heller, Patrick. 1996, 'Social Capital as a Product of Class Mobilisation and State Intervention : Industrial workers in Kerala, India', *World Development*, Vol. 24, No. 6, p. 1057.
159. Report of *the Working Group on District Planning,* 1984, *op.cit.*, p.92, par. 10.3.
160. Thomas Issac, T.M., 2000, 'The Story of People's Plan', *Panchayati Raj Update,* (September), p.7.

4

METHODOLOGY OF DISTRICT PLANNING

We may now turn to the district of Midnapore which is the main theatre of decentralized district planning operations in our study. The reason for according representive status to the district of Midnapore is obvious. Midnapore is in fact the first district in the state and also in the country that started a serious experiment in decentralized planning in the eighties. The present methodology of decentralized district planning followed in the state of West Bengal is in fact the replica of the model developed in this district incorporating therein the organisational innovations conceived in the People's Campaign programme in Kerala. It will not be inappropriate to point out here that the scheme of village Planning introduced in Kerala has been almost borrowed from the experiments carried out in this district during the Seventh and Eighth Five-year Plans.[1] The methodology of decentralized district planning and its status in the state can only be comprehended empirically through the examination of its methodology and implementation in the district of Midnapore.

Note : Due to administrative reasons, the district is now divided into two : *Purba Medinipur* (East Midnapore) and *Paschim Medinipur* (West Midnapore) since January 2002. This study was undertaken and completed before the bifurcation of the district and, therefore, the undivided status of the district has been retained in this study to make it more relevant. Now the two districts consist of eight subdivisions, four in each, one more (Egra) created after the bifurcation of the district. The data, references and information included in this book are equally relevant to both the situations, pre and post-division periods. Hence, the word 'district' wherever used in this book refers to the undivided district of Midnapore which now comprises both the East and the West.

The Zilla Parishad of Midnapore and subsequently the District Planning Committee initiated a bold step to introduce the process of formulation of district plans on the basis of programmes prepared by the villagers themselves. The experience gathered through action-research for preparation of work programmes for village based planning since the end of nineteen eighty 'coupled with the decision of the West Bengal Government in 1985 to decentralise planning up to Block level enabled the district to adopt and to implement' the methodology of decentralized district planning for rural development.[2] A brief presentation of the district profile will thus be the starting point in the order.

PROFILE OF THE DISTRICT

Geographical Characteristics

The district of Midnapore, the southern-most district of the Burdwan Division is situated between 21°36′ 35′ and 22°57′10″ north latitude and between 86°33′50″ and 88°12′40″ east latitude.[3]

The headquarter of the undivided district, Midnapore, was situated on the north bank of the river Kasai. Midnapore, the name itself is a derivation of the vernacular 'Medinipur, meaning the city of the world.'[4] On the north, the district is bound by the district of Bankura and on the east, the river Hooghly and its tributary, the Rupnarayana separate it from the 24 Parganas, Howrah and Hooghly. The coastline of the Bay of Bengal and the district of Balasore in Orissa are at its south ; while on the west, the boundary merges with the districts of Mayurbhanj in Orissa and Singbhum and Manbhum of formerly Bihar.

The land pattern of the districts is quite unique in some respects. Some parts of the land under Tamluk, Ghatal and Haldia sub-divisions are low-lying and prone to flood. A vast area of the districts is under either forest cover or uncultivable and barren having wide scope for fodder cultivation. The climate in Jhargram, Midnapore and part of Ghatal sub-divisions being drier with less than average rainfall and large forest area has a good prospect for dairy, goat and sheep farming. The western part with the red laterite formation is threatened by a potential erosion of top-soil and causing siltation of the rivers in the eastern part of the district, which ultimately results in drainage congestion and recurrent floods.

In view of its differential geographical features, the district is one of the most varied of the districts in the state. In terms of agro-climatic diversity, the district encompasses the saline, coastal belt in Contai, Egra, Haldia and Tamluk sub-divisions, drought prone zones in Jhargram and Sadar sub-divisions, flood-prone areas like Ghatal and Moyna, laterite zones in North-Eastern Ghatal, Chandrakona, Garbeta and alluvial zones in Panskura, Sabang, Dantan etc. Broadly speaking, the district is divided into two natural parts. It is bifurcated by the metalled road from Raniganj and Bankura which passes through the district from north to south. The eastern part of the district is purely alluvial with a flat and fertile soil and is fully cultivated. The western half is undulating, the high lands of Central India terminates here in long rolling waves of laterite rocks, and most of the surface consists of alternate ridges and depressions.

India is divided into fifteen Agro-climatic regions for the purpose of effective planning and management. For scientific and effective management of resources and formulation of regional plans, the districts of West Bengal are divided into three regions: (i) Eastern Himalayan Region, Zone-II, (ii) Lower Gangetic Plain Region, Zone-III, and (iii) Eastern Plateau and Hill Region, Zone-IV. According to this classification, Midnapore is included in Zone-III, i.e. Lower Gangetic Plain Region, Sub-Zone coastal, saline and laterite. Out of 54 blocks of the district, 14 blocks fall under the Coastal Zone, 17 under the Laterite and 23 blocks under the Alluvial Zone.[5] The average rainfall in the district for the last ten years (up to 1997) is around 1639.85 mm but it varies in the area from east to west. These averages, however, are composed of very wide variations not only from season to season, but also from year to year.[6] It may be noted that though both Contai and Jhargram have similar amount of rainfall, it is the difference in soil-characteristics and topography which makes Jhargram sub-division drought-prone. Because of the presence of the Bay of Bengal, cyclones and heavy rainfalls are normal features of the coastal areas of the district. Due to topography, lack of drainage, heavy deformation leading to erosion and silting of river beds there have often been serious floods in certain areas when other areas suffer acutely from scarcity of water.

The district (undivided) is mainly an agricultural district though some important industrial complexes like Haldia, Kharagpur and Jhargram have occupied important places in the industrial map of the state. Besides the large industries at Haldia and medium industrial estates at Kharagpur and Jhargam, there is a steady growth and development of village and small industries all over the district. Various types of small and medium industries based on agriculture, forest, animal-husbandry, textile-handloom, chemicals, engineering, building materials and ceramic have been set up in the district with assistance from the government and the banks under different schemes. In spite of all these, the district still remains a major agricultural district with a sharing of 16.30 per cent in production of food grains in the state.[7]

Demographic Features

The largest and the most populous of the districts of West Bengal, the undivided district had an area of 14,081 sq. kilometres with a population of 8,331,912 (Census 1991) comprising 12.28 per cent of the total population of the state. In terms of population, the district was bigger than not only each of the north-eastern states, except Assam, but also Jammu and Kashmir (7,718,700) and Himachal Pradesh (5,111,079). The figures relating to population reveal that the increase in the growth rate in the district during the 1981-91 decade was just 1.44 per cent over and above the previous one.[8] Moreover, the growth rate of population reflects a 2.99 per cent increase over the total population in this century from 1901 to 1991. The district stood at fifth position in the state in order of sex ratio which is 944 per 1000 males. The sex composition of the population in the district is dismaying in the sense that the sex ratio has declined during 1981-91 in comparison to that of 1971-81 while there is a marginal improvement in the state as a whole.[9] Of the total population of the district, the Scheduled Castes and Scheduled Tribes constitute 16.34 and 8.28 per cent respectively. The urban population constitutes 9.85 per cent of the total population of the district and thus represents an increase of 1.36 per cent in the ten years between 1981 and 1991.[10]

The undivided district was the largest in West Bengal also in terms of the number of villages included in it. It consisted of 10,446 inhabited villages with 593 people living per sq. kilometre. The percentage of literacy was 57.64 as per Census 1991. But as a result of Total Literacy Campaign (TLC) launched in the district since 1990 the overall effective literacy rate in the district has exceeded ninety per cent.[11] Distribution of population according to different categories of workers constitutes a basic demographic characteristic of the population. In the district, the main workers consisting of cultivators, agricultural labourers, household manufactures and other workers constitute 30.43 per cent while marginal workers and non-workers represent 4.76 and 64.81 per cent respectively.[12]

Administrative Divisions

During the initial days of the British administration, all the three functions – revenue, judicial and police – were vested in the Collector, though for a very short span of time.[13] At present the administration of the districts is vested in the District Magistrates who are assisted by a few Additional District Magistrates (ADMs). The ADMs usually relieve the District Magistrates of some of their routine works. For the purposes of general administration, the districts are now divided into eight sub-divisions comprising 54 blocks, 25 blocks in *Purba Medinipur* and 29 in *Paschim Medinipur*. Each of the sub-divisions is under the charge of a Sub-divisional Officer. The development administration of the blocks was previously the exclusive domain of the Block Development Officer, an officer of the state cadre, created under the Community Development Programme in the fifties. Now a block has become co-terminous with Panchayat Samiti and the Samiti now looks after the total developmental aspects of the block and the Block Development Officer acts as the Executive Officer of the concerned Panchayat Samiti. In respect of general administration of the district, there is to some extent a sharing of responsibilities between the general administration headed by the District Magistrate and the Zilla Parishad.

Panchayati Raj Institutions today perform various activities. As elected local-self organisations, they have to perform a variety of functions, both obligatory and optional. With this end in view, the Panchayati Raj Institutions are established in the district. There is the Zilla Parishad at the apex of the three-tier Panchayati raj structure which is composed as per the Act of the Government. Below the Zilla Parishad, there are Panchayat Samitis at the block levels, each consisting of a few Gram Panchayats. At present, there are 514 Gram Panchayats in the districts, the lowest tier of the Panchayati raj system. These bodies are spread over all the 54 blocks on an average of 8-9 Gram Panchayats per Panchayat Samiti. Under the existing conditions of effective decentralization, the Panchayati raj bodies have become the centres of 'development policies that might be attempted by any provincial Third World Government trying to alter the socio-economic conditions in favour of the lower classes.'[14]

To make the panchayats able to cope with the development works, different categories of full time staff at different tiers have been appointed. Infrastructural facilities including their own buildings to house their offices have been built. The provision for creation of *Gram Sansads* within the area of Gram Panchayats has been implemented in the districts and at present there are 6463 *Gram Sansads* covering 514 Gram Panchayats of the districts.[15]

The local and development affairs of the urban areas are being looked after by the municipalities and two special purpose bodies (Digha and Haldia development authorities). The districts have a long tradition of municipal system, though limited only to a few towns. Most of the existing municipalities have been in existence for well over a period of hundred years.[16] There are at present 13 municipalities consisting of 237 municipal wards. The plans and activities of these bodies are coordinated and supervised by the District Urban Development Agency (DUDA) created in the district.

Historic Contributions

The undivided district of Midnapore occupies a place of pride in the history of freedom movement in India. During the 18th and

19th centuries, there were various 'subaltern movements' in the district notable among which were the *Chuar* (1799) and *Paik Rebellions* (1817).[17] It was also a strong bastion of terrorist movements in the twenties and thirties of this century. Three successive District Magistrates, Paddy, Douglas and Burge, were killed in three successive years in the thirties.[18] The people of Midnapore also took an active part in different movements under the leadership of Mahatma Gandhi against the British rule since the days of the partition of Bengal and faced courageously the stormy days of Union Board Boycott, Non-Cooperation and Salt Movements. Most significant had been their active involvement and participation in the Quit India Movement of 1942 when they could establish *National Governments* in the sub-divisions of Contai and Tamluk in the district of Midnapore.[19]

In recent years, the district has once again come to the front line. It is the first district in India that started the experiment of 'Village-based District Planning' in 1985-86. Just five years after the introduction of decentralized planning, the 'Total Literacy and Immunization Programme' was launched in the district which took the shape of a people's movement. Another experiment of people's participation is the successful planning and implementation of the schemes of Social Forestry through the establishment of People's Forest Protection Groups. These experiments highlight the simple hypothesis that organizational infrastructure of the district is conducive to the successful implementation of decentralized district planning through people's participation.

INTRODUCTION OF DISTRICT PLANNING

The Approach Paper of the Seventh Five-Year Plan emphasized the role of decentralized planning but it was all the more surprising that the Seventh Five-Year Plan contained only two sentences on decentralized planning in the preface written by the Deputy Chairman. The comment runs thus: "District and block level planning has yet to take firm roots. Without the introduction of effective block level/district level planning, the impact of large flows of money through the various anti-poverty programmes will remain limited."[20] Notwithstanding such a limited appraisal, the Government of West Bengal decided to introduce decentralized planning from the beginning of the

Seventh Plan. The decision of the State Government regarding formulation and implementation of District and Block Level Plans was taken in October 1984. Accordingly, attempts were made to introduce decentralized planning in the districts. But due to a variety of reasons, including the General Elections in December 1984, it took almost six months to have a scheme of decentralized district planning when the State Planning Board worked out 'Guidelines for District Plan for 1985-86' relating to formulation and implementation of decentralized planning throughout the state.[21] The State Government also decided to develop an integrated organizational structure at the district and block levels through the formation of Block Planning Committee (BPC), the District Planning Committee (DPC), and the District Planning and Co-ordination Council (DPCC). As a result, a lot of enthusiasm was generated in bringing down the planning process to the levels of blocks and gram panchayats. West Bengal is one of the few states in the country that has established the role and primacy of the people representatives in the local self-governing bodies in respect of formulation and implementation of development plans through effective articulation and integration of the needs and priorities of the common people. The degree and extent of popular participation have also been widened in the state through the organization and functioning of *Gram Sansads.*

In conformity with the decisions of the State Government, the district authorities of Midnapore under the leadership of the Zilla Parishad decided to start 'Village Based District Planning' from the first year of the Seventh Plan to find out an alternative model of development for the people of the district.[22] The Eighth Five-Year Plan of the district was also modelled and implemented within the broad framework and norms already developed for the Seventh Plan. The priority plan outlined at the villages and Action Plans prepared at the Gram Panchayats were integrated into Block Plans and again integrating the same in the District Plan and incorporating therein the District Sector schemes and municipality-specific schemes, the district plan was formulated. The process of decentralized district planning started as a movement in the district at the beginning of the Seventh Plan proved to be successful in ensuring higher generation of growth in a self-reliant fashion. This brings about sustainable development for the maximum number of people with special emphasis on the poorer and weaker sections of the community. Thus the district planning in Midnapore is not an independent but an integrated process. The village level plans and the municipality-specific panchayat plans provide the basis on which the district plan works. Hence, no evaluation of district planning is possible without an understanding of the entire decentralized planning process in the district starting from the village level.

In this context, it is necessary to point out that after the recent modifications, the planning structure in West Bengal comprises four distinct levels in a district : (i) Village level (ii) Gram Panchayat level, (iii) Block level, and (vi) District level. Each of these four levels have been provided with the required autonomy and authority in its own sphere of decision-making. The present structure now in operation throughout the state may be presented with the help of a diagram presented in Figure 1. Though the broad goals of planning are almost the same at all the levels ranging from the villages to the district yet due to differences in the infrastructural facilities and availability of resources, the priorities and the level of consideration may be different at each level. Naturally, the types of schemes and projects that cannot be included in the Gram Panchayat Plan may have to be considered under the Block Level Schemes. Similarly, the schemes not feasible for implementation under the Block Plan may be incorporated in the District Plan since the district is better equipped with planning infrastructure than the block. Thus the principles of both autonomy and integration have been accommodated in the planning methodology.

As pointed out earlier, the plan budget of the State Government is divided into two segments, one relating to the *State Sector Schemes* and the other incorporating *District Sector Schemes*. The concept of 'district sector' was something new to the district authorities, since the district authorities were familiar only with the 'state sector' from the very beginning of the planning era. The District Planning Committee through their interactions with the State Planning Board and the State Government identified some important items of development and planning like, (a) Area specific agricultural production; (b) Extension of technical services, storage and marketing facilities; (c) Minor irrigation; (d) IRDP including TRYSEM; (e) NREP and RLEGP proposal (f) Social Forestry; (g) Minimum Needs Programmes; (h) Pisciculture; (i) Animal Husbandry; (j) Cottage and small industries, sericulture; (k) District and lower level roads; etc. as District Sector Schemes for the purpose of formulation of district plans.[23] In the above context and in the overall perspectives of the planning of the district, the basic objectives of the district plan were underlined. The district plan

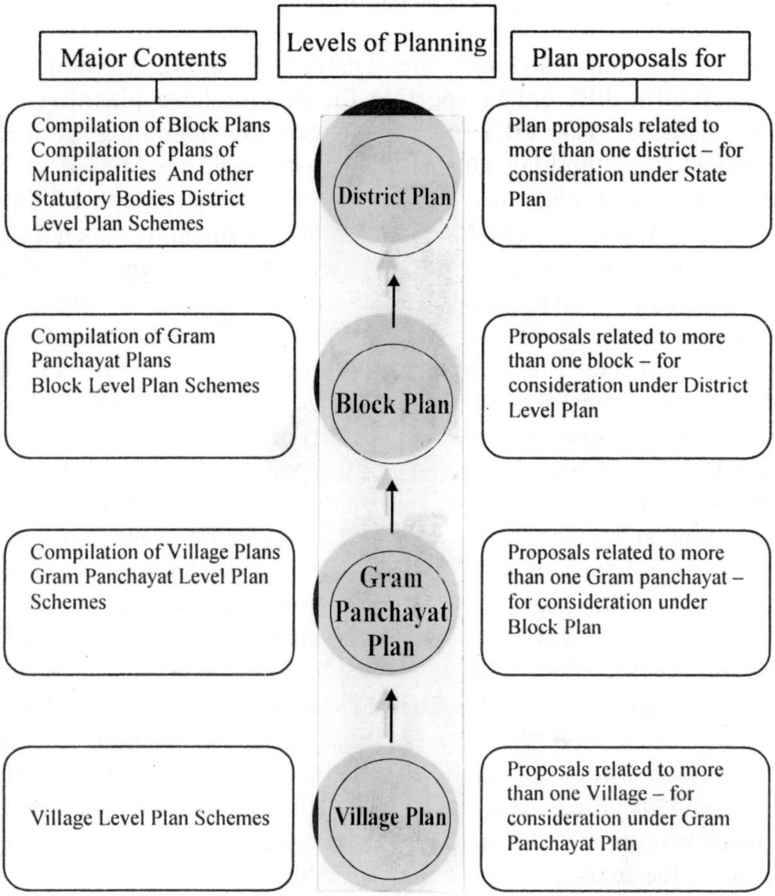

Figure 4.1 : Structure of Village Based District Plan

of Midnapore is designed to ensure best utilization of the available resources both financial (institutional and non-institutional) as well as local (geo-physical and socio-economic), to generate growth in a self-reliant fashion from an investment pattern in order to bring about maximum sustainable development of maximum number of people with special emphasis on the deprived majority of the population.[24]

PERSPECTIVES OF PLANNING IN THE DISTRICT

The Zilla Parishad and the District Planning Committee visualised a different perspective for decentralized planning in the district. The Zilla Parishad, since the beginning of the eighties, was thinking about a target-oriented, need-based and resource-based planning strategy for the development of the district.[25] It was thought that the main task of planning was not to determine how best to utilise the money allotted by the government or financed by the banks but to use the endeavour with the basic task of changing the society. Since the conscious people and their organizations were considered to be the main forces for transforming the society, the district authorities deliberately chose the alternative model of planning based on the maximum possible participation of the people — particularly the poorer, the deprived working people — in the process of planning and plan implementation.[26] It may be noted that the basic foundation of the district planning in Midnapore was provided by the success of Land Reforms measures undertaken in the district.[27] Such a conclusion is strengthened from the fact that up to 1984 almost three lakh acres of land were vested in the district out of which two lakh acres were distributed to 4.22 lakh beneficiaries. Of the beneficiaries, people belonging to the Scheduled Castes and Scheduled Tribes constituted 28.68 per cent and 22.66 per cent respectively. It may also be noted that the contribution of this district in land reforms was around 24 per cent of the total achievement made in the state. Similarly, 2.91 lakh *bargadars* of the district were able to record their right to cultivation, thus representing 22 per cent of the state's share.[28]

The logic behind this alternative model is convincing. Removal of imbalances and disparities is an important objective of decentralized planning. The problem of imbalances is not confined to the states or the districts, it exists even within a district. In a large district like Midnapore, characterised by diverse agro-climatic regions, incongruous soil types and textures, differential pattern of land holdings, uneven rate of economic growth, a structural homogenous development strategy for the entire district is not helpful. Moreover, the problem of imbalances may exist within a block also. While formulating plans for a particular area, the policy makers are required to set up goals and to find out strategies to iron out the intra-district and even intra-block disparities.[29] The main objective of planning as set forth by the District Planning Committee was to find out the optimum way for attaining the best possible results for the villages, panchayats and the districts. A concurrent survey of 40 sample villages of Midnapore, covering 6,192 households having 34,527 persons, was conducted under the auspices of the Zilla Parishad and the District Planning Committee to understand the class-caste composition of the villages and the different, often contradictory, interests of the various socio-economic groups. The survey identified the level of productivity of each economic sector, with a view to understanding the differences between the various classes in the sector, as well as the level of under-utilisation and mis-utilisation of the productive forces. The study also highlighted the extent and nature of stratification of rural society along the class and caste lines, as well as the discrimination between the sexes.[30] The finding provided an important input in developing the model of 'Village Based District Plan' in the district. The District Planning Committee underlined the philosophy of motivating the villagers to use their improved conditions as a tool for ushering in a new society. The main social force of the district live in the villages and consists of the rural poor, the landless, marginal and other poor peasants, the artisans, the tribes and the scheduled castes. The best way for them to know their country is to concentrate their attention, to start with, on the smallest spatial unit of the society, i.e. their own village, for understanding the problems and for taking actions to change it. Moreover, there is no spatial unit, above the village, where all the adults can assemble to discuss a problem. Discussions above the village level can be held only through the representatives depriving thereby the overwhelming majority of the people of the knowledge and consciousness which could occur to them in the process of discussions on, and deliberations about, planning of their own villages.

The District Planning Committee viewed decentralized planning as the conscious designing of the best possible coordinated programmes for changing the present reality to achieve a target.[31] With a view to achieving this conscious coordination, the villages were considered as the micro-units of decentralized planning. Only in the village meetings, large number of villagers, the adult inhabitants, can exchange their views regarding their resources, needs and welfare thereby enhancing both the self-confidence of the people and at once educating others about their priorities and needs. This conscious interaction among the people provides the basis of mutual training for themselves. In such village meetings, different categories and groups of people find an opportunity to come out openly and concretely about their needs, problems and expectations. These meetings also strengthen the linkages between the villagers on the one hand and the representatives of the panchayats and the government departments on the other.

PLANNING DESIGN IN THE DISTRICT

To understand the district planning of Midnapore it is necessary to examine the planning methodology together with the implementation process starting from the village level since the village plan is the first tier in the entire process of decentralized planning. The Guidelines issued by the State Planning Board stated the objective of formulation and implementation of district and block Level plans only.[32] But the District Planning Committees in Midnapore decided to come down to the Gram Panchayats and villages for the reasons mentioned above. However, only in a small number of villages the idea of formulation of village plan was realised. But in most of the villages the people were involved in the collection of data, setting up of priorities, selection of work-sites and beneficiaries and in discussions on the proposals and schemes of the panchayats. In fact, the call for 'planning by the villagers' or the 'village based planning' was a campaign during the Seventh Plan with a view to developing a planning culture and social consciousness.[33] The Zilla Parishad and the district authorities were eager to give the decentralized planning process the shape of an organized movement in the district.

Before the introduction of the 'village-based district planing' in Midnapore in 1985-86, the District Planning Committee published various documents, approach papers, guidelines etc. and sent those papers to all the panchayat samitis, municipalities, gram panchayats and different government departments located in the district. Subsequently, 30,000 leaflets were printed in the name of the *Sabhadhipati* of the Zilla Parishad addressing directly the people on the utility of village based district planning and the tasks to be performed by the villagers.[34]

During the Eighth Plan period, a conscious attempt was made by the panchayat leadership and the district administration to integrate decentralized planning movement with the total literacy campaign of the district. Attempts were made to motivate the people, both in rural and urban areas, to be involved in development and planning activities through the course contents of reading materials for the post-literacy programmes of the district. Again to assess the level of consciousness of the neo-literates, they were induced to put forward their own perception of development and suggestions thereof.[35] A separate sheet of paper, '*Unnayan Bhabna*' (development ideas) was added in which the neo-literates were asked to give their proposals for the development of the localities. The District Planning Committee took a policy decision to involve people in the activities connected with decentralized planning for developing an environment of mutual interactions and lasting relationship between the people and the planning agencies.[36]

DATA-BASE FOR PLANNING

Plan document is a final product of a long exercise involving various steps in the process of formulation of plans. Planning involves a hierarchy of priorities at the appropriate levels on the basis of availability of resources, both material and human. The District Planning Committee needs in-depth data and information covering all the area coming within the scope of district planning. The Working Group on District Planning (1982) classified the information required for district planning under six heads: resources, demographic, agro-economic, socio-economic, infrastructure and sectoral. Nevertheless, it recognized the scope of 'innovations as warranted by individual circumstances' at the district level.[37]

Anyway, a sound data-base is a precondition for the success of decentralized district planning. Earlier, the entire planning process was mainly dependent on the conventional methods of data collection. Data collected from conventional sources may be used for planning at different levels, from village level to the national level. The collection of information from primary and secondary sources is a difficult task. Again the information gathered from the sectoral departments located within the district are often inadequate for comprehensive planning.[38] There are deficiencies at the district level because of some historical and technical reasons. Availability and reliability of information are the two basic conditions for any fruitful exercise. Though the need for improving planning methodology and capabilities is emphasized repeatedly, the importance of data-base is hardly realised. The Working Group on District Planning points out many deficiencies in the present data-base and suggests various methods and tools for improving the data bank.[39] It may be stated that decentalized district planning does not have any chance of success if the basic data available are not dependable. Hence, there is the need for serious and organized attempts for building up data-base at different levels.

The problem of collecting information was well comprehended by the District Planning Committee in Midnapore while launching the district plan. The Committee made a clear distinction between two ways of collecting information. The first method of data collection may be executed through deputing some trained investigators from outside who could go to the remote target area for collecting information according to a format supplied from the district headquarters. The information thus collected is placed before the experts for analysis and subsequent use. The alternative method, in the main, is to gather information collectively by the villagers as a whole, or in groups, through discussions and to record the same by a group of educated people of the village itself. The recording could be read out in the village meeting for verification and correction, if necessary. In the instant case, the District Planning Committee has adopted this alternative method of data collection. It has developed two forms – Form No. 1 and 2, and Compilation Sheet No. 1 for the purpose of collection of data. It has also classified the categories of data to be collected. The District Planning Committee has identified eighteen heads for collection of information in Form No.1 and these are related to subjects like drinking water sources, health facilities, land pattern and irrigation facilities, live-stock and modern implements, education and infrastructural facilities. Similarly, information collected on thirteen other items are arranged in Form 2. In fact, the information sought for under Form 2 are related to the requirements of the village and the exploration of possibilities of implementation of such essential requirements through the planning.[40]

All these village level data are tabulated village-wise at the Gram Panchayats and Gram Panchayat-wise at the Panchayat Samitis and are submitted to the Zilla Parishad for processing. Again, the information so collected are re-arranged block-wise at the district level. To get the group total for a particular spatial unit (like a village, a Gram Panchayat or a Panchayat Samiti) the tabulator has to enter in a horizontal line the data from Form 1 in one sheet and from Form 2 in another sheet such relevant information for each concrete cluster (relevant villages for a particular Gram Panchayat, or relevant Gram Panchayat for a specific Panchayat Samiti etc.) as necessary and to add together the data so entered.[41] In addition to the preparation of information schedules and formats for collection of information from the villages, the District Planning Committee circulated a detailed guideline highlighting the types and characters of data and the method of collection of such data. The information collected through the proposed method are integrated with the secondary data available from the sectoral offices of the State Government.[42]

During the initial phase of launching of decentralized planning, the District Planning Committee decided to classify the data available with the Zilla Parishad into four broad categories: *Schedule I*, Information about the conditions of families; *Schedule II*, General conditions of the village; *Schedule III*, Scope of execution of existing schemes of development by linking individual schemes to the particular families; *Schedule IV*, Identification of projects and schemes eligible for execution at the village as a whole. Subsequently. the schedules have been simplified with necessary modifications relevant for decentralized district planning in the context of changing perspectives.[43] It should be noted here that initially the District Planning Committee insisted on collection of data on factors like land-ownership, productivity, income of different types of families, wage structure, wages, condition of education and the level of literacy, status of health, land-use pattern, village forestry, animal-keeping, consumption of industrial goods and rural industrialization etc. which could be changed by human action. Other data were considered irrelevant in the context of village-based district planning. The approach adopted by the Planning Committee was participatory one. It advised the line cadres to report to it for taking necessary action should they found irrelevant elements or the missing of relevant ones at the time of classification of information.[44] The restructured methodology of decentralized district planning as worked out by the District Planning Committee in 1996 is more or less akin to that followed during the preceding two five-year plans. The Committee has concretised the area of information to be collected at the village level for up-dating the data-bank for decentralized district planning.

Now the information is broadly classified in two categories: information on households and information about the general conditions of the individual villages or wards. Household information consists of inputs like the number of family members, land and other sources of family income, education etc. The District Planning Committee has identified twelve areas for preparation of 'Household Registers' on the basis of information collected from household survey. The items of information included in the 'Household Register' may be presented below:

Schedule A

Household Register

1. Name of the head of the family
2. Category: Community/Caste
3. Percentage of the total population of the village/ward
4. Education/level of literacy
5. Land and pattern of land-use
6. Income from agriculture
7. Income from industry/trade/service
8. Wage
9. Other income
10. Total Income
11. Residence
12. Status of the household

The District Planning Committee has also adopted its own yardstick for determining the status of the individual households on the basis of annual income. Likewise 'Resource Register' includes information relating to the general and infrastructural conditions of the concerned locality. It includes data on twenty items identified by the committee relating to the spatial unit like area, population and families within the locality under survey.[45]

Schedule B

Resource Register

1. Area of the village/population/families
2. Provisions for drinking water
3. Arrangements for education
4. Education and culture
5. Information regarding health and hygiene
6. Cultivable land and land patterns
7. Type of crops and outputs
8. Projects and profit-based cultivation
9. Irrigation facilities and sources
10. Self-employment projects with number of man-days
11. Fisheries and Fish industry
12. Information regarding loans and investments
13. Types of modern agricultural implements

14. Provisions for electricity
15. Non-conventional energy
16. Number of workers
17. Number of beneficiaries from government
18. Information regarding *pattadar, bargadar* and landless
19. Irrigation system and the status of the farmers
20. Particulars about village and small industries.

The scheme of maintaining these two registers is being followed in this district since the introduction of 'village based district plans' in the mid-eighties. Now emphasis is placed on periodical up-dating of the information already available. Attempts have also been made for preservation of information at all the stages starting from *Gram Sansads* and *wards*.[46] *Iswar Chandra Jana Chetna Kendra* at each of the *Gram Sansads* in the panchayat areas and at the wards under the municipalities are being established to organize the programmes of Basic Literacy and Post-Literacy in the district. The District Planning Committee has outlined the methodology to transform the literacy centres into centres for local development and the *Iswar Chandra Jana Chetana Kendra* is considered as the first step of decentralized district planning.[47] The information so gathered and entered in the Household Registers and Resource Registers are cross-checked and verified with the data already available with line departments of the government and the Bureau of Statistics to ascertain the authenticity. After collection of information and their systematic arrangements, the process of decentralized planning starts at different levels.[48]

Based on the experiences gathered over the years in the concrete situation of Midnapore, the State Government has elaborated the methodology for developing data-base for decentralized planning. The Government is convinced that development of a data bank can never attain complete success unless the villagers do actively participate in the process and accordingly, it has outlined a comprehensive scheme of data collection through para-wise group meeting instead of the conventional method of door to door survey. For this purpose, each village is divided into a few *paras* (neighbourhood) and separate meetings are organised by the survey team to collect information. With the help of the local panchayats, the surveyors are required to launch extensive campaign programmes before holding such meetings for mobilisation of common people especially the women and the marginal sections of the community. Moreover, it is suggested that one of the surveyors could be selected from among the women volunteers and separate meetings for the women may be organised, if necessary, to ensure their active participation. To overcome the problem of absence, two to three meetings in the neighbourhood and even survey of the individual families through door to door visits also are suggested in the Guidelines for obtaining accurate information when no body from these particular families turns up at such meetings.

Another improvement upon the process of data collection is the provision for structuring of the methodology of resource appraisal. As a result of land reforms undertaken in the state, the number of people having direct access to land resources has increased. Both production and productivity have also been increased considerably. In spite of more than a decade of experiments in decentralized planning in the state, a systematic appraisal and mapping of natural resources like land, water, vegetation, technical skill, instruments is yet to be developed. But information on these material resources are necessary for planning particularly in the fields of agriculture and employment generation.[49] The experiments conducted in some DPEP blocks of Purulia (W.B.) for implementing Micro-Watershed Plans have accelerated the feasiblity of conducting such kind of appraisal of land and water resources and formulation of village level plans on the basis of available data to make them 'much more produciton-oriented, down-to-earth and effective.'[50]

As mentioned earliar, the idea of resource mapping has been adapted from the Kerala methodology and thus it supplements the scheme of preparing 'Resource Register' conceived earliar in Midnapore district and subsequently followed in other parts of the state. The design of resource mapping is now more structured and covers a wide range of specified information together with relevant mapping on the following aspects :

1. Terrain Feature Data (Information on characteristics of land): type of ownership, soil texure, depth of top soil, colour and quality of soil, water holding capacity, slope

of land, soil drainage, types and extent of erosion, soil conservation measures, problems encountered by the users etc. ;

2. Land use Data (Information on land use) : type of ownership of land, pattern and intensity of use, major crops and average yield, crop rotation and yield thereof, source of irrigation, use of fertilizer and pesticides, reasons for under-utilisation, user's perception of land use, etc. of each plot of land in each mouza ; and
3. Water Resource Data (Information on the sources of water): description of the source, plot number, ownership, year of construction, depth of water level and fluctuations thereof, use of water, mode of lifting, diameter of well, maintenance status, perception of users, etc.[51]

Separate kinds of formats are prescribed for each category of information. The elements of information involved are of different categories ; some of these can be produced in formats and not on maps. Again, there are some information which may be represented through both maps and formats. Collection of information in the formats and preparation of the draft maps need to be taken up simultaneously in order to avoid confusion and duplication. In this process the role of the villagers is most vital for having accurate information and hence the team members are required to ensure the involvement of the villagers in the entire process of survey. After collection of information and the preparation of maps, the survey team, with the help of the Trainers Team, will prepare a report on the basis of formats with special emphasis on analysis of data and drawing a problem-map reflecting the major problems of the village.

Apart from the utility of the reports and maps for village-based planning, these may also be used for other administrative purposes, Hence, the forms and formats will be arranged serially and bound village-wise for systematic maintenance and timely availability. Since the panchayats are involved in the preparation of the socio-economic reports and resource maps right from the field survey, preservation and their use are vested with the gram panchayats.

PRIORITIZATION IN PLANNING

In the light of information and needs, the District Planning Committee outlines the major objectives and priorities of the district plan. Usually the basic objectives and strategies are included in the approach paper of the Five-Year Plan on the basis of which Annual District Plans are formulated. Naturally, the objectives and strategies of district plans change after a considerable period of time. Within the broad spectrum of basic objectives, priorities and targets are determined by the District Planning Committee and these are included in the Annual Action Plans of the various implementing agencies at various levels.

The overall strategy of both the Seventh and Eighth Five-Year Plans of the district was streamlined on a three point programme: (a) to involve the maximum number of people without consideration of their political or community affiliations in the process of decentralized planning in such a way as to make them realise that they are doing their own jobs, (b) to determine the priorities in such a way as to make the poorest of the poor get the maximum benefits and play a decisive role in planning and development since the society is inegalitarian and highly stratified in character, and (c) to help the people to realise the limitations and constraints through selection of priorities and schemes.[52] While deciding priorities, two principles were more or less followed by the District Planning Committee during the initial phase of district planning: *first*, one-third of the funds available for district planning was spent for irrigation programmes, not more than one-third of the allotment for road construction and the balance of the funds was spent for other programmes. *Secondly*, roughly seventy per cent of the total amount was set apart for planning below the district level and the balance was meant for district level schemes.[53]

The District Planning Committee has endorsed the basic objectives of the District Plan outlined previously and has re-emphasized the strategy to fulfil the five basic needs of food, clothing, shelter, education and health of the people of the district. This is to be done by properly accommodating the district sector subjects within the overall framework of the National-cum-State Plan by an effective utilization of the available resources, and, taking into account the local factors, both geographical and socio-economic.[54] In fact, the basic objectives and strategies of the district plan have remained more or less unchanged since the introduction of decentralized district planning in Midnapore in 1985 though the priorities have been changed from time to time. Thus the District Planning Committee decided to give the highest priority to the Power Sector as was done in the Eighth Plan period. It proposed an allocation of Rs.25.57 crore for this sector in the first year of the Ninth Plan (1997-98) thereby proposing 27.39 per cent allotment for this sector.[55] Though incidental, it may be noted that the State Government also accorded top priority to power sector and has earmarked an additional amount of Rs.70 crore from outside the plan budget of the state.[56]

PROJECTIONS AND TIME-FRAME

After analysing the information collected from village survey, the department of statistics and other departments at the corresponding levels, the different planning bodies prepare priorities and formulate plan projections reflecting one through annual plan and the other through five-year plans. During the Seventh Five-Year Plan, there was a deliberate and conscious attempt towards formulation of three categories of plans: *One*, Annual Plan; *two*, Five-Year Plan; and, *three*, Perspective Plan, spreading over a period of ten to fifteen years. The schemes which were expected to be completed within a year were included in the Annual Plan, and those requiring more than a year in the Five-Year Plan and those requiring much longer period were included in the Perspective Plan.[57] These three aspects of the plan combined together constituted the plan for the target area, and of these three plans, the most important and the primary one was the perspective plan which provided the perspectives, orientation, continuity and the direction of change in a concrete situation. But since the Eighth Five-Year Plan, Annual and Five-Year Plans only are being prepared.[58] These two plans are now formulated at appropriate levels in consideration of the potentialities of physical resources of the locality. Subsequently, projections are made on different sectoral planning like irrigation, agriculture, forestry, industry, health, education, urban development etc. and targets are fixed in the light of available financial and infrastructural inputs. During the formulation of district plans, a total review of the existing infrastructural facilities available in the district particularly in respect of link roads, transport services, market facilities and power supply is also made so that schemes and projects for development of infrastructure are included in the district plan.

The need for a time-frame for comprehensive planning arises out of the fact that all the projects, programmes and schemes identified cannot be implemented simultaneously and all at a time due to both sequential and resource constraints. The formulation of concrete and time-bound programmes to counter the twin problems of poverty and inequitable distribution of resources acts as a check on the 'push' towards the cities.[59] Though the perspective plan was not formally abandoned, the Ninth Five-Year Plan of the district was viewed from two angles only: *one*, from the angle of five separate but integrated and well-linked annual plans; and the *second*, from a single comprehensive five-year plan.[60] The District Planning Committee has also developed two schedules in such a way as to ensure complete integration and linkage between the annual plans and the five-year plans at both the Gram Panchayat and village levels.[61] Recently, the State Government has made some modifications in the methodology and time-schedule of planning. According to this schedule, the process of planning at the *Gram Sansad* level starts in the month of November preceding the year of planning.[62] Moreover, a programme under the Convergent Community Action (CCA) has been devised as an updated and holistic strategy to ensure community participation in planning, implementation and monitoring of decentralized district planning.

FORMULATION OF PLANS

The methodology of decentralized district planning marks a revolutionary break with the previous one and creates an integrated planning process at four different levels: Village Level

(*Gram Sansad*), Gram Panchayat Level, Block Level and District Level.

At the Micro Levels

The lowest unit or the micro unit of planning in the district is the *Gram Sansad* in the rural areas and *wards* in the urban areas. To avoid confusion and misunderstanding on the criteria for inclusion of a particular scheme or a proposal at the appropriate level it has been decided to include only those items in the village plan that could be implemented at the village level. The schemes and projects which are considered useful and relevant for a particular village but which could not be included in the plan of the said village, may be included in the Panchayat Plans, if they affect more than one village. Similarly, in the municipal areas the Ward Committees are required to formulate their plans and proposals at the ward level. The criteria of classification of schemes between the Ward Level Schemes and Municipal Level Schemes are similar to those of the Village and Gram Panchayat Level Schemes.

During the beginning of the Seventh Five-Year Plan there were 518 Gram Panchayats comprising the inhabited villages in the rural areas while there were 155 municipal wards in the urban areas.[63] Though attempts were made for decentralization in planning down to the village level by the District Planning Committee in the beginning of the Seventh Plan there was no proposal or scheme for decentralization in urban areas below the municipality level.[64] Thanks to the success in the experiments of decentralization through Panchayati Raj Institutions and the changes resulting from land reforms and other pro-people policies of the State Government, the District Planning Committee became increasingly pre-occupied with the development programmes in rural area. On the other hand, the urge for decentralized planning by involving the people at the grassroots level was lacking in most of the municipalities.[55] Indifferent attitude of the municipal leadership in ensuring people's involvement in area development programmes of the district is almost a common feature.[66]

Prior to the commencement of the Ninth Plan, the villages were considered as the ground units of planning. But from the first year of the Ninth Plan, the *Gram Sansads* and the W*ards* in both rural and urban areas respectively have been identified as the primary working units of district plan. This change in the level of planning has been necessitated due to two important factors. Under the amended provisions of the Act, *Gram Sansads* have been created and empowered with some basic tasks in the formulation of plan priorities and the selection of development schemes.[67] Secondly, the huge size of the district is a major obstacle in initiating the process at the village level in the absence of any organizational structure at the villages.[68] There are more than eleven thousand villages and municipal wards in the district. The number of primary units of district planning has been drastically reduced by more than fifty per cent through identifying the *Gram Sansads* as the micro units of planning. It is a fact that even after intensive campaigning throughout the district during the entire span of Seventh Five-Year Plan, village planning could only be introduced in 700 villages in the district.[69]

Since there was no separate body for planning at the Gram Panchayat level, formulation of plans was designed to take place at an extended meeting of the members of Gram Panchayats, local school teachers, social organisers, and others called specially for the purpose during the years under Ninth Plan. The District Planning Committee also enumerated an exhaustive list of twenty-two subjects to be covered under planning at the Gram Panchayat level.[70] The plans of the Gram Panchayats were formulated according to the format supplied by the District Planning Committee and forwarded to the Panchayat Samiti, the middle tier of the Panchayati raj system, for necessary follow-up.

Village Plans

Formulation of plans at the villages remained almost incomplete throughout the state in the Ninth Plan. Again, whatever the villagers formulated while preparing plans for their villages was merely a list of priorities or a charter of demands.[71] Still now in most of the villages, people are guided by an impression that their role is primarily confined to ventilating their needs and demands through village plans so that the government or the panchayats could provide funds to meet them. After an assessment of the situation, the government felt the need to remove such misconceptions by convincing the people that planning does not mean the articulation of or enlisting the needs and demands, neither it is a task of selecting beneficiaries and preparing schemes within the allocations made by the government. It has been a constant endeavour on the part of both government and the panchayats to make the people conscious that planning has to be visualised in terms of convergence of their own resources and efforts on the one hand, and the institutional or government support on the other. Accordingly, the government has refined the methodology of formulation of village plans detailing out all the necessary modalities in this respect.[72]

Moreover, the Government after considering all the aspects involved in the vital question as to which type of village is to be treated viable in the context of village based planning, has decided to consider a 'populated mouza (revenue village)' as an appropriate unit for this purpose. Since the village needs to be a viable unit for planning, the villagers may consider an amalgamation of adjacent mouzas to be a unit for planning, if the size of a single mouza is too small to be a sound unit for planning, and if all the villagers think it both logical and necessary to combine a number of contiguous mouzas for effective management of resources and better mobilisation of people under a common programme of planning and development. However, in case of any problem or dispute in this regard, the Government authourises the Gram Panchayat concerned to settle the differences.

The Government has also constituted a 'Task Force on Decentralization of Power in Rural Areas' to examine all aspects of decentralization with special emphasis on (i) concretisation of the *gram Sansad*-based block plans, (ii) formulation of a scheme for involvings NGOs in the process of planning, (iii) elaboration of the methodology for integration of *Gram Sansad* and Gram Panchayat plans with district and state level plans, and (iv) strengthening of panchayat organizations including reorganisation of the existing *Sthayee Samitis*.[73]

The Socio-Economic Survey and the Resource Survey provide the ground realities on which the priorities and possibilities of an area plan may converge. Hence after the completion of the survey, the entire data generated and the maps prepared through such survey are placed before the *Gram Sansad* for finalisation. The teams of volunteers organise and conduct workshops at appropriate time and place to provide opportunity for the selected representatives of the villages to interact with the volunteers, the government functionaries and the panchayat members. A draft village plan is formulated in these meetings after analysis of data, exchange of opinions, evaluation of needs and priorities. The draft plan is placed at the *Gram Sansad* meetings for approval after necessary additions and modifications. This revised methodology of decentralized district planning worked out for operation since the first year of the Tenth Plan consists of *four chapters*. The *first chapter* incorporates the geographical location, history and demographic features and other related information of the village. The *second chapter* contains the proplems of the village and the needs thereof. The *third chapter* deals with information on village resources while the *fourth* contains the action plan (Annual Plan) for the following year and for the next five years (Five-Year Plan). A model format developed for preparing the village plan for the sake of convenience and uniformity throughout the state is reproduced in Format 1.

Format 1

Village based Action Plan								Name of the Village : Name of the Gram Panchayat :				
Subject	Nature of Project	Work done in last 5 years	What can be done		Funds required		Source of Funds					Expected results	Remarks
			One year	Five year	One year	Five year	Village own	Gram Panc-hayat	Govt.	Bank	Others		
1	2	3	4(A)	4(B)	5(A)	5(B)	6(A)	6(B)	6(C)	6(D)	6(E)	7	8

Source : Institute of Panchayats and Rural Development, Government of West Bengal, 2001.

Gram Panchayat Plan

Though the methodology detailed out is meant for the formulation of plans starting from the level of villages (*Gram Sansads*), the State Government seems to be more determined to implement the process of plan formulation upwards from the Gram Panchayat levels for the present, if not feasible from further below. Hence it has concretised a detailed methodology for formulation of Gram Panchayat Plans commensurating with the Tenth Plan.[74] Following Kerala's People's Campaign Programme for popularising decentralized planning, the planning process in West Bengal has been conceived to be implemented through *six* interrelated stages:[75]

Stage I starts with the completion of the training of the panchayat members and officials and is devoted to the collection of information from the villages for building up database for planning. The Socio-Economic Survey and the Resource Survey conducted by a team of volunteers comprise information on individual households and a picture of the entire village including a Resource Map.

Stage II collected information through survey are verified, collated and analysed by the survey team with the help of *Krishi Prajukti Sahayak, Bhumi Sahayak, Health Workers, Anganwadi Workers,* school teachers and others. The entire work of data collection is supervised by the gram panchayats and up-dating of the inventory is vested with them.

Stage III, in this phase Special *Gram Sansad* meetings are organised, quite similar to the Special *Gram Sabhas* in Kerala, for the purpose of preparing plans. In the said meetings detailed discussions on the outlines prepared by the Task Forces on *six different sectors*, i.e. (a) education, (b) health, (c) women's development, (d) agriculture, irrigation, animal husbandry and fishery, (e) cottage, small industry and trade, and (f) infrastructure are organised. After initial discussions, the participants are divided into *six sectoral groups* for meaningful participation and the synopsis prepared on individual sectors there is placed before the respective groups for detailed discussions and suggestions on the identification of problems, prioritisation of development schemes and availability of local resources. Plenary session is held after deliberations by the respective groups to place the summary of the discussions. Then the chairperson sums up the discussions and announces the follow-up actions.

Stage IV is confined to the concretisation of the sectoral plans. In this phase, the Task Force prepares the draft plans on the basis of data generated earlier and the needs and priorities of the people expressed in the Special *Gram Sansad* meetings.

Stage V, in this phase Development Seminars are organised at the gram panchayats and are attended by the gram panchayat members, the Local Resource Persons, ten to twelve representatives from each of the *Gram Sansads*, Task Force members, Government functionaries attached to the Gram Panchayats and Blocks, representatives of the NGOs, local persons interested and experienced in development, and local representatives of all the political parties. In the said seminars, the draft sectoral plans are discussed and revised, if necessary, with additions, modifications and deletion.

Stage VI is devoted to the preparation of the Gram Panchayat Plan. The drafts prepared by the Task Force and the suggestions mooted in the Development Seminars are accommodated in the Gram Panchayat Plans, Two plans are prepared—the *Outline Development Plan* (ODP) for a period of five years synchronising with the Five-Year Plan and the *Annual Plan* on the basis of ODP. In subsequent years covered under the Five-Year Plan, only the Annual Plans are prepared. Like the Village Plan, the Gram Panchayat Plan also contains *four chapters* covering the same contents though a few additional issues may have to be addressed to in Gram Panchayat Plans depending on the local situation of a particular gram panchayat since decentralized planning is always situation-specific. However, the format prepared by the Government for Gram Panchayat Plan is also quite similar to that of the village plan excepting the necessary changes required for a gram panchayat. However, as pointed out, the Gram Panchayat Plans will have to accommodate three distinct aspects:[76]

(i) Compilation of all the Village Plans under the Gram Panchayat concerned;

(ii) Incorporation of the Gram Panchayat level plan schemes taking into account the schemes and proposals involving interest of more than one village, originated at the village level but could not be included in a particular village plan; and

(iii) Inclusion of proposals catering to the interest of more than one Gram Panchayat for consideration at the block level.

At the Blocks and Municipalities

The schemes and projects which are not included in the Gram Panchayat Plans or the schemes and projects considered relevant for more than one Gram Panchayat or a cluster of Gram Panchayats in the same Panchayat Samiti (block level) are taken up at the block level. Municipal plans are also formulated by the municipalities. During the initial phase of district planning, the Block Planning Committees were given the authority to approve their own schemes and priority-proposals having beneficial effects confined to the block and involving estimated costs not exceeding Rupees fifty thousand in each case. They could, however, prepare schemes covering command areas which extended over the adjoining blocks and proposals involving more than Rupees fifty thousand, subject to the approval of the DPC.[77] At present there is no such financial limit on the proposals.The Block Planning Committees submit their plans and proposals to the District Planning Committee for information and incorporation in the district plans.

The Block Planning Committee, apart from classifying the schemes into 'Block Level Schemes' and 'District Level Schemes', re-arranges all the schemes according to the format specified by the District Planning Committee.[78] During the first year of the Seventh Plan, the district plan was divided into seventeen sectors[79] which were increased to twenty-five in the Eighth Plan through bifurcation of the old ones and the creation of new sectors like Labour and Employment (AEP/SESRU) and Special Rural Development (IRDP/DPAP/JRY).[80] At present, the blocks and the municipalities are entitled to formulate plans and priorities for twenty-nine sectors[81] on the basis of Gram

Panchayat Plans. The outlay limits of Block and Municipal plans are determined after obtaining detailed information from the sectoral departments of the State Government. In the absence of such information, the Block Planning Committees and the Municipalities prepare their Annual Plans on the basis of an increase of ten per cent over and above the actual allocation in the plan sector in the previous year.[82]

The Block Planning Committee prepares the block plans on the basis of Gram Panchayat Plans. Attempts are now being made in the district for preparation of plans at municipalities on the basis of proposals and priorities suggested by the newly constituted ward committees.[83] In addition to further classification of the 'remaining schemes', submitted by the Gram Panchayats, into Block Level Schemes and District Level Schemes, all the schemes are re-aligned and re-arranged as per departmental programmes. The village plans and Gram Panchayats plans are also integrated in the block plans. The differences and similarities in scope and priority of village plans and Gram Panchayat Plans are identified and integrated, wherever possible, into the block plans to make it a total exercise. In this way, a two-way integration, vertical integration between the Gram Panchayat plans and district plans, and horizontal integration between the various departments of the government, are achieved at the block level. At the block and municipality level two sets of plans are prepared : *One,* an Annual Plan, and *another,* a Perspective Plan, now for five years. The perspective plan is relatively more abstract and in most cases provides the parameters and framework for the annual plan which actually contains the details.[84] Since the practice of block planning exercise is relatively an older one than the municipal planning, the experiments in block planning has undergone some changes since its introduction. During the Seventh Five-Year Plan, the block plan included the following parts: introduction, block profile, different departmental plans with information on schemes and physical and financial targets together with sources of funds. During the Eighth Plan period, the previous format was revised and it contained five chapters to include information on current profile of the block; review of the last plan in respect of both physical and financial aspects; proposed outlay of the departments and block level-based and department-wise allocation; particulars regarding schemes and projects together with sources of funds; and the analysis of department-wise physical targets with names of schemes.[85] In addition to these, the block plans were required to include special notes on the accommodation of schemes and projects for the scheduled castes and tribes in both outlays and physical targets. Moreover, prioritization of schemes was also outlined in the Eighth Plan. Minor changes have been introduced recently in the formats for the preparation of annual block and municipality plans. Now the block and municipal plans comprise the following: (i) Profile of the block or municipality, (ii-a) Financial review of the previous plan, (ii-b) Physical review, (iii) Sectoral outlay matrix, (iv) Sectoral Plan, and (v) Break-up of physical targets.[86]

The Block Planning Committees and Municipalities give priority to 'spill-over' or 'on-going schemes' before taking up new set of schemes. Moreover, the District Planning Committee has identified the sectors for which the Blocks and Municipalities are required to prepare plans. It may be noted here that the Gram Panchayat plans are not shown Gram Panchayat-wise separately in the Block Plans. In fact, there is no scope for the projection of schemes and plan proposals of individual Gram Panchayats. In the format prescribed for block planning, the block is considered as a whole and distinctions between projects and expenditure in terms of sectors, sources of financing etc. are shown. However, within each sub-sector, specific projects are spelt out in details indicating their nature, location, physical targets etc.

The Block Plan incorporates the schemes and proposals for execution by the block itself as well as those transferred by the Zilla Parishad, the government departments and the municipalities. Moreover, Credit Plans of the block and the projects under Centrally Sponsored Schemes are included in the block plan.[87] Naturally, the problem of integration and linkages among these different kinds of schemes and projects becomes a major issue in decentralized district planning which is proposed to be considered in a separate chapter while examining the infrastructural arrangements for planning. In the methodology of 'village based district planning', the Block Planning Committee prepares plan at the block level as per the parameters set by the District Planning Committee and the Guidelines issued by the State Planning Board.[88] The Guidelines, though modified from time to time, contain the basic principles of decentralized district planning. Under the existing structure of decentralized planning, the block and municipality-specific schemes are again aggregated at the district level and after incorporating all the district sector schemes and municipality-specific schemes, the district plan is prepared.[89]

At the District Level

Formulation of plans at the district level is a complicated task since there are various agencies and departments engaged in the process of planning. Moreover, the coordination and integration of the plans prepared by the panchayats, municipalities and line departments take place at this level. While preparing the district plan it is necessary to ensure that the schemes and projects included in the district plan reflect the priorities and needs identified at different levels by the people of respective areas and by their representatives. At the same time, it is to be ascertained that the district plan is inter-sectorally and inter-regionally well balanced and integrated.

Hence, the formulation of a plan at the district level will be partial and incomplete if all the development programmes are not considered and integrated with other schemes of the district. This is most important since most of the programmes require sufficient linkages.[90] The realisation of a target in a particular sector depends not only on the effort and functioning of that sector but also on the quantum and content of assistance from the related sectors. Linkages, both forward and backward, can be established through getting inputs from and supplying outputs to other sectors. Thus the essence of district planning lies in a two-way transaction in the agencies of planning and implementation.[91] All these are highly sophisticated activities and are performed by the District Planning Committee which prepares the draft district plan with assistance from different agencies and departments. This assistance is mainly secured through the information networks developed by different sub-committees of the District Planning Committee.[92] The district planning aims at integrating the national goals and objectives with the local needs and priorities. It is linked vertically downwards to the local area plans and integrated upwards with the state and national plans and thus helps to achieve coordination between micro-level and macro-level planning. This process of functional integration is sometimes labelled as 'Nesting of Plans' which is important in combining the 'top down' and 'bottom up' approaches.[93] Thus the existing process of district planning may be viewed as a continuous cycle covering the articulation and integration of popular needs reflected through the block and municipality-specific projects, prioritization of various schemes and proposals and different aspects of resource allocation and mobilization in the district as a whole.

Under the existing methodology, the District Plan of Midnapore covers various aspects of resource assessment, identification of needs, prioritization of projects and formulation of total plans for the district spreading over twenty-nine sectoral departments of the State Government. As pointed out previously, the district plan is both an extension and improvement upon the block and municipality-specific plans of the district. It contains the essential elements reflected usually through *five chapters*.[94]

Chapter I	District Profile
Chapter II	Review of the previous plan: (A) Financial Review, (B) Physical Review
Chapter III	Sectoral Outlay Matrix, Outlay Matrix for Blocks and Municipalities
Chapter IV	Sectoral Plan: Physical and Financial
Chapter V	Physical Targets : Block/Municipality-wise break-up

The District Plan also contains a synopsis of Credit Plan which is included in Chapter IV. Both the Five-Year and Annual Plans are prepared by the Development and Planning Cell of the District Planning Committee highlighting the problems and difficulties and incorporating the suggestions and proposals received from different sub-committees of the District Planning Committee.

ROUTE CHART IN PLANNING

The methodology of decentralized district planning outlined above contains a route chart in the entire planning process. The plans formulated at the village level are submitted to the Gram Panchayat for transmission through the Block Planning Committee to the District Planning Committee for inclusion in the district plan. The methodology of district planning based on micro planning at *Gram Sansad* level does not keep the village plan or *Gram Sansad* plan in isolation but integrates the same in a system of linkages[95] at various levels of planning and thus ensures an integrated and total approach. The village plans are submitted to the Gram Panchayat and after scrutiny the Gram Panchayat divides the higher level schemes formulated at the *Gram Sansads* into 'Gram Panchayat Level Schemes' and 'the remaining schemes'. Thus Planning at the Gram Panchayat level consists of three inter-related processes: *first,* collection and articulation of all the micro plans from the below; *secondly,* identification and examination of proposals and priorities having scope for the involvement of and impacts upon two or more villages for exploring the possibilities of inclusion within the Gram Panchayat Plan; and *thirdly,* preparation of two lists of priorities relating to (i) the schemes and projects to be undertaken by the Gram Panchayat itself in its own plan proposals and (ii) the schemes which cannot be taken up at the Gram Panchayat level but to be referred to the Panchayat Samiti for possible inclusion in the Block Plan. Apart from some points specific to the Gram Panchayats, the steps and methodology applied in case of village plans are also followed in the formulation of the Gram Panchayat Plans. The symmetry between the village plan (*Gram Sansad* Plans) and the Gram Panchayat Plan is maintained through the formats prescribed for these two levels which are same only with the exception of an additional column in respect of Gram Panchayats. Uniform formats have also been prepared by the District Planning Committee to help the process of integration of Gram Panchayat

Plans with the Block plans. This mechanism of integration and linkages is crucial in the whole process of planning to achieve cohesion and comprehensiveness in development programmes within the district as a whole.

The Block Planning Committee, keeping in view the budgetary limits, social needs and priorities of different projects and schemes relating to different sectors, prepares the Block Plans and submits the same to the District Planning Committee. The Municipalities simultaneously prepare their plans furnishing therein the Sectoral Outlay Matrix together with rough cost-estimates and submit the same to the District Planning Committee for integration and coordination with the district plan.[96] Similarly, the district level officers of each department of the Government prepare project schemes for the proposed outlay kept apart for inter-block and district level schemes, since block level and panchayat level schemes are integrated into the block plans on the basis of block-wise disaggregation of the available funds. The district level officers before the finalisation of their sectoral schemes consult the District Planning and Co-ordination Sub-Committee. Once the selection of project schemes for each sector is finalised at the block and the district levels and their costs estimated, the compiled plan becomes the annual plan of that particular sector (department) of the district level. The sectoral plan thus formulated and approved by the District Planning Committee is forwarded to the head of the respective departments at the state level.

Likewise, the District Planning Committee, with the help of the District Planning Cell and the Sub-Committees of the DPC integrates the Block Plans, Municipal-specific Plans, Panchayat Plans and the district level schemes and projects into a Draft showing therein the outlay for each sector and the sources of funds. The annual district plan also incorporates credit plan of the district apart from those of the Centrally Sponsored Schemes and the District Plan Schemes introduced since 1985-86.[97] The route chart also includes the transmission of the Draft District Plan to the State Planning Board for consideration and approval. Usually, the District Planning Committee submits its plan within November each year. Under the existing rules, the District Planning Committee is required to forward the draft development plan of the district to the State Planning Board within one month from the date when the Committee adopts the draft plan for the district or within such date as may be specified by the Government.[98] It is needless to say that the State Plans are submitted to the Planning Commission for approval. Thus the district planning process is a comprehensive exercise starting from the village to the district level and at the same time serving as a bridge in a hierarchy of development plans connecting the grassroots plans to the National Plan. A schematic presentation of the planning methodology followed at present in the district is shown in Figure 4.2.

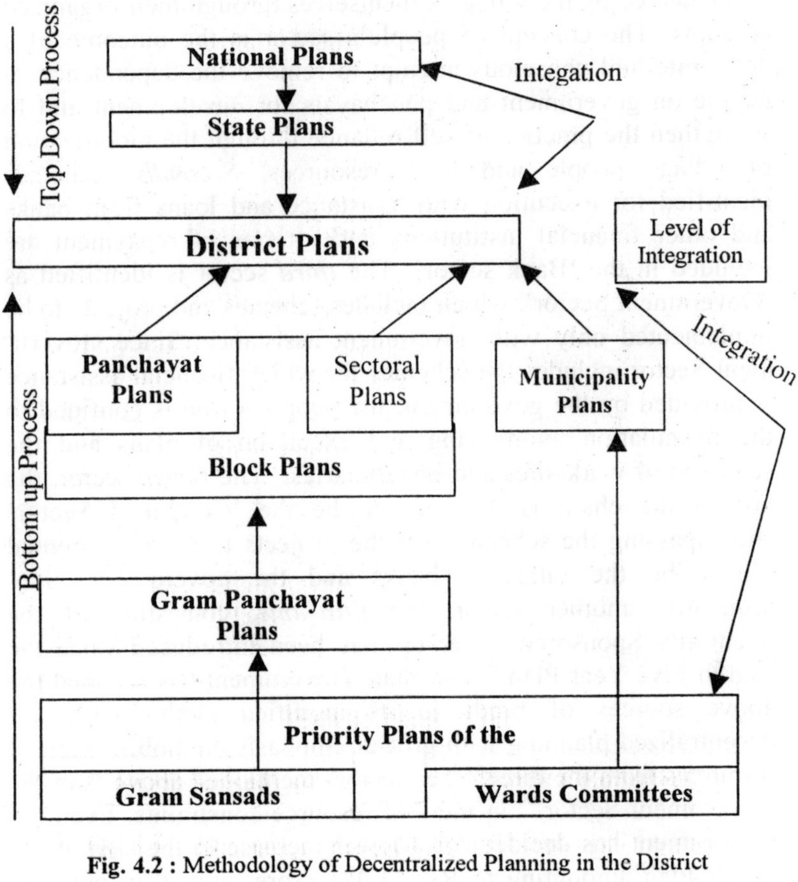

Fig. 4.2 : Methodology of Decentralized Planning in the District

RESOURCE MOBILIZATION AND CREDIT PLANNING

The planning methodology developed by the District Planning Committee in Midnapore not only creates an integrated planning process at different levels but also identifies the sources of funds for decentralized district planning. The District Planning Committee classified the sources of funds originally into four sectors: *the People's Sector, the Bank Sector, the Government Sector* and *the Combined Sector*. Subsequently in the Eighth Plan period, one more sector was added to the existing four. The most important sector in the process is identified as the 'People's Sector', which includes the schemes and proposals that may be implemented by the villagers themselves through their organized attempts. The concept of people's sector is the outcome of a deliberate and conscious attempt to remove the dependence of people on government and panchayats for development and to strengthen the practice of self-reliance through the mobilization of village people and local resources. *Secondly*, schemes identified for execution with assistance and loans from banks and other financial institutions under terms of repayment are included in the 'Bank sector'. The *third* sector is identified as 'Government Sector', which includes schemes and projects to be implemented only with government assistance. Since Government Sector includes the schemes for which financial assistance is provided by the government, the people's role is confined to the formulation, monitoring and execution of plans and the selection of work-sites and beneficiaries. The *fourth* sector, the last in the chain is designed to be the 'Combined Sector' encompassing the schemes and the projects to be implemented jointly by the villagers, banks and the government. Subsequently, another sector, the *fifth one*, consisting of the 'Centrally Sponsored Schemes' has been introduced since the Eighth Five Year Plan.[99] The State Government has retained the above sources of funds in its modified methodology for decentralized planning with greater emphasis on mobilisation of resources from the three other sectors mentioned above than the Government Sector[100] in view of resource constraints. Even the Government has decided for a lower increase in the size of the Tenth Plan amounting to Rs. 33,071 crore, only fifty per cent higher than the nominal expenditure made during the Ninth Plan.[101]

Of the five sectors mentioned above, the first two, viz., the People's Sector and the Bank Sector are most vital since active and direct contributions of the people are required for the implementation of the schemes and projects included in these sectors. Ten primary tasks are identified and included in the category of People's sector which can be implemented by the people themselves, while the Bank Sector includes six such items for execution with financial support from the banks.[102]

Under the decentralized planning process, apart from the final examination of the schemes and projects included in the block and municipality-specific plans, district level schemes are formulated on the basis of priorities and needs indicated by the *Gram Sansad*, ward committee, panchayats and municipalities. Consideration of such priorities and needs in the formulation of district level schemes arises as these cannot be included in the respective plan either partly or fully. Such schemes are treated as District Plan Schemes and are executed under allocations from District Plan Fund. The fund allocated for District Plan Schemes is placed with the District Planning Committee for coordinating and filling up of the gaps between requirements and achievements, which again reallocates a certain portion of the funds to the Block Planning Committee, Municipalities and other agencies.[103]

The District Planning Committee formulates district plan on the basis of allocations of funds through District Plan Schemes, Sectoral allocations and allocations under Centrally Sponsored Schemes. Under the existing practice, the District Planning Committee appropriates 30 per cent of the plan funds received from the government while reallocating 20 per cent to the Panchayat Samitis and the balance for the Gram Panchayats.[104] The existing procedure of allocation and vertical sharing of funds between the three tiers of Panchayati raj bodies in West Bengal conforms to the recommendations of the State Finance Commission (1995).[105] The rationale for a larger allocation for the base tier, i.e. Gram Panchayats follows from the fact that the Gram Panchayats are the bodies which are primarily responsible for meeting the local needs and priorities. On the other hand, the disparities in the ratio of sharing the allocations between the upper two tiers, i.e. Zilla Parishad and Panchayat Samiti arises from the expectation that the Zilla Parishad would undertake relatively larger projects and provide for overall administrative and technical supervision.[106]

There are two points which deserve to be mentioned in this regard. The district plan contains a proposal on Credit Plan for the district and a brief write-up for every sector included in the plan document. It is the usual practice to highlight the objectives of the plans and to assess objectively the cumulative targets and achievements attained up to the preceding year through such write-up. Moreover, specific problems relating to the priorities, needs, infrastructural potentialities, system capabilities, availability of resources are also raised. In addition, the suggestions for the launching of new state level projects and laying more emphasis on the on-going projects are also included in such write-up. Secondly, plan for credit for district plan has now become an integral part of the district planning. The inclusion of Credit Plan as a sector in district plan is an attempt towards introduction of decentralized credit planning aiming at the removal of disparities in Credit-Deposit Ratio in the district.[107] Since the introduction of the decentralized planning in the district, organised attempts have been made for planning the scarce credit resources among the different sectors and regions at both the blocks and the district according to the objectives and priorities of the district plan. The monitoring, coordination and control of credit schemes and proposals of the financial institutions, mainly the banks, are designed at the district level through the District Level Co-ordination Committee. Through quarterly meetings of the DLCC, the Zilla parishad and the District Planning Committee interact with the banks and review the progress of implementation of the credit plan and the targets.[108] The credit policies are determined beforehand through the DLCC with a view to reducing the disparities in the flow of credits between different sectors and areas within the district. Each of the banks located within a block prepares individual credit plan annually and the Block Credit Plan is formulated by integrating and consolidating the annual credit plans of the individual banks at the meeting of the Block Level Co-ordination

Committee (BLCC). In the municipal areas, there is no such committee and this coordinating role is played by the municipalities. At the district level, the Block Credit Plans and Municipal Credit proposals are integrated and consolidated into the District Credit Plan which is finalised and included in the draft plan of the district.

After having a first-hand experience in village-based district planning for more than a decade, the newly formed District Planning Committee (under the Act of 1994) in its first meeting has taken a decision to carry on the process of decentralized district planning but has restructured the levels of planning. Now the lowest spatial units of decentralized planning in the district are identified with the *Gram Sansads* in rural areas and *Wards* in the municipal areas.[109] The District Planning Committee has also introduced minor changes in the methodo-logy of decentralized planning to make the planning process more flexible and participatory. However, major changes have been made so far as the organizational structure is concerned. Examination of the organizational structure of district planning will be made in the subsequent chapters. At this stage it may only be noted that the whole idea of district planning has undergone a sea-change following the enactment of the Amend-ments in 1992. But in case of the district of Midnapore the broad principles and processes followed during the Seventh and Eighth Plans have remained almost unchanged so far.

From the above review of the methodology of decentralized district planning in Midnapore, it is clear that most of the essential prerequisites[110] for decentralized district planning are, by and large, satisfied in the district. Apart from political commitments and policy support, sustained actions from the State Government for decentralized district planning are regular features. The district leadership has also initiated some important methodological steps like building up of data-base at various levels, disaggregation of sectoral outlays and their consequent integration with the district plan, delegation of administrative and financial powers, introduction of both horizontal and vertical linkages in the planning process for the success of district planning. The District Planning Committee through its planning methodology has also been able to crystallise the local needs and priorities within the broad framework of national and state-level objectives. The review of physical, economic and human endowments are also taken into account in deciding objectives and priorities. Moreover, the listing and mapping of resources of the locality through Resource Register are also considered and subsequently accommodated in the District Plan.[111]

Notes and References

1. *Samanwita Jana Udyoge Sahabhagi Parikalpana* (in Bengali), 2001, September, Government of West Bengal, State Institute of Panchayat and Rural Development and Department of Panchayat and Rural Development, Kolkata, p.1.
2. Chaudhury, Binoy Krishna, 1987, 'Foreword' to *The Rural People of Midnapore District*, Kharagpur : IIT, Rural Development Centre.
3. *District Statistical Handbook*, 1996-97, Government of West Bengal, Calcutta, p.1, Table 1.1.
4. O'Malley, L.S.S. 1995, *Bengal District Gazetteers* (1st Reprint), Government of West Bengal, p.1.
5. *Records of District Planning Committee*, District Planning Cell. Also, *District Annual Plan*, 1996-97, Midnapore, p. –d.
6. *District Annual Plan, ibid.*, p.I/2.
7. *West Bengal Statistical Report*, 1994-95, Government of West Bengal and *District Annual Plan, op.cit.*, p. –c.
8. *Census of India*, 1991, Series – 26, Paper 1 of 1991, West Bengal, pp.31, 57-58, 64 & 99.
9. *Census of India, op.cit.*, pp.88-89 and *District Statistical Handbook, Op.cit.*, p.19.
10. *Census of India,op.cit.*, p.31.
11. *District Statistical Handbook, op.cit.*, p.66. And *Census of India, op.cit.*, p.m.
12. *Census of India*, 1991, reproduced in *District Statistical Handbook, op.cit.*, p.32.
13. Bhattacharya, Tarundeb. 1979, *Medinipur* (in Bengali), Calcutta: Firma KLM Pvt. Ltd., p.153.
14. Mallick, Ross. 1993, *Development Policy of a Communist Government*, U.K.: Cambridge University Press, p.1.
15. *Records of the District Panchayat Office*, 1998, Midnapore.
16. O'Malley, *op.cit.*, pp.189-92.
17. *Ibid.*, pp.50-54.

18. Dash, Binode Sankar. (ed.), 1989, *Medinipur: Itihas-O-Sanskritir Bibartan,* (in Bengali), Calcutta: Sahityaloka, Vol.I, pp.258-60.
19. Jana, Anil Kumar. 1993, *Quit India Movement in Bengal,* New Delhi: Indian Publishers Distributors, pp.19-41.
20. *Seventh Five-Year Plan,* 1986, Government of India, New Delhi, *Preface.*
21. Government of West Bengal, *Guidelines of the West Bengal State Planning Board,* March 12, 1985.
22. *An Outline of Methodology,* 1985, District Planning Committee, Midnapore, p.1.
23. *District Annual Plan* (Revised), 1985-86, Midnapore, p. 3:1.
24. *District Seventh Five-Year Plan,* 1985-90, Midnapore, *Objectives and Targets.*
25. *Proceedings of the meeting of the District Planning and Co-ordination Council,* Midnapore, dated 17-5-1988.
26. *An Outline of Methodology, 1985, op.cit.,* p.8.
27. Lieten, G.K. 1996, Development, Devolution and Democracy, New Delhi: Sage, p.37.

    Also, *Interview with Mr. H.K. Samanta, Sabhadhipati,* Midnapore Zilla Parishad dated 4-8-1998.

    Saha, Anamitra and Swaminathan, Madhura. 1994, 'Agricultural Growth in West Bengal in the 1980s', *Economic and Political Weekly,* March 26, pp.A/2 – A/4.
28. *Left Front Government and Land Reforms,* 1984, Government of West Bengal, Calcutta.
29. Nanjudappa, D.N. 1991, 'Concepts, Approaches and Techniques of Decentralized Planning' in B.N. Yugandhar and Amitava Mukherjee (eds.), *Readings in Decentralized Planning,* New Delhi: Concept Publishing Company, Vol. I, p.18.
30. *The Rural People of Midnapore District,* 1986, Rural Development Centre, IIT, Kharagpur and Midnpaore Zilla Parishad, Kharagpur: Rural Development Centre, IIT, pp.V-VI, *Preface.*
31. *Gram Bhittik Zella Parikalpanar Paddhatigata Ruparekha* (in Bengali), 1985, District Planning Committee, Midnapore, pp.1-8.
32. Government of West Bengal. 1985, *Guidelines, op.cit.,* par. 2.
33. *Discussions with* Mr. M.N. Goray, Formerly member of the D.P.C., Midnapore and *ex-Sabhapati,* Dantan I Panchayat Samiti on different dates.

    Note: The exact number of the villages could not be ascertained from the records available with the District Planning Cell of the DPC. However, it appears from the office record that village plans were formulated in about 700 villages of the district.
34. *Records of the District Planning Committee,* Midnapore, District Planning Cell. Also, *Medinipur Zellar Janaganer Kachhe Abedan,* D.P.C., September 1985.

35. Report on the *Evaluation of Post-Literacy Programme,* 1995, Quoted in *Samaj Jijnasa,* Vol. I, No.1, 1996, Vidyasagar Centre for Social Sciences, Midnapore, pp.77-79.
36. *Gram Bhittik Block Parikalpanar Paddhati-O-Prayoger Ruparekha,* (in Bengali), 1989, District Planning Committee, Midnapore, p.6.
37. Report of the *Working Group on District Planning,* 1984, Government of India, New Delhi, Vol. I, pp.52-53, par. 6.18.
38. Thaha, M. 1991, 'Database for Decentralized Planning' in Yugandhar and Mukherjee (eds.), *op.cit.,* p.121.
39. Report of the *Working Group on District Planning,* 1984, *op.cit.,* p.53, par(s). 6.20 & 6.23.
40. *An Outline of Methodology,* 1985, District Planning Committee, Midnapore, pp.33-34.
41. *Ibid.,* p.35.
42. *The Rural People of Midnapore District,* 1986, *op.cit.,* p.107.
43. *Records of the District Planning Committee,* Midnapore.
    Note: During 1980-81, a detailed survey was conducted jointly by the Zilla Parishad, Midnapore and Rural Development Centre, IIT, Kharagpur to study the conditions of the families and villages in the district of Midnapore.
44. *An Outline of Methodology, op.cit.,* p.10.
45. *Medinipur Zellar Gram Bhittik Parikalpana Rachanar Ruparekha-O-Unnayaner Pratichhabi,*(in Bengali), 1996, District Planning Committee, Midnapore, pp.9-10.
46. *Proceedings of the meeting of the District Planning Committee,* Midnapore, dated 19-9-1996.
47. As referred to in 43, *op.cit.,* p.4.
48. *Ibid.*
49. *No. 1/PA/JS(DG) /P & RD/5 – M – 19/99 Government of West Bengal,* Panchayat and Rural Development, Kolkata, dated 2 January, 2002.
50. *Village-Based Planning and Development,* Government of West Bengal, *op. cit,* p.19.
51. *Samanwita Jana Udyoge Sahabhagi Parikalpana,* 2002, *Government of West Bengal,* Department of Panchayat and Rural Development, and State Institute of Panchayats and Rural Development in collaboration with UNICEF, Kolkata.
    Also, Annexure to *No. 1/PA/JS(DG)/P & RD/5- M-19/99, ibid.*
52. *Eighth Five-Year Plan, Perspectives and Issues,* 1990, Midnapore, District Planning Committee, pp.1-14.
53. *Interview with Mr. A. Mandal,* District Planning Officer, dated 19-8-1997.
54. *Interview with Mr. H.K. Samanta, op.cit.*
55. *A Prelude to the Ninth Plan,* 1997, District Planning Committee, Midnapore. Also, *Proceedings of the meeting of the DPC* dated 20-8-1997.

56. Finance Minister of West Bengal, *The Ananda Bazar Patrika,* Calcutta, 24-8-1997.
57. *An Outline of Methodology, op.cit.,* p.22.
58. *Gram Bhittik Block Parikalpanar Paddhati-O-Prayoger Ruparekha,* (in Bengali), 1989, *op.cit.,* p.21.
59. Myrdal, Gunnar. 1968, *Asian Drama,* England: Penguin, Vol. I, p.471.
60. As referred to in 45, *op.cit.,* p.12.
61. *Proceedings of the meeting of the D.P.C.* dated, 19-9-1996.
62. *No : 183 (18) PA / JS (D.G.) / P & R.D.* dated 1 November, 1999, *Government of West Bengal,* Department of Panchayat and Rural Development, Kolkata.
63. *Records of the District Panchayat Office* and *District Urban Development Agency,* Midnapore.
64. *Interview with Mr. Bijali Ghosh,* Project Officer, DUDA, Midnapore dated 19-8-97.
65. *Interview with Mr. A. Mandal, op.cit.*
66. Report on the *Evaluation of Post-Literacy Programme,* 1995, *op.cit.,* pp.77-79.
67. *West Bengal Panchayat* (*Amendment*) Act, 1994, Section 16-A.
68. *Interview with Mr. H.K. Samanta, op.cit.*
69. *Gram Bhittik Block Parikalpanar Paddhati-O-Prayoger Ruparekha* (in Bengali), 1989, *op.cit.,* p.3.
70. *Medinipur Zellar Gram Bhittik Prikalpana Rachanar Ruparekha-O-Unnayaner Pratichhabi,* (in Bengali), 1996, *op.cit.,* pp.14-18.
71. *Village-Based Planning and Development,* 2001, *Government of West Bengal,* State Institute of Panchayats and Rural Development, p. 47.
72. *Ibid.,* pp. 58-59.
73. *GO. No. 574/PA/JS(DG)/P&RD/O/Trg./5 M-17/2001,* dated, 9 November, 2001, Government of West Bengal.
74. *Village-Based Planning and Development, op. cit.,* pp.61, 63.
75. Sarkar, D. and Ghosh, B.D. 1999, 'Outlines of the Proposed Model for Participatory Planning', *Workshop on People's Participation in Development,* Calcutta, 15-16 December.

    Also, *No. 183(18) PA/JS(DG)/P & RD,* dated 1-11-1999, and *No. 1/PA/JS(DG)/P & RD/ 5M—19/99 dated* 2 January, 2002, *Government of West Bengal,* Department of Panchayat and Rural Development, Kolkata. Also, *Records of the State Institute of Panchayats and Rural Development,* Government of West Bengal.
76. *Village-Based Planning and Development, op. cit.,* p. 64.
77. Government of West Bengal, *Resolution No.3230/P-IS-6/85 dated* 12-5-1985.
78. District Planning Committee, *Memo No.773(120) Development and Planning Cell* dated 24-6-1997, *Formats* - IIIA, IIIB, IV & V.

79. *District Annual Plan* 1992-93, District Planning Committee, Midnapore.
80. *Ibid.*
81. District Planning Committee, *Memo No.773(120) Development and Planning Cell* dated 24-6-1997.
82. *Ibid.*
83. *Ibid.* Also *interview with Mr. B. Ghosh, op.cit.*
84. *Gram Bhittik Block Parikalpanar Paddhati-O-Prayoger Ruparekha* (in Bengali), 1989, *op.cit.*, pp.21-23.
85. *Ibid.*, pp.22-23.
86. District Planning Committee, *Memo No.773(120),op.cit.*
87. *Ibid.*
88. Government of West Bengal, 1985, *Guidelines, op.cit.*
89. *Medinipur Zellar Gram Bhittik Parikalpana Rachanar Ruparekha-O-Unnayaner Pratichhabi,* 1996, *op.cit.*
90. Nanjudappa, D.N. 1991, *op.cit.*, pp.19-22.
91. *Ibid.*, p.22.
92. *Note*: Previously this was achieved through the Working Group of the District Planning Committee. Now, the Sub-Committees of the DPC have taken over these functions.
93. Benninger, Christopher C. 1991, 'District Planning Methods and Techniques : An Overview' in Yugandhar and Mukherjee ed., *op.cit.*, p.387.
94. *District Annual Plan,* 1996-97 and *A Prelude to Ninth Plan,* 1997, *op.cit.*
95. *An Outline of Methodology, op.cit.*, p.31.
96. District Planning Committee, *Memo No.773(120) op.cit.*
97. Government of West Bengal, *No.6372/P/1F-8/85* dated 28-8-1985, Development and Planning Department, Calcutta.
98. *West Bengal District Planning Committee Rules,* 1994, Government of West Bengal, *Rule 28.*
99. *Gram Bhittik Block Parikalpanar Paddhati-O-Ruparekha,* 1989, *op.cit.*, p.7.
100. Sarkar, Dibyendu and Ghosh, B.D. 1999, 'Outlines of the Proposed Model for Participatory Planning', *op. cit.*
101. *Tenth Five-Year Plan*, (2002 – 2007) *op. cit.* , p. (x).
102. *Gram Bhittik Zella Parikalpanar Paddhatigata Ruparekha* (in Bengali), 1985, District Planning Committee, pp.9-12.
103. *Gramonnayan Prakalpa Parichayika, (in Bengali),* 1994, State Institute of Panchayat and Rural Development, Government of West Bengal, p.17.
104. Finance Minister of West Bengal, *The Ganashakti,* Calcutta, dated 24-8-1997.
105. Recommendations of the *State Finance Commission,* 1985, Government of West Bengal, Calcutta, pp.44-45, par(s). 6.27 and 6.30.
106. *Ibid.*

107. *Interview with Mr. H.K. Samanta, op.cit.*
108. *Ibid.*
109. *Proceedings of the meeting of the DPC,* dated 19-9-1996.
110. Report of the *Working Group on District Planning,* 1984, *op.cit.*, p.41, par.5.2.
111. *Ibid.*, pp.46-47, par.5.30.

5

PLANNING MACHINERY IN THE DISTRICT

Decentralized district planning is both a concept and a process. As a process it requires an organizational set-up for its formulation and effective implementation. Formulation of an effective methodology is an unproductive exercise unless the operational issues like the choice of appropriate implementing agencies and organizations are considered as an integral part of the planning process. This chapter seeks to highlight the organizational arrangements available in the district for the actualization of decentralized district planning.

NEED FOR AN INTEGRATED ORGANIZATION

As examined in the previous chapters, decentralized planning involves a complicated process and hence necessitates an administrative or organizational infrastructure that may ensure 'efficiency, effectiveness and responsiveness of planning' at the various stages.[1] The Committee to review the Existing Administrative Arrangements for Rural Development and Poverty Alleviation Programmes (CAARD) aptly observed:

> "An organizational structure requires to be built up for integrated planning, effective implementation, better management, closer monitoring and concurrent evaluation to ensure optimal use of resources and delivery of benefits to those for whom they are meant. This should also keep in view national objectives, state priorities, regional

> requirements, local needs and people's aspirations. *The structure at the district level will, therefore, have a dual function of integrated area planning and effective implementation.*"[2] (emphasis added)

Moreover, planning involves (a) appraisal of past trends and performance, (b) assessment of major current problems and identification of measures for future development. Again, it tries to review the resources that were available at the preceding plan and the scope of their availability in future. "These appraisals and surveys call for the cooperation of a large number of agencies and institutions, both within and outside the government."[3]

Under our constitutional system, a two-tier administrative political device has been created: the Central Government and the State Governments. There is no government below the states; there are only government departments. Hence, the philosophy of decentralized district planning calls for an effective institutional arrangement at the district level where planners, bureaucrats and the people, may be through their representatives, can interact on the formulation and implementation of the district plan. Such interactions and exchanges may be meaningful only if the government, not *ad hoc*, creates a standing body. The Working Group on Block Level Planning, popularly known as Dantwala Committee, also stressed the need for strengthening the planning capability at the district level. It recommended the setting up of a planning team at the district level with the responsibility of formulating block plans.[4] It is a good beginning that the 74th Constitution Amendment Act (1992) provides for the creation of such a body named 'District Planning Committee' at the district level. But district planning cannot be viewed in isolation. It is well knit within a system of National-State-District decentralized planning system. Hence, the study of planning machinery at the district level needs to be examined with a brief reference to the planning machinery available at the centre and the states.

PLANNING ORGANIZATIONS ABOVE THE DISTRICT

At the National Level

National Development Council

With a view to strengthening and mobilizing the efforts and resources in support of the plans and also promoting interactions and consultations between the Central and the State Governments on plan proposals and economic policies, there is the National Development Council (NDC) at the apex of the planning heirarchy.[5] It consists of the Prime Minister, Cabinet Ministers of the Union, the Chief Ministers of the States and Union Territories and members of the Planning Commission. The Council is presided over by the Prime Minister who is the Chairman of the Planning Commission. The National Development Council acts through a number of Committees like Committee on Population, Committee on Employment, Committee on Literacy etc. It has also set up a committee on Micro-Level Planning in the early nineties for the actualisation of decentralized planning. The functions of the National Development Council include *inter alia*, formulation of guidelines, consideration of the national plan formulated by the Planning Commission, consideration of issues of social and economic policies relating to national development and review of the working of the plan from time to time.[6]

Planning Commission

Below the National Development Council there is the Planning Commission, considered to be a 'Super Cabinet' by the Administrative Reforms Commission, 1966 (ARC),[7] which is responsible for organizing and coordinating the process of formulation of both five-year and annual plans. The Planning Commission is a product of a Cabinet Resolution of the Government of India (15th March, 1950) and is headed by the Prime Minister as Chairman, though the Administrative Reforms Commission strongly argued in favour of its close association with the Commission, but not in the capacity of its chairman.[8]

Similar was the recommendation of the ARC with respect to the inclusion of the Finance Minister in the Planning Commission.[9] The Deputy Chairman of the Commission acts as the technical and administrative head. The Planning Commission works as a collective body, though each member takes charge of one or more subjects and directs the study of programme in a year.[10] Other members of the Planning Commission belong to both official and non-official categories. The Planning Commission comes under the Ministry of Planning and functions through several technical and subject divisions, each of which is headed by a senior officer, mostly designated as Adviser. At present, there are 31 such divisions under the Planning Commission. Apart from the divisions mentioned above, which are primarily concerned with the preparation, monitoring and evaluation of plans, the Commission works through the Steering Groups, Working Groups and a well organized Secretariat.[11]

The Working Groups consisting of official and non-official members are broad-based and maintain a regular and close contact with the planning bodies in the states.[12] Moreover, the Commission is assisted by other agencies like the Programme Evaluation Organization (PEO), National Informatics Centre (NIC) etc.[13] Over the years, the Planning Commission has grown enormously in staff strength and establishment and hence immediate steps for the reduction in strength and expenditure has been suggested by the experts.[14]

Formulation of guidelines and the preparation of national plan in a federal set-up are a complicated task, which requires the Planning Commission to act as, an 'Economic Cabinet not merely for the Union but also for the States.'[15] Thus it involves an interaction with the states. The process of the formulation of plan usually starts with the preparation of the Approach Paper by the Working Groups indicating therein the issues, approaches and strategies for discussion. The approach paper based on the reports of the Working Groups and the details received from the states and union territories is circulated among the states for observation and comments before it is considered by the NDC. The paper finalised by the NDC, highlights the broad objectives and strategies for realising the goals.[16] The Planning Commission which is neither a creation of the Constitution, nor a product of parliament, is responsible for the formulation of long-term development plans and it recommends those to the Union Cabinet. While making recommendations, it has to act in close understanding and consultation with the ministries of the Central Government and the State Governments. Thus the responsibility of policy decisions and implementation is vested in the governments. In fact, the Planning Commission has been preoccupied excessively with executive activities at the cost of its vital duties of the formulation of national plans.[17]

On the basis of the approach paper, the state planning bodies prepare their five-year plans. The plans of the districts together with sectoral plans are integrated into the state plans and the draft plans of the states are prepared and submitted to the Planning Commission and to their respective legislatures. The state level draft plans are discussed at the central level. The plan of a state is thus the product of a compromise between the state and the centre worked out through mutual discussions on the basis of interests and concerns of both the sides.[18] Similarly, the respective ministries prepare the sectoral plans of the Central Government. Finally, the state plans and the sectoral plans are brought together by the Planning Commission and accordingly, the National Plan is finalised. The Five-Year Plan is formally endorsed by the Union Cabinet and then presented to Parliament for approval. Once finalised, it is communicated to different implementing agencies and bodies for execution though the scope for some adjustments is always available particularly in the sectoral allocations. The methodology of formulation of both the Five-Year Plan and the Annual Plan is more or less the same excepting that the Annual Plan is prepared on the basis of the Five-Year Plan and hence it constitutes a part of it. Usually, the preparation of an annual plan starts in September-October and after finalisation, it is integrated with the annual budget of the respective government. In case of five-year plans, the process begins at least two years before the end of the previous plan.

At the State Level

At the state level, there is the State Planning Board, (SPB) with the overall responsibilities of formulation, monitoring and supervision of state plans. The Administrative Reforms Commission assigns the following functions to the State Planning Boards: formulation of plans for the most effective and balanced utilization of the resources of the state; determination of plan priorities within the framework of national plan; providing assistance to the district authorities and to coordinate district plans with the state plan; identification and removal of the factors creating bottlenecks and strengthening the conditions for successful implementation of plans and review of progress of implementation of plans and programmes.[19] These huge functions are carried out by the State Planning Boards with the help of State Planning Department and the ministries of the State Government. At present all the States in India have a Planning Board or a Planning Committee headed by either the Chief Minister or a Senior Cabinet Minister, though the size and composition of State Planning Board vary from state to state and from time to time.

In West Bengal, the State Planning Board is now composed of 11 members including the Chief Minister as the Chairman.[20] At the administrative level, there is the Development and Planning Department of the State Government. The Planning Secretary, assisted by a Joint Secretary and a few Deputy Secretaries, looks after the administration of the Planning Department. The Department helps the State Planning Board in the process of formulation, monitoring and evaluation of five-year and annual plans. It may be mentioned here that even before the states could initiate steps for strengthening the state planning machinery, the Planning Commission emphasized the need for creating a separate agency of planning at the state-levels. The State Planning Board in West Bengal, like its counterparts in Karnataka, Kerala and Gujarat, has been able to make some impact on the system of planning through improving and strengthening the decentralized planning process. It has been able to enhance the standard of decentralized planning by evolving more effective and rational methods of formulation of plans. A demarcation of activities has also been done between the state and the district plans on the basis of twin norms of location and coverage of benefits,[21] though the common view is that this classification is not always accurate and scientific and many of the activities which ought to have been done by the districts, are sometimes retained at the state level.[22] To overcome these problems, Regional Planning Committees below the state level have been constituted in some states like Andhra Pradesh.[23] But there is no such committee at the level between the state and the districts in West Bengal.

The Planning activities at the state level are generally carried out by the Planning Department of the Government. In West Bengal, the Department of Development and Planning is a separate department outside the Finance Department. While the State Planning Board carries out a good number of functions, the main functions of the State Planning Board relate to the preparation of five-year plans, annual plans, and monitoring, review and evaluation of district planning activities. It takes the help of the Bureau of Applied Economics and Statistics of the State Government in the formulation of plans and conduct of evaluation. Besides, the Board ensures continuous and effective linkages among the Central Government, State Government and District Planning Committees.[24]

Planning Bodies below the State

Planning in India has so far been basically unitary and sectoral in nature and largely confined to the central and the state levels. Though there were attempts towards introducing decentralized planning since the Gadgil days, it was in fact only a few states in India, which made some progress in this direction before the Seventh Plan. District Planning in West Bengal was only launched with the commencement of the Seventh Plan.[25] Naturally the creation of separate machinery for planning at the district level and below was not contemplated by the state prior to it. In West Bengal, the planning activities at the district level were considered to be the functions of the district administration. Prior to 1985, the planning and development affairs of the district were looked after by the District Planning Board, which was chaired by the District Magistrate. The Board was composed of the District Planning Officer, the district level officers of technical and development departments and some non-official members.[26] This arrangement was replaced subsequenttly by the establishment of District Level Co-ordination Committees (DLCC). In the beginning of 1985, the DLCC was reconstituted and redesignated as the District Planning and Co-ordination Council.[27]

Planning Organizations created in the Eighties

The Government of West Bengal decided to set up a separate district planning machinery at each of the districts save Calcutta and to sanction some posts to lend support to the district planning authorities in the formulation and implementation of district level plans.[28] The Planning machinery at the district level was organized in two tiers, one, the District Planning and Co-ordination Council (DPCC), and the other, its executive arm, the District Planning Committee (DPC). Following the Guidelines of the State Planning Board (SPB), Block Planning Committees (BPC) were also constituted at the block levels.

District Level Committees

At the district level, the apex body in the decentralized planning organization was designated as the District Planning and Co-ordination Council (DPCC). It was formed under the Chairmanship of a State Cabinet Minister hailing from the district. Since there was more than one Minister belonging to this district, the Chairmanship was rotational. The DPCC was a large body consisting of all the MLAs (thirty-seven) and Members of Parliament (five) elected from the district, Chairpersons of the Municipalities (twelve), *Sabhapatis* of the Panchayat Samitis (fifty-four), *Karmadhyakshas* of the Zilla Parishad (ten) and around a hundred district level officers. The *Sabhadhipati* of the Zilla Parishad was the Vice-Chairman and the District Magistrate was the Member-Secretary of the DPCC. Moreover, the Commissioner of the Burdwan Division was a permanent invitee to the Council.[29]

The District Planning and Coordination Council, by virtue of its composition, was a deliberative and coordinating body, which used to meet twice annually in the initial years of the Seventh Plan to discuss and approve the district plan. Subsequently, the meetings of the DPCC became irregular and it turned to be almost a ritual for the DPCC to meet once in a year to approve the plan formulated by the District Planning Committee.[30] However, the Council was entrusted with the power of reviewing the progress of the district plan schemes and programmes from time to time. Apart from performing the functions of review and monitoring, it provided a forum for interactions and linkages between the State Government and the district planners. Though the rules relating to the formation of the District Planning and Co-ordination Council did not make any specific provision for the inclusion of all the ministers hailing from the district, it is noticed that most of the ministers elected from the district would attend such meetings.[31] Even the Chief Minister was present in a meeting to see for himself the working of the Council.[32] The ministers attended the meeting and very often discussed the issues and problems of the government. Sometimes they could give suggestions for augmentation of own resources of the district and for effective implementation of the plan proposals and development schemes.[33] Members of all categories, both elected and ex-officio, including government officials, would discuss various problems and made suggestions at those meetings. It is interesting to note that even the MLAs considered the DPCC as an important forum for airing their views and placing specific proposals for developments in their respective constituencies and in some cases they were effective participants.[34]

The District Planning and Co-ordination Council, apart from streamlining the planning and development policies of the district, played its role in the prioritization of development schemes and proposals for development of the district. The views expressed and suggestions made at the meetings of the DPCC were taken into account for inclusion in the meetings of the Working Groups formed under the District Planning Committee.[35] Thus through the DPCC, coordination and integration of all planning activities of the district were brought about and better interactions between departmental officials and elected representatives were ensured in respect of formulation, implementation and monitoring of plans and development schemes at the district level. The District Planning and

Coordination Council came to exist in the district since the introduction of decentralized district planning in Midnapore and continued to function till the enactment of the West Bengal District Planning Committee Act, 1994. Subsequently, the District Planning Committee has been formed. Under the said Act there is no provision for constitution of the District Planning and Coordination Council. In fact the DPCC, which had been in existence since 1985, ceased to exist with the passing of the DPC Act. It has not been reconstituted so far, though the State Government is contemplating to re-establish it to accommodate all the local MLAs and MPs in the process of district planning in the state.[36]

The most effective institution in the organizational hierarchy of decentralized district planning worked out by the government at the district level was the District Planning Committee (DPC). It was envisaged as somewhat similar to the executive committee formed in a number of states. The District Planning Committee of Midnapore was constituted for the first time in 1985 in terms of a resolution of the State Government.[37] It was a large body composed of the *Karmadhyakshas* of the Standing Committee of the Zilla Parishad, *Sabhapatis* of all Panchayat Samitis of the district, Chairmen of all the municipalities, one representative from each of the two statutory bodies of the district and district level officers of all administrative departments located in the district. The Sub-divisional Officers belonging to the district were included in the District Planning Committee as invitee members. Moreover, the district level officers of different banks were also invited to the meetings of the DPC as and when required. The *Sabhadhipati* of the Zilla Parishad and the District Magistrate were designated as Chairman and Member-Secretary of the District Planning Committee respectively.[38]

The functions of the District Planning Committee under decentralized district planning are multifarious. It has to harmonise the plans at various levels of the hierarchy. The district planning in Midnapore is methodologically conceived as a device to integrate together the formulation and implementation of plans at different stages starting from the below. Naturally the District Planning Committee has to take into account the local needs and priorities in the context of availability of natural and human resources in the district.[39] The powers and functions of the first District Planning Committee were specified by the State Government.[40] Broadly the District Planning Committee had to formulate the district plan within the framework for the decentralized planning process in which the formulation of plan schemes up to the value of Rupees fifty thousand was left to the Block Planning Committees and such schemes were discussed and finalised by the Block Planning Committee and subsequently included in the district plan. Proposals and schemes limited within the value of Rupees five lakh were formulated by the District Planning Committee and approved by the DPCC. Schemes exceeding the earmarked amount of Rupees five lakh were sent to the State Planning Board for approval. Similarly, as indicated in the previous chapters, the schemes affecting a district or districts other than individual district, were also sent to the State Planning Board for incorporation in the State Plan. The DPC used to meet once in a quarter during the Seventh Plan period but subsequently the meetings of the DPC turned to be irregular and most functions of the DPC were performed by its Working Group and the Standing Committees of the Zilla Parishad.[41]

Originally the District Planning Committee started functioning in an effective manner with the help of the Working Group formed by it. But gradually, the DPC became ineffective and irregular in its functioning. To overcome these problems and to ensure better monitoring and coordination of different schemes and programmes within the district, the State Government decided to constitute a Standing Committee under the District Planning and Coordination Council in early 1992.[42] The Standing Committee in the district was formed with a minister, elected from this district, the *Sabhadhipati* of the Zilla Parishad, one MP and one MLA each from the different political parties from the district as decided by the Minister in consultation with the concerned political parties. The Minister was nominated as the Chairman and the District Magistrate as the Member-Secretary. The district level officers were used to be invited as and when required. The decision for constitution of the Standing Committee of the DPCC was a much needed one in view of the large size of both the DPCC and DPC and also in the context of increasing functions *vis-à-vis* the growing difficulties in the functioning of these bodies. The Committee acted as a 'Steering Committee of the DPC' for all practical purposes and was in tune with the recommendations of the Working Group on District Planning.[43] The Committee was very much active since its first meeting and sought to plug the gaps whenever and whichever noticed.[44]

In the decentralized district planning in Midnapore, the Working Groups enjoyed a vital place in the organizational set-up. Originally one Working Group was formed by the district administration in April 1985 with all the *Karmadhyakshas*, some district level officers and a few persons from outside the government departments to monitor the introduction and formulation of district plans. Since then it was reconstituted several times to make it more effective and active. The group was first reconstituted in August 1986 and was given a complete shape with nineteen members, both official and non-official.[45] The Working Group, created on the suggestion of the District Planning Committee, was headed by the *Sabhadhipati* of the Zilla Parishad.[46] The group was originally concerned with the training of the Volunteers and Planning Cadres at the block levels.[47] Subsequently the scope of its functioning was extended to the monitoring of formulation and implementation of district plan. The Working Group used to hold separate subject-wise meetings with the district level officers of the government departments to review the achievements of targets in respect of plans of the different sectors like agriculture, industry, fishery etc. To ensure effective participation of the members and to improve effectiveness in the functioning of the Group, it used to meet regularly on every second Thursday of a month. Later on, arrangements were made for weekly meeting of the Group at Zilla Parishad to have constant monitoring on the progress of decentralized planning. To ensure expeditious and effective functioning in the planning organization and to avoid communication gap subject-wise agenda for the next meetings were identified at the preceding meeting. The time for holding the meetings was fixed. This arrangement for structuring the schedule of meetings was very much helpful in ensuring regularity and effectiveness.[48]

During the Eighth Plan, separate Working Groups in place of the earlier one, were constituted under the District Planning Committee to deal with the different categories of subjects of the district plan. Following the Guidelines of the State Planning Board, ten such Working Groups were formed in the district, viz., (i) *Krishi-Sech-O-Samabay* Working Group, (ii) *Purta Karya* Working Group, (iii) *Silpa-O-Kshudra Silpa* Working Group, (iv) *Sakti-O-Aprachalita Sakti* Working Group, (v) *Nagar Unnayan* Working Group, (vi) *Gram Unnayan-O-Janakalyan* Working Group, (vii) *Ban-O-Bhumi Sanskar* Working Group, (viii) *Janasasthya* Working Group, (ix) *Siksha* Working Group, and (x) *Matsya-O-Pashupalan* Working Group. These Working Groups were comparatively small and compact in size and were composed of members ranging from 10 to 12 drawn from both the elected and official categories.[49] Since the DPC and the DPCC were large bodies and were accustomed to deliberations and discussions, the Working Groups were the real effective wings in the district planning organization. Each Working Group had a convenor selected from the State Cadre of the government and hence the initiatives were taken by them under the supervision of the *Karmadhyakshas* and overall guidance of the *Sabhadhipati* and the District Magistrate. An examination of the proceedings of the meetings of different Working Groups during the Eighth Plan period reveals that the presence of the *Sabhadhipati*, District Magistrate and District Planning Officer was almost a regular phenomenon.[50] Apart from being the core committees of the DPC for initiation, supervision, coordination and monitoring of the planning process, the Working Groups were also the platforms for meaningful interactions between the bureaucrats and the elected representatives. As a result, the scope for misgivings between the functionaries of the District Planning Committee and the sectoral managers was reduced to the minimum.[51]

The District Planning Committee developed its own machinery to have the full knowledge of the allotment of funds and the status of the schemes and projects of the district, which together constituted the Annual District Plan. Moreover, the DPC held periodic monitoring meetings to review the progress in physical achievements of different projects as well as the extent of utilisation of the sectoral allocations. It could monitor and review the performance of different agencies operating in the district and took steps for the removal of tensions and lacuna by suggesting remedial steps.[52] Thus the District Planning Committee fulfilled the task of functioning as an umbrella organization nesting the plans of individual sectoral departments and organizations and integrating them 'into a common and consistent framework, subserving to a central strategy formulated for the district as a whole'.[53]

Block Planning Committee

Following the 'Guidelines' of the State Government for decentralized district planning, the Block Planning Committees were constituted in the first half of 1985 throughout the district.[54] It may be noted here that the blocks are coterminous with the Panchayat Samitis in the state. The Block Planning Committees (BPC) were formed at the block levels with the *Sabhapati* of the Panchayat Samiti as Chairman and the Block Development Officer as the Member-Secretary of the BPC. The Block Planning Committee included the *Karmadhyakshas* of the *Sthayee Samitis* (Standing Committees) of the Panchayat Samiti, *Pradhans* of the Gram Panchayats located within the territorial jurisdiction of the Panchayat Samiti and the block level officers of the government departments.[55] Thus it was a comparatively small body which was required to meet once in every two months to coordinate and review the schemes prepared by it, schemes run by the panchayats and the schemes jointly implemented by panchayats, departments or by other agencies functioning within the block area.

Though the Guidelines issued by the State Planning Board did not provide room for the creation of an institution analogous to that of the DPCC, the Block Planning Coordination Committees (BPCC) were formed in the district with the *Sabhapati, Sahakari-Sabhapati*, *Karmadhyakshas* of the Panchayat Samiti, the Block Development Officer and a few reputed local people of the block. The Coordination Committee (BPCC) would discuss the projects for inclusion in the block plan. The BDO was the convenor of the BPCC, which acted more in an informal manner. The meetings of the BPCC were attended by all block level departmental officers to ensure coordination of departmental and non-departmental plans of different sectors and sub-sectors.[56] Practically the role of the BPCC was advisory in nature and the actual works were done by a small planning group composed of the *Sabhapati*, Block Development Officer, the Sub-Assistant Engineer and the Planning and Evaluation Officer of the block. This group prepared the block plan, which was considered and approved by the Block Planning Committee.

The functions of the Block Planning Committee were quite analogous to those of the District Planning Committee under the 1985 Model, save and except the level of functioning. Under the methodology of district planning adopted in the eighties in the district, the Block Planning Committees (BPC) formulated the Block Plans integrating the proposals and schemes of the Gram Panchayats and the block level departments having a command area within the block. It was empowered to approve block-specific schemes with estimated cost limited to Rupees fifty thousand and to forward schemes involving more costs than the prescribed ceiling to the DPC for approval. Moreover, the BPC enjoyed the power to prepare such schemes for consideration and approval of the DPC as involved the area covering more than one block. In addition to these functions, the Block Planning Committee had the authority to coordinate and review all schemes prepared and implemented within the block.[57]

Though the methodology of district planning worked out in the district in 1985, considered the village based Gram Panchayat plan as the starting point in the hierarchy of decentralized planning, yet it did not contemplate the idea of creating an organization for planning below the block level. Similarly, there was no planning body at the municipality level. Thus the Gram Panchayats were entrusted with the planning activities at the Gram Panchayat level[58] as well as at the village level.

Present Planning Machinery

The District Planning Committee of Midnapore, like its counterparts in other districts of West Bengal, has been functioning since the beginning of the Seventh Five-Year Plan, but it did not have any *locus standi.* It was created by a Resolution of the State Government after the introduction of the decentralized district planning as an administrative innovation. The 74th Constitution Amendment Act, 1992 has accorded constitutional recognition to the institution of District Planning Committee to enable it to function as a sound planning and implementing machinery at the district level. It may be mentioned here that neither the Planning Commission nor the State Planning Board is a constitutional body.

District Planning Committee

The 74th Constitution Amendment calls upon every state to constitute a 'District Planning Committee (DPC) to consolidate the plans prepared by the panchayats and the municipalities in the district and to prepare a draft development plan for the district as a whole' (*Article* 243-ZD). The said Act also provides for the broad Guidelines to be followed by the District Planning Committee in preparing draft development plans. However, the Act empowers the states to formulate their own rules relating to the composition and functioning of the DPC and the manner in which the membership of the committee would be determined. Further the manner in which the chairpersons of the DPC are to be chosen and the functions to be discharged by the DPC have also been left to the State Legislatures. Apart from the District Planning Committee, the Act also incorporates a provision for the establishment of Metropolitan Planning Committees in the metropolitan areas within the state. Thus the 74th Amendment Act may be viewed as a great leap in the concrete direction of developing suitable machinery for decentralized planning. It may also be said that the Act resolves in this way the old dilemma nourished since the Gadgil era about the appropriate level of decentralized planning.

It has already been pointed out in the previous chapters that the State Government was moving in the direction of decentralized planning since the middle of the eighties in its own way. Hence, it took no time in enacting the Conformity Act incorporating the provisions for the establishment of District Planning Committees as per constitutional requirements.[59]

Subsequently, the District Planning Committee Rules have been framed by the government enumerating therein the rules for composition of District Planning Committee and the conduct of election of the members of the DPC.[60]

Pursuant to the District Planning Committee Act, 1994 and the Rules made thereunder, the District Planning Committee of Midnapore was constituted by the Government in 1995.[61] Since the strength of the Zilla Parishad was 108, the Committee was composed of one hundred members out of which 74 and 6 members were elected from amongst the members of the Zilla Parishad and Municipalities of the district respectively. They were elected by the members of the Zilla Parishad and Municipalities of the district in accordance with the system of proportional representation by means of a single transferable vote.[62] It may be noted here that the *Sabhadhipati* of the Zilla Parishad, the *Sabhapatis* of the Panchayat Samitis and the Chairmen of the Municipalities are not eligible for such election. The remaining 20 members were nominated by the State Government. The nominated members included the *Sabhadhipati* of the Zilla Parishad and the District Magistrate, *Sabhapatis* of the Panchayat Samitis and Chairmen of Municipalities, Members of Parliament and State Legislative Assembly, Economists and Social Workers. A close scrutiny of the composition of the District Planning Committee revealed that the members nominated by the State Government included the *Sabhadhipati* of Zilla Parishad, the District Magistrate, one member of Lok Sabha, five members of the State Assembly, six *Sabhapatis* of Panchayat Samitis, two representatives from two Statutory Bodies of the district, viz., Digha Development Authority and Haldia Development Authority, two university teachers from the Economics Department, one Chairman of a Municipality and a social worker.[63] The *Sabhadhipati* of the Zilla Parishad is the Chairperson and the District Magistrate is designated as the Secretary of the District Planning Committee. The District Planning Committee Act of the State also provides for the post of a Vice-Chairperson who is selected by the members of the DPC from amongst them after the constitution of the District Planning Committee.[64] Thus, as expected by the experts, the District Planning Committee represents a happy blending of 'local autonomy, administrative capability and planning expertise' through its present composition.[65]

Now after the division of the district into two districts — *Purba (East) Medinipur* and *Paschim (West) Medinipur*, two separate District Planning Committees have been constituted in March 2002. Each of the Committees (East and West) now consists of 60 members of which (i) 43 members are elected by the elected members of the Zilla Parishad from amongst them ; (ii) 5 members are elected by, and from amongst, the elected members of the Municipalities within the district ; and (iii) 12 members are appointed by the State Government under provisions of the DPC Rules, 1994. Accordingly, the District Planning Committee constituted in 1995 has been dissolved.[66]

Under the existing arrangement, the District Planning Committee enjoys such powers as its predecessor used to enjoy under 1985 Model. It consolidates the plans prepared by the panchayats and municipalities and prepares the draft development plan for the district as a whole. Beside these twin powers, such other powers may be assigned to it as the State Government may consider necessary.[67]

During the Seventh and the Eighth Five-Year Plans, the District Planning Committee acted through a number of committees and sub-committees. Under the present DPC Act (1994), there is a provision for constitution of sub-committees including Urban Development Sub-Committee for the smooth and effective functioning of the DPC. The constitution and functioning of the sub-committees have been outlined subsequently. The District Planning Committee of Midnapore (West) functions through the sub-committees formed by it. Now there are 12 sub-committees on different areas of development and planning, viz., (i) District Planning and Co-ordination, (ii) Urban Development, (iii) Special Area Development, (iv) Cottage Industries Power and Non-conventional Energy, (v) Education, Culture, Sports and Youth Services, (vi) Agriculture, Irrigation and Co-operatives, (vii) Child-Women Development, Relief and Welfare, (viii) Public Health, Family Welfare and Environment, (ix) Food and Supplies, (x) Public Works, Roads and Transport; (xi) Forest and Land Reforms, (xii) Fishery and Animal Resources Development. A diagrammatic presentation of the sub-committees of the DPC that follows in Figure 3 will help a comprehensive understanding of the organizational structure at the district level.

Of these sub-committees, the first three are headed by the *Sabhadhipati* of the Zilla Parishad and the remaining nine by the concerned *Karmadhyakshas* of the Zilla Parishad.[68] Under the present set-up, the Secretaries of the sub-committees are district level government officials. Moreover, all the *Karmadhyakshas* of the Zilla Parishad have been accommodated in different sub-committees of the District Planning Committee in the capacity of chairpersons. Thus the composition of the sub-committees provides a standing platform for organizational linkage between the panchayats and the government departments.

The District Planning and Co-ordination Sub-Committee is the most important one and it has taken over the functions of the Standing Committee of the erstwhile DPCC. It is the largest Sub-Committee of the DPC comprising thirty-eight members besides the invitees. It includes among others all the leading district level officers of the State Government and the Sub-divisional Officers on the one hand, and the *Karmadh-yakshas* of the Zilla Parishad and Planning experts, on the other.[69]

The Chairperson of the DPC heads this Sub-Committee and the District Magistrate acts as the Secretary.[70] The meeting of the Sub-Committee is held usually once in every three months. The Secretary convenes the meeting of the Sub-Committee in consultation with the Chairperson and maintains all records of proceedings and takes follow-up action. The functions of the District Planning and Co-ordination Sub-Committee are wide and it advises and assists the DPC in the preparation of the District Plan integrating and consolidating the annual plans and programmes of the panchayats, municipalities, government departments and other development authorities of the district. It shall 'prepare a draft development plan' and shall coordinate the overall functioning of different development agencies in the implementation of the development plan for the district.'[71] The District Planning and Co-ordination Sub-Committee has been given enormous powers under the statutory provisions of the State Government. Its powers may appear to be real, since the DPC itself is a large body and may find little time to go into the

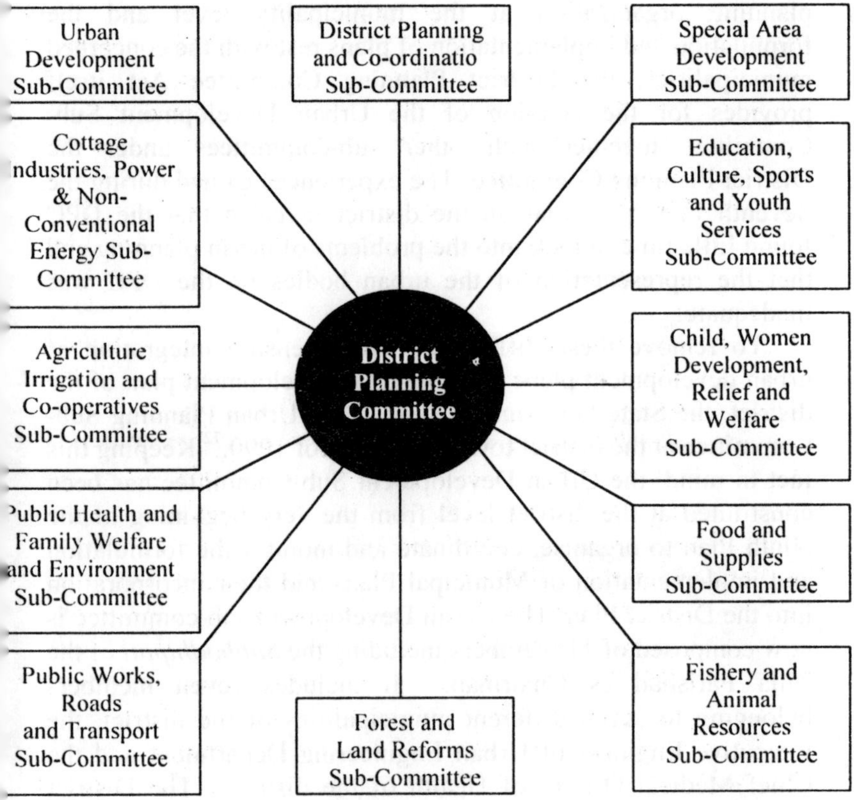

Fig. 5.1 : District Planning Committee and its Sub-Committees

details of planning and implementation. Usually the DPC, as experiences suggest, prefers to delegate powers to the sub-committees. Thus under the existing arrangement, the Planning and Coordination Sub-Committee initiates, supervises, monitors, coordinates and controls the formulation and implementation of the district plan and acts as the executive committee of the District Planning Committee.

Judged from a different perspective, the Urban Development Sub-Committee of the DPC, besides the District Planning and Coordination Sub-Committee, occupies an important place in the planning machinery of the district. Since there is no separate planning organization at the municipality level and the formulation and implementation of plans rest with the concerned municipalities, the District Planning Committee Act itself provides for the creation of the Urban Development Sub-Committee together with other sub-committees under the District Planning Committee. The experiences gained during the Seventh Five-Year Plan in the district revealed that the DPC found little time to look into the problems of urban planning and that the representation of the urban bodies on the DPC was inadequate.

To remove these difficulties and to ensure integration of urban development plans with the total development plan of the district, the State Government formed the Urban Planning Sub-Committee at the district towards the end of 1990.[72] Keeping this fact in mind, the Urban Development Sub-Committee has been constituted at the district level from the very beginning of the Ninth Plan to organise, coordinate and monitor the formulation and implementation of Municipal Plans and their incorporation into the District Plan. The Urban Development sub-committee is now composed of 11 members including the *Sabhadhipati* of the Zilla Parishad as Chairman. It includes seven members belonging to seven different municipalities of the district, the Executive Engineer of Urban Engineering Department and the Chief Medical Officer of Health of the district. The District Planning Officer is the Secretary of the Sub-Committee.[73] The Sub-Committee discharges its functions in close relation with the District Urban Development Agency (DUDA), set up in 1992.[74] It compiles the municipal plans before their inclusion in the district plan and undertakes the review and monitoring of the urban schemes. Apart from these functions, the Sub-Committee decides financial allocations for different municipal-specific development schemes.

All other sub-committees of the District Planning Committee, excepting the Special Area Development Sub-Committee, have been formed in the district keeping symmetry with the Standing Committees of the Zilla Parishad. In case of Special Area Development Sub-Committee, all the members other than the Chairman are official members. The Additional District Magistrate (Development) is the Secretary of this Sub-

Committee. The Sub-Committee also includes representatives, Executive Officers or Administrators, from the six area development authorities functioning in the district. It monitors and coordinates the development and planning activities of the area development bodies and approves their action plans after incorporating them in the district plan.[75] The rest of the sub-committees are sector-based and comprise both the official and non-official members.

In the district planning process, the District Planning Cell occupies an important place. It should be noted that, on the recommendations of the Working Group on District Planning[76] and with financial support and assistance from the Planning Commission[77] District Planning Cells have been created in different districts of the state. In this district, the District Planning Cell has been functioning since 1985 as an effective wing of the District Planning Committee to carry out major functions of the district planning, including the preparation of 'resource inventory, project appraisal and selection, setting of priorities and plan formulation for the district.'[78] The District Planning Cell also reviews and monitors the implementation of the district plan on behalf of the DPC. It prepares resource paper of the district with the help of other district level departments and compiles the sectoral targets and outlays.

The Planning Cell is headed by the District Planning Officer who, in turn, is assisted by four permanent staff: One Economist-cum-Credit Planner, a Sub-Assistant Engineer, one Upper Division Clerk and a Lower Division Clerk. These four posts have been created in 1985.[79] Since then the volume of work at the Planning Cell has increased manifold but additional posts have not been sanctioned. The Cell functions with the help of staff deputed from other wings of the Collectorate by the District Magistrate from time to time. Moreover, some important functions of the Planning Cell are carried out in a regular way by the Development Department of the district. Again, the statistical and computerised assistance is made available from a local unit of NRDMS, a project sponsored by the CASSARD, Government of India.[80]

The first District Planning Committee under the Act started functioning from September 1996 which was the last year of the

Eighth Five-Year Plan. The Committee has decided to pursue the same approach and methodology that was adopted while introducing decentralized district planning or the village based district planning in the district and followed all through the Seventh and Eighth Plans. Naturally, the machinery and institutions identified and created previously for district planning remained functional and operative under the existing arrangements. For proper understanding of the Planning machinery at the district after the District Planning Committee Act, 1994, a diagram showing the organizational hierarchy in planning is given in Figure 4. The only change that has been made by the present DPC is that the *Gram Sabha*, the grassroots organization involved in planning has been replaced by the *Gram Sansad* in rural areas. Similarly, the *Wards* at the municipal areas have been assigned the responsibilities of micro-planning at the grassroots.[81] Hence the study of district planning machinery would remain incomplete without reference to the planning organizations available below the district level.

Machinery below the District

The 74th Amendment has constitutionalized the practice of decentralized planning through making provisions for the establishment of District Planning Committee at the district level and entrusting to it the duties of consolidating the plans of the panchayats and municipalities and preparing the draft development plan for the district as a whole. But the Act does not make any reference to the creation of planning machinery below the district level. It is also a fact that the Amendment does not even recognize the planning bodies created at the Union and the States. The District Planning Committee Act passed in the State, in pursuance of the stipulations of the Amendment, reinforces the position outlined in the Constitution. The State Act is silent in this respect, nor does it abolish the planning organizations created below the district under the model developed in 1985. However the situation is altogether different in this district, since the DPC has decided to retain the planning structure developed below the district level in 1985 with only minor modifications in the composition of the Block Planning Committee.[82] To ensure greater participation from all corners, the Block Planning Committee now includes the *Sabhapati* of the Panchayat Samiti, all officers functioning at the block level including the Sub-Assistant Engineer, the Block Development Officer, *Karmadhyakshas* of the Standing Committees of the Panchayat Samiti, members of the Zilla Parishad elected from that block, *Pradhans* of the Gram Panchayats, local MLA, District Resource Persons of the Mass Literacy Programme, members of the Panchayat Samiti, representatives of the banks and representatives of voluntary agencies operating in the block.[83] Thus it is now a larger body in comparison to the previous committee created under 1985 model. Though the DPC Guidelines do not elaborate the *modus operandi* of the Block Planning Committee, it is obvious that the Panchayat Samiti would act as the core institution in block level planning since the preparation of the five-year plan and annual plan is also considered as an important function of the Samiti under the State Panchayat Act.[84]

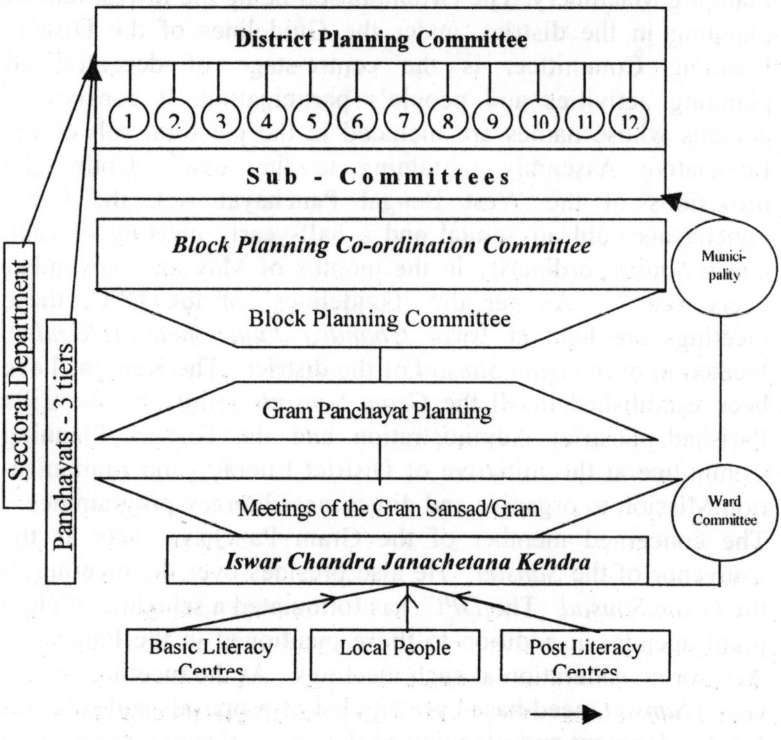

Fig. 5.2 : Organizational Structure of District Planning Machinery

The usual forum created by the District Planning Committee at the Gram Panchayat level is the Gram Panchayat Planning Committee which meets only to discuss and deliberate on the draft panchayat plan of the Gram Panchayat.[85] In reality it is not a 'committee' but a session of some selected persons of the locality including the government officials and panchayat members to accord approval to the draft plan. The said session is convened and presided over by the Gram Pradhan and is attended by all members of the Gram Panchayat, members of the Panchayat Samiti elected from that area, educationists and representatives of local NGOs, Field Staff of the government working at the Gram Panchayat level, officers of the Panchayat Samiti and representatives of the banks, Scheduled Castes and Scheduled Tribes.[86]

The situation is more or less the same below the Gram Panchayat, i.e. at the level of *Gram Sansad* where there is no Planning Machinery. The *Gram Sansad* being the lowest unit of planning in the district, under the Guidelines of the District Planning Committee, is the centre-stage of decentralized planning activities and people's participation. It consists of persons whose names are included in the electoral roll of the Legislative Assembly pertaining to the area.[87] Under the provisions of the West Bengal Panchayat Act, the Gram Panchayats hold an annual and a half-yearly meeting of each *Gram Sansad* ordinarily in the months of May and November every year.[88] As per the 'Guidelines' of the DPC, these meetings are held at *Iswar Chandra Jana Chetana Kendra,* located in each *Gram Sansad* of the district. The Kendras have been established in all the *Gram Sansads* jointly by the Zilla Parishad, District Administration and the District Planning Committee at the initiative of District Literacy and Immunization Mission to organize and direct mass literacy programmes.[89] The concerned member of the Gram Panchayat acts as the Convenor of the *Sansad.* He also presides over the meeting of the *Gram Sansad.* The *DPC* has formulated a schedule of eight point agenda, in addition to those mentioned in the Panchayat Act, for consideration at such meetings. At the meetings of the *Gram Sansad*, need-based priority list of proposals and schemes for development and planning of the area, selection of sites, list of beneficiaries, extent of contributions from villages, time schedule and rough cost estimates are prepared. Subsequently, these are submitted to the Gram Panchayat for incorporation in the Panchayat Plan after scrutiny.[90]

Other Planning Organizations

Apart from the organizations created exclusively for the formulation and implementation of district plans, there are many other agencies and organizations at both the district level and the below, which play their role in the preparation of five-year plan and annual plans. The Panchayati Raj Institutions at different tiers play the most active part in the process. The Zilla Parishad, Panchayat Samitis and the Gram Panchayats draw their plans according to the Guidelines of the State Planning Board. Again, a substantial part of the district plan is made up of departmental plans, and hence the role of various departments in the formulation of district plan is also important. But a department is not a part of the formal structure created for the purpose of planning. Thus the involvement and the role of the departments in the implementation of district plans are proposed to be dealt with in the following chapter in course of examining the implementation of planning in the district. Moreover, the scope of involvement of the sectoral departments in the formulation of departmental plans has been discussed in the preceding chapter.

The role of the District Rural Development Agency (DRDA) is also important in this connection since it is the key agency created in 1980 for the implementation of Integrated Rural Development Programmes and similar other programmes. Because of its important role, the State Government has made the *Sabhadhipati* of the Zilla Parishad the Chairman of the DRDA and the District Magistrate the Vice-Chairman, while in some other states the District Magistrate continues to chair the body. The DRDA is a large body comprising the official, ex-officio and non-official members, which plays a pivotal role for the .development of rural poor. It identifies their problems, prepares appropriate schemes, mobilises credit, provides incentives and coordinates the rural development activities in the district. It acts through a Governing Body which is again assisted by an Executive Committee consisting of the Chairman, the Vice-Chairman, Project Officer and the district level officers and any other officers whose services are considered necessary for planning and implementation of schemes and projects. The establishment of the agency includes Project Officer, Assistant Project Officers and other technical and non-technical members. It prepares action plans that are incorporated in the district plan and are executed through the PRI. Thus the agency is tied into the panchayat framework and its independent functioning is lost.[91]

The Panchayati raj provides another set of statutory organizations which is engaged in the formulation and implementation of decentralized area plans of the district. The Panchayati Raj Institutions act as the complementary organizations in the entire process starting from the *Gram Sansad* to the district. They provide necessary inputs and support for the statutory planning committees at the various levels. Again, the Constitution itself visualises both the Panchayati Raj Institutions and the Municipalities as the 'institutions of self-government'[92] having endowed them with the responsibilities of 'the preparation of plans for economic development and social justice.'[93] The statutory provisions enacted by the State Government in the aftermath of the Constitutional Amendments reinforce the position outlined in the Constitution. The Amendments made in the State Panchayat Act confer the responsibilities upon all the tiers of the panchayats to prepare perspective plan as well as annual plans for their respective areas.[94]

The Zilla Parishad, as the apex organization of the three-tier Panchayati Raj Institutions, is responsible for organizing and achieving the overall development of the district. After the introduction of decentralized planning, the role and authority of the Zilla Parishad over district development administration has been consolidated. Now it acts as the 'interface between the district's political institutions and the state government'.[95] It enjoys the powers of supervision, inspection and monitoring over the Panchayat Samitis and the Gram Panchayats for the effective management of development plans apart from those of preparing the same.[96] Since the Zilla Parishad operates at the district level, it enjoys close proximity and easy access to different district level departments of State Government and thus ensures the effective and meaningful interaction and coordination between the departments and panchayat bodies. Again, the association of the District Magistrate as both the Executive Officer of the Zilla Parishad and the Secretary of the District Planning Committee has succeeded in asserting the role of the Zilla Parishad in the administration of the district.

The Zilla Parishad functions mainly through the Standing Committees, each headed by a *Karmadhyaksha.* Executive responsibilities are vested with the *Karmadhyakshas,* which are further strengthened by making them responsible for 'financial and executive administration' in respect of the programmes and schemes under the control of the Standing Committees.[97] At present there are *ten Standing Committees* formed on the basis of sectoral division of responsibilities, namely: (i) *Artha, Sanstha, Unnayan-O-Parikalpana,* (ii) *Janasasthya-O-Paribesh,* (iii) *Purtakarya-O-Paribahan,* (iv) *Krishi Sech-O-Samabaya,* (v) *Shiksha, Sanskriti, Tathya-O-Krira,* (vi) *Khudra Silpa, Tran-O-Janakalyan,* (vii) *Bon-O-Bhumi Sanskar,* (viii) *Matsya-O-Prani Sampad Bikash,* (ix) *Khadya-O-Sarbaraha* and (x) *Bidyut-O-Achiracharit Shakti Sthayee Samitis.*[98] The *Sabhadhipati* of the Zilla Parishad himself is the ex-officio *chairman* of the *Artha, Sanstha, Unnayan-O-Parikalpana Sthayee Samiti.*[99] It may be noted that the District Planning Committee has twelve sub-committees of which ten such sub-committees are the counterparts of the Standing Committees of the Zilla Parishad, which have common sectoral area. The jurisdictions and functions of the sub-committees of the DPC and the Standing Committees of the Zilla Parishad seem to be apparently overlapping and incongruous. Each of the Standing Committees is headed by a *Karmadhyaksha,* a non-official elected personality of the Zilla Parishad. The Secretary of the Zilla Parishad acts as the Secretary to all the Standing Committees which are dominated mostly by non-official members. The functioning of the Standing Committee has also strengthened the mechanism of decentralized planning in another way. Since the draft proposals of departmental schemes are exclusively prepared by the government departments, it is found that the views of the Panchayati raj bodies could not be accommodated immediately in the district annual plan because of the delay in the submission of the draft plan by the departments to the District Planning Committee. This problem is minimised to a large extent through interactions at the meetings of the Standing Committee before hand.[100] Thus through the functioning of the Standing Committees 'the horizontal coordination at the district level'[101] is achieved and the projects and schemes implemented by the sectoral departments are 'coordinated both from the sectoral and locational points of view.'[102]

Moreover, the Zilla Parishad has a Coordination Committee (*Samanway Samiti*) consisting of the *Sabhadhipati, Sahakari-Sabhadhipati*, *Karmadhyakshas*, the Executive Officer and the Additional Executive Officer of the Zilla Parishad. The Secretary of the Zilla Parishad is the Secretary of this committee. This is a high power committee which, as the nomenclature suggests, coordinates all activities of the Zilla Parishad. Moreover, the coordination and integration of block and municipal plans relating to policy issues take place here through this committee.[103] This supervisory role of the Zilla Parishad does not create any problem due to the organic linkage and functional cooperation established among the three tiers of the panchayat hierarchy. All *Gram Pradhans* are the ex-officio members of the Panchayat Samiti and all *Sabhapatis* of the Panchayat Samitis are the ex-officio members of the Zilla Parishad.

The scope of activities of the Panchayat Samiti in the formulation and implementation of block plans is very wide. It can undertake schemes on different subjects ranging from agriculture to public utility and coordinate and integrate Gram Panchayat Plans and schemes in the block plan. It may execute the Gram Panchayat schemes itself or may provide assistance for proper execution, if requested by the Gram Panchayats.[104] It possesses wide general powers of supervision over the Gram Panchayats and may inspect and direct their activities.[105] The Panchayat Samiti discharges the development and planning functions usually with a very small establishment consisting of a Sub-Assistant Engineer, one Upper Division Clerk and a Peon.[106] It depends upon the services of the establishment of the block which is ensured more or less through the Block Development Officer and the Panchayat Extension Officer who are the Executive Officer and the Secretary of the Panchayat Samiti respectively.[107]

The Panchayat Samiti while discharging its functions, acts through a number of Standing Committees each with its own sectoral functions. At present there are ten Standing Committees at the Panchayat Samiti,[108] each of which consists of both official and elected members, more or less in equal proportion and is headed by a *Karmadhyaksha.* Apart from these Standing Committees, there is a Coordination Committee comprising the *Sabhapati, Sahakari-Sabhapati*, all the *Karmadhyakshas* and the Executive Officer. The Committee usually meets once in a month and coordinates the planning and development activities of the block and reviews the functioning of the Standing Committees. The relevant Standing Committee scrutinises, supervises and monitors the plans and execution of schemes and plans proposed and undertaken by the Gram Panchayats. The Standing Committees examine the larger projects submitted by a Gram Panchayat or by a group of adjoining Gram Panchayats and consolidate the schemes into a large one for execution by the Panchayat Samiti after their inclusion in the block plan.[109] All projects whether proposed by the panchayats or the government departments are scrutinised and approved by the relevant Standing Committee of the Panchayat Samiti before they are included in the block plan. The decisions and recommendations are communicated to the *Sabhapati* of the Panchayat Samiti for consideration in monthly or special meetings. After being approved by the Panchayat Samiti, the block plan is prepared as per format and submitted to the Block Planning Committee for discussion and approval.[110] In this way, the idea of block level planning as a means to accelerate the process of decentralization is structured organizationally. This helps to speed up the process of development and also to improve qualitatively by making it responsive to the local needs.[111]

The Municipalities, unlike their rural counterparts, have no separate planning machinery at the municipality level. The formulation and implementation of municipal plans are entirely the responsibilities of the concerned municipality. The municipalities have their own staff including both the field and technical persons who prepare the draft plan for consideration of the municipal bodies.[112] The District Planning Committee has identified the wards at the municipalities as the lowest unit of decentralized district planning in urban areas.[113] The Councillor elected from the ward is the *ex-officio* Chairperson of the Ward Committee of the particular ward.[114] Since there is no machinery for planning, the Ward Committees look after the planning activities of the wards. List of projects and schemes on priority basis and the names of beneficiaries, time-schedule and estimated cost are prepared by the Ward Committees for inclusion in the Municipality Plan. The Ward Committees meet usually once in a year to formulate the list of priorities and the schemes for development of the locality.[115]

The role of Gram Panchayat in the hierarchy of decentralized district planning is of crucial importance in the district since it is the grassroots organization in the panchayat system where people have an easy access to ventilate their needs and priorities as well as their grievances. The District Planning Committee being aware of this has decided to organize decentralized planning from the Gram Panchayat level where the schemes, proposals and priorities identified by the *Gram Sansads* are subsequently articulated and integrated in the draft plan of the panchayat. Apart from these functions of articulation and integration, the Gram Panchayat formulates its own plan and forwards inter-panchayat plans to the Panchayat Samiti for consideration.[116] But there is no separate planning machinery at the Gram Panchayat level and the Gram Panchayat itself is the statutory organization which prepares a development plan and annual plans for the area and revises and updates the same, if required, due to non-availability of resources or for other reasons. It also implements schemes for 'economic development and social justice' drawn by it or entrusted to it.[117] Though there is no provision for Standing Committees at the Gram Panchayat level in West Bengal, there is a scope for delegation of powers, functions and duties of the Gram Panchayat to one member or a group of members, severally or jointly, for effective functioning of the panchayat.[118] All the Gram Panchayats in the district have organized collective functioning through the creation of such groups and delegations of powers and functions.[119] Each group has a convenor nominated by the Gram Panchayat. The Convenor is responsible for convening the meetings of the group, coordinating the functions of its members and preparing the reports on actions taken or proposed to be taken in any matter falling within its jurisdiction. For all practical purposes, the group functions as the counterparts of the Standing Committees created in some states.[120]

The establishment and the staff-strength of the Gram Panchayat are small. The *Pradhan*, as the chief executive of the Gram Panchayat, is overburdened with duties. He is assisted by the *Upa-Pradhan* and other members of the Gram Panchayat. There is a Secretary who assists the *Pradhan* in his administrative works. Each Gram Panchayat has a Job Assistant who acts as the counterpart of the SAE of the block at the Gram Panchayat level. The Job Assistant with his minimum technical expertise helps the *Pradhan* in the preparation, supervision and implementation of Panchayat plans. Besides, there are a few *Chowkidars* and *Dafadars* who also assist in the functioning of the Gram Panchayats. Recently two posts, one of *Gram Karmi* and another of *Gram Sahayak*, have been created by the State Government for all the Gram Panchayats in the states. The Gram Panchayat discharges the planning functions with the help of these staff, panchayat members and local people.

It is evident from the above review that the planning organization in the district consists of a multiplicity of organizations, which are engaged in some way or the other in the formulation, implementation and monitoring of decentralized district plan. However, it is not possible to 'erase' the various existing agencies which play their role in the process of planning.[121] Naturally, there may arise scope for an overlapping of functions between the various agencies. In the present case, such a situation may emerge between the Sub-Committees (previously, the Working Groups) of the District Planning Committees and the Standing Committees of the Zilla Parishad. The decentralized district planning is based on the philosophy of inter-sectoral, intra-sectoral, inter-regional and intra-regional harmony and coordination. To achieve this balance and integration and to avoid contradictions a working principle has been developed in this district according to which the Standing Committees of the Zilla Parishad look after the formulation and implementation of the panchayat plans of all the three tiers while the sub-committees of the District Planning Committee prepare and monitor the departmental plans which are approved by the DPC and implemented by the departments more or less independently.[122]

The function of the planning machinery at the district is to translate the policy decisions into a concrete document, which is again put into practice by implementing agencies. Thus considered from a broad point of view, decentralized planning requires coordination, cooperation and commitment at all the levels of its machinery ranging from the Centre down to the organizations in the field at the *Wards* and *Gram Sansads* through the various organizations, government departments, planning bodies, local government institutions etc. Decentralized district planning is a joint responsibility of many interacting administrative and operational organizations and other groups comprising experts in the field of planning. It also requires the active support and involvement of the political elite, the bureaucracy and, above all, the people for its success.

Notes and References

1. Report of the *Committee to Review the Existing Administrative Arrangements for Rural Development and Poverty Alleviation Programmes,* 1985, (CAARD), Government of India, New Delhi, p.24, par.4.1, *(Hereinafter referred to as Report of the CAARD).*
2. *Ibid.*, p.44, par.6.22.
3. Rudra, Ashok. 1974, *Proceedings of the Inter-regional Seminar on Organization and Administration of Development Planning Agencies,* New York: United Nations, Vol. I, Page.41.
4. Report or the *Working Group on Block Level Planning*, 1978, Government of India, Planning Commission, Vol. II, Chap.X, par.11.
5. Report of the *Commission on Centre-State Relations,* 1988, Government of India, New Delhi, p.363.
6. Desai, P.B. 1979, *Planning in India,* New Delhi : Vikas, p.31.
7. Quoted in Maheswari, S.R. 1972, *The Administrative Reforms Commission,* Agra : Lakshmi Narain Agarwal, p.95.
8. Report of the *Administrative Reforms Commission,* (ARC) 1966, par.137. Quoted in *ibid.* p.219.

9. *Ibid.*, p.219, par.138.
10. Agarwal, P.P. 1957, 'The Planning Commission', *The Indian Journal of Public Administration*, Vol. III, p.332.
11. *Induction Material*, 1988, Internal Work Study Unit, Planning Commission, New Delhi: Government of India Publications, pp.7-15.
    Mozoomdar, Ajit. 1996, 'The Rise and Decline of Development Planning in India', in Kuldeep Mathur (ed.), *Development Policy and Public Administration*, New Delhi : Sage Publications, p.54.
12. Report of the *Administrative Reforms Commission*, par.152, *op. cit.* p.222.
13. *Annual Report*, 1993, Planning Commission, Government of India, New Delhi, pp.6-7 and 105-109.
14. Report of the *Administrative Reforms Commission*, par.161, *op.cit.* p.225.
15. Chandra, Ashok. 1958, *Indian Administration*, London : George Allen and Unwin, p.92.
16. Sinha, Arun. 1990, 'Decentralized District Planning : The Indian Experience' in R.P. Misra (ed.), *District Planning : A Hand Book*, New Delhi : Concept Publishing Company, pp.20-21.
17. Report of the *Administrative Reforms Commission*, par.160, *op.cit.*, p.225.
18. Misra, Baidyanath. 1972, *Capitalism, Socialism and Planning*, New Delhi: Oxford and IBH Publishing Company, pp.199-200.
19. Maheswari, S.R. 1972, *op. cit.* pp.99-100.
20. Government of West Bengal, *Resolution* No.2337/20-2/90 dated 16-7-1991.
21. Government of West Bengal 1985, *Guidelines of the State Planning Board* dated 12-3-1985 and State Planning Board *D.O. No.1068-1082, SPB/1S-4/85* dated 29-3-1985.
22. Joshi, B.M. 1989, 'Evaluation and Practice of Decentralized Planning in India', *The Indian Journal of Public Administration*, January-March, pp.98-113.
23. Somasekhara, N.S. 1985, *State Planning in India : Techniques, Procedures and Management*, Vol. II, Delhi: Himalaya Publishing House, pp.17-18.
24. Palanidurai, K.V. 1993 in Rakesh Hooja and B.Y. Raju (eds.), *Decentralized Planning in Multi-Level Framework*, Jaipur : Rawat Publications, pp.191-206.
25. Report of the *CAARD*, 1985, *op.cit.*, p.25, par.4.5.
    Also, The Government of West Bengal, 1985, The *Guidelines, op.cit.*
26. Report of the *CAARD*, 1985, *op.cit.*, p.15, par.3.4.
27. Government of West Bengal, *Resolution No. 3230/P-1S-6/85* dated 24-5-1985.
28. State Planning Board, Government of West Bengal, *D.O. Letter of the Vice-Chairman, SPB addressed to the Sabhadhipati(s) of the Zilla Parishads* dated 12-3-1985.
29. *Records of the District Planning Committee*, Midnapore.

30. *Interview with Mr. A. Mandal,* District Planning Officer, dated 19-8-1997.
31. *Proceedings of the meetings of the District Planning Co-ordination Council* held on 9-1-1987, 17-5-1988 and 17-8-1991.
32. *Ibid.*, dated 17-5-1988.
33. *Ibid.*, dated 17-8-1991 and 21-7-1992.
34. *Ibid.*, dated 9-1-1987 and 21-7-1992.
35. *Ibid.*, dated 21-7-1992.
36. *The Asian Age,* Calcutta, dated 20 August 1998.
37. *Gram Bhittik Zella Parikalpanar Paddhatigata Ruparekha* (in Bengali) 1985. District Planning Committee, Midnapore, p.2, and *Resolution,* Government of West Bengal, *op.cit.*
38. Government of West Bengal, *Resolution, op.cit.*, and *Gram Bhittik Zella Parikalpanar Ruparekha op.cit.* p.2.
39. Report of the *Working Group on District Planning,* 1994, Government of India, New Delhi, Vol. I, pp.46-47, par. 5.30.
40. Government of West Bengal, *Resolution, op.cit.*
41. *Interview with Mr. A. Mandal, op.cit.*
42. Government of West Bengal, *Chief Secretary, No. 96/92-CS* dated 28-2-1992.
43. Report of the *Working Group, op.cit.*, p.47 par. 5.31.
44. *Proceedings of the meeting of the Standing Committee of the DPC* dated 8-4-1992.
45. *Order of the District Magistrate* dated 1-8-1986.
46. *District Planning Committee,* Midnapore, *No.913(50)* dated 17-7-1987.
47. *Ibid.*
48. *Records of the District Planning Committee,* 1987-88.
49. *Records of the D.P.C.* Midnapore, 1990-91.
50. *Proceedings of the meetings of the Working Group of the DPC* held in 1991 and 1992.

    Also, *interview with Mr. N.Chatterjee,* District Planning Officer dated 21-5-1995.
51. *Interview with Mr. N. Chatterjee, ibid. and corroborated by Mr. H.K. Samanta, Sabhadhipati,* dated 27-8-1997.
52. *Interview with Mr. H.K. Samanta, ibid.*
53. Report of the *Working Group,* p.76, par.8.11.
54. *Gram Bhittik Zella Parikalpanar Paddhatigata Ruparekha* 1985, *op.cit.* p..2. Also, *Resolution No. 3230, op.cit.*
55. *Resolution, op.cit.*
56. *Interview with Mr. N. Chatterjee, op.cit.*

    Also discussed with Mr. M.N. Goray, Formerly *Sabhapati* of Dantan I Panchayat Samiti.
57. *An Outline of Methodology of Village Based Decentralized Planning,* 1985, District Planning Committee, p.32.
58. *Gram Bhittik Zella Parikalpanar Paddhatigata Ruparekha, op.cit.*, p.17 and *Gram Bhittik Block Parikalpanar Paddhati-O-Prayoger Ruparekha* 1989, *op.cit.*, p.20.
59. *The Calcutta Gazette, Extraordinary,* dated 3-5-1994.

60. *Ibid.*, dated 28-9-1994.
61. Government of West Bengal, *Notification No.2888/DP/2M-1/95* dated 27-10-1995.
62. *The West Bengal District Planning Committee Rules,* 1994, Rule 4(A).
63. *The Calcutta Gazette,* Extraordinary, dated 10-7-1996.
64. *The West Bengal State Planning Committee Act,* 1994, Section 4 (2).
65. Report of the *CAARD, 1985,* p.28 par.4.12.
66. G.O.No. 785/DP/O/DP/2M-03/2002, dated 8 March, 2002. And, No. 786/DP/O/DP/2M-3/2002, dated 8 March, 2002, Government of West Bengal, Department of Development and Planning, Kolkata.
67. The West Bengal District Planning Committee Act, 1994, Sec.10(1).
68. *Proceedings of the meeting of the* D.P.C., *op.cit.*, dated 19-9-1996.
69. *Ibid.*
70. *Ibid.*
71. *The West Bengal District Planning Committee Rules,* 1994, Rule.26(5).
72. The Government of West Bengal, *No.5186 DP/1S-12/89* dated 22-11-1990.
73. *Proceedings of the meeting of the DPC* dated 19-9-1996.
74. *Interview with Mr. Bijali Ghosh,* Project Officer, DUDA, Midnapore dated 19-8-1997.
75. *Proceedings of the meeting of the Special Area Development Sub-Committee,* dated 11-3-1997.
76. Report of the *Working Group on District Planning,* 1984, *op.cit.*, p.48, par(s). 5.35 and 5.36.
77. *Planning Commission,* Government of India, *No. PC(P)35/WB/85-MLP* dated 19-2-1986 addressed to Planning Secretary, Government of West Bengal.
78. Report of the *CAARD, 1985,* p.26, par.4.9.
79. Government of West Bengal, *Department of Planning and Development, No.10131/P/1E-5-85* pt. I, dated 24-12-1985.
80. *Interview with Mr. N. Ghorai,* Economist-cum-Credit Planner, District Planning Cell, Midnapore, dated 21-8-1997.
81 *Proceedings of the First meeting of the DPC* dated 19-9-1996.
82. *Ibid.*
83. *Medinipur Zellar Gram Bhittik Parikalpana Rachanar Ruparekha-O-Unnayaner Pratichhabi,* (in Bengali), 1996, DPC, Midnapore, p.7.
84. *The West Bengal Panchayat Act,* 1973, Section 109(1).
85. *Ibid.*, p.8.
86. *Ibid.*, p.6.
87. *The West Bengal Panchayat Act,* 1973, Section. 16A.
88. *Ibid.*, Section. 16A(2).
89. Interview with *Mr. A. Mandal, op.cit.*
90. *As in 82*, p.8.
91. Webster, Neil. 1992, *Panchayati Raj in the Decentralization of Development Planning in West Bengal,* Calcutta : K.P. Bagchi & Co., p.35 and *Interview with Mr. D.C. Das,* Project Officer, DRDA, dated 1-9-1998.
92. *The Constitution of India,* Arts. 243G and 243Q.

93. *Ibid.*, Arts. 243G(a) and 243W(a)(i).
94. *The West Bengal Panchayat Act, 1973* Section 19(1), 109(1) and 153(1).
95. Webster, 1992, *op.cit.*, p.31.
96. *The West Bengal Panchayat Act,* 1973, Sections 163(1) and 153.
97. *Ibid.*, Section 172(5)(a).
98. *Ibid.*, Section 171(1).
99. *Ibid.*, Section 172.
100. *Ibid.*
101. Report of the *CAARD, 1985*, p.67, par. 9.17.
102. Report of the *Working Group on District Planning*, 1984, p.78. par. 8.21.
103. *The West Bengal Panchayat Act,* 1973, Sec.153(1)(e). And *interview with Mr. N. Chatterjee, op.cit.*
104. *Ibid.*, Section 153(2).
105. *Ibid.*, Section 115(1) & (2).
106. *Interview with Mr. N.Ghorai, op.cit.*
107. *The West Bengal Panchayat Act,* 1973, Section 119(1) & (1-A).
108. *Ibid.*, Section. 124(1).
109. *Interview with Mr. H.K. Samanta, op.cit.*, dated 14-4-1998.
110. *Interview with Mr. A. Mandal, op.cit.*
111. Somasekhara, N.S. 1985, *op.cit.*, p.18.
112. *Interview with Mr. Bijali Ghosh, op.cit.*
113. *As in 82*, pp.8-9.
114. *The West Bengal Municipality Act,* 1994, Section 123(1).
115. *Interview with Mr. Bijali Ghosh, op.cit.*
116. *Proceedings of the meeting of the DPC* dated 19-9-1996.
117. *The West Bengal Panchayat Act, 1973,* Section 19(1).
118. *Ibid.*, Section 32A.
119. *Interview with Mr. H.K. Samanta, op.cit.*, dated 4-8-1998.
120. The *Madhya Pradesh Panchayati Raj Adhiniyam,* 1993, Section 46 and *Kurukshetra,* 1998 (April), p.7.
121. Report of the *Working Group on District Planning,* 1984, *op.cit.*, pp.75-76, par.8.8.
122. *Interview with Mr. H.K. Samanta, op.cit.*, dated 14-4-1998.

6

IMPLEMENTATION OF DECENTRALIZED DISTRICT PLANNING

A PRELUDE TO IMPLEMENTATION

Against the background of a sustained campaign for decentralized district planning since the Gadgil era, the District Planning Committee of Midnapore decided not to make the district planning a mere carbon copy or the replica of the national planning. The District Planning Committee (DPC) undertook the task of rectifying the gaps and pitfalls of the earlier planning process and set the motion to organise 'village based district planning' as a people's movement by emphasising the aim of development from within and not from without. The political leadership of the district authorities had a very clear vision of decentralized planning and was committed to formulate district plan in Midnapore on the ground realities.[1] To make the planning more pro-people and in order to attach the planning process to the needs and requirements of the people, it decided to consider the development of villages and localities in the light of the involvement of the local people. The development administration during the first four decades since independence was always guided by a philosophy of paternalistic management in which the bureaucrats and the politicians established themselves as the masters of development.[2]

Campaign for District Planning

To counterbalance the prevalent notion about planning and to involve as many people as possible, the Zilla Parishad leadership along with the key officials of the district administration visited different Panchayat Samitis of the district between January and February, 1985 to explain the need for decentralized area planning and to motivate the block and panchayat leadership to identify the resources, needs and priorities of individual villages and Gram Panchayats.[3] Simultaneously, the Panchayat Samitis of the district were advised to identify their problems on priority basis through consultations with the people for subsequent accommodation within the development plans of the district. Accordingly, a concerted attempt was made by the DPC for developing village level workers for planning throughout the district.[4]

The objective situation arising out of the implementation of NREP schemes created a positive attitude in the rural people. This attitudinal change and a positive interest were developed in them as a result of their day-to-day experience when they came across the panchayat activities in maintaining and repairing the existing rural assets like irrigation canals, roads, buildings, embankments, *boro-bundhs* (small embankments for irrigation during dry seasons) and tube-wells. Naturally, the response was spontaneous and encouraging in some of the blocks when the Zilla Parishad started to raise Planning Cadres for decentralized district planning. The District Planning Committee adopted a very careful and cautious approach for motivating and persuading all sections of the community to get them involved in the process of planning.[5] As a preliminary measure, District Planning Committee, Zilla Parishad and the Rural Development Centre of the IIT, Kharagpur, made joint efforts for the preparation of village level plans. In eight blocks of the district the preparation of village plan was done with top priority and unusual enthusiasm as a result of which villagers took part in the formulation of their own plans. These plans were subsequently integrated into the concerned Gram Panchayat Plans and thereafter into the Block and District Plans.[6]

Prevalent Scenario

The institutional mechanism for interactions between the panchayats and the villagers and also among the villagers themselves was already in existence in the district. There were the statutory obligations on the part of the Gram Panchayats for holding within the local limits of a *Gram* an annual and a half-yearly meeting for each *Gram Sabha*[7] on such date, place and hour as might be decided by the Gram Panchayat. The statutory provisions in the state (under the Panchayat Amendment Act of 1984) for ensuring people's participation in planning and development at the grassroots level were exemplary. The relevant Act contained in itself a time schedule for holding the meetings, the procedure for convening the meetings and the subjects of discussions for such meetings. It is noteworthy, in this connection, that the statutory provisions for people's involvement were introduced in the early eighties in West Bengal.[8] The practice of organizing public meetings at the village levels periodically to review the progress of works, select sites of development schemes, determine priorities and to prepare lists of beneficiaries was introduced in some of the blocks in this district after the devastating floods of 1978 to meet the requirements of reconstruction.[9]

The method of people's participation at the grassroots level was further strengthened in the district after the Second General Panchayat Elections in the state (1983). The ruling Left Front of West Bengal worked out a detailed guideline for the management of the affairs of the Panchayats through people's involvement.[10] After the Second General Panchayat Elections, 'Village Committees', under the auspices of the '*Krishak Sabha*', a frontal organization of the CPI(M), the leading partner of the Left Front Government, were formed in most of the blocks of the district for identification and execution of village schemes and implementation of welfare programmes. This process of organized participation of the village people in selection and implementation of village level programmes strengthened the scope of devolution of decision-making power to the public at large.[11] The formation of the village committees paved the way for organized participation of the village people in decentralized planning in subsequent years, though there were serious weaknesses and limitations in understanding the philosophy of decentralized district planning.[12]

The strategy adopted in Midnapore in raising peoples interest in decentralized planning and building planning culture could not be sustained and the outputs were shortlived. Naturally, the State Government was contemplating an alternative methodology for a sustainable environment in which decentralized planning could flourish. Inspired by the success of Kerala's People's compaign, awareness generation programmes have been devised by the Government recently through a comprehensive strategy involving (a) the conventional method of distribution of printed materials, use of electronic devices, organising cultural programmes, exhibition of posters etc. and (b) the community interactive strategy through Participatory Rural Appraisal method. The strategy has been devised to build up awareness and interest of the community people in which small group meetings are organised in the neighbourhoods prior to the meeting of the entire community. The concept of neighbourhood meetings is adapted from the experiments carried out in Midnapore in which 30-35 people belonging to a particular cluster of a households used to take part.[13]

Collection of Data

The need and importance of comprehensive and reliable database for district planning were already felt by the District Planning Committee since the beginning. The data needed for planning were related to the scope and content of the plan. It has been noted earlier that the District Planning Committee preferred to develop its own village-based data inventory with the help of local people. It is a fact that the previous attempts towards creation of a database in the country did not extend beyond coordination and collation of local level statistical and administrative data for district planning, which compelled the Planning Commission to issue a format for the collection of data at the village, block and district levels in a prescribed, pre-coded schedule covering a wide range of items.[14]

The Working Group on District Planning (1982-84) pinpointing the limitations of both the NSS rounds and IRDP surveys commented: "The data collected through primary surveys under IRD, on the other hand, are of varying degrees of reliability, as the surveys have not always been designed systematically. With more experience, it is hoped that these surveys will be better designed and would yield better quality information. The alternative to these two sources of information would only be that of conducting fresh primary surveys at the district level. Necessarily, such surveys would be costly and time-consuming. Under such circumstances, the Group feels that to start with, the district planning exercise may incorporate the results of such surveys as are readily available, duly cross-checked with other information and refined to the extent possible."[15] The District authorities, being aware of such limitations, have undertaken a programme to conduct micro-level surveys at the interval of every five years, preferably before the preparation of each five year plan.[16]

At the beginning, the District Planning Committee decided to enrich itself with the information already collected under the initiatives of the Directorate of Panchayat, West Bengal during the primary survey conducted at the micro level for implementing the IRD programme.[17] But there were certain inadequacies in those information. It has already been pointed out that the District Planning Committee took the lead even before the Planning Commission asked the State Governments to arrange the collection of the required data for storage and retrieval on a regular basis through NICNET (DISNIC). The DPC decided to have the information collected through household and village surveys according to the schedules and formats prepared and supplied by it. The surveys were conducted with the help of village-level volunteers. Two to three volunteers for each village were selected by the Gram Panchayats.[18] The programme, though initially began with much interests, could not be continued with desired success. The decentralized district planning had to be introduced on the basis of the data then available with the administration.

The first attempt towards the creation of a data bank for decentralized planning at the district level was made in 1985 by the District Planning Committee through a fresh survey of the villages. The committee prepared a detailed note for the guidance of the panchayat workers and village level volunteers for the collection of required information from the villages.[19] Pending the development of such a bank, the committee took the help of an external organization for collection of data of 40 sample villages in the district. Similarly with a view to strengthening the data-base with inputs on current developments, the DPC undertook another micro-level survey of the villages prior to the commencement of the Eighth Plan jointly with the District Planning and Development Society, an NGO, the District Rural Development Centre of the IIT, Kharagpur. This time, the sample area was extended to 766 inhabited villages spreading over 22 blocks of the district and the schedule meant for collection of data was made household-based and simplified by reducing the elements for investigation from 48 to 28 only.[20] The third attempt towards collection and analysis of detailed information about the households and villages to meet the pre-conditions of decentralized district planning has been visualised recently by the District Planning Committee.[21]

Development of Planning Cadres

In spite of all these efforts of the District Planning Committee and the Zilla Parishad, the state of planning at the villages during the first year of the Seventh Plan was microscopic. This was soon realized and the district authorities took a decision to develop Planning Cadres for planning and plan implementations through mutual training process. Each of the Panchayat Samitis and Block Organizations was asked to make utmost effort to train up at least 15 to 25 planning cadres per block who could, in turn, initiate the process of training 15 to 20 cadres per Gram Panchayat. These village level cadres were required to act as the main organizers of regular village level meetings both for the villagers as a whole, as well as separately for the various deprived groups of the village, so that they might put their effective imprint on the whole village meeting. The *Sabhapatis* of the Panchayat Samitis and the Block Development Officers were accordingly requested by the DPC to select sincere planning cadres, both male and female, at least 2 for each Gram Panchayat, and to convene the group meetings immediately.[22]

The District Planning Committee did not remain satisfied with transmitting the ideas to the block and panchayat leadership. It constituted a Group of Instructors for Training consisting of eleven members of the Working Group of the District Planning

Committee and entrusted it with the responsibilities of conducting training programmes in the blocks. Subsequently, monthly phase-wise training camps were organized and this programme continued for a year starting on and from 21-4-1987.[23] As a part of this training course, the camps were held in each month on a particular date fixed for a period of the next three months for a cluster of blocks. The blocks included in a particular cluster sponsored three trainees of either sex who previously took part in the preparation of Village Register and Household Survey Schedule during 1986. The cadres were trained in such a way as to enable them to conduct training camps at villages and Gram Panchayat levels simultaneously on the tasks and responsibilities of village level workers.[24] The Instructors for village level planning cadres worked out a total training plan and prepared materials for training of the cadres.

The District Planning Committee was pragmatic in its approach and was guided by the 'Stage approach' based on the famous Chinese proverb: 'The journey of a thousand miles must start with a single step.'[25] At the first stage, it identified one-third of the blocks, 18 out of 54, for organizing the training programmes. The blocks which showed considerable interest in launching the village based district planning, were included in the first phase training programme. The course-materials for training devised by the Instructors were reviewed thoroughly in the light of suggestions made in the District Level Seminar held on 19-6-1987.[26] The training course was designed to make the cadres acquire cognitive and analytical skills in dealing with the technical aspect as well as the human aspect of planning. The District Planning Committee also devised the programmes for mutual interactions among the sectoral functionaries at the district level so that they could adopt a comprehensive view of planning. The mutual training process initiated by the DPC helped to establish forward and backward linkages in both the government departments and the Panchayati raj bodies.

At the training programmes, the planning cadres were usually imparted the knowledge pertaining to decentralized planning and decentralization, planning process, methods of collection of data and information, preparation of priorities and the tools and techniques of planning. Thus the training packages were common for all the categories of the cadres. Such a common package had both advantages and limitations. It is usually recommended that in a decentralized operational context different training packages are necessary to deal with the individual requirements of the planning cadres.[27] Anyway, the scope for mutual and open interactions between the instructors and the cadres helped to overcome the shortcomings and develop a common attitude towards the problems.

At the first training camp of the planning cadres, there were general discussions on different aspects relating to the methodology of decentralized planning. Both the Planning Cadres and the Instructors visited different places under the blocks to meet the panchayat functionaries, government officials belonging to different departments and participated in the planning activities at the block levels within one month after the first training camp. They convened meetings at the village levels in consultation with the panchayat representatives immediately after they acquired first hand knowledge about the scheme implemented at different levels by the gram panchayats, panchayat samitis and government departments. In such meetings, they interacted with the people and apprised them of the various aspects of the planning methodology and assuaged their feelings.[28] Through mutual interactions, the cadres tried to learn the basic thrust of the people and their reactions about the planning methodology, both subjectively and objectively. In the meetings, the planning cadres developed intimate knowledge about the particular village and its people. They collected detailed information regarding the percolation of government benefits to the people of the village during the preceding five years. In the next training camp, they submitted a detailed write-up as to the experiences they gathered during the last one month. Then the cadres prepared the Village Registers, since basic inputs were already available with them, after the completion of the above noted tasks [29] Simultaneously, the DPC sought the assistance of Midnapore Planning and Development Society, an NGO, to implement the training programmes. The society organized five training camps in each month and at the first phase, planning cadres belonging to 17 blocks were introduced to the decentralized planning methodology.[30]

To monitor the progress and implementation of decentralized planning, a Working Group was constituted at the beginning of the Seventh Plan. It consisted of the *Sabhadhipati*, District Magistrate, *Karmadhyakshas* of the Zilla Parishad, some district level officers, experts and others. The group was reconstituted on 1-8-1986 and was asked specifically to look after the affairs of mutual training at block level and to coordinate and monitor the process and progress of district planning.[31] It may be noted that, thus after the passage of almost two years the District Planning Committee took up the decision to revamp the implementation machinery of the district planning at the village level through activating the planning cadres.[32] The Working Group could not give much attention to the preparation of the Household Registers, though much progress was noticed in respect of Household Surveys. It is evident from the proceedings of the meetings of the Working Group of the DPC that it concentrated most on the preparation of Village Registers. Since the village was identified as the basic unit of decentralized district planning in Midnapore, the district authorities were more concerned with the data of the village as a whole and preferred to leave the intra-village peculiarities to be addressed by the villagers themselves. This may be viewed, as an incomplete approach in the context of comprehensive planning, but it was not possible to go into the minute details of a village under the then prevalent conditions. Subsequently, the Working Group of the District Planning Committee laid maximum emphasis on the preparation of Village Schedules on the basis of village surveys. The village profile thus prepared was updated with the data available with other agencies such as DRDA, District Industrial Centre, Blocks and other Government Departments and were used for planning at different stages.[33]

As has been discussed in the previous chapter, the methodology of district planning as worked out and put into operation by the District Planning Committee was village-based. Though it has been claimed by the district authorities that village plans were prepared in about 700 villages of the district during the Seventh Five-Year Plan[33], no systematic record is available to ascertain the actual progress. However, there is no dearth of records available at different Gram Panchayats, which suggest that plans in the form of prioritization of schemes and proposals indicating preferences of implementation were formulated in most of the villages. Most of the Gram Panchayats and all Panchayat Samitis formulated their annual and five-year plans during the Seventh and Eighth Plans and on the basis of block plans and municipal plans, district annual action plans were prepared during this period.[35]

Besides raising the Development Cadres, arrangements have now been made for continuous training of the planning volunteers, chairpersons and members of the panchayats and municipalities, and persons connected with planning activities. At the state level, a team of *State Resource Persons* (SRP) has been constituted with the faculties of the State Institute of Panchayats and Rural Development, retired and experienced government functionaries, and persons having expertise and completence in the field of planning and development. The team provides district level training for the *Key Resource Persons* (KRP) consisting of two persons from each of the blocks and sub-divisions of the district and three persons from the district head-quarters. Similarly, the Panchayat Development Workers selected at the gram panchayat levels are trained by the KRPs. Moreover, arrangements have been made for training of the panchayat members and other officials working at different levels.[36]

Prioritization in Implementation

The introduction of the Eighth Five-Year Plan in the district was delayed for two years following the delay in the commencement of the National Plan. The Eighth Five-Year Plan could not be started in 1990 at the national level. The Planning Commission decided to start the same from 1992-93 with a new document (fourth version in the order) approved by the National Development Council on May 23, 1992.[37] Thus the Eighth Plan was a late starter. The Eighth Five-Year Plan of the district was formulated in time by the District Planning Committee on the basis of three basic principles included in the methodology: participation of the people in preparation, implementation and evaluation of plans; identification of schemes and proposals for maximization of benefits for the weaker sections and lower strata of the society; and, building up of consciousness among the people about the need for fundamental changes.[38] Thus the methodology, strategy and objectives of the Eighth Plan were similar to those of the Seventh Plan in the district. Naturally the process and mechanism of implementation were also similar in character. By that time, the District Planning Committee and the development administration of the district gained considerable experience which helped them to be realistic in their approaches. There was scanty rainfall and nature turned hostile that year. Moreover, the enthusiasm and interest developed in the people and the panchayats during the initial days of the village based district planning began to recede.[39] To meet this compulsion of circumstances, the District Planning Committee decided to recast the sectoral priorities and prepare Time Schedule for implementation of the process step by step. The different stages and agencies for implementation of the schemes and projects included in the priority schedule were also identified by the DPC. The District Planning Committee streamlined and ensured the sources for mobilization of funds for the execution of each of the categories of projects.[40]

Formulation of five-year plan and annual plan in the district did not only include proposals for expenditure on various sectors, but also indicated the scope and extent of the mobilization of resources from all sources available in the district. A brief scrutiny of the priority schedule as mentioned reflects the pragmatic character of approach the DPC followed in actualising the decentralized district planning in Midnapore. It identified ten sectors for immediate implementation during the second half of the Eighth Plan. In terms of according priority, the status-matrix of these sectors were to some extent different from those of the sectors, originally included in the Eighth Plan document. Thus the decision of the District Planning Committee in rearranging the priorities in 1994-95 constituted a part of the Action Plan of the district for 1994-95.[41] However, it may be noted here that the DPC did not introduce the scheme of rearranging the priorities in district planning for the first time in 1994-95. Changes in prioritization of sectors in course of execution of the District Annual Plan (1992-93) were also necessitated in 1992 due to a variety of factors like resource crunch and hostile nature.[42] In fact, prioritization and rearrangement in priorities of schemes and proposals were concomitant with the process of planning and constituted the most vital part of the Annual Action Plan of the district. The modified priority schedule is presented below in the form of a table for understanding the extent of autonomy enjoyed by the DPC in course of the implementation of district plan.

Table 6.1 : Modifications in Priorities (1994-95)

Sectors identified	Sources of Funds	Implementing/ Monitoring Agency / Authority
1. *Agriculture (i)* (a) Replacement of traditional cultivation of kharif paddy in the up-lands by crops like wheat, ground nuts, maize, *arhar* in the red and laterite undulating tracts of the district. (b) Extension of horticultural crops like cashew, guava, papayas, etc. in sand and laterite areas and coconut in coastal belts on the banks of canals, roadsides etc.	(a) Finance by individual cultivators mainly. (b) Programmes of Agricultural Department. (c) JRY for S.C. & S.T. people and G.P.Schemes for general categories.	Gram Panchayats.
2. *Agriculture (ii)* Increase of level of productivity by maximising irrigation and drainage facilities ensuring flow of improved inputs and (c) using organic manure particularly *azolla*, blue, green algae and green manure through construction of bio-gas plants, compost pits etc.	(a) Loans from banks (under credit plans) and subsidy from government for bio-gas plants. (b) JRY for people belonging to target group and G.P. funds for others for the construction of compost pits.	Gram Panchayats (with assistance from banks).
3. *Irrigation* Re-excavation of the existing sources of irrigation, excavation of small new sources, dug wells, selection of labour-intensive and collective projects, construction of water channels, *bundhs* and canals etc. Supply of pump sets. (c) Electrical conversion of RLI., completion of underground pipe-lines with PVC pipes, modernization of RLI schemes under IDA assistance.	(a) E. A. S. (schemes) in the selected blocks. (b) M. W. S. and IJRY in other blocks: @ Rs.20-25 lacs per block. (c) Pump sets under IRDP and MT loans. (d) Major schemes ear-marked for Zilla Parishad. (e) Schemes under CSMI. SSPP, SCP & ITDP. (f) CADC (Debra & Tamluk) and Jhargram Development Board.	Panchayat Samitis & Zilla Parishad. CADA(s) and Jhargram Development Board.
4. *Use of Lands*	—	—

(Contd.)

5. *Fisheries*		
(a) Short time *magur* culture in the laterite zones, Demonstration for *galda* culture in all the blocks; production of juvenile *prawns* in small water bodies constructed in low lying areas alongside the river;	(a) Schemes for excavation of tanks and water resources for irrigation purposes. (financed under irrigation schemes)	Panchayat Samitis and Zilla Parishad
	(b) State Fisheries Development Corporation	SFDA and FFDA
(b) Brackish water fish farming in the eastern and southern part of the district;	(c) Loans from banks under credit plans	
(c) Establishment of *prawn hatchery* and construction of windmill for augmentation of fish production.	(d) National coastal Development Corporation through Directorate of Fisheries, W.B.	
6. *Power*	—	—
7. *Construction and repairing of Primary School Buildings.*	—	—
8. *Play Grounds*	—	—
9. *Construction and repairing of roads*		
(a) Village link-roads (b) Setting up of culverts and (c) Construction of small bridges	(a) JRY Schemes of the blocks (b) EAS for the selected blocks (c) General funds of the Panchayat Samiti (d) District Plan Funds	Gram Panchayats, Panchayat Samitis and the Zilla Parishad
10.(a) Construction of houses for the target people and	(a) Indira Awas Yojana (b) Group loan from HUDCO through Panchayat Samitis	Panchayat Samitis
(b) Low cost latrines	(c) Individual contribution by the beneficiaries, subsidy from Panchayat Samitis & Zilla Parishad and loans from Government	Panchayat Samitis through Ram Krishna Mission Lokasiksha Parisad (NGO)

Source : Compiled from the records of the Development and Planning Cell. Also, District Annual Plan of Midnapore, 1994-95.

From the table presented above, it appears that considering the distribution pattern of rainfall, land and soil conditions, drainage position etc., District Planning Committee put special emphasis on crop planning in agricultural sector. Cultivation of traditional kharif paddy was substituted to the maximum possible extent by alternative crops requiring comparatively less irrigation. Moreover, together with agriculture, special attention was given to the extension in production of horticultural crops. Again, in view of the gradual increase in both prices and quantum of consumption of fertilisers in the district (from 42095 M.T. in 1984 to 90926 M.T. in 1991-92)[43], it recommended the use of organic manure and the construction of bio-gas plants. As a result of the changed emphasis through prioritization of sectors, the district was able to achieve cent per cent of the targets in food grains production. The figures collected from the agricultural department revealed that the rice production went up from 20.97 lakh M.T. during 1993-94 to 23.92 lakh M.T. in 1994-95.[44]

Similarly in the revised list of priorities, fishery sector was asked to augment fish production through utilisation of untapped resources and application of non-conventional pisciculture. The DPC planned to exploit the advantages of temporary and short lived ponds, reservoirs, catchment areas during rainy season by introducing short-time projects like *magur culture,* capture fishery, brackish water fishery, prawn culture etc. Naturally, attainments in respect of fish production as well as welfare of the fishermen were a commendable success. In production of fish, the rate of growth was encouraging, i.e. about 12.5 per cent during the last four years of the Eighth Plan. As a result of appropriation of untapped but potential resources and the non-conventional methods and varieties such as, prawn hatchery, fresh water Prawn culture, marine fishery along the coastal line etc., the level of table fish production was increased from 1200 kg per hectare to 1400 kg per hectare amounting to 39,179 M.T. in 1994-95.[45] The table produced above does not only reflect the changes made in the priorities of the district plan but also identifies the sources of funds and the agencies for implementing and monitoring. The identification of sources of funds and the agencies in the context of overall perspectives and changed realities in the district gave the process of district planning a new direction.[46] The scope for modification in prioritization in the course of implementation of plans is an additional advantage that paves the way for learning through experience.[47]

It has already been pointed out in the first chapter that decentralized planning is not contrary to the national planning ; rather it is complementary to the goals and broad objectives of the national and state plans. This year the State Government has indentified the following *broad thrust areas*[48] for the Tenth Plan (2002 – 2007) :

Agriculture,
(i) Industry and Food processing, especially cottage and small scale,
(ii) Overall development and employment generation,
(iii) Education,
(iv) Health, and
(v) Infrastructure.

Based on this assessment and anticipating the active role of the local bodies, the State Government has also proposed a *crash programme* concentrating on a few areas which include :

(i) Achievement of universal primary education,
(ii) Assured functioning of all primary health centres and sub-centres,
(iii) Universal access to safe drinking water,
(iv) Full coverage of rural electrification, and
(v) Extension of provision for at least double-cropping to the farmers.

It is interesting to note here that both the DPCs of Midnapore have accepted the proposed of crash programmes and has accordingly identified the *priority areas* for the Tenth Plan of the districts.[49]

Preparation of Time Schedule

Planning is a consecutive and sequential process. This is truer in the case of decentralized planning, because it involves various stages and a number of processes which cannot be adhered to at once and at the same time. Moreover, a step needs to be initiated only after the completion of the preceding step. Hence a proper time framing or schedule is required. In planning there are two aspects of time elements. First, a time schedule is required for the formulation of plans and secondly, for the implementation as well. The District Planning Committee of Midnapore was convinced of this aspect and accordingly, it prepared a time schedule for both planning and implementation. Time schedule was prepared by the DPC for execution and implementation of individual schemes and projects.

Time framing is important in the formulation of plans. Delay in execution affects the concerned scheme or project or at best the future programmes of the executing agency. But failure in respect of formulation of plan at any stage under the decentralized planning process may affect the entire exercise.[50] Hence, the District Planning Committee took the utmost care for timely preparation of plans by different bodies and accordingly prepared time schedule for each element of work during both the Seventh and Eighth Plans. The DPC was possibly guided by the scientific technique of plotting the progress of work against time. The time schedule prepared by the DPC included the time that the job would require under the given conditions. The first set of time-schedule was generally based on the expectations about a certain span of time required for formulation of a particular plan or scheme. In case of failure in accomplishing the task, a revised set of time frame was considered by the DPC.

The District Planning Committee developed a preliminary time schedule for the preparation of plans on the lines suggested by the State Government in June 1986.[51] It decided that the planning exercise should commence from the very beginning of a financial year so as to complete the process of finalisation of the district plan in consultation with the State Planning Board by the next November. As per the proposed time frame, the government departments used to submit information on antici-pated flow of funds from their respective departmental budget at the meetings with the District Planning Committee and the Block Planning Committees and discuss the priority, location and type of schemes to be taken up under the district and block plans within 15 July of the year. Thereafter, the departments would submit their draft plans and proposals to the District Planning Committee and Block Planning Committee by the first week of August in Formats DP-I and DP-II as mentioned in the previous chapter. The Gram Panchayats after taking the village plans into consideration and the Block Planning Committee integrating the Gram Panchayat Plans with the block level plans and proposals would formulate their plans by the June of each year. Finally, the draft district plans were used to be approved by July-August of that year by the District Planning and Co-ordination Council.[52]

The District Planning Committee worked out a similar programme for the execution of plans and schemes as well. Thus the annual action plans for each individual department were prepared taking note of the expected period for completion of each scheme. As for example, for the construction of a house with latrine or a smokeless *chullah* under Indira Aawas Yojana or re-excavation of an irrigation canal under Million Wells Scheme, a period of three months was scheduled.[53] Again, construction of a *Chathal* at Rajbundh in Salboni block and the construction of a sluice-cum-irrigation canal at Majuria under Keshpore block were allowed 60 and 120 days respectively for completion.[54] Similarly, time-bound programmes were also drawn up for schemes and projects coming within the purview of government departments for execution though there were failures due to delays in providing allotments by the government.[55] Sometimes, execution of a work was also delayed by the implementing agency itself.[56]

Such schemes as could not be completed within the stipulated period covered under a certain financial year were taken up as running schemes in the subsequent year and were, accordingly, included in the concerned annual action plan of the succeeding year. Thus there was no problem regarding the implementation of sectoral plans executed through the government departments located within the district. But there were restrictions in respect of carrying over the funds of JRY exceeding 15 per cent by the Gram panchayats.[57] The Gram panchayats were required to utilize the funds allotted according to annual action plan of the district within the financial year in which it was made available to them. If the carry-over funds were more than the above mentioned percentage of the funds received during a particular year, the Zilla Parishad could impose a cut on the share of Gram panchayat to the extent of excess unspent balance. The fund so deducted could be spent by the Zilla Parishad, within the area of the concerned locality through Panchayat Samiti with the help of Beneficiary Committee.

The time-frame thus worked out, though it helped the District Planning Committee to exercise its supervision and monitor the progress at the district level, could not be strictly followed at different levels.[58] Accordingly, the District Planning Committee developed a modified schedule in April 1994.[59] The modified schedule was an improvement upon the original and it continued to guide the planning operations of the district during the Eighth Plan and was by and large followed by the lower level planning bodies and the departments. In the modified schedule, the whole plan of work is divided into the five well-linked steps. The revised Time Schedule is given in table form in Table 6.2 to have a close review of the scheme of dividing a total work into a number of phases for effective implementation.

Table 6.2 : Time Schedule for District Planning

No. of Phases	Target Span of time	Works to be done at the appropriate levels
I	3-6-94 to 15-6-94	1. Identification of such schemes/projects by the Panchayat Samitis as may be determined directly by themselves. 2. Transfer of the items/subjects falling under the jurisdiction of the GPs to the Gram Panchayats (GP) for planning.
II	16-6-94 to 22.6.94	1. Classification of the schemes and projects by the GP into two categories: (a) those to be directly dealt with by the G.P. itself and (b) those to be referred to the villages for discussions and prioritization. 2. Discussions on the proposals and schemes as mentioned above in 1(b) in phase II.
III	13-6-94 to 30-6-94	1. Finalisation of the lists of projects and beneficiaries in the meetings of the villagers to be held at Post-Literacy Centres (meeting to be convened by the GP) 2. Evaluation and reporting by the GP on the attendance and participation of the people at the above meetings.
IV	1-7-94 to 7-7-94	1. Formulation and finalisation of Gram Panchayat Plans by the GP on the basis of village plans and lists of priorities, and its own priorities and requirements. 2. Submission of Panchayat Plans to the Block Planning Committee.
V	5-7-94 to 10-7-94	1. Formulation of Block Plans by the Block Planning Committee integrating therein the GP Plans, proposals and priorities of the Panchayat Samiti and the schemes and projects for earmarked sectors of the PS / Block. 2. Submission of Block Plans to the District Planning Committee as per formats prescribed for it.

Source: Based on the records of the DPC, Midnapore, 1994-95 and a Brochure captioned *Kayekti Agradhikar Kshetra, Bikendribhuta Parikalpana-O-Medinipur Zella* (in Bengali) published by the Zilla Parishad, Midnapore, 1994.

The experience in the Ninth Plan in following the time-schedule in different districts was not at all encouraging. There were some constraints in ensuring integration of the plans prepared at the lower levels with those of the higher tiers, apart from the continuous problem of tailing behind the schedule in almost all the districts. Moreover, there was no uniformity in approach in the schedules prepared by individual districts. To overcome these problems, the State Government has come out with a fresh time-frame for formulation of decentralized plans at the Gram Panchayat levels. The revised schedule has been prepared with a view to implementing the methodology of decentralized planning in the state from 2001-2002 onwards. The modified time-frame together with schedule of activities is presented below:

Table 6.3 : Revised Time Schedule for the Districts

Sl. No.	Types of Activities	Period
1.	Preliminary discussions at *Gram Sansads*	18-30 November, 1999
2.	Identification of DRPs	December
3.	Identification of KRPs	December
4.	Identification of Task Forces	February 2000
5.	Training of DRPs	January – April
6.	Training of KRPs and Task Forces	May – August
7.	*Gram Sansad Meetings* for discussions on planning	May
8.	District Seminar on Planning	August – September
9.	Block Seminar on Planning	September – October
10.	Data Collection	September – November
11.	*Gram Sansad* Meetings for Formulation of Plans	November
12.	Preparation of Draft Gram Panchayat Plan	December
13.	G P Development Seminar	January 2001
14.	Finalisation of GP Plans	January 2001

Note : Based on the records of the State Government (W.B.).

Very often planning is viewed to be a process consisting only of determination of some targets about certain programmes and setting up of strategies and the laying down of a set of policies in a document. This is not an adequate understanding of planning. Planning is very much an administrative process, a problem of management of economics and hence implementation is an important aspect of planning. Thus the formulation of methodology and the implementation thereof are the twin elements involved in the operation of successful planning. Both these parts are inter-linked and they interact upon one another. Objective formulation of plans is dependent on the feedback from the implementation process.

IMPLEMENTATION OF PLANS

Whatever the flow of funds, the implementation of the projects and schemes were carried out generally in the way in which plans were formulated at different levels within the district. Funds were allotted to the executing agencies in the district according to the approved outlay of the district plan. Departmental budget allocations meant for a district are separated and made known to the district beforehand to enable the District Planning Committee to prepare the Draft Development Plan of the district as a whole incorporating therein the Departmental Plans, Panchayat Plans, Municipal Plans and other Rural Development Programmes within such allocations called the *divisible pool*. The *divisible pool* reserved for the district has progressively increased over the years and now about 50 per cent of the total State Plan allocation is made available to the *divisible pool* of the districts on an average basis.

Departmental Plans

Departmental plans and projects covered the largest percentage of the plan outlay in this district. It constituted nearly 52 per cent of the plan expenditure under district plan for the first four years of the Eighth Plan.[60] The projects which came under the category of departmental or sectoral plans were executed generally by the district and block level departments. Apart from the schemes included in the category of sectoral schemes and projects, the district level departments would execute such state level schemes within the district as were related to the development of overall infrastructural priorities of the state. These were kept outside the scope of district plan and were assigned to the state sector priorities. Usually, no problem other than the inadequate and untimely flow of funds was faced by the respective executing agencies in the implementation of the sectoral plans.[61] From an analysis of the proceedings of the DPCC (1992), it appears that the annual plan of 1992-93 could not be implemented as per the approved outlay due to shortage of funds. To meet the financial constraints, the district administration had to tap other sources of revenue collection at the district level and the sources like Small Savings, Motor Vehicles Fees, Excise Duty, Stamp Duty, Entertainment Tax, Land Revenue etc. were identified for this purpose.[62]

Since the major part of the district plan relates to the departmental plans, the roles of different departments (the implementing agencies), Standing Committees of the Zilla Parishad, Panchayat Samitis and Working Groups or Sub-Committees of the District Planning Committee are particularly important. The Working Groups (now the Sub-Committees) of the DPC review and monitor the projects and schemes on a regular basis. These groups sit with the departmental officers, executing agencies and the Panchayat Samitis, interact on the progress of execution on a regular basis and provide guidance wherever necessary.[63] The departments received cooperation from the Panchayati raj bodies in the execution of schemes at all the levels. The cases of misunderstanding between the panchayats and the sectoral departments were marginal. There are about 100 departments in the district. In some cases, there were differences between the panchayats and the departments of agriculture, irrigation and minor irrigation. But such differences were resolved at the intervention of the functionaries of the Zilla Parishad.[64] Funds to the district level agencies were released by the State Government quarterly and accordingly, no major problem arose in the implementation of the project schemes of the district, except delays in some cases. But the problem of delay could not come to the forefront since the schemes were executed through contractors and they were paid long after the execution of schemes.[65]

Municipal Plans

The formulation and implementation of municipal plans were entirely the responsibility of the concerned municipalities. It has earlier been pointed out that the DPC was mainly preoccupied with planning at blocks, gram panchayats and villages. During the Seventh Plan, the District Planning Committee could not bring urban planning of the district into the fold of the district plan. Following the formation of the Urban Planning Sub-Committee under the DPC as per Government Guidelines[66] the issues relating to municipal plans were taken up by the DPC. Subsequently, District Urban Development Agency (DUDA) was set-up for monitoring and coordinating the development and planning activities of the urban local bodies of the district. However, the tasks of formulation and implementation of plans were left to the municipalities. Projects under *Nehru Rozgar Yojana* (NRY) Programme with its two branches, i.e. Scheme for Urban Wage Employment (SUWE) and Scheme for Urban Micro Enterprize (SUME) were prepared and implemented by the municipalities themselves. The first scheme was an employment generation scheme while the second was an individual scheme for the upliftment of the urban poor. About 100 branches of the banks were engaged in this programme of the district. 25 per cent of the funds for SUME was provided by the Government as subsidy and was released to the concerned bank against individual scheme. There were also other schemes like Urban Basic Services for the Poor (UBSP), Integrated Low Cost Sanitation Scheme (ILCS), *Prime Minister's Rozgar Yojana* (PMRY), Basic Minimum Services (BMS) etc. which were implemented through the municipalities on the basis of annual action plan of the municipality. It may be noted here that the *Nehru Rojgar Yojana* and Prime Minister's Integrated Urban Poverty Eradication schemes have been later clubbed together into a unified programme – *Swarna Jayanti Sahari Rojgar Yojana*. Besides, two other new programmes, namely, National Slum Development Programme and Basic Minimum Services, have also been introduced as Centre-State joint ventures to improve the health, education, environment and infrastructural support exclusively in slum areas. The basic principles of formulating and implementing all these programmes have been developed on the lines followed in respect of other programmes.[67]

The plans prepared by the municipalities were used to be integrated into the district plan. Since funds were released to the municipalities directly through State Urban Development Agency (SUDA), without any information to the district authority in most cases, the role of the District Urban Development Agency (DUDA) in coordinating and monitoring the schemes of municipalities was very insignificant.[68] However, the involvement of the target-people in the preparation and execution of the schemes was ensured by the municipalities.[69] From a review of the district plan outlay (approved) for three successive years, 1992-93, 1993-94 and 1994-95, it appears that the municipal plans constituted 8.87 per cent of the district plan while the percentage of urban population of the district as per 1991 census is around 9.85 per cent. The figure shows apparently a disproportionate trend but this is due to the fact that most of the schemes and projects were implemented by the municipalities themselves, without bringing those under the umbrella of the district plan.[70]

Panchayat Plans

The Zilla Parishad, Panchayat Samitis and the Gram Panchayats execute the projects which are usually formulated by them. The Zilla Parishad publishes each year an Annual Action Plan showing therein the project-schemes to be executed by the Zilla Parishad, Panchayat Samitis and the Gram Panchayats in the district. These action plans contain information regarding the nature and location of the projects, their executing agencies and cost break-ups in terms of cash and kinds, time required for completion and the employment opportunities to be created in terms of mandays. The Zilla Parishad at the district level, Panchayat Samitis at the block level and the Gram Panchayats at the gram panchayat level, apart from executing the projects and schemes under JRY, IRDP and other special development programmes, execute the schemes financed under 'District Plan Schemes Funds' and those financed by their own resources. While the schemes and projects included in the sectoral plans of the government departments are mostly executed through the contractors under the supervision of the implementing agencies, most of the projects under the Panchayati raj bodies are executed by the panchayats (including Zilla Parishads) themselves. Usually the supervision and monitoring of Gram Panchayat projects are done by the Gram Panchayats themselves. But in case of projects entrusted to the Gram Panchayat by the Zilla Parishad or Panchayat Samiti, the roles of the Zilla Parishad or the Panchayat Samiti become important. In all such cases, the Zilla Parishad or the concerned Panchayat Samiti constitutes 'Beneficiary Committee' within the Gram Panchayat normally consisting of the *Gram Pradhan*, Sub-Assistant Engineer of the block, one or two beneficiaries of the project, residing in the locality, the Village Level Worker (VLW) and a member of the Panchayat Samiti or the Zilla Parishad, as the case may be, elected from that locality. Again, the role of the *Gram Pradhan* becomes marginal when the schemes of the Zilla Parishad, Panchayat Samiti or of a government department is executed within the area of a particular Gram Panchayat. The *Pradhan* is usually requested to provide necessary help for the execution of such schemes. The scope and extent of this formal or informal cooperation by the *Gram Pradhan*, however, differs from place to place and from situation to situation. When the leadership of both the entrusting and executing agencies belong to the same political party or group, the area of cooperation and linkages become stronger. Even in cases of political differences between the Gram Panchayat and the higher level Panchayat organizations, execution of projects and schemes takes place through a working relationship between these levels.[71]

The importance of credit planning for the success of the decentralized planning was visualised by the District Planning Committee and accordingly credit planning was incorporated as a part of the District Plan. Though there is no statutory body for organizing and monitoring the flow of credits for development and planning of the district, there is a plan and a sustained attempt on the part of the Zilla Parishad and the District Planning Committee to motivate the banks and other financial institutions located within the district to enhance their targets and ensure regular fund flow. The Zilla Parishad undertakes quarterly review of the credit position of the banks and other agencies with the help of the District Level Co-ordination Committee (DLCC).

In the blocks of the districts, the Block Level Co-ordination Committee (BLCC) coordinates the activities of the banks located within the block and finalises the Block Credit Plan by incorporating and consolidating the annual credit plan of each of the banks. In urban areas, this is done by the municipalities and the banks. For all practical purposes, this job is primarily done by the main branch of the Lead Bank of the locality in consultation with other banks. Similarly, the Block and Municipal Credit Plans are in turn aggregated at the district level to constitute the Annual Credit Plan of the district. This task of integrating and consolidating the Block Credit Plans into the District Credit Plan is supervised by the DLCC constituted under the Lead Bank Scheme.

Rural Development Programmes

Besides the departmental schemes and projects executed in conformity with the district plan, Special Rural Development Programmes of the district constitute a major part of the district plan in which the involvement, volition and autonomy of the District Planning Committee and the Panchayati raj bodies are prominent. Hence, the implementation process of the schemes under the Rural Development Programmes in this district during the last two five-year plans deserves a close scrutiny. It may be noted that the organizational arrangement for both formulation and implementation of plans in this district has been examined exclusively in the previous chapter.

Special Rural Development Programmes like Integrated Rural Development Programme (IRDP), *Jawahar Rozgar Yojana* (JRY), with its sub-schemes including *Indira Aawas Yojana* (IAY), *Million Wells Schemes* (MWS), *Integrated Jawahar Rozgar Yojana* (IJRY), Innovative and Special Employment Schemes (SES-JRY – Third Stream), Schemes for Development of Women and Children in Rural Areas (DWCRA), and Training of Rural Youth for Self-employment (TRYSEM) have been implemented all over the district under the overall planning of the District Planning Committee since the commencement of the Eighth Five-Year Plan. It may be noted that JRY was launched from April 1, 1989 by merging the

National Rural Employment Programme (NREP) and Rural Landless Employment Guarantee Programme (RLEGP). These schemes, excepting DPAP, are target-oriented schemes sponsored by the Central Government for the amelioration of poverty in rural areas with the specific intention of ensuring additional employment opportunities to labourers and artisans and creation of rural assets side by side. The Drought Prone Areas Programme (DPAP) is an area-specific centrally sponsored scheme to restore ecological balance as well as to provide integrated development of the project area. It is a special area programme introduced during the Fourth Plan in seven blocks of Jhargram Subdivision of the district. These schemes are finally approved by the District Planning Committee and are implemented through respective implementing agencies as per guidelines. Funds required for implementation of different schemes under these programmes are shared by the Central and the State Governments at the ratio of 80 : 20.[72]

The three main development programmes — IRDP, JRY and DPAP — constitute a sector called *Special Rural Development Programme* in the district plan. Annual Action Plans are formulated separately in respect of these development programmes, i.e. Action Plan on IRDP and plans on allied schemes by the Zilla Parishad through the District Rural Development Agency (DRDA), Action Plans on JRY (NREP and RLEGP before April 1989) by the Zilla Parishad and Action Plans on DPAP schemes by DPAP agency. In the action plans, review of activities undertaken, target *vis-à-vis* achievement, perspective plans and approach to plans etc. are analysed. As mentioned earlier, DPAP is also an important Centrally Sponsored Scheme included in the category of sectors of district planning. Major thrust in the programme is on activities related to soil conservation, levelling of lands, irrigation, aforestation, pasture and fodder development. Apart from these, there are other schemes like animal husbandry, dairy, fisheries, sericulture which directly contribute to the basic objectives of the programme of prevention of drought in the identified blocks.[73]

Different programmes under DPAP are implemented through the Panchayati raj bodies after the annual action plan is prepared by the DRDA.[74] As regards planning and implementation, the general problem associated with this programme is that major success could not be achieved as there were no clear guidelines for the identification of watershed areas. Though the policy decision to merge watershed development projects with DPAP was taken in 1987, concrete plans could not be formulated by the District Planning Committee in this respect. Recently, the Government has advised the district authorities to appropriate the entire fund of the DPAP for micro watershed development.[75] The District Planning Committee has accordingly initiated steps for integrating watershed projects with the district plan.[76]

Prior to the launching of district plan in Midnapore, the formulation, reviews and monitoring of the schemes of rural development were done on *ad hoc* basis and naturally there were repetitions in identification and execution of these programmes. But since the commencement of the District Annual Plan of 1985-86, linkage and integration have been achieved in these respects through the District Planning Committee.[77]

Integrated Rural Development Programme (IRDP) is a major poverty alleviation programme of rural development in the district. An analysis of the implementation of the schemes under IRDP reveals that there has been steady progress in (a) identification and coverage of target families, (b) financial coverage and (c) per family investments. In 1984-85, the last year of the Sixth Plan, there were only 32,400 families in the district covered under IRDP while in 1985-86, 43,340 families (new) were added to it. Till 1997, 4,19,051 families have been given assistance through IRDP. It may be noted that there are 5,34,748 families in the district who live below the poverty line.[78] Thus more than 76 per cent of the target-families of the district have been included in the programme and a total amount of Rs.194 crore has been spent for this purpose. As the available report during 1994-95 shows, 3836 rural youths were trained up under TRYSEM and 165 groups consisting of 2267 beneficiaries have been formed under DWCRA.[79] These groups are involved in traditional activities like mat-making, pottery, tailoring, piggery etc. and new types of activities like production and manufacturing of *papad*, spice, polythene bag have been added to the traditional ones. More than fifty per cent of the beneficiaries are scheduled castes, tribes and women who have become aware of their role and position in the society as a result of their being economically self-reliant through group activities. IRDP is thus sometimes treated as an approach and a strategy which 'aims at the total development of the area and the people by bringing about necessary institutional and attitudinal changes....'[80] Schemes under IRDP are formulated by the DRDA under the leadership of the *Sabhadhipati* at the district level and are implemented through the panchayats at different levels and as such linkages and coordination in formulation and implementation between the IRDP and other development schemes of the district have been fully ensured through the District Planning Committee. In the initial years of the launching of the programme, certain difficulties were felt in the implementation of the IRDP schemes due to delays in releasing subsidies from the government to the bank concerned. As a result of this delay, release of loan to the identified beneficiaries by the bank took longer period. Moreover, the targets could not be achieved in several cases due to differences between the panchayats and the banks in the identification of beneficiaries. But these initial hurdles were removed later on through active intervention of the Zilla Parishad.[81]

Jawahar Rozgar Yojana (JRY) is the single largest employment generating programme implemented through the district plans of Midnapore. It consisted of JRY First stream, JRY Second stream (Integrated JRY) and JRY— Third stream (Innovative and Special Employment Schemes). Since the scheme was launched in 1989, the last year of Seventh Plan it could not be included in the Draft Eighth Five-Year Plan. However, in the subsequent annual plans of the district it was included as an important programme for the creation of employment and assets by strengthening the rural infrastructure. At present, JRY (consisting of First and Third streams, since Second stream has been discontinued from 1996-97) together with *Indira Aawas Yojana* and Million Wells Scheme is implemented as a sub-sector of the district plan.

Since 1989-90, under JRY 323.59 lakh mandays have been generated. The importance and role of these Rural Development Programmes can be assessed from the simple fact that during 1994-95 alone, an amount of Rs.6483.82 lakh has been spent under JRY, IJRY and EAS programmes and economically productive assets, like rural roads (2410 kms), Link road (280 kms), Social forestry (24000 hectares), Water and soil conservation measuring 12,400 hectares, minor irrigation covering 8070 hectares, primary school buildings (1177 nos.), secondary school buildings (100 nos.), play ground (80 nos.), and rural electrification in 38 villages have been created.[82] A brief financial review of the Eighth Five-Year Plan (1992-97) reveals that during the first four years of the Eighth Plan, an amount of Rs.204,34.33 lakh was spent against the available outlay of Rs.243,12.31 lakh and thus the achievement exceeded 84 per cent of the fund made available to the district.[83] The performance of the district in the implementation of poverty alleviation programmes is highly encouraging. To cite an example, during 1994-95, total mandays generated in the state was 184.79 lakh out of which 36·77 lakh mandays were created in Midnapore alone. During the said period Central Government's contribution under Employment Assurance Scheme was found to be the highest in the district.[84]

The *Jawahar Rozgar Yojana* together with its sub-streams constituted the major component of the Special Rural Development Sector in the district plan. Judged in terms of inter-district performance, the district topped the list in the field of employment generation under JRY in a number of occasions.[85] Out of the approved Plan outlay of Rs.857.66 crore during 1992-93 to 1996-97, the share of Special Rural Development Programmes (SRDP) was around 38 per cent and that of the JRY alone was above 31 per cent. In fact, SRDP was the largest among the twenty-nine sectors identified and incorporated in the District Annual Plans and Eighth Five-Year Plan (1992-97). Again, the share of the JRY among the schemes, in the category of Special Rural Development Programme, was above 82 per cent.[86] Moreover, the District Planning Committee, Zilla Parishad and the panchayats enjoy the highest degree of volition in the execution of these programmes under the overall guidelines of the governments. Hence, a brief review of the process of formulation and implementation of JRY schemes through the district plan is necessary. The administrative arrangement in respect of JRY schemes has been discussed in the last chapter.

Under the general guidelines of the JRY, 80 per cent of the funds allotted to the district was distributed to the 514 Gram Panchayats of the district and the balance 20 per cent was kept for utilization at the district level for inter-block and inter-panchayat works after providing for earmarked sectors. Out of the amount so available to the Zilla Parishad, 5 per cent and 10 per cent respectively were spent towards meeting the administrative costs and the maintenance costs of the social assets created previously under JRY, NREP and RLEGP schemes. During the Eighth Plan, the balance was placed with the District Planning Committee for utilization by it in the following order: 35 per cent for economically productive assets, 25 per cent for social forestry, 15 per cent for schemes benefiting the Scheduled Castes and Scheduled Tribes, and the remaining 25 per cent for other schemes including construction of roads and buildings.[87] Subsequently, the head-wise allocation schedule was changed by the Zilla Parishad under instructions from the Central Government, and the percentage of allocations on social forestry was reduced from 25 per cent to 17.5 per cent and that on schemes benefiting the Scheduled Castes and Tribes was increased to 22.5 per cent from 15 per cent. Thus the Action Plans for *Jawahar Rozgar Yojana* correspond to the District Annual Plan and cover Earmarked Sectors, Zilla Parishad Sectors of General JRY and the Gram Panchayat Sectors.

From an examination of the implementation process, it appears that planning bodies of different levels are involved in the formulation of plans in respect of JRY schemes while the implementation is left to the Panchayati raj organizations in the district. At present the District Planning Committee formulates plan for *Indira Aawas Yojana* and Million Well Schemes, in addition to the schemes covered under the share of the Zilla Parishad in JRY. The Panchayat Samiti formulates priority lists and proposals for the selection of schemes for incorporation in the district plan, conducts technical scrutiny and approves the Gram Panchayat projects. Besides, the Panchayat Samitis implement such projects and schemes as are assigned to them by the Zilla Parishad. There is no sectoral earmarking of the JRY fund at the Gram Panchayat level except that 22.5 per cent is reserved for the schemes benefiting the Scheduled Castes and

Tribes and that all the schemes are executed by the beneficiaries themselves. JRY action plans equivalent to the value of 125 per cent of the funds allocated in the previous year are prepared before the beginning of each financial year by the Zilla Parishad and the Gram Panchayats for their portion of funds respectively. While preparing the annual action plans, completion of incomplete works are given priority over the taking up of new ones. The preparation of plans for JRY schemes at the Gram Panchayat level is discussed thoroughly in the meetings of the Gram Panchayats preceded by discussions at *Gram Sansad* levels. Moreover, sufficient care is taken to safeguard the interests of the weaker sections including the Scheduled Castes, Scheduled Tribes and women of the society at the time of preparation of schemes and projects.[89] It may also be noted that the involvement of the people of the locality has been ensured through the *Gram Sansads* which have acquired statutory recognition by the relevant Acts. For effective formulation and implementation of schemes, the Zilla Parishad has introduced 'Scheme Bank' for efficient and need-based selection of technically sound and viable irrigation projects under Million Wells Scheme of the JRY from 1993-94 on the suggestion of the State Government.[90]

From the above analysis, it is established that the implementation of Centrally Sponsored Schemes as a sector under the district plan is a total success. During the last twelve years starting from 1985-86, this sector has ensured an overall achievement of 86.71 per cent of the approved outlay of the district plan. From another point of view, the implementation of these schemes through the district plan by involving the panchayats and the people has devolved administrative experience and responsibilities to the democratically elected representatives. Side by side, it has also promoted a cooperative and interacting relationship between the bureaucrats and the political functionaries, which is perhaps the most valuable asset created in a democratic set-up. It may be noted that in other states, excepting only a few, these programmes are implemented by the bureaucracy through the DRDA which is headed by the District Magistrate.[91] But in West Bengal and especially in this district the DRDA acts as the development agency of the elected

Zilla Parishad. This delegation of authority to the panchayats through planning and implementation of these and other similar types of programmes has encouraged a parallel decentralization in activities of the political parties and other organizations.[92]

VILLAGE PLANNING BY VILLAGERS

The study of decentralized district planning in Midnapore will remain incomplete unless the experiment of 'Village Planning by Villagers' in the district is examined in brief. The Planning by villagers is an integral part of the district and it was introduced for the first time in May 1985, through the formation of two village committees at the first instance. The main reason behind such an experiment was to conduct action-research to identify the methodology of village based plan implementation process.[93] Another aspect that shaped the minds of leadership was that the deprived groups might find their salvation only as an integral part of the salvation of other deprived groups and of the society as a whole. Otherwise these groups could be induced by interested groups to fight each other. Thus viewed, it was necessary for a deprived group not only to understand its own condition but also the conditions of other deprived groups so that they may be united to fight poverty in an organized manner.[94]

Since there was no organization for planning and development below the Gram Panchayat, two 'Village Level Committees' were set-up by the District Planning Committee, one in Daharpur under Makrampur Gram Panchayat in Narayangarh Block and another for a cluster of villages - Garrow, Balad-duba and Jualbhanga in Garh-Salboni Gram Panchayat under Jhargram Block.[95] The Village Level Committees (VLC) created by the DPC consisted of nine members including the *Sabhapati* of the concerned Panchayat Samiti, the respective member of the Zilla Parishad and the Gram Panchayat representing that village and the *Pradhan* of the Gram Panchayat concerned, all as ex-officio members. In addition to these ex-officio members, three to four persons who participated in planning or in collecting village data, were included in the said committee. One of the members of the 'Village Level Committee' was designated as convenor of the committee.[96]

Within the broad framework of block planning, the annual plans of the concerned villages were prepared after organized and detailed discussions with the adult inhabitants of the village at village meetings. Such meetings were attended mostly by the people of the poorer sections, the small and marginal farmers, agricultural labourers and village artisans. Special schemes were undertaken for the women in consultation with them.[97] Annual Plans were divided into four quarterly plans for effective implementation. Following the methodology of the village based district planning, the village level committees formulated plans for their respective villages and classified the schemes and proposals into three categories.

The classification of village development schemes into three categories reflect the maturity in understanding the problems in the light of resource planning for comprehensive development. The schemes involving the labour and initiative of the villagers were included in the *first category* which could be implemented by the villagers themselves. Capital based and labour intensive schemes were included in the *second category* for implementation by individuals and groups with financial support from banks and cooperatives. The *third category* of schemes related to water transmission arrangements through River Lift Irrigation (RLI), Shallow Tubewells, Shallow tubewells with submersible pumpsets, surface flow and drainage schemes, Health, Family Welfare and Nutrition programmes. The proposals under the *third category* were expected to be implemented only under financial and technical assistance from the government under different State and Centrally Sponsored Schemes. Apart from these three, a *fourth category* was also contemplated later as a joint venture of the villagers, panchayats, government and banks. The schemes and proposals coming under this head were expected to be implemented with contributions of labour from the villagers and resources from these agencies. Distribution of agricultural inputs like *minikits;* excavation and improvement of tanks; establishment of agro-service centres, bio-gas plants; and construction of houses, pisciculture and social forestry schemes and the like were categorised under this joint venture.[98] The classification and grouping of the schemes and projects into four distinct categories and the provision of direct contribution of the villagers started the process of reducing their dependency on the government and panchayats for the development of their locality.

Of the sectors mentioned above, the sectors included in the first two categories deserve special mention since active and direct contributions of the people were required for the implementation of the schemes and projects included in these sectors. The following ten primary tasks were identified and included in the *first category* which could be implemented by the people themselves:[99]

(a) Conservation of at least one pond or a water source for exclusive use for the purpose of drinking;
(b) Construction and maintenance of public convenience and pit latrines;
(c) Construction of compost pits for each household;
(d) Construction of community warehouse to protect small and marginal farmers from distress sale of their paddy;
(e) Repairing and maintenance of village-roads, small embankments, small gaps and culverts;
(f) Popularization and practice of the norms of health and hygiene, particularly the care of the child and the mother;
(g) Eradication of illiteracy by organizing and motivating the youths of the locality,
(h) Protection of cottage and village industries through the campaigning for the use of indigenous goods and products and discouragement of the use of foreign goods;
(i) Holding of regular village meetings for collection of information, discussions and formulation of plans for the village; and, above all,
(j) Building up of active and self-reliant organizations of women, deprived and working people.

In the *second category*, some tasks were identified, which might be undertaken by the villagers with assistance from banks and other financial institutions. The concept of Bank Sector was a product of the provisions for borrowing funds from banks or cooperatives as seed capital for the implementation of the schemes and repayment of the same with interests in due course. The major items included in this sector were of general nature and required to be worked out in details in conformity with the credit policy of the banks *vis-à-vis* the viability of the projects. The following items formed the core of this sector:

(a) Improvements in agriculture;
(b) Provisions for irrigation facilities;
(c) Organization of cooperative warehouse or *grain-gola* in each Gram Panchayat;
(d) Establishment of cottage and small industries;
(e) Organization of pisciculture; and
(f) Establishment of small trades and business etc.

The District Planning Committee sanctioned Rupees one lakh to each of the two Village Level Committees (VLC) as government fund for the implementation of their plans and the amount was placed at the disposal of the Executive Officer (EO) of the respective Panchayat Samiti. The Executive Officer was advised to release funds to the Village Level Committee on submission of requirements and the VLC used to submit utilisation certificate of the last allotment to the Extension Officer (Block) at the time of placing further requirements. After a few months, it was experienced that this procedure of fund-flow to the VLC caused delay in the implementation of schemes and projects and hence an alternative method was devised. According to the revised method, the District Planning Committee decided to allow the VLC to open accounts at the nearest branch of any nationalized bank to be operated jointly by any two of the *Gram Pradhan*, the President and the Convenor of the Village Level Committee. This simplified procedure of operating village plan funds accelerated the process of implementation.[100] At the same time, a modified system of account keeping was also developed. The VLC maintained the Cash Book, Scheme Allotment Register and Cheque Register and placed details of receipts and payments in the periodical meetings of the villagers. The permissible limit of cash in hand was fixed at Rs.200 only and the VLC was required to submit accounts to the District Planning Officer every month.[101]

The functioning of these two village committees received appreciation from all quarters. The District Planning Committee was inspired and emboldened by the success of these committees and decided to carry out the experiments in five more villages in the following year. Accordingly, five village level committees were constituted at the villages in five blocks, (a) Rajnagar in Dantan-I, (b) Bhangadali in Salboni, (c) Nimki Mohar in Sabang, (d) Aurai-Beliachatta in Contai-II and (e) Baligeria in Nayagram. This time, due to paucity of funds, each VLC was sanctioned Rupees fifty thousand as Plan Fund by the District Planning Committee. The Village Level Committees, by merging government's contribution with the contribution of the villagers together, were able to transform 19 acres of fallow land into cultivable one by levelling the same; re-excavation of three ponds, construction of 1.5 km long village road; construction of a school building, a club house, 12 compost pits, 5 dug-wells and 31 pit-latrines; extension of irrigation facilities to fifty bighas of land by constructing a small *bundh* on a drain beside the *pucca* road at Daharpur.[102] Similarly, an irrigation canal was excavated at Jualbhanga to facilitate the flow of water from Kangshabati Canal which resulted in an additional yield of 20 tones of paddy a year. The total cost involved in this project included voluntary contribution of 200 mandays by the villagers. Apart from these achievements, the Jualbhanga Village Level Committee was able to organize coaching classes for poor students and its counterpart at Daharpur provided a pair of laying birds for each of the helpless poor widows of the village at a subsidised rate of Rs.25 per pair.[103]

The achievements in the sphere of creation and maintenance of permanent assets and in respect of accomplishing the immediate tasks were not negligible. Performance of the village level committees in terms of achievements and raising the level of consciousness of the villagers strengthened the concept of alternative model of decentralized planning. A close look into the stages of formulation and implementation of these village plans by the villagers leads us to a few conclusions. The planning by villagers developed a sense of participation in the poorer sections of the community including the women. The female inhabitants of Daharpur village through mutual discussions with the Village Level Committee pointed out three problems faced by them regularly. The problems identified by them were related to drinking water, public conveniences and nutrition and they submitted their proposals for solutions. On being motivated by the women, the villagers came forward and shielded the surroundings of fifteen dug wells with bricks and concrete, incurring an expenditure of Rs.250 per well against an estimated cost of Rs.750 to Rs.1000 as per schedule of the government, to prevent the inflow of polluted water in the monsoons. Similarly, pit-latrines were constructed by the villagers themselves involving a total cost of Rs.200 only per latrine out of which Rs.75 was borne by the benefited family by providing own labour.[104] However, the major achievement of the villagers cannot be understood without going through the non-material achievements that the VLCs were able to attain.

The experience of village planning carried out by the Village Level Committee in Village Aunrai-Beliachatta under Contai-II Panchayat Samiti also confirm the success of village-based district planning in Midnapore. The programme of 'village plan by villagers' was undertaken at the village Aunrai-Beliachatta in the second year of the Seventh Five-Year Plan (1986-87). In the initial year of planning in this village, the Village Level Committee allotted rupees six thousand to enable ten efficient *bidi* workers to organize a small *bidi* manufacturing industry. The workers gave a brand name to their product and developed their own marketing schemes. This helped the workers to increase their weekly income from the previous level of Rs.63 per head per week to Rs.83 registering an increase of Rs.20 per worker. In this village, it became also possible in a year to initiate organized action for substituting private money lending system, involving a high rate of interest, obligation and dependence on the part of the poor, by introducing loans from banks with relatively low rate of interest.[105]

From the above accounts, it is established that the programme of 'Village based district planning' was intended to be an organized movement of the people to completely transform the elitist planning and plan implementation process by people's planning process or the village-based district planning process as officially adopted by the District Planning Committee of

Midnapore. There were both successes and constraints in village planning. Constraints were again both structural and technical. Whatever may be the achievements and failure in terms of quantification, the experiment of 'Planning by villagers' in Midnapore provides the clue for answering the question: who are to be the immediate beneficiaries of planning?[106]

Notes and References

1. Proceedings of the *District Level Seminar on Alternative Strategy of Planning*, organized by the Zilla Parishad, Midnapore, at Zilla Parishad, Midnapore, dated 19-6-1987.
2. Misra, R.P. 1991, 'On the Task of District Planning' in B.N. Yugandhar and Amitava Mukherjee (eds.), *Readings in Decentralized Planning*, New Delhi: Concept Publishing Company, Vol. I, pp.10-11.
3. *Discussions with Mr. M.N. Goray*, Formerly member of the DPC and ex-*Sabhapati* of Dantan I Panchayat Samiti on different dates.
4. District Planning Committee, *Memo No. 460(19)/Development and Planning Cell*, dated 9-4-1987 and *No. 934(50)/Dev. and Planning Cell*, dated 21-7-1987.
5. *Sabhadhipati, Zilla Parishad, Proceedings of the Seminar, op.cit.*
6. *Gram Bhittik Block Parikalpanar Paddhati-O-Prayoger Ruparekha*, 1989 (in Bengali), District Planning Committee, Midnapore, p.3.
7. *Note:* Now it is designated as *Gram Sansad* vide the *West Bengal Panchayat (Amendment) Act, 1994*.
8. Inserted by the *West Bengal Panchayat Amendment Act*, 1984.
9. *Interview with Mr. H.K. Samanta*, Chairman, DPC, dated 4-8-1998.
10. Dasgupta, Sailen. 1983, *Gram Panchayat Parichalanar Nirdeshika* (in Bengali), Left Front, Calcutta, pp.3-5.
11. Gent, John Echeverri. 1993, *The State and the Poor: Public Policy and Political Development in India and the United States*, Berkeley: California University Press, p.148.
12. *Note:* This was stated by the *Karmadhyaksha, Krishi, Sech-O-Samabay Sthayee Samiti* of the Zilla Parishad, Midnapore and a member of the First DPC in his report at the *Seminar, op.cit.* (19-6-1987).
13. Sarkar, D. and Ghosh, B.D. 1999, 'Outlines of the Proposed Model for Participatory Planning'. *Seminar on* 'People's Participation in Development', Kolkata, 15-16 December.
14. Report of the *Working Group on District Planning*, 1984, Government of India, New Delhi, Vol. I. pp.52-53, par(s).6.16 & 6.18 and *Database on Village Level Indicators*, 1987, Planning Commission, New Delhi.
15. Report of the *Working Group, ibid.*, p.53, par.6.21.
16. *Interview with Mr. A. Mandal*, District Planning Officer, dated 19-8-1997.
17. *Gram Sambandhiya Tathyabali*, 1981 (in Bengali), Department of Panchayat and Community Development, Government of West Bengal.
18. *Records of the District Planning Committee*, Midnapore.

19. *Parikalpana Paddhati, Samaysuchi abong Talika Puraner Niyamabali,* 1985 (in Bengali), Zilla Parishad, Midnapore.
20. *Mr. H.K. Samanta,* Formerly Chairman, DPC at the State-Level *Seminar on Decentralization: Devolution and Participation* organized by the State Planning Board, West Bengal, at Calcutta, dated 20-22 November, 1998.
21. *Proceedings of the meeting of the DPC,* dated 19-9-1996.
22. District Planning Committee, *Memo No. 903(75)/Development and Planning Cell,* dated 2-8-1986.
23. *Ibid., No. 934(50)/Development and Planning Cell,* dated 21-7-1987.
24. *Ibid., No. 460(19)/ Development and Planning Cell,* dated 9-4-1987.
25. Quoted in the Report of the *Working Group on District Planning, op.cit.,* p.93, par.10.4.
26. *Proceedings of the Meeting of the Instructors for Village Level Planning Cadres,* District Planning Committee, dated 2-7-1987.
27. Recommendations of the *Expert Group on District Planning* at L.B.S. Academy on 11-13 June, 1990, Quoted in Yugandhar and Mukherjee, 1991, *op.cit.,* p.455.
28. *Records of the District Planning Committee.*
29. *Ibid.* Also corroborated by *Mr. N. Chatterjee,* District Planning Officer, dated 21-5-1995.
30. *Proceedings of the meeting of the Instructors,* DPC, Midnapore, *op.cit.*
31. District Planning Committee, *Memo No.903(75)/Development and Planning Cell, op.cit.*
32. District Planning Committee, *Memo No. 913(50)/Development and Planning Cell,* dated 17-7-1997.
33. *Interview with Mr. H.K. Samanta, op. cit.,* dated 19-8-1997.
34. *Gram Bhittik Block Parikalpanar Paddhati-O-Prayoger Ruparekha,* 1989 (in Bengali) *op.cit.,* p.3.
35. *Interview with Mr. H.K. Samanta, op.cit.*
36. *No. 183(18) PA/JS(DG)/P & RD* dated 1-11-1999 and Sarker, D. and Ghosh, B.D. 1999, 'Outlines of the Proposed Model for Participatory Planning' *op.cit.*
37. Datt, R. and Sundharam, K.P.M. 1995, *Indian Economy,* New Delhi: S. Chand, p.260.
38. *District Eighth Five-Year Plan,* 1992-97.
39. *District Annual Plan,* 1993-94, *Preface.*
40. *Kayekti Agradhikar Kshetra, Bikendribhuta Parikalpana-O-Medinipur Zella* (booklet in Bengali). April 1994.
41. *Ibid.*
42. *Proceedings of the meeting of the DPCC,* dated 20-7-1992.
43. *District Annual Plan* – 1993-94, 'Economic Review'.
44. *Ibid.*
45. *District Annual Plan* – 1996-97.
46. *Interview with Mr.* H.K. Samanta, *op.cit.*
47. Report of the *Working Group on District Planning, op.cit.,* p.21, par.3.4.
48. *Tenth Five-Year Plan,* West Bengal (2002 – 2007), Department of Development and Planning. Kolkata, Vol. I, p. (xi).
49. *Records of the Planning Cell,* District Planning Committee, Midnapore.
50. *Ibid.,* p.58, par. 6.58.

51. Government of West Bengal, *No. 2720(45)/DP/15-21/86, Department of Development and Planning* dated 19-4-1986.
52. *Proceedings of the meetings of the DPCC* dated 17-8-1991 & 21-7-1992 and *No.713(54)/1/6/ Development and Planning*, dated 2-6-1986.
53. *JRY, District Annual Action Plan* - 1996-97.
54. *JRY, District Annual Plan* – 1989-90.
55. *Proceedings of the meetings of the DPCC*, dated 17-8-1991 & 21-8-1992.
56. *Statement of the Chairman, DPC* published in the *Ananda Bazar Patrika*, dated 1-8-1997, subsequently corroborated by him, *op. cit.*, dated 19-8-1997.
57. *Jawahar Rozgar Yojana – Manual*, 1994, Government of India, New Delhi, par.15.
58. *Proceedings of the meeting of the DPCC* dated 24-3-1990.
59. *Records of the DPC.*
60. *A Prelude to the Ninth Plan*, 1997, District Planning Committee, Midnapore, p.7.
61. *Proceedings of the meeting of the DPCC*, dated 17-8-1991.
62. *Ibid.*, dated 21-7-1992.
63. *Proceedings of the meetings of the Working Group of the DPC*, Midnapore, dated 15-7-1987 (re: Agriculture), and 24-8-1987 (re: Roads, PWD Sector); *Proceedings of the meeting of the Sub-Committees* of the DPC, dated 10-3-1997.
64. *Interview with Mr. H.K. Samanta, op.cit.* and *Mr. A. Mandal, op.cit.*
65. *Interview with Mr. A. Mandal, op.cit.*
66. Government of West Bengal, *No.5186/DP/1S-12/89*, dated 22-11-1990, Department of Development and Planning; and *No. 2114(16)/DP/1S /91*, dated 21-6-1991.
67. *Interview with Mr. H.K. Samanta* dated 4-8-1998.
68. *Proceedings of the Annual General Meeting of the District Urban Development Agency* (DUDA), Midnapore, dated 11-7-1996.
69. *Interview with Mr. Bijali Ghosh*, Project Officer, DUDA, Midnapore, dated 19-8-1997.
70. *Interview with Mr. A. Mandal, op.cit.*, dated 21-8-1997.
71. Lieten, G.K. 1996, Development Devolution and Democracy, New Delhi: Sage Publications, p.224.
    Interview with Mr. H.K. Samanta, dated 19-8-1997, and *Mr. A. Mandal, op.cit.*
72. *Jawahar Rozgar Yojana – Manual*, 1994, *op.cit.*
73. *District Annual Plan* – 1997-98, *op.cit.*
74. *District Annual Plan* – 1996-97, *op.cit.*
75. Government of West Bengal, *No. 942/PA/JS/RD*, dated 17-9-1997, Department of Panchayat and Rural Development.
76. Proceedings of the *Seminar on Land Use Planning* organized by Development and Planning Department, Midnapore, dated 21-7-1997.
77. *District Eighth Five-Year Plan* – 1992-97.
78. *Records of the DPC*, Development and Planning Cell, Midnapore.
79. *District Annual Plan* – 1996-97, *op.cit.*
80. Khanna, S.K. and Malhotra, S.L. 1977, *Integrated Rural Development*, New Delhi: Abhinav, pp.16-17.

81. Discussions with *Mr. M.N. Goray, op.cit.* and *Mr. S. Majumdar*, a member of the District Planning Committee, Midnapore on different dates.
82. *District Annual Plan* – 1996-97. Chapter on 'A brief Review', *op.cit.*
83. *A Prelude to the Ninth Plan, op.cit.*, pp.8-9.
84. *Report of the Department of Rural Development* – 1993-94.
    Chatterjee, Biswanath. 1998, 'Poverty, Role of State and Participatory Development in West Bengal: A Critical Review', *paper presented at the State Level Seminar on 'Decentralization: Devolution and Participation', op.cit.*
85. Chatterjee, 1998, *op.cit.*
86. *A Prelude to the Ninth Plan, op.cit.*, p.7.
87. *Jawahar Rozgar Yojana Project Guidelines,* 1989, Midnapore Zilla Parishad, p.5.
88. Government of India, *No. V-11011/7/90-RE-1,* dated 17-11-1992.
89. *Interview with Mr. D.C. Das,* Project Officer, DRDA, Midnapore, dated 1-9-1998.
90. Government of West Bengal, *NO.5717(16)/RD,* dated 1-9-1992, Department of Panchayat and Rural Development.
91. Maheswari, S.R. 1985, *Rural Development in India,* New Delhi: Sage Publications, Second edition, p.137.
92. Gent, John Echiverri, 1993, *op.cit.*, pp.151-52.
    Webster, Neil. 1992, *Panchayati Raj in the Decentralization of Development Planning in West Bengal*, Calcutta: K. P. Bagchi & Co., p.115.
93. Mishra, S.K. and Bose, A.N. 1987, *Village Planning by the Villagers,* Zilla Parishad, Midnapore, '*Preface*'.
94. *The Rural People of Midnapore District* – 1986, Zilla Parishad, Midnapore and Rural Development Centre, I.I.T., Kharagpur, pp.15-17.
95. *Grambasider Tairi Gram Parikalpana,* 1985, DPC and *records of the DPC,* 1987.
96. *Records of the Zilla Parishad,* Midnapore.
97. *Records of the DPC, 1987.*
98. *Ibid.*
99. *Gram Bhittik Zella Parikalpanar Paddhatigata Ruparekha, 1989, op.cit.*
100. *Records of the DPC,* 1987.
101. *Ibid.*
102. Maiti, R.K. 1987, District Planning Officer '*Gram Bhittik Zella Parikalpana Tairir Andolane Gramstar Committeeguli theke Abhijnata,* (in Bengali), unpublished report available with the DPC, Midnapore.
103. *Records of the DPC.* Corroborated by *Mr. H.P. Jana* of Daharpur Village. *Notes:* Mr. Jana was one of the main organizers of Daharpur Village Planning and an active worker of the District Planning Committee.
104. *Maiti, op.cit.*
105. *Records of the DPC, Report on Village Planning at Aunrai-Beliachatta,* DPC, Midnapore.
106. *Vice-Chairman, State Planning Board,* West Bengal. D.O. Letter to *Sabhadhipati*(s) dated 12-3-1985.

7

ISSUES, CONSTRAINTS AND CHOICES

Planning is generally viewed as the effective utilisation of the potential resources available to the society and, in this sense, it is guided by the aim of working out a rational solution to different problems. This does not mean that planning involves the mere aggregation of Central and State Government projects. "Planning is a direction",[1] and the direction in decentralized district planning is more direct and less ambiguous. Professor V.K.R.V. Rao made some observations three decades ago, which are relevant still today:

> "The whole *raison d'etre* of district planning rests not only on technical grounds but also on the involvement and participation of the people of the district. What is meant by grassroots planning is that it is not only technically more efficient but also operationally more efficient because the psychology it creates of a movement for development and social and economic change because of popular participation."[2]

Thus decentralized planning creates an atmosphere in which the ideas and ideals of democratic governance are translated into actions within the limited sphere. The Working Group on District Planning appointed by the Planning Commission elaborates the objectives of district planning in the same direction. It observes that district planning enables "a better perception of the needs of the local areas, makes better informed decision-making possible, gives people a better voice in decisions concerning their development and welfare, serves to achieve better coordination and integration among programmes, enables felt needs of the people to be taken into account, ensures effective participation of the people, serves to build up a measure of self-reliance by mobilizing resources of the community in kind or money, making development self-sustaining and enables better exploitation of local resources and growth potentials of local area for improving productivity and increasing production."[3]

ISSUES AND CONSTRAINTS

Decentralized planning in the context of rapid globalization is difficult to be actualised. Lack of autonomy at the lower levels, absence of strong political will and commitments, bias towards centralization, inadequate scope for people's participation, apathy of the political elite and indifferent attitude of the bureaucracy appear to be the general constraints in making the decentralized planning experiment a success story. Given this background, the decentralized planning raises some major issues together with certain constraints which deserve serious consideration in general and in the concrete situation in the district.

People's Participation

The first and the most vital issue involved in the context of decentralized planning here is the question of people's participation. People's participation is both a means and an end. It is a means to attain greater control and authority over the environment to improve the conditions of living. It is an end in the sense that it tries to create an atmosphere which may nourish the dignity and psychological satisfaction of having a say in creating and maintaining the environment of decision-making.

The concept of popular participation may be viewed from three analytically separate but inter-connected elements: participation in decision making, participation in implementation of the schemes and projects and participation in the benefits awarded. Thus the concept implies that if people have the opportunity to be involved in implementing the decisions they have arrived at, with a reasonable hope of deriving a just share of benefits, then this form of participation helps in building up both the institution and the individual.[4] It is now established that failure to engage all the available human resources in the process of development planning may act as a brake on economic growth and helps little to solve the problems of social and political instability. Existence of institutions is the necessary prerequisite for effective popular participation. Mere pronouncement, without creating necessary and viable infrastructure for participation, is meaningless.

In the context of planning, public participation means the participation of citizens in the decision-making process in the various stages of planning: (i) formulation of plans, programmes and projects, (ii) their implementation, and (iii) evaluation of attainment of the goals of the programmes. Decentralized planning in the true sense of the term envisages the percolation of decision-making authority in the formulation and implementation of plans to the lower levels, to the people and their representatives, the panchayats. For transferring the authority of decision-making, the government and the political executives would have to create a local level planning capability.

The urge for ensuring people's participation in planning and development has been felt since the days of the Community Development Programme, which called upon to organize villagers' efforts in development schemes and projects initiated by the bureaucracy. But the Programme failed due to a lack of popular participation, over-bureaucratization and imposition from the above. The local context was virtually absent and there was no organized attempt to motivate local people for their involvement in planning, implementation and monitoring of the development programmes.[5] The active participation of the people especially of those for whom the benefits of the plan were intended to be addressed is the most vital condition for the success of any scheme or project.[6]

The need for people's participation in planning is nowhere better stated than in India's five-year plans. It was gradually realised by the Planning Commission that "this aim cannot be fulfilled unless, as was pointed out in the First Five-Year Plan, there is an agency in the village which represents the community as a whole and can assume responsibility and initiative for developing the resources of the village and providing the necessary leadership."[7] The Panchayati Raj Institutions provided an elaborate mechanism for people's involvement in planning but this mechanism for people's participation has been the subject of considerable erosion and gradual disintegration over the years.[8]

In early 1950s, the States were advised to prepare District and Village Plans and to provide an institutional base for people's active participation in development planning and a number of committees were set up by the Government of India to study the issues connected with grassroots-level planning and implementation. The establishment of the Working Group on Block Level Planning, the Asoka Mehta Committee on Panchayati Raj Institutions and the Planning Commission's Working Group on District Planning marked the beginning of an era towards real decentralization. These groups analysed the issue from different perspectives and context and recommended appropriate organizational designs for planning and plan implementation.[9]

The Working Group on District Planning viewed development planning 'as a three-way model' and identified 'the schemes, the machinery and the people' as the three components of district planning.[10] It observed that for the successful implementation of this model, "the schemes must be well-conceived, the machinery must be adequate in quality and quantity and the people must be alive to their rights and obligations. Public participation in planning is an area where the divergence between theory and practice, rhetoric and reality has been the most striking as revealed from a critical study of our plans at the various levels."[11] The Working Group, therefore, recommended (i) adequate representation of people, social groups and voluntary agencies in the district planning bodies; (ii) involvement of local leaders, teachers, students and local people in the planning stage including collection of data and conduct of survey; (iii) assessment of needs and priorities, identification of beneficiaries and the adoption of strategies and schemes through interactions with people in village sittings and open forums; (iv) participation of the people in the implementation of plan and projects through ensuring individual and social contributions, assisting administration and enlisting themselves in programmes for possible benefits; (v) involvement of people in monitoring and evaluation of projects and (vi) the association of universities and other academic institutions in the various tasks of plan formulation.[12]

The recommendations of the Working Group are wider and represent a catalogue to ensure effective participation of the people in the diversified activities of district planning. But the scope of direct participation of people is very much limited and cannot go beyond a certain stage while the scope of involvement through representatives is relatively greater. The Working Group on Block Level Planning, though it emphasised the necessity and importance of public participation at all the stages of planning, adopted a very cautious approach to the issue mainly due to the heterogeneous character of the rural population and their inadequate understanding of problems and technical constraints.[13] It is well established that "people can make a contribution to the planning process only if they are presented with a well articulated and feasible framework of approaches, objectives, measures and alternatives. If, however, they are asked to indicate their needs in a vacuum, they are bound to put up a charter of demands, which will be far beyond the capacities of the Government. The correct stage to consult the people and their representative organization is, therefore, after an analysis of relevant information has been undertaken and a broad framework is drawn up and not at the starting point of the planning process."[14]

Indirect Participation

Under the existing infrastructure of decentralized planning the scope for people's participation is ensured in two ways: *direct participation* of the people at the lower levels, especially at the *Gram Sansads* and *Ward Committees* and *indirect participation* through their representatives elected in the panchayat bodies and the municipalities. The scope of indirect participation is wider because the Panchayati raj bodies and urban bodies, like the Nagar Panchayats, Municipal Councils and Municipal Corporations, are now established and these bodies have been entrusted with the functions of planning and development by the various

State Acts. All these acts attempt to elevate the panchayats and the municipalities as institutions of self-government. The 74th Amendment Act accords constitutional status to the District Planning Committee and calls upon every state to constitute the DPC at the district level for consolidating 'the plans prepared by the panchayats and municipalities in the district and to prepare a draft development plan for the district as a whole'.[15] Similarly, the Metropolitan Planning Committee is proposed for discharging the same functions in the metropolitan areas (Article 243ZE).

Thus participation of people 'at every stage of planning including pre-planning, strategy setting, scheme formulation, monitoring and review, not merely at the time of plan finalisation'[16] through their representatives, has been constitutionalized and operationalised by the Panchayat Acts and the District Planning Committee Act of the States including West Bengal. The role of Panchayati raj bodies in decentralized planning in West Bengal has been examined at length while discussing implementation and planning machinery in the district. Through a number of amendments to the West Bengal Panchayat Act, 1973, the scope and mechanism of involvement of Panchayati Raj Institutions in the planning process have been strengthened. The panchayats at all the three tiers have been crowned with the powers and duties of preparation of development plans and annual plans for their respective areas.[17] Again, the members of the Zilla Parishad, the apex tier in the panchayati system, and the municipalities are represented in the District Planning Committee by way of election and nomination. Thus the scope of people's participation in planning through representatives exists at all the levels. The DPC acts as the final planning body at the district level to 'consolidate the plans prepared by the panchayats and the municipalities ...... and prepare a draft development plan for the district as a whole'.[18] Hence, a question may be raised relating to the *locus standi* of the Draft Development Plan of the district *vis-à-vis* the plans prepared by the panchayats and the municipalities. The stipulations of the Constitution included in Article 243ZD may help to find out clues for solution of the possible contradiction but it does not rule out the possibilities of confusion.

Direct Participation

Apart from the institutional mechanism of indirect people's participation, the scope for direct involvement in planning has been created and subsequently institutionalised through an amendment to the West Bengal Panchayat Act. It is to be noted here that the scope of direct participation of some selected people of the locality in the formulation of plans still exists in Midnapore at the Gram Panchayat and Panchayat Samiti levels in a limited way.[19] It is interesting that the concept of public accountability and involvement in the Panchayati raj system through the institution of *Gram Sabha* (changed to *Gram Sansad*) was introduced in West Bengal even before the 73rd Amendment Act could deal with the question.[20] Similarly, the provisions for 'Ward Committees' in the urban areas have been incorporated in the Municipal Act. Though the constitution of Ward Committee in larger municipalities having a population of three lakhs or above is obligatory, and, in other cases, optional under the Act,[21] now it has been the general practice in West Bengal to have Ward Committees in all the municipalities and corporations.[22] Both the *Gram Sansads* and the Ward Committees are composed of the citizens of the respective areas, and they are empowered under the relevant acts to identify proposals and beneficiaries and determine schemes for development of the area. In Midnapore, there has been a conscious and deliberate attempt on the part of the Zilla Parishad and the DPC to activate the *Gram Sansads* as the primary units of planning. From a current report on the involvement of *Gram Sansads*, it is found that out of 5069 *Gram Sansads* (as in 1997), meeting could be organized only in 4473 till the end of May, 1997.[23] The activities and role of the Ward Committee, though formed in all the municipalities, are insignificant and, in most cases, they seldom meet to discuss the annual reports, schemes and proposals for inclusion in the municipal plans. Thus the scope of direct participation of citizens in the urban areas of the district is not effective.[24]

The situation is different in the panchayat areas of the district. The literacy movement in the district found a solid base in rural areas. A study conducted in 1994 and 1995 concluded that the progress of literacy campaign was satisfactory in the rural areas while it was much below the expectation in the urban areas.[25] Naturally, the *Iswar Chandra Jana Chetana Kendras* established in the Post-Literacy (PLC) period at different *Gram Sansads* of the district are more effective than their urban counterparts. The lowest level of direct people's participation is the *Kendra* which is also considered as the lowest steps in district planning hierarchy.

The institutional mechanism for interactions between the panchayats and the villagers and among the villagers themselves was already in existence in the district even prior to the amendments in the State Panchayat Act. The practice of organizing village meetings periodically to review the progress of works, to select work-sites, to determine priorities and to prepare lists of beneficiaries was introduced in the blocks of the district after the devastating floods in 1978[26] under the leadership of the *Krishak Sabha.* But the strategy of involving the people was met with partial success because of the fluid political situation then prevalent in the state and the involvement of the CPI(M), the dominant partner of the State Government, in 'highly conflictual politics of land distribution, registration of share-croppers, the granting of ownership rights of homestead land to the occupants …..'[27]

After the Panchayat election of 1983, the situation was different and a shift 'towards the reformist politics of development management, the resolution of village conflicts, the management of village affairs' was noticeable[28] and the Left Front of West Bengal worked out a detailed guideline for the management of rural affairs through people's involvement.[29] Naturally, the 'Village Committees' formed at the villages paid dividends and paved the way for organized participation of the village people in decentralized planning in subsequent years, though there were serious gaps and limitations in understanding the philosophy of decentralized planning.[30] The institution of Village Committees and subsequently the *Gram Sansads* has made decision-making more accessible to the public at large. But the effectiveness of this institution depends upon a variety of conditions: it requires to be an active body, meeting regularly, discussing common issues and deciding the question of plan and development. On the question of regularity in holding meetings and the percentage of attendance, the experience of the district suggests that these two conditions are difficult to be attained. Even after the practice of functioning in a coordinated way for a considerable period of time, these bodies have not been working effectively and the meetings have either been irregular or marked with absence of the majority of the village people. The all-India picture is more disheartening in this respect.[31] There was a report from Himachal Pradesh where the directions from the government followed by camping by high profiles even failed to ensure people's participation in Gram Sabha meetings. The meetings were fixed for 1 July, 2001 but could not be held in around 90 per cent of the panchayats in the district of *Mandi in Himachal Pradesh* for want of quorum. Gram Sabha meetings could only be held in 45 gram panchayats out of 422 in the district.[32] The report from Madhya Pradesh is more frustrating. Failing to hold the meeting of the *Pathari Gram Sabha* after convening the same twelve times, special efforts were made to hold it again on 19 December, 2001 but the requirement of quorum could not be met. All arrangements including an appeal from the Chief Executive Officer of Vidisha Zilla Parishad could move only seven persons including the *Sarpanch*, Gram Sabha-in-Charge and *Gram Sewak* to turn up at the venue of the meeting which was postponed for the thirteenth time.[33]

A report on the situation in this district brings out the point that the meetings of the *Gram Sansads* are not held regularly and not even the statutory requirements of the State Panchayat Act are satisfied.[34] There are other problems as well. In some cases, majority of the villagers attending the meetings come from a few extended families or close-knit social groups. Moreover, the meetings are most often overwhelmingly dominated by the male population of the locality and as such the participation of women appears to be negligible. Even sometimes those who attend the meetings belong to the dominant party or group of parties of the village and those who do not belong to that party or group usually prefer to keep themselves away from such meetings or to remain as passive observers. Whatever may be the reasons, it is ascertained from personal interactions with a crosssection of villagers that they do not find any interest in *Gram Sansad* meetings. Again, the *Gram*

Sansad meets twice a year to transact certain items of business and there is no further scope for organized interactions.

Regular meeting of the *Gram Sansad* is one of the conditions for the success of this institutional innovation. The other conditions are the attendance and active participation at such meetings. The general picture is that the meetings are often not held because of the lack of a quorum despite government efforts to boost attendance.[35] An investigation was conducted to examine the extent of popular participation at the *Gram Sansads* of a Gram Panchayat which attained a very successful performance record during the Seventh Plan period. From the investigation, it is established that none of the ten such meetings could ensure the participation of at least ten per cent of the adult population of the respective villages.[36] The following Table 7.1 prepared on the basis of information available relating to that Gram Panchayat establishes the point.

Table- 7.1 : People's Participation at *Gram Sabha* Meetings

Keshpur No.10 Gram Panchayat Keshpur Panchayat Samiti : Midnapore November – 1994							
Sl. No.	Name of the Gram Sabha	*No. of electors	No. of Members of G.P.	People attended Male	Female	Total	Percentage of attendance
1	2	3	4	5			6
1.	Mahishda	728	2	54	4	58	7.97
2.	Keshpur	805	2	66	6	72	8.94
3.	Kalaberah	420	1	27	3	30	7.14
4.	Garaipur	416	1	33	3	36	8.65
5.	Ichhapur	751	2	49	2	51	6.79
6.	Bikalchak	430	1	18	1	19	4.41
7.	Beldoba	470	1	29	3	32	6.80
8.	Gar Gajpota	801	2	58	7	65	8.11
9.	Elna	819	2	55	11	66	8.05
10.	Bajir Chak	758	2	58	9	67	8.84
	Average attendance:						7.57

* *Notes* : as per Electoral Rolls, 1992.
Source : Records of the Gram Panchayat

It appears from Table 7.1 that the concerned Gram Panchayat consisted of 10 *Gram Sabhas* (now *Gram Sansads*) in which half-yearly meetings were held in November 1994. In all the meetings, attendance of village people was below 10 per cent and the average attendance was around 7.6 per cent. But on the issue of inclusion of proposals passed at such meetings, it is interesting to note that all the schemes and projects proposed by the respective *Gram Sansads* in their lists of 'first priorities' were included in the Gram Panchayat Plan subsequently.[37] But accommodation of village proposals or priorities in Gram Panchayat plan is not enough. It is the active participation of people in decentralized planning which is the index of its success.[38]

The picture, as depicted in above Table 7.1, has changed considerably over the years. Recently, under the initiative of the local political leadership, Bhagwanpur-I Panchayat Samiti decided to organize the meetings effectively in all the 100 *Gram Sansads* spreading over 9 Gram Panchayats of the block. All these meetings were scheduled on a particular day, i.e. on October 8, 1996, mostly at *Iswar Chandra Jana Chetana Kendra.* Two training programmes for the purpose of imparting training on the preparation of village plans and the functioning of the panchayats were organized at two different places of the block on October 2, 1996, which were attended by the members of the Gram Panchayat and Panchayat Samiti, all village level workers, volunteers from *Gram Sansads* and members from NGOs. The participants were apprised of the need, techniques and the art of village planning by the *Sabhapati*, BDO, Extension Officers and other resource persons. The date, time, venue and agenda of the proposed meetings were widely publicised through walling, handouts and door to door campaign. Invitations were sent to individual members of each household through letters, delivered by the members of the Panchayat Samiti and the Gram Panchayats themselves, local political leaders, volunteers and organizers of post-literacy centres. While delivering the letters, they also took the opportunity to interact with the adult members of the family. As a result of this campaign and organized planning, the proposed meetings of the *Sansads* were successful with an average attendance above 11 per cent.[39]

It is all the more encouraging that the progress achieved in the said block has been sustained and the meetings of the *Gram*

Sansads have been organized in the subsequent months.[40] The position was further improved in 1997 and it was evident that people's attendance stood at between ten and twenty per cent at the annual meetings of the *Gram Sansads* in different panchayat samitis.[41] Again, intensive political campaign and frequent monitoring by the panchayat leaders and the block officials motivated the people of some blocks, like Sutahata-I to such an extent that it resulted in the attendance of 45 to 50 per cent of the village people at the meetings of some *Gram Sansads* in November, 1998.[42] But the success attained in Sutahata-I cannot be construed as the general picture of the whole district. There are some complaints regarding irregularities in holding the meetings within the time-schedule, fixed by the government.[43] It is established that organized people's participation has taken place in those villages where the political parties and panchayats have joined together to achieve the desired changes.[44]

Mobilization of the People

People's participation cannot be ensured in a vacuum. Political will of the government and organized mobilization of the people may create an atmosphere where the conditions of democratic governance may take place. More than thirty million voters of West Bengal periodically have been electing their representatives to the Panchayati raj without interruptions for the last 20 years. In the last panchayat elections (1998), more than sixty per cent of the voters of the state have cast their votes.[45] In Midnapore, the situation is not different: 48.43 lakh electors have elected 8,591 representatives including a large number of Scheduled Caste, Scheduled Tribe and Women candidates, which strengthen the willingness and ability of the people for participation in decision-making. The class composition of the newly elected panchayat members of the district is not available and may require a separate study. But it can be seen that there is now a significant representation on the panchayat bodies from among the poorer and more marginal social groups. A general view of their composition may be traced from the table given below which consolidates the experiment of people's participation in development planning and self-governing activities of the district.

Table 7.2 : Composition of PRIs in Midnapore (1998-2003)

Tiers	Total Seats 1998	MEN			WOMEN			Percentage to the total	
		General	S/C	S/T	General	S/C	S/T	Men	Wome
GP	7188	2740	1210	663	1813	458	304	64.18	35.82
PS	1295	509	215	123	321	81	46	65.41	34.59
ZP	108	44	18	10	26	8	2	66.66	33.34

Source: District Panchayat Office, Midnapore.

The above Table 7.2 is an indicator to a number of directions. The last panchayat election is a kind of 'social renewal' of commitment to the people. The renewal prescribes a new place for women in society and thus it has brought about a 'revolution in the countryside'.[46] With the renewal of 'commitments to the masses', the planning process becomes more relevant than ever before.[47]

As stated in Chapter 3, the organized mobilization of the people — peasants, agricultural workers and middle class, to a certain extent — has taken place through a number of programmes and activities undertaken by the government since 1977. The panchayats and organized mobilization of the people have helped strict enforcement of the Minimum Wages Act for the agricultural workers, and achievement of *Operation Barga* in the district. Though child labour may still exist, there are no reports of bonded labour in the district and the reports of police atrocities and custodial violence are also rare.[48]

Since the commencement of the Eighth Plan in the district, there was a conscious and deliberate attempt on the part of the district authorities and the Zilla Parishad to transform the decentralized planning process into a mass movement by linking it with the literacy movement of the district.[49] The decentralized planning experiment received much impetus from the literacy campaign of the district on the one hand and provided support for the campaign on the other, by strengthening and consolidating the process of development in the villages and the wards.

The strategy worked out for implementation of both these programmes is identical in nature. The objective is also identical since both the programmes are designed to develop and strengthen the community consciousness together with a sense of self-dependence of the people in general and the weaker sections of the community in particular. The organizational structure of the literacy campaign is chalked out, more or less, corresponding to the structure developed for decentralized planning, from the village to the district, through the involvement of the panchayats, municipalities, government departments, political parties and non-government organizations. A five-tier committee structure for rural areas and a four-tier structure for urban areas are created to conduct the campaign.[50] Previously, the villages and the wards were considered as base units in literacy campaign. Now the *Gram Sansads* have been identified in place of the 'villages' and *Iswar Chandra Jana Chetana Kendras* have been established at the *Gram Sansads* and the *Wards* to organize and conduct the continuing education programmes. The *Kendras* have also been entrusted with the task of organizing decentralized planning.[51] Moreover, the materials for instruction have been designed to motivate the learners to participate in the activities of local development and planning. Thus both organizational and objective linkages have been established between these two programmmes which ultimately consolidate the infrastructure for decentralized planning in the district.

From the above review it is clear that irregularities in holding the meetings of the *Gram Sansads* and the *wards*, ineffectiveness of such meetings and inadequate participation of the people at the meetings are the major constraints that may stand in the way of actualization of participatory decentralized planning.

Flow of Funds

Decentralized district planning due to its closer proximity with people raises their expectations to a higher level and performance demands a sound resource base at the district and block levels. Funds for decentralized planning at the district level and below is composed of (i) own income of the Local

Bodies, (ii) funds from the State Government and (iii) funds allotted through a host of Centrally Sponsored Schemes on the basis of cost-sharing between the Centre and the States. Funds, other than the District Plan Fund and matching grants, may flow from the state to the line departments located in the district.

Mobilization by Local Bodies

An important aspect of decentralized planning is the scope for mobilization of resources lying at the command of the local institutions. Under the existing system, the scope for such mobilization exists at all the three levels of the panchayats and municipalities, though the scope of the Panchayat Samiti is comparatively limited.[52] The local bodies are empowered to levy taxes and collect various types of tolls and fees to support their normal and plan budgets. The earnings of the local bodies have increased manifold over the years and most of the panchayats, municipalities, besides the Zilla Parishad, have attained remarkable success in this regard.[53] Though no record is available to segregate the expenditure incurred by the Panchayat Samitis and Gram Panchayats of the district on plan and non-plan heads, the income of the Zilla Parishad is inadequate to meet the normal budgetary requirements of the Zilla Parishad. Again, it is revealed from detailed discussions with a sizeable cross-section of the functionaries of the Municipalities, Panchayat Samitis and Gram Panchayats of the district that all these bodies have been able to augment their own resources to a greater extent in the last ten years, yet in most cases they are unable to meet their regular and contingency expenditure.[54] Moreover, the experience suggests that neither the sources of local resources are effectively tapped, nor are the own assets managed properly at all the levels, mainly due to a lack of organizational set-up and planning. The local bodies do not make a proper project appraisal and there is no idea of likely returns.[55]

Devolution of Funds

The decentralized district planning aims at changing the total complexion of planning below the state level by transferring the task of decision-making in formulation and implementation of plans to the district. This changing complexion necessitates an uninterrupted flow of funds to the districts and then to the lower levels. After identification of area between the state and the districts, there is the need for automatic devolution of funds to the districts and also powers to aùgment their own resources.[56] Transfer of resources for district planning has thus become an issue of vital importance but still the system has not yet been stabilized though the Planning Commission thought of allocation of resources up to the block-level in its 'Guidelines for District Planning'.[55]

Sectoral Fund

There is no uniform or well-accepted procedure in deciding the share between the district and the state sectors. The Working Group on District Planning, while emphasising the maintenance of a balance between local needs and overriding national and state priorities through consultations and exchange of information,[58] recommended the distribution of divisible plan outlays 'among the districts on the basis of three elements, viz., population, area and level of development.'[59] There are certain factors which influence the pattern of sharing between the state and the districts. The classification of sectors as the district and the state subjects, the infrastructural status of the district *vis-à-vis* the state and the number of districts within the state are the elements involved in the process of allocations of plan outlays for the districts.[60]

The procedure that came to be followed in West Bengal from the second year of the Seventh Plan has been discussed in Chapter 4. The procedure is that each department indicates in advance the flow of funds to the districts from its plan budget each year. On receipt of information, the district level officers disaggregates the district fund in consultation with the District Planning Committee. This part of the departmental outlay is divisible and has gradually been increased over the years. Now "a little more than 50 per cent of the entire state budget is devolved down to district or below."[61] Out of plan allocations of the district, 30 per cent is utilised by the Zilla Parishad, 20 per cent by the Panchayat Samitis while the remaining 50 per cent goes to the Gram Panchayats.[62] In addition to this, provisions have been made for sharing of taxes and tax assignments to implement fiscal decentralization and entitlements of the panchayats and municipalities have been identified by the State Finance Commission.[63]

As pointed out previously, resource mobilization for district planning in Midnapore was visualized originally through four sectors. Subsequently, another sector comprising Centrally Sponsored Scheme has been added.[64] During the last two successsive five-year plans, government funds have been allotted to the district through three heads: Sectoral allocations through the departments, District Plan Fund (DPF) and Centrally Sponsored Schemes (CSS). Schemes under the first two heads are earmarked by the State Government and in case of the third, the Central Government shares funds with the state on a ratio of 80:20.

It is revealed from an analysis of the flow of funds from the State Government during the Seventh and Eighth Plans that even after making allowances for substantial increases in the priority sectors of agriculture, irrigation, power, the minimum needs programmes and a rise in Central assistance towards schemes of integrated rural development at the district and block levels, the gap between the requirements and the availability of resources continue to be significant. The following Table 7.3 substantiates the above statement.

Table 7.3 : Flow of Government Funds

(*Rs. in crore*)

Years	Proposed Total outlay	Govt. outlay	Available Govt. outlay
1992-93	295.17	175.36	81.93
1993-94	327.40	203.61	133.91
1994-95	480.37	273.82	186.42
1995-96	469.05	296.80	183.64
1996-97	611.17	356.21	230.99
Total	2183.16	1305.80	608.89

Source: District Planning Cell, DPC, Midnapore.

From Table 7.3, it is evident that the outlay of the Eighth Plan of the district was Rs.2183.16 crore out of which departmenttal outlay was Rs. 1305.80 crore. It is assessed that the actual fund flow during the last five years as against the proposed outlay was only 27.89 per cent and against the government outlay it was around 46.63 per cent. Thus the constraint of inadequate flow of funds still haunts the district planning in Midnapore. There is another important problem. The fund which is devolved to the sectors in a district comes under the direct control of the government departments and the local bodies find little or no scope in the selection of departmental schemes and priorities unless they are asked for. Though there is scope for intervention by the District Planning Committee through its sub-committees, there is little scope at the block level since the departments decide on their own ways without consulting the Panchayat Samitis.[65]

The State Government allocates fund to the DPC under District Plan Schemes Fund in addition to the funds released through sectoral departments. The DPC also receives special grants on the basis of performance in mobilizing small savings. The government has introduced a scheme of decentralized resource mobilization in the districts since November 1992. According to this scheme, if the collection of the district under any of the heads, viz., registration fee, amusement tax, royalty and cess on minor mineral resources, and motor vehicle tax exceeds the stipulated target, 50 per cent of the additional collection is ploughed back to the respective district through the District Planning Committee.[66] This scheme of incentive grants to encourage additional mobilization of local resources is commendable and an improvement over the allocation formula of plan funds for the district.[67]

With the deepening of the local self-governing institutions under active support from the State Government, the decentralized planning process has also been strengthened in the state. To consolidate this process further, the State Government has been trying to institutionalise the system through a good number of measures including the introduction of a special budget-head called 'District Plan Schemes Fund' or the DPF since 1985-86. In addition to the divisible pool, the allotment of funds to the districts under this head during the first decade of decentralized planning shows a progressive trend except brakes for two-three years. Table 7.4 will confirm the position.

Table 7.4 : Flow of District Plan Schemes Fund 1985 - 86 to 1995 - 96

Year	Fund allotted (in crore) to the districts
1985 - 86	16.53
1986 - 87	12.18
1987 - 88	15.28
1988 - 89	33.34
1989 - 90	63.48
1990 - 91	49.15
1991 - 92	04.68
1992 - 93	01.54
1993 - 94	04.50
1994 - 95	56.57
1995 - 96	57.91

Source : Records of the Department of Development and Planning, Government of West Bengal.

District Plan Fund

The District Plan Fund (DPF) is entirely under the custody of the DPC. It has been created in 1985-86 with a meagre amount of Rs.1.17 crore for the district[68] for implementation of district plan schemes and block plan schemes. Since then funds have been allocated by the State Planning Board. Funds so received are reallocated by the DPC to the blocks, municipalities and other agencies.[69] During the first six years of its introduction, i.e. up to 1990-91, the District Planning Committee received a grant of Rs.18.19 crore out of which Rs.16.51 crore representing 90.75 per cent has been utilised by the DPC.[70] But there was no allotment from the government in this account in two successive years, viz., 1992-93 and 1993-94. Again, during the last three years of the Eighth Plan, Rs.4.10, 5.76 and 1.74 crore respectively were released to the district under District Plan Fund. However, the main problem lies in the fact that in all these three years the funds were tied to specific schemes or sectors which goes against the very concept of decentralized planning: 'it is necessary to place some funds at its (DPC) disposal which are not tied to any departmental schemes and which may be used towards small schemes meant to meet the local priorities, needs and aspirations of the local community' to give some meaning to the concept of district planning.[71]

In the meantime, the situation has changed marginally. Since the financial year 1997-98, the State Government has been releasing occasionally some *untied funds* for the district plan.[72] But the constraints are not removed. Still the fund under DPF is both meagre and irregular. The State Finance Commission suggested the 'transmission of funds at regular intervals' on the basis of 'entitlements.[73] It is estimated, on the basis of the State Budget for 1995-96, that this district was entitled to have Rs.69 crore while it received just Rs.5.76 crore during 1995-96.[74] However, there have been some improvements recently in this regard. A scrutiny reveals that the State Government provided *untied funds* for decentralized planning programmes during 2000-2001 to the tune of Rs. 100 crore. In 2001-2002, the budgetary support in this sphere was increased to Rs. 120.95 crore and the provision for Rs. 546.15 crore in 2002-03 has been made as against a proposed allocation of Rs. 2702.15 crore in this respect under the Tenth Five-Year Plan.[75] If the recommendations of the Second State Finance Commission are implemented by the Government shortly, the decentralized planning will be further strengthened. The Government of India has been also releasing *untied funds* on the recommendations of the Eleventh Finance Commission which is also channelised to the panchayats and municipalities following the *Guidelines* outlined by the First State Finance Commission.

Rural Development Fund

Another important source of fund for district planning has been the Rural Development Programmes sponsored by the Central Government. Before the commencement of the Eighth Plan, the Centrally Sponsored Schemes (CSS) were executed outside the purview of district planning on *ad hoc* basis from time to time. But since the introduction of the Eighth Plan, coordinated efforts have been made to implement these schemes as integral parts of the annual plan of the district.[76] Since the year-wise allotments are known to the district beforehand in most cases, the identification of projects and scheme-wise break-ups are made and shown in the action plans for implementation by the respective implementing agencies.

Apart from the IRDP, DPAP and JRY which constitute a separate sector in the district plan, Employment Assurance Schemes (EAS) are also implemented by the Panchayat Samitis and an amount of Rs.113.11 crore was received in 1996-97.[77] Similarly, funds released to the municipalities for urban development are now included in the district plan.[78] But the funds for urban development are released through a variety of channels and no complete record is available either with the District Urban Development Agency or the District Develop-ment Department.[79] The non-availability of information on the flow of funds for urban development and their subsequent non-inclusion in the overall district plan create problems in spatial planning.

Rural Development Programmes still constitute a major part of the district planning. By including the schemes in the district plan, both the sectoral and the spatial balance have been achieved within a set of constraints.[80] The constraints mainly relate to local irrelevance, economic inefficiency, internal inconsistency and non-viability. But a concerted attempt is going on to remove these constraints through review programmes and regular interactions conducted by the DRDA and the DPC.[81] Flow of funds from this sector to the district during the last two five-year plans may be viewed with the help of following Table 7.5.

Table 7.5 : Flow of Funds to Rural Development Programmes (1992-97)

Schemes	VIIth Plan Outlays		VIIIth Plan Outlays	
	Approved	Available	Approved	Available
IRDP	27.58	21.13 (76.6%)	49.96	44.57 (89.2%)
JRY	352.95	380.58 (107.8%)	265.70	243.12 (91.5%)
DPAP	5.32	3.65 (68.6%)	6.99	6.05 (86.6%)

Notes : Percentage of availability to the total is given in the brackets.

Source : (i) *Eighth Five-Year Plan, 1992-97, Midnapore, pp.II/A,24-26.*

(ii) *Annual Plan,* 1996-97, Midnapore pp.IV/44-49.

(iii) *A Prelude to the IXth Plan,* DPC, Midnapore, 1997, pp.7-8.

From Table 7.5, it appears that the flow of funds to the district and integration thereof with the district planning is highly satisfactory. The overall availability of fund in this sector is 91 per cent of the approved outlay, while the flow of fund is just 71 per cent in case of sectoral allocations from the government during the Eighth Plan period. But it creates problems in other direction. These schemes are carried out according to the guidelines of the Central Government without any regard to local needs and priorities. In such circumstances, the programmes increase the dependence and destroy the autonomy of the local bodies.

Another problem that confronts the formulation and implementation of district plans incorporating therein the various Rural Development Programmes under the Centrally Sponsored Schemes, is the sudden discontinuance of running schemes and the launching of new ones. During the Ninth Five-Year Plan, IRDP, JRY, EAS and MWS were replaced by JGSY, EAS and SGSY and again from April 2002, JGSY and EAS were replaced by *Sampoorna Grameen Rozgar Yojana* (SGRY). The resultant problem faced by the District Planning Committee is to develop new methodology for their accommodation and communicate them to the tiers below the district for their implementation. The problem is serious because, unlike some other states, these programmes are executed by the panchayats and municipalities here in the state. Naturally it takes more than three months between the launching of a new programme or the restructuring of implementing agencies and the actual execution of such programmes at the ground level.

Bank Credit

Planning of scarce credit resources among different sectors of economy is a strategic instrument in decentralized planning. In a situation where the flow of credit is uneven between various sectors of economy and among different regions in the country, credit planning has become an important and integral part of the planning exercise.[82] The District Planning Committee, being well aware of the importance of credit planning, took the initiative to introduce a rational approach in investments and credits by the financial institutions. When the DPC first started functioning, total investments made by the nationalised banks located in the district stood around Rs.5 crore as against a deposit of Rs.25 crore in 1985.[83] Credit plan of the district in the Seventh Plan period was formulated by the 'Lead Bank' but a steady growth was noticed in the credit-deposit ratio as a result of intervention by the Zilla Parishad.[84]

Subsequently, the DPC has initiated steps for effective monitoring through interactions with representatives of the banks on a regular basis. The District Level Coordination Committee (DLCC) has been activated by the Zilla Parishad and the DPC and this has led to an increase in both the number of banks and the amount of investments.[85] Again, the prevalent bias towards credit in developed blocks and urban areas of the district has been checked and a parity has been attained through planned efforts by the district authorities.[86]

A review in this regard shows that out of a total credit-target of Rs.193.96 crore during 1994-95, the achievement was only Rs.144.09 crore, i.e. 74.29 per cent. Credit-Deposit Ratio, which is often viewed as one of the indicators to assess the credit flow *vis-à-vis* economic development of the district, has declined from 37 per cent in 1994 to 34 per cent in 1995.[87] The position has been further deteriorated in 1995-96 when it came down to 31.78 per cent only, involving an investment of Rs.402 crore as against the deposit of Rs.1265 crore as in 1996.[88] Judged from the viewpoint of achievements during the Eighth Plan, the DPC has been able to raise the percentage of investment by the banks. The DPC estimated a target of Rs.641.29 crore during this period, while the achievement was recorded at Rs.497.86 crore, thereby registering a 77.63 per cent mobilization of the estimated credit.[89]

Thus the situation in credit flow in the district is no less favourable, though the decline in C.D. Ratio is the prime concern of the day. However, there is an organized attempt on the part of the District Planning Committee and the Zilla Parishad to motivate the banks and other financial institutions to enhance their investment-targets and expedite the process of sanctioning funds to the beneficiaries. The Zilla Parishad interacts on a regular basis with the banks through the Block Level

Coordination Committees (BLCC) and the District Level Coordination Committee (DLCC).

Coordination and Linkage

Decentralized planning implies the formulation and implementation of an integrated and balanced proposal for development on a concrete understanding of the resources, problems, needs and priorities. Thus district planning is not an isolated phenomenon; it is necessarily a holistic exercise having a two-way process. It includes, *first,* a broad outline and priorities which reflect the goals, objectives and strategies adopted by the centre and the states. *Secondly*, it is also related to the local needs, varieties and resources. In this sense, district planning is not a mere 'target area planning', rather it is more comprehensive operating in a multi-level planning framework: it ensures internal integration between the sectoral and spatial plans; and on the other hand, coordinates with the national plan through the establishment of 'backward' and 'forward' linkages. District planning demands 'inputs' from other sectors and supply 'outputs' to various other departments or agencies. The establishment of the linkages, backward and forward, calls for understanding of the interdependence of the different sectors of development.[90]

Formulation and implementation of plans again require both horizontal and vertical integration for their success. Another aspect which is involved in district planning is that it should seek to establish organic linkages with the developmental efforts outside the district sector schemes in order to check the growth of lopsided development in other spheres to ensure balanced development of the district.[91]

To ensure integrated planning and coordinated implementation, the working Group on District Planning visualises the District Planning Committee 'as an umbrella organization nesting the plans of individual department and agencies' in to the common framework of district planning.[92] It further suggests the empowerment of the District Planning Committee for allocation of funds to various sectoral departments. The Committee to review the existing Administrative Arrangements for Rural

Development and Poverty Alleviation Programmes (CAARD)[93] is non-committal on this issue and leaves it to the discretion of the states. Notwithstanding, it recommends the setting up of a State Development Council in each state on the model of the National Development Council for integration of the plans into a common framework.[94]

The idea of the creation of a State Development Council at the state level seems to be a wise suggestion for introducing inter-district linkages but it has not so far received adequate support in most of the states. In West Bengal, the Government is contemplating the revival of the District Planning Coordination Council[95] but not the establishment of State Development Council. Whatever may be the case, the DPC has to secure the integration and linkages in the whole process at various levels. The integration and linkage in the decentralized district planning are now ensured in two ways : *organizationally* and *functionally*. Organizationally, the tiers of the Panchayati Raj Institutions are not isolated from each other, they are organically linked in that the *Pradhans* of the Gram Panchayats falling under the territorial jurisdiction of a Panchayat Samiti are the *ex-officio* members of that Panchayat Samiti. Again, all the *Sabhapatis* of the Panchayat Samiti are *ex-officio* members of the Zilla Parishad. To make this integration more effective, the mechanism of organic linkages has been incorporated in the formation of the District Planning Committees in West Bengal.[96]

The District Planning Committee now appears as 'a social instrument of decision-making' comprising the planning experts and people's representatives from the panchayats and municipalities and thus an integration of 'local autonomy, administrative capability and planning expertise is achieved.'[97] The scope of similar linkages also exists in the composition of the Block Planning Committees (BPC) in this district.[98] But the establishment available to the DPC and the BPC is poor and inadequate. As a result, effective functioning of these bodies is hampered. The situation at the Gram Panchayat level is worse still.

On the question of organizational linkages, two issues are involved: *first*, under the existing infrastructure, the functions of district planning are carried out, setting aside the role of the DPC and the departments, by the Panchayati raj bodies. For all practical purposes, it is the Standing Committees of the Panchayat Samitis and the Zilla Parishad which, under the compulsions of circumstances, have taken over the real power from the parent bodies making them mostly deliberative. But there is no organizational linkage between these Standing Committees and the relevant lower tier of the panchayats. There is neither the provision for *ex-officio* membership from the Panchayat Samitis to the Standing Committees of the Zilla Parishad, nor is there the scope for inclusion of Members-in-Charge of the Gram Panchayat into the Standing Committee of the Panchayat Samiti. *Secondly*, there is no scope for organizational linkage among the Zilla Parishads at the State level. These two issues may create constraints in ensuring the vertical and horizontal linkage at the inter-district and intra-district levels.

There is another tension area, though not prominent in the present case due to political compulsions, that dominates the relationship between the functions of the panchayats and the District Planning Committee. The concept of 'area plan' has been institutionalized through the Amendments. The panchayats and municipalities have been declared as 'institutions of self-governments' and are empowered to prepare Action Plans or final plans. The District Planning Committee exists outside the family of PRIs but it is authorised to prepare the draft development plan of the district as a whole in which the panchayat plans are also integrated. Hence, the situation is ripe for a dilemma in the functioning of the Panchayats *vis-à-vis* the District Planning Committee should there be a change in the *modus operandi* of the political actors or in the political processes in the district. Again, the effectiveness of the panchayats in ensuring coordination and linkage with the government departments are seriously hampered since the line departments are much insulated and the panchayats do not have the minimum administrative machinery to bring these vertical hierarchies within their coordinating discipline. Shortage of staff at all the level of the panchayats especially below the district, is a major problem that threatens the future of these 'institutions of self-government'.

In the methodology of district planning, the planning process starts at the level of *Gram Sansads* and *Wards*[99] and ends at the district level with the formulation of the district plan. Thus the finalisation of the district plan is the end product of a long process which integrates the common men in the villages or wards with the district plan. But there is no organizational mechanism for regular linkages, forward and backward, between the ordinary citizen and the Gram Panchayat save and except through the panchayat members and the two meetings of the *Gram Sansads* and Ward Committees in minicipalities, mostly irregular and inadequate.

It appears from experience that there still exists some gaps in communication and cooperation from the sectoral departments of the district. Traditionally, the sectoral departments prefer to be guided by their allegiance to the departmental hierarchy. Their bond with the higher authority is so firm and strong that even the active intervention by the District Magistrate fails to motivate them to cooperate with the District Planning Committee and the Zilla Parishad.[100] It is widely believed that there is still scope for improvement in the attitudes and functioning of some of the sectoral departments.[101] It has also become a common practice of some government officials to pass on their responsibilities to the panchayats, especially at the grassroots, instead of going to the people to explain the policy of the government or to have personal interactions with the local people.[102] But success of decentralized district planning depends largely on the active involvement of the people who may be motivated by the field officers in an effective manner. The indifferent attitude of the government officials is a major hindrance.

The uniqueness of the district planning in Midnapore lies in the fact that a clear demarcation of areas and functions of each of the planning tiers starting from the village level has been worked out in the methodology. The methodology seeks to plug the possible loopholes of confusion and conflicts which are usually common in a multi-level planning arrangement. Since the district plan is structured beforehand by the DPC through a process of integration and linkage at all the levels, the 'Principle of Nesting and Integration' in decentralized planning is followed.[103]

In the planning framework of the district, the Block Planning Committee plays a crucial role. It helps to create a planning culture to get the plans of the Gram Panchayats correctly prepared, and have the effective implementation by the agencies. It performs two functions: *one* integration of the needs and priorities of village plans and panchayat plans fully into the block plans, and *two*, vertical coordination and integration between the village plans, panchayat plans and the district plans. The integration of planning activities, though streamlined both functionally and organizationally within the panchayats and planning bodies, constraints still remain to be addressed in the sphere of proper linkage between the departments and the planning bodies at all the levels, prominently at the block levels.

The planning process in the district has since been revamped to overcome the problems, mainly in the sphere of maintaining linkage and integration, in the meantime. The formulation of Annual Plan of 1985-86 was not at all encouraging due to inordinate delays on the part of some of the departments in communicating the district-wise break-up in due time. There were also similar problems in 1986-87, when some departments could not furnish relevant information in prescribed forms, known as DP-I and DP-II.[104] Again, the information submitted by the departments were based on guess-work and without verification. The district level departments, however, did not have the communication from their parent departments, as a result of which some of them failed to furnish details to the District Planning Committee.[105] Thus the linkages between the departments, the District Planning Committee and the Zilla Parishad is not regular and smooth. Still now the District Planning Committee depends on the guess-work and formulates the drafts in some cases on the basis of ten per cent increase in the proposed outlay compared to the last year's actual allocation in the plan sector.[106]

One of the major constraints, related to the issue of linkage, is the 'stubborn persistence' on departmental and sectoral planning by the government departments at the local levels, rather than on spatial planning where the district becomes a unit.[107] The planning exercise in Midnapore is not free from this constraint.[108] In a broader sense, coordination depends upon the administrative pattern, procedures and planning. Problems in coordination arise due to prevalent structure of sectoral departments, which leads to dual loyalty for district officials, to the sectoral hierarchy, on the one hand, and to the development administration, on the other.[109] Inadequate communication leads to delay in the formulation and implementation of plans. Hence, phasing of planning activities into time-based schedules is a part of the plan itself and 'is the conversion of a project action plan into an operating time-table'.[110]

Time-Schedule

To remove these difficulties, the government decided to work out a time-schedule in 1986-87, and in conformity with the schedule, the planning exercise began from the beginning of the financial year. This enabled the departments to complete their respective exercises of the Annual Plan for 1987-88 on time and helped the completion of the process of consultation with the DPC by September every year. The government prepared the schedule in such a way as to enable the State Planning Department to submit the State Plan Document to the Planning Commission by the first week of December.[111] The Working Group on District Planning also emphasises the need of time-schedule and expeditious communication to the DPC on the resource position for maintenance of planning cycle and qualitative improvement of multi-level decentralized planning.[112]

The District Planning Committee, as we have seen in Chapter 6, was very much conscious of this situation and was guided by a tentative time-schedule in respect of preparation of district plan. The time-schedule prepared initially by the DPC overlooked some of the vital points and was sketchy since it did not deal with the time factors involved below the district level. But it was realised subsequently that the survival of the 'village based district planning' was dependent on the effective and proper planning at the grassroots in time. Accordingly the time-schedule was modified by the DPC.

The revised time-schedule covered both the aspects of planning: formulation and implementation. As a result, the annual action plans were prepared by the different implementing agencies on the basis of the expected time of completion of each scheme. It is evident from the review of implementation of projects and schemes that there were failures in maintaining the time-schedule due to delays in receipt of allotments from the state.[113] In some cases, the DPC failed to maintain the time-schedule due to the delaying habits of the officials and the departments.[114] Execution of works was also sometimes delayed by the executing agencies themselves.[115] Delay in the execution of schemes or projects results in increases in project costs and uncertainties relating to the implementation of succeeding schemes. But delay in formulation of plans affects the entire process. So delay is a major constraint in district planning. Since there are various stages and agencies in the process of decentralized planning, the scope for delay in execution and consequent deviation from the time-schedule becomes recurrent phenomena in the district.

Monitoring and Evaluation

Decentralized planning requires proper monitoring and evaluation at all the stages from the formulation to implementation of plans. It involves a long way from the village to the district, sectors of which are mostly unorganized. In such a situation, effective and desired outcome is ensured through proper monitoring and evaluation by small committees or Working Groups.[116] The Working Group on District Planning (1984) while suggesting the establishment of 'a separate monitoring cell' stressed the introduction of 'modern concepts in management' based on sound information and cartographic system.[117]

The practice of departmental monitoring by the higher authorities is an old one. But when we come down to decentralized planning, we confront a weak monitoring system. In West Bengal, the district administration used to monitor the implementation of development schemes and projects prior to the emergence of District Planning Committee in 1985 and was heavily pre-occupied with the achievement of targets and the distribution of benefits. In most cases, higher targets and achievements were the usual reports prepared by manipulation without taking the unknown and the unaccounted factors into consideration.[118]

In the present situation, the District Planning Committee seeks to change the prevalent system in monitoring and coordination through the formation of Working Groups and Sub-Committees of the DPC. Since the Zilla Parishad and the District Planning Committee are lacking in technical expertise for the formulation of plans, and the Standing Committees of the Zilla Parishad are overburdened, the formation of working groups and, subsequently, the sub-committees to monitor, supervise and evaluate the progress of district planning is a concrete step in the right direction.

Monitoring and evaluation at the district level were done by the Working Group once in a month during the Seventh Plan. The Group would meet the district level line agencies and officials to review the progress in the implementation of different projects. It also used to meet the *Sabhapatis* of the Panchayat Samitis, Block Development Officers to take stock of the situation which provided the scope for interactions both upward and downward from time to time.[119] Moreover, the functionaries of the Zilla Parishad and the District Planning Officer very often visited the blocks to provide guideline for planning and execution of schemes. From the Eighth Plan onwards, separate sector-based Working Groups were formed and separate meetings of the Working Group were organized.[120] But the proceedings of the meeting of the Working Groups reveal that monitoring and evaluation was inadequate and unorganized. Moreover, the information supplied to the DPC by different agencies were incomplete and inconsistent in nature.[121]

Apart from the Working Groups, a Standing Committee and an Urban Development Committee were formed during the Eighth Plan. At present, there are twelve sub-committees including the Urban Development Sub-Committee and District Planning and Coordination Sub-Committee. These sub-committees together with the Standing Committees of the Zilla Parishad coordinate the total activities of the decentralized district planning and provide organizational and functional linkages between the local self-bodies and the sectoral departments of the government. It is also seen that a functional division has been worked out to avoid possible overlapping of functions between the Sub-Committees of the District Planning Committee and the Standing Committees of the Zilla Parishad. But a problem may crop up, as there is no arrangement for interactions on a regular basis. Previously, monthly meetings of the Working Groups were designed for this purpose but could not be followed after a few years.[122] So far no planning has been made for discussions at regular intervals. Effective monitoring and timely interactions demand the strengthening of the sub-committees of the DPC.

Again, at the Gram Panchayat and Panchayat Samiti levels, there is no Working Group to monitor and evaluate the progress. The Standing Committees of the Panchayat Samiti review the progress under the overall supervision of the Block Planning Coordination Committee (BPCC). Moreover, monitoring of progress of running projects takes place regularly in the monthly meetings of the Panchayat Samiti in case of some blocks, while in some other blocks, such discussions are held as and when problems of serious nature crop up in course of the execution of projects. At the Gram Panchayat levels, monitoring and supervision are undertaken by the *Gram Pradhan, Upa-Pradhan* and the Job Assistant. Besides, the local members belonging to Panchayat Samiti, the Gram Panchayat members supervise the execution and progress of respective schemes and projects with the help of local 'beneficiary committees'.[123]

The beneficiary committees, though not the substitutes of the working groups or sub-committees of the DPC at the grassroots due to their inherent limitations in scope and capabilities, have become the effective organizations in ensuring durability, cost-efficiency and utilities of the projects. Though the committees are formed in most cases accommodating local people having different shades of opinion, a tendency has mostly developed to include the supporters of the local panchayat leaders or the neutral and passive participants from the locality.[124] As a result, the committees sometimes fail to discharge their duties effectively. Again, the limitation arises from the fact that the committees have no role in the formulation of plans of the locality.

Data Collection

In the previous chapter, the steps taken by the District Planning Committee for developing a sound database have been discussed. As already mentioned, the DPC adopted an alternative method of data collection for district planning. The survey was conducted with the volunteers raised at the village and panchayat levels initially. At a later stage, attempts were made for the enrolment of volunteers at the ward levels of the municipalities and developing Planning Cadres to cover the entire district.[125]

The organization for collection of information was well-planned but it could not have the desired outcome. Raising of Planning Cadres became very difficult at the beginning because during the survey conducted for IRDP the workers were paid reasonably but in the instant case, the volunteers were asked to carry out their jobs without remuneration. Secondly, there were difficulties in collecting required information since large number of villagers was reluctant to give out the same. Besides, people belonging to the minority communities were not eager to disclose information on private matters, like birth control measures etc.[126]

Again, the progress in preparation of Household Registers and Resource Registers was not at all encouraging. Till the end of 1986, registers relating to 651 villages could only be prepared[127] and the preparation of registers was left half-done in subsequent years. The District Planning Committee was dependent on outside organizations, like Rural Development Centre of the IIT, for development of data bank. But the population covered by the RDC in its survey was extremely limited. It collected information from 40 villages which constituted only 0.4 per cent of total number of villages. Leaving aside the question of representative character of the sample population, the finalisation of the summary sheet was too delayed to be used during the Seventh Plan period.[128]

Role of Bureaucracy

The overall situation in district planning now brings us to the issue of role performance by the administrators in a decentralized perspective. In the decentralized planning arrangement, the role of the administrators is mostly affected by the relationship between the administrators and the political leaders, which necessarily involves a behavioural dimension. Both interact in concrete situations and the interactions are influenced by the problems and demands of development administration. The concept of development administration and the role perception of administrators have undergone conside-rable changes in the district over the last two decades. Sufficient consensus has developed between the two, which tends to mitigate the tension, conflict and tug of war. For example, with regard to matters relating to the distribution of benefits, selection of priorities or choice of work-sites for the poor, both the groups have developed a common perception.[129]

It is gathered from interactions with the officials and the panchayat functionaries at the district level that both political leaders and administrative wings prefer to supplement each other and function in an atmosphere of cooperation, mutual trust and confidence. The *Sabhadhipati* was a leading member of the district committee of his party having a long experience in panchayat administration. His political clout combined with his statutory position in administrative hierarchy ensured cooperation from both the panchayat bodies and the administration. Though no special study has been made on the aspect of official and non-official relationship, enquiries reveal that the areas of misunderstanding and tension have gradually been reduced mostly by government policies. Day to day problems are erased through interactions at different bodies and intervention by the *Sabhadhipati* and the District Magistrate.[130]

The role of the District Magistrate is very crucial in the process of district planning. Under our administrative set-up, the District Magistrate is both an important and indispensable personality. The office of the District Magistrate combines in itself both the regulatory and developmental functions. He is also the Collector of the district and hence looks after the revenue administration as well. He coordinates and supervises the functions of the officers posted at the district level and the below. Thus his office is a centre of both information and communications. He is both the Chief Executive Officer of the

Zilla Parishad and the Secretary of the District Planning Committee. In these capacities, he plays three important roles. He assists the Zilla Parishad and the District Planning Committee in the formulation and implementation of plans and programmes of the district. He exercises control over a large contingent of district bureaucracy. He also assists the Zilla Parishad and the DPC in the supervision of the planning process below the district level. Thus he is responsible for the removal of administrative difficulties, inter-departmental conflicts and undue delays at the district level. In such a situation, the role performance of the District Magistrate demands initiative, vision and accommodative leadership. Seniority and experience may strengthen his capabilities. But the general constraint is that the District Magistrate is too burdened to look after all these things of a district like this one, the largest in India. At the district level there are about 100 committees of various nature, with the District Magistrate heading roughly half of them and the *Sabhadhipati* the other half and the committee system is time-consuming and costly.[131]

Success of decentralized planning mostly depends upon how efficiently and closely the field administrators motivate people and how they perceive their role and establish rapport with the villagers. The role of the bureaucracy below the district level especially at the blocks is most vital. But the position is vulnerable at block levels where, apart from the Block Development Officer, a number of field officers are involved in development planning. These officers possess identical status in the administrative hierarchy. Since the division of labour is based on power rather than on work,[132] there is an inherent tendency to exert authority in the communication pattern.

At the block level, the pattern of relationship between the officials and non-official functionaries is not so smooth as it exists at the district level. Since the block and the Panchayat Samitis are units closed to the field, engaged mostly in the implementation of programmes, the scope of differences is relatively wider. But the situation has changed considerably in the district after the first decade of Left Front rule.[133] The compulsions of circumstances and the logic of development administration have brought the two closer, though there is scope for improvement.[134]

Involvement of Political Parties

The inadequacy and ineffectiveness viewed at different levels of formal organizations for decentralized planning are compensated by the political parties, especially the CPI(M), the dominant party in the district. It has developed its frontal organizations and party base throughout the entire district. Party officials frequently visit the work-sites, panchayat offices and government departments to take a regular stock of the situation and to pursue the implementation of schemes and projects. Before arriving at a decision at the panchayats, the panchayat functionaries belonging to the party get the issues discussed and clinched beforehand at the appropriate party forum — district committee, zonal committee, local committee and the branch. Moreover, *Anchal Samanvay Samiti* (Gram Panchayat Co-ordination Committee) at the Gram Panchayat level and *Block Samanvay Samiti* (Block Coordination Committee) at the Panchayat Samiti level are established in most of the blocks of the district. These committees consisting of local party leaders and panchayat functionaries take decisions on policy issues of local importance, determine major schemes and projects and monitor implementation of works.[135] Internal audit of gram panchayat funds by party functionaries and check-up meetings for monitoring development programmes are also organized at party levels at scheduled intervals.[136]

At the district level, there is a panchayat party team of the district committee which meets on a fixed day in a week to review and monitor the works of panchayats and the Zilla Parishad.[137] Moreover, the issues and activities relating to panchayats and planning are discussed and reviewed in each month by the district committee of the party.[138] But the role of other political parties is insignificant. The opposition parties are mostly unorganized and have developed an anti-establishment attitude towards the programmes initiated by the pro-government panchayats, which constitute the majority in this district. They are accustomed to the agitating role and less interested in popularising the process of decentralized planning. It is doubtful whether all the political parties have realised the philosophy and essence of decentralization. However, their opposition to the process of development and planning is not so strong that it may create major problems in implementation of schemes and projects.[139] After the Panchayat Elections of 1998 and especially the Assembly Elections (Mays, 2001), the political atmosphere in the district has been changed and now almost all the political parties are extending their support for the model wherever planning activities are initiated. The general acceptance of the development design by the political parties has strengthened the scope of cooperation and involvement of the people in the process further.

Experiments in Village Planning

The unique experiment of *Planning by the villagers* was started in 1985 but had to be abandoned unofficially just almost after two years. The District Planning Committee decided not to carry on the experiments in future due to paucity of funds and lack of organizational infrastructure below the Gram Panchayat level. Even at the block level and also at the district level, the organizational support was too inadequate to organize the experiment of *planning by the villagers* at the grassroots throughout the district, consisting of more than ten thousand villages.[140] However, there is a different view. It is believed in some quarters that the real cause for untimely abandonment of village plans in the district is to be traced to political opposition and not the necessities of economic or administrative realities. The informed sources attribute to the cause of rolling back the experiment by the villagers to the existence of forces opposed to such changes within the society.[141] They are somehow convinced that the proposed methodology and mechanism of village planning intended to bring about a fundamental change in the correlation of class forces in the long run and as such the privileged section organized disguised but deliberate attempts to sabotage the process of village planning.[142] Experiences gained at Daharpur does not negate this type of apprehension. However, an in-depth and separate study is required to examine whether the process of 'embourgeoisement'[143] or the socio-political constraints had ever played any role in the discontinuance of this novel but potential experiment in the district.

Autonomy in District Planning

The above analysis leads us to the issue of the autonomy in decentralized district planning. The issue of autonomy of the District Planning Committee and other lower level organizations is to be understood in the light of autonomy enjoyed by the 'institutions of self-government', the panchayats and the municipalities, which have been entrusted with the responsibilities of 'preparation of plans for economic development and social justice' in the Constitution. The DPC has been created to consolidate the plans prepared by the panchayats and municipalities and prepare a draft development plan for the district. Hence, constitutionally, the DPC is not to be viewed as an agency which only tackles some of the needs, those that are centrally supported and can be provided by bureaucratic means. Rather, the DPC is supposed to be an organ of definite activities, free from interference from the higher level and also an instrument of development and planning in the district.

Under the existing system, the State Government exercises a considerable measure of control over the activities of district planning; it makes allocations of funds, mostly tied to a sector or schemes, besides sectoral allocations. It prepares the guidelines, determines the priorities and intervenes whenever it likes. The DPC has no control over the sectoral funds. Allocation of tied funds and larger share for the departments lead to a distortion of the autonomy in district planning. Effective functioning of the DPC not only requires the devolved functions but also demands that such functions should be accompanied by the devolution of resources as well as the power to exercise control over the instruments. But the DPC has no control over the machinery for development and planning available at the district.

People's participation strengthens local autonomy but there are certain constraints to people's participation. These constraints emerge from inadequate administrative arrangements, opposition from within the system and incomplete devolution of funds and authority to the lower levels from the state. Inadequate understanding of the ideology of decentralization and the absence of village level organizations for articulation and integration of interests also hamper people's participation. The problems like deviation from time-schedule, gaps in monitoring and evaluation or failures in data-collection challenge the success of district planning but gaps in the decentralization-participation scheme will betray the whole philosophy.

THE CHOICES

The issues and constraints identified and raised lead us to find out the choices that may strengthen the infrastructure of decentralized planning. The entire discourse on decentralized planning is concentrated on the focal point that the 'people' is the common denominator among a variety of actors, very often overlapping, entangled and enmeshed in the process. Indirect participation provides little scope while direct participation may result in sporadic expressions of views by the citizens. To overcome these constraints, there is a need for organized direct participation which may be strengthened through creative participation of the people at the grassroots. The functioning of the *Gram Sansads* and *Ward Committees* needs to be planned, organized, regularised and made effective. This calls for the heightening of the willingness and capacity of the common citizens. Creation of planning culture and awareness building may enhance both the motivation and the capabilities on the part of the people.

The experiments of 'planning by villagers' or 'village planning' have not so far met with complete success. The existing conditions do not encourage a fresh start at this stage. In this context, the methodology of people's campaign followed in Kerala at the grassroots levels to motivate and involve the people in the process of planning may be viewed as a brake on 'elite governance with periodic election ceremonials'.[144] Involvement of the people is a continuous and self-sustaining activity and as such it cannot be fully ensured through an annual and a half yearly meeting of the *Gram Sansads* or the *Ward*

Committees. It means that people are to be involved in the whole process of the development effort — planning, execution, monitoring and evaluation. Creative participation of the people in planning is the *raison d'etre* of decentralized planning.

The *Gram Sansads* and the *Ward Committees* are the broad platforms where the citizens may find a scope to interact with each other and put forward their suggestions. Planned and meaningful interactions demand information, prior consultations and working ideas. An organization of the people, like a *Village Committee* at the village level, may be formed on an annual basis by the villagers themselves. The Village Committee will act as a task force for organizing the *Gram Sansads*. The scope of functioning of village committees are to be widened to include all community activities of the village.[145] But in no case should the village committees be construed as substitutes for *Gram Sansads*. This organizational device may be designed for the wards in urban areas as well, by creating smaller wards, if necessary. Besides constituting village committees taking a cluster of adjoining households as a unit for representation through some regulatory provisions as a strategy to ensure effective and continuous functioning of the *Gram Sansads*, holding of meetings of a *para* (a cluster of households) to discuss a particular sector of planning may be considered as an additional choice. But it should be kept in mind that in most of the countries of the Third World, the participation of the people in decentralized planning is not very high and the 'rules of the decentralization game are the outcome of a complex set of historical, institutional and political factors'.[146]

Various recommendations have been made to activate the *Gram Sabha* from time to time with a view to enhancing the scope and extent of people's participation in development activities. *The Task Force on Panchayati Raj* (1999), constituted by the Government of India, has recommended vast changes to make the Gram Sabhas effective. The major recommendations of the Task Force include the appointment of government or higher level panchayat officers as observers for Gram Sabha meetings, holding of Gram Sabha meetings through out the state or the country in the form of '*Gram Sabha Abhiyana*' spreading over a period of two weeks, identification of pro-people programmes in the *Gram Sabha* meetings, due consideration of the recommendations of the *Gram Sabha* meetings by the Gram Panchayats and the introduction of the system of reporting the reasons to the *Gram Sabhas* in case of non-compliance of the recommendations by the Gram Panchayats.[147] The *Gram Sabhas* and the *Gram Sansads* have a vital role to play in making the Gram Panchayat responsive, accountable and effective. Hence, these are required to be empowered with substantial authority so that they may influence the course of actions and decisions of the Gram Panchayats in an effective manner.

The present phase of limited decentralization, due to lack of mobilization of local resources, inadequate and irregular flow of funds and practice of tied funds, needs to be crossed over through the introduction of a sound principle of resource mobilization from the state. Formulation of district plan and annual action plans can be made in a meaningful way only when there is certainty in respect of availability of actual funds. The State Finance Commission (1995) has dealt with entitlements to the local level bodies in the form of 'untied funds' and grants. The report also contains suggestions on generation and management of funds by the local bodies themselves. The obsession of the lower level bodies largely with the psychology of spending needs to be removed. The flow of funds to the district and the levels below the district should be guided by the recommendations of the State Finance Commission.[148] The practice of releasing tied funds through the District Plan Schemes Fund (DPF) should be discontinued. Similar is the situation with regard to grants released by the Central Government under different poverty alleviation programmes. These programmes are carried out according to the guidelines and norms of the Centre, and the implementing agencies are denied the scope for diversion or reallocation to suit the local needs and variations. In such circumstances, the programmes increase the dependence and destroy the autonomy of the local agencies. Though there is a strong argument in favour of 'controlled decentralization'[149] in the Indian context, the Centrally Sponsored Schemes should in the larger interest, be discontinued and the allotments be channelled to the appropriate bodies in conformity with the financial principles of decentralized district planning.

Decentralization in planning necessitates the tapping of resources at the local levels and the local bodies must be induced and motivated to augment their own resources for planning and development of their locality. The people may also be motivated through organized and regular meetings of the *Gram Sansads* and the *Ward Committees* to contribute in the form of capital or labour components for development works at the local level. Such contributions will ensure maintenance, durability and cost-efficiency of projects.[150] The scheme of *people's sector* and *joint sector* is a novel idea that needs to be translated into concrete action plans. The introduction of the provision for incentive outlay matched by the contributions from the people and the local bodies, in conformity with the practices followed in Gujarat, may act as an impetus for augmenting local resources. Simultaneously the existing system of 'vertical and horizontal tax overlapping' should be removed to strengthen the tax effort and spending power of the local bodies.[151] The local resources are not only to be tapped but to be managed efficiently through proper project appraisal, and hence the solution seems to be the effective financial management at all the levels under the supervision of financial experts.

There is an urgency in introducing the elements of flexibility in allocations and reallocations of funds at the district level. The practice followed in Maharashtra in respect of reallocation of plan funds based on periodical reviews by the District Planning and Development Council deserves positive consideration. To bring balanced development corresponding to the needs, resources and priorities of the locality and to remove sectoral disparities, a holistic approach is necessary in district planning. In this regard, the proposal for devolution of entire plan allotments earmarked for a district to the respective District Planning Committee for further devolution to the various sectors and lower level planning bodies is an alternative choice. Introduction of a fresh route of fund-flow may finally lead to another issue: the question of setting up a third tier of government at the district level[152] to which the entire responsibilities of planning, implementation and monitoring could be transferred.

Though the Working Group on District Planning does not favour such an idea at this stage,[153] it seems to be an appropriate choice for the present, especially after the Constitutional Amendments.

The policy prescriptions arrived at in the foregoing review open up another sphere where concrete policy decision is required. The area is related to the proper designing of administrative machinery for decentralized district planning. The problem of linkage and coordination is a major concern in multi-level planning. Integration and coordination are necessary at the stages of both formulation and implementation of plans. The choice in decentralized planning is not confined to the manipulation of something at the final stage by 'pruning something here or increasing something there'[154] but to carry on constant interactions not only after the formulation of the plan but also before and during the process of programme formulation. The imperatives of decentralized planning call for the building up of a discrete organization for planning at the district level and the level below the district. The District Planning Committee is naturally called upon to act as an 'umbrella organization' accommodating the differentiation at the administrative levels. The role perception demands that the DPC will have to be strengthened both quantitatively and qualitatively. This requires that the District Planning Cell should be revamped with additional manpower. Task-specific wings are to be created within the cell so that each wing can look after a specific function allotted to it. The cell together with other district level organizations engaged in development planning looks like a huge apparatus but in reality such organizations are separate agencies independent of the District Planning Committee.

The first choice in the process of revamping the district planning machinery is to bring the entire establishment connected with development activities of the district under the functional control of the District Planning Committee. There is no reason to retain the separate existence of organizations like District Rural Development Agency (DRDA) and the District Urban Development Agency (DUDA). The sooner they are merged with the District Planning Committee, the better for the harmonious and integrated development of the district. Merging of the DRDA and DUDA with the District Planning Committee will enhance the scope for harmonious supervision of different agencies for implementation of different programmes. In fact after the constitution of the DPC, independent existence of these agencies is without any reason. In Kerala, the District Rural Development Agencies (DRDA) have been merged with District Panchayats; Project Directors of the DRDA are now in-charge of the distribution of plan funds of the blocks and gram panchayats, and poverty alleviation programmes of the district panchayats. The state of Karnataka made a similar attempt in the eighties and the experience was encouraging. The District Planning Cell needs to be strengthened organizationally with engagement of both experts and technical staff so that the Planning Cell may act as the planning secretariat at the district level under the control of the District Planning Committee. The cell would ensure horizontal linkages and control over the officers of the department in the district. The cell must include a separate wing for constant monitoring and evaluation not at the end of a particular project but appraisal in course of implementation, which may serve as feedback.

The intricacies of decentralized planning require the creation of planning organization at the block level as well. The block level planning establishment is more important because most of the programmes require linkage, both forward and upward, which is possible at the block levels. Hence, the choice is clear which requires the creation of a separate planning establishment at block levels. The Panchayat Samitis and Gram Panchayats suffer from inadequate staff strength. To ensure effective decentralization in rural areas, the Panchayat Samitis and Gram Panchayats should be strengthened with additional manpower. The devolution of functions and funds to the lower levels should also accompany the transfer of qualified and trained personnel to all the levels. The technical and engineering personnel posted at the blocks may be assigned to a group of gram panchayats, if posting of one such person exclusively at one gram panchayat considered difficult at the present instance, since gram panchayats have become the nerve centres of development activities at the base level. There is also the need for developing mechanisms for monitoring and supervision of the projects and schemes at the lower levels. The need for strengthening the audit system, formation of committees for inter-tier linkages, introduction of social audit and formulation of guidelines for identification of beneficiaries are long felt to ensure transparency and openess in the functioning of local self-governing bodies. Moreover, an enabling provision should be included in the Constitution empowering the state governments to confer on all the local self-governing bodies full power of administrative and functional control over such staff as are transferred to them following the scheme of decentralization.

Similarly, the issue of planning at the urban areas needs serious consideration. Unlike their rural counterparts, the urban local bodies are not organized hierarchically, nor are they linked with either the local authorities or the district administration, except indirectly through the District Planning Committee.[155] The linkage between the municipalities and the DPC is ensured, but what is lacking is the absence of a separate planning body at the municipality level, the creation of which in a broad based nature is the crying need of the process. Under the present arrangement, the DPC seems to be the only forum where panchayat and municipality plans and plans of different line departments of the government are coordinated. But the district is too high a level for such coordination. Hence, there is no alternative to the establishment of effective planning organizations at the levels below the district, particularly at the blocks and municipalities. At the state level, the creation of a State Development Council, a counterpart of the National Development Council, is a worthwhile suggestion. Gujarat has shown the way in this respect. The Gujarat Panchayat Act, 1993 provides for the constitution of the Gujarat State Council for panchayats on the pattern of the Inter-state Council constituted under Article 263 of the Constitution. Similar councils may be set up in all the states under the Chairmanship of the Chief Minister. In order to develop consensual approach in development and to foster the spirit of democratic functioning, the Leader of the Opposition may be nominated as the Vice-chairperson of the Council. It may also be noted here that the State of Kerala has also made a lasting contribution to the decentralization experiments through creating the institution of *Ombudsman* for the local bodies of the state. The *Ombudsman* is headed by a High Court Judge and includes six other members.

There are other prerequisites like effective data base, operating time schedule, prioritization etc. but these are not policy issues involved in decentralized planning.[156] But there are other dimensions which need to be examined closely. The scope and extent of decentralized planning are to be decided first by setting aside the confusions and uncertainties developed around the role and functioning of the Panchayats, Municipalities, District Planning Committees and the State Government in the process of decentralized planning. The cloud of contradictions and confusions created by the 73rd and 74th Amendments has cast its shadow over the provisions enumerated in the State Act as well.

The Constitution visualises both the panchayats and the municipalities as 'institutions of self-government, in charge of economic development and social justice'. Simultaneously it also seeks to constitute a District Planning Committee to 'consolidate the plans prepared by the Panchayats and the Municipalities in the district and to prepare a draft development plan for the district as a whole'. The statutory provisions of the state reinforce the same position. Now a question arises relating to the *locus standi* of the draft development plan of the district *vis-à-vis* the plans prepared by the panchayats and the municipalities. The stipulations of Article 243ZD may provide clues for solution, not the solution itself. A clear demarcation of operational jurisdictions by way of both differentiation and integration is necessary without overlooking the spirit and philosophy of the twin Amendments. The panchayats should be categorically declared as the 'institutions of self-government' and hence Article 243G needs to be recast. Similar amendments are also necessary to Article 243W to spell out the powers, authorities and responsibilities of the municipalities in clear terms.

There is still a grey area in the process of decentralized planning. The DPC prepares the draft plan for the district, which is forwarded to the State Government for approval with such modifications, as the government may deem fit. If that were the situation, the whole concept of decentralized planning becomes meaningless and the autonomy of the District Planning

Committee is lost. Decentralized planning may have a chance to move towards final stage in the process of decentralization only after achieving the extensive devolution of both powers and resources to the district level. 'The shedding of power' is an act of self-abnegation but it is the imperative of the present moment.[157] Decentralized district planning is a *fait accompli* today. Hence there is no scope for fresh choice. The real choice remains between putting it in mere papers and actually implementing it on the ground. No doubt it is going to be a challenging task. Shaking off past practices is difficult, yet conditions are now ripe to ring in the new.

Notes and References

1. *Sixth Five-Year Plan*, 1981, Government of India, New Deli, Preface, pp. iii-iv.
2. Hooja, Rakesh, 1994, 'Decentralized Planning and the Hanumantha Rao Report' in Asha Kaushik (ed.), *Democratic Concerns: The Indian Experience : Essays in Honour of Professor Iqbal Narain*, Vol.II, Jaipur: Aalekh, p.295.
3. Report of *the Working Group on District Planning*, 1984, Government of India, New Delhi, Vol. I, p.22, par.3.6.
4. *MIT Report*, No.17. 1969, *The Role of Popular Participation in Development*, USA: MIT, pp.23-25.
5. Rajan, M.A.S. 1990, 'District Plans, Monitoring and the Poor — An Administrator's Viewpoint', *Indian Journal of Public Administration*, Vol. XXXI (April-June), No.2, pp.211-15.
6. Subramanian, V. 1975, 'The Citizen and Planning', *op.cit.* Vol. XXI, (July-September), No.3, p.357.
7. *Second Five-Year Plan*, 1957, Government of India, New Delhi, p.150.
8. *Seventh Five-Year Plan*, 1986, *op.cit.*, p.62.
9. Report of *the Committee to Review the Existing Administrative Arrangements for Rural Development and Poverty Alleviation Programmes*, (hereinafter referred to as Report of the CAARD), 1985, Government of India, New Delhi, p.24, par.4.3.
10. Report of *the Working Group on District Planning*, 1984, *op.cit.*, pp.81-82, par.8.35.
11. *Ibid.*
12. *Ibid.*, pp.84-85, par(s). 8.50(1) to 8.50(13).
13. Report of *the Working Group on Block Level Planning*, 1978, Government of India, New Delhi, Vol. II, Chap. X, p.142, par.16.
14. Sarup, Anand. 1978, Quoted in *ibid.*, pp.37-8, par.3.34.
15. *The Constitution 73rd & 74th Amendment Acts* (1992), Article 243ZD.

16. Report of *the Working Group on District Planning*, 1984, *op.cit.*, p.83, par.8.45.
17. *The West Bengal Panchayat Act*, 1973 (as amended), Sections 19, 109 and 153.
18. *The West Bengal District Planning Committee Act*, 1994, Section 10(1).
19. *Medinipur Zellar Grambhittik Parikalpanar Ruparekha 'O' Unnayaner Pratichhabi* (in Bengali), 1996, District Planning Committee, pp.6-7.
20. *The West Bengal Panchayat Amendment Act*, 1992, Section 7 and *The West Bengal Panchayat Amendment Act*, 1994, Section 10.
21. *The West Bengal Municipal Act*, 1994, Section 123(1).
22. Mukhopadhyay, Asok. 1995, *Seminar Paper*, Seminar organized by the Institute of Social Sciences, New Delhi in Calcutta on November 24-25, 1995.
23. *Proceedings of the meeting of the district Vigilance and Monitoring Committee*, Midnapore, dated 27-8-1997.
24. Interview with *Mr. Bijali Ghosh*, Project Officer, District Urban Development Agency, Midnapore, dated 19-8-1997.
25. *Samaj Jijnasa*, 1996, Vidyasagar Centre for Social Sciences, Midnapore, Inaugural Number, p.79.
26. *Interview with H.K. Samanta, Sabhadhipati*, Midnapore Zilla Parishad, dated 27-8-1997.
27. Webster, Neil. 1992, 'Panchayati Raj in West Bengal: Popular Participation for the People or the Party?' *Development and Change*, Sage, Vol.23, No.4, p.144.
28. *Ibid.*
29. Dasgupta, Sailen. 1983, *Gram Panchayat Parichalanar Nirdeshika* (in Bengali), Left Front Committee, Calcutta, pp.3-5.
30. Report submitted by the *Karmadhyaksha* of the Zilla Parishad at a seminar, 'Alternative Strategy of Planning' organized by the Zilla Parishad, Midnapore, dated 19-6-1987.
31. *The Telegraph*, Calcutta, 10 July, 1997.
32. *Panchayati Raj Update*, 2001 (July), Vol. VIII, No. 7, p. 3.
33. *Ibid.*, 2001 (December), Vol. VIII, No. 12, p. 4.
34. *Proceedings of the District Vigilance and Monitoring Committee*, 1997, *op.cit.*
35. *The Telegraph, op.cit.*
36. *Note:* The meetings were held village-wise on the basis of earlier concept of *Gram Sabha.*
37. Report of the Annual General Meeting of Keshpur No.10 Gram Panchayat held on 24-2-1995.
38. Ostargaard, Geoffrey. 1985, *Non-violent Revolution in India*, New Delhi: Gandhi Peace Foundation, p.31.
39. *Report submitted by Mr. Subrata Mahapatra, Sabhapati* of Bhagwanpur-I Panchayat Samiti, dated 20-8-1997.
40. *Report of the District Vigilance and Monitoring Committee, op.cit.*
41. *Records of the District Panchayat Office*, Midnapore.
42. *Discussions with Mr. H.K. Samanta*, Formerly Chairman DPC, dated 20-11-1998.

43. *The Sabyasachi* (local daily), Midnapore dated 30-11-1998.
44. Discussions with *Mr. H.K. Samanta, op.cit.* and *Mr. Sankar Majumdar*, Member of the DPC. Subsequently verified from the *Sabhapatis* of different Panchayat Samitis of the district.
45. *The Statesman*, Calcutta, dated 30 May, 1998.
46. Lieten, G.K. 1996, *Development, Devolution and Democracy*, New Delhi: Sage Publications, p.218.
47. Sarup, Anand and Brahme, Sulabha. 1990, *Planning for the Millions*, New Delhi: Wiley Eastern Limited, p.149.
48. Sarkar, Dipak. 1998, *The Ganashakti*, (Special Issue on Development in Midnapore), Calcutta, 15 May, 1998.
49. *Interview with Mr. H.K. Samanta, op.cit.*, dated 27-8-1997.
50. Report on the *Evaluation of Midnapore Total Literacy Campaign*, 1992, LIM Cell, Midnapore, p.3.
51. *Proceedings of the meeting of the District Planning Committee* (DPC), Midnapore, dated 19-9-1996.
52. Recommendations of *the State Finance Commission*, West Bengal, 1995, Government of West Bengal, Calcutta, pp.148-54, Annexure-VIA and VIB.
53. Records available at the District Panchayat Office and the Development and Planning Department of the district.
54. *Discussions with Mr. H.K. Samanta, op.cit.* dated 20-11-1998. *The Ananda Bazar Patrika*, Calcutta, dated 17-12-1998.
55. Mukarji, Nirmal and Bandyopadhyay, D. 1993, *New Horizons for West Bengal's Panchayats* (A Report for the Government of West Bengal), Government of West Bengal, Calcutta, p.9.
56. Joshi, B.M. 1989, 'Evolution and Practice of Decentralized Planning in India', *Indian Journal of Public Administration*, Vol. XXXV, No.1, p.111.
57. Sharma, P.N. 1991, 'Decentralized District and Sub-District Planning: Shorting out the Basic Issues' in B.N. Yugandhar and Amitava Mukherjee (eds.), *Readings in Decentralized Planning*, New Delhi: Concept Publishing Company, p.81.
58. Report of the *Working Group on District Planning*, *op.cit.*, p.29, par.4.12.
59. *Ibid.* p.43, par.5.10.
60. Krishan, Gopal. 1991, 'Resource Transfer under Decentralized District Planning: Some Issues' in Yugandhar and Mukherjee (eds.), *op.cit.* p.144.
61. Sundaram, K.V. 1997. *Decentralized Multi-Level Planning*, New Delhi: Concept Publishing Company, p.323.
62. *The Asian Age*, Calcutta, dated 21 August, 1997.
63. Recommendations of *the State Finance Commission*, *West Bengal*, 1995, *op.cit.*, pp.122-25, and 148-51.
64. *Gram Bhittik Block Parikalpanar Paddhati-O-Prayoger Ruparekha* (in Bengali), 1989, District Planning Committee, Midnapore, p.7.
65. *Note:* This conclusion has been arrived at after detailed discussions with a representative number of *Sabhapatis* of the Panchayat Samitis (six) of the district. Also, endorsed by *Mr. S. Majumdar*, a member of the DPC, Midnapore.

66. VANI. 1995, *State Panchayat Acts: A Critical Review*, Voluntary Action Network India, New Delhi, p.190.
    Also. Government of West Bengal, *No. 2441(17)DP/1F-7/95*, dated 27-6-1997, Department of Development and Planning, Calcutta.
67. Report of *the Working Group on District Planning, op.cit.*, pp.43-44, par.5.12.
68. Government of West Bengal, *No.6372/P/1F-8/85 dated 28-8-1985, op.cit.*
69. District Planning Committee, *Order dated 5-5-1995*, signed by the Additional District Magistrate, Midnapore.
70. Government of West Bengal, *No.2441(17)DP/1F-7/95, dated 26-7-1997*, Department of Development and Planning.
71. Report of the *CAARD, op.cit.*, p.31, par.4.21 (iv).
72. *Finance Minister of West Bengal in a Seminar* on 'Decentralization: Devolution and Participation' organized by the State Planning Board, Government of West Bengal, dated 20-22 November, 1998, Calcutta. Also corroborated by *Mr. H.K. Samanta, op.cit.*
73. Recommendations of the *State Finance Commission*, 1995, *op.cit*, p.4, par(s). 2.10 and 2.11.
74. *Ibid.*, pp.4 & 112.
75. *Records* of the Department of Development and Planning, *Government of West Bengal.*
76. *District Eighth Five-Year Plan*, District Planning Committee, Midnapore, p.iv/108.
77. *Annual Action Plan*, 1996-97, Employment Assurance Scheme, Midnapore.
78. *Proceedings of the Annual General Meeting of the District Urban Development Agency* (DUDA), Midnapore, dated 28-7-1997.
79. *Ibid.*, dated 11-7-1996. Also *corroborated by Mr. Bijali Ghosh*, Project Officer, DUDA, Midnapore dated 12-8-1997.
80. Misra, R.P. and Sundaram, K.V. 1980, *Multi-Level Planning and Integrated Development*, New Delhi : Heritage Publishers, pp.20-21.
81. *Interview with Mr. H.K. Samanta*, Chairman, DRDA, *op.cit.*
82. Nanjudappa, D.M. 1991, 'Concepts, Approaches and Techniques of Decentralized Planning' in Yugandhar and Mukherjee (eds.), *op.cit.* p.26. Report of the *Working Group on District Planning, op.cit.*, pp.80-81, par(s). 8.26 and 8.27.
83. *District Seventh Five-Year Plan, op.cit.*, p.3.8.
84. *District Eighth Five-Year Plan, op.cit.*, p.IV/362.
85. *District Seventh Five-Year Plan, op.cit.*, Table No. XXII, and *District Annual Plan*, 1996-97, *op.cit.*, p.1/14.
86. *Interview with Mr. H.K. Samanta*, dated 4-8-1998.
87. *District Annual Plan*, 1996-97, *op.cit.*, p.IV/152-53.
88. *Panchayati Raj* (in Bengali), 1997 (March-April), Government of West Bengal, p.4.
89. *A Prelude to the Ninth Plan, District Planning Committee, Midnapore*, pp.10-11.
90. *Nanjudappa*, 1991, *op.cit.*, pp.21-22.

91. Benninger, Christopher C. 1991, 'District Planning Methods and Techniques' in Yugandhar and Mukherjee (eds.), *op.cit.*, p.381.
92. Report of the *Working Group on District Planning,* 1984, *op.cit.*, pp.76-77, par.8.11
93. *Ibid.*, pp.77-78, par.8.16.
94. Report of the *CAARD, op.cit.*, p.28, par.4.14.
95. *The Ganashakti,* Calcutta, dated 21-8-1997.
96. *The West Bengal District Planning Committee Act,* 1994, Section 3(2) and 3(3).
97. Report of *the Working Group on District Planning,* 1984, *op.cit., p.44,* par.5.16.
98. Government of West Bengal, *Resolution No.* 3230/P-1S-6/85, dated 24-5-1985, *op.cit.*
    Medinipur Zellar Grambhittik Parikalpana Rachanar Ruparekha O Unnayaner Pratichhabi, DPC, *op.cit.*, p.7.
99. *Guideline of the DPC,* Midnapore, approved by the DPC in its meeting, dated 19-9-1996.
100. Reported in the *Chhapa Khabar* (a local daily), dated 30-9-1997. Subsequently verified at an interview.
101. Mukarji and Bandyopadhyay, 1993, *op.cit.*, p.5, par.3.3. This view is also held by most of the *Sabhapatis* of Panchayat Samitis and *Karmadhyakshas* of the Zilla Parishad.
102. *Note:* Such a conclusion is drawn after discussions with a sizeable number of panchayat members of Dantan-I, Keshiary and Narayangarh blocks of the district.
103. Sundaram, K.V. 1989, 'Multi-level Planning: Concepts, Principles and Some Aspects of its application of Sectoral Planning' in Sundarban, Ramesh and Tiwari (eds.), *Regional Planning and Development,* New Delhi: Heritage Publishers, Vol. I, pp.101-102.
104. *Interview with Mr. N. Chatterjee,* District Planning Officer, dated 21-5-1995.
105. Government of West Bengal, *No.2720(45)/DP/15-21/86,* dated 19-4-1986, *op.cit.*
106. District Planning Committee, *No.773 (120)* dated, 24-6-1997, Midnapore.
107. Jain, R.B. 1984, 'Planning in the Third World', *Indian Journal of Public Administration,* Vol. XXX, No.3 (July-September), p.559.
108. Reported by *Mr. H.K. Samanta, op.cit.*
     The Ananda Bazaar Patrika, Calcutta, 1 August, 1997.
109. Sridharan, L. 1990, 'Coordination in Development Administration', *Indian Journal of Public Administration,* Vol. XXXVI, No.2 (April-June), p.172.
110. Meredith and Mantel, Quoted in Amitava Mukherjee, 1992, *Studies in Multi-Level Planning-III : Methodology and Database for Decentralized Planning,* Part-C, New Delhi : Heritage Publishers, p.352.
111. Government of West Bengal, *No.2720(45)/DP/15-21/86,* dated 19-4-1986, and *No. 3328(46)/DP/1M-21/86,* dated 19-5-1986.
     Also, *Corroborated by Mr. N. Chatterjee, op.cit.*

112. Report of the *Working Group on District Planning, op.cit.*, pp.58 & 72, part(s). 6.58 and 7.107.
113. *Proceedings of the DPCC*, dated 17-8-1991 and 21-7-1992.
114. Government of West Bengal, *No.3328(46)DP/1M-21/86*, dated 19-5-1986, Development and Planning Department.
    Proceedings of the meeting of the DPC Sub-Committee (PWD), dated 10-3-1997, item-B.
115. *The Ananda Bazar Patrika*, Calcutta, dated 1-8-1997.
116. Report of the *Working Group on District Planning, 1984, op.cit.*, p.94, par.10.8.
117. *Ibid.*, p.95 par(s). 10.9 & 10.10.
118. Rajan, M.A.S. 1990, *op.cit.*, pp.212-16.
119. *Proceedings of the meeting of the working Group* (Monitoring), dated 8-1-1987, DPC, Midnapore.
120. *Proceedings of the meetings of the Working Group*, dated 26-6-1987 (Fishery) and 24-8-1987 (PWD).
121. *Ibid.*, dated 17-8-1987 (PHE).
122. Interview with *Mr. A. Mandal*, DPLO, Midnapore, dated, 19-8-1997.
123. *Interview with Mr. A. Mandal, op.cit.* Corroborated by the *Sabhapatis* of Dantan I, Narayangarh and Keshiary Panchayat Samitis of the district.
124. *Note:* This conclusion is drawn after having detailed discussions with a sizeable number of Gram Panchayat members and some members of the Beneficiary Committees of No. 1 (Alikosa), 2 (Tarrui) and 3 (Manoharpur) Gram Panchayats of Dantan I Block. The same view is also held by some *Sabhapatis* of the Panchayat Samitis of the district.
125. District Planning Committee, No. 903(75)/dated, 2-8-1986, Midnapore.
126. *Records of the DPC*, Midnapore. *Corroborated by Mr. M.N. Goray*, Formerly *Sabhapati* and member of the DPC in course of discussions. Also, *Proceedings of the Seminar organized by the Zilla Parishad, op.cit.* dated 19-6-1987.
127. *Proceedings of the meeting of the Working Group*, dated 8-1-1987, District Planning Committee.
128. *Ibid.*
129. *Interview with Mr. H.K. Samanta and Mr. A. Mandal, op.cit.*
130. *Interview with Mr. A. Mandal and Mr. N. Chatterjee, op.cit.*
    Also, endorsed by the *Sabhapatis* of some Panchayat Samitis and the *Karmadhyakshas* of the Zilla Parishad.
131. Mukarji and Bandyopadhyay, 1993, *op.cit.*, p.6, par.3.14.
132. Simon, H.A. 1957, *Administrative Behaviour*, New York, USA: The Free Press, p.9.
133. *Interview with Mr. H.K. Samanta*, and *Mr. A. Mandal, op.cit.*
134. Mukarji and Bandyopadhyay, 1993, *op.cit.*, p.8, par.3.13.
    This view is also endorsed by the *Sabhapatis* of some Panchayat Samitis and *Karmadhyakshas* of the Zilla Parishad
135. Lieten, G.K. 1992, *Development, Devolution and Democracy*, New Delhi : Sage Publications, p.143.

This is ascertained from discussions with the *Sabhapatis* and most of the *Gram Pradhans* of Dantan I, Keshiary and Narayangarh Panchayat Samitis.

Also, corroborated by *Mr. H.K. Samanta, op.cit.*, dated 27-8-1997.

136. *Panchayat Parichalana Prasange Nirdeshabali* (in Bengali), 1983, Left Front Committee, Calcutta.

Panchayat Parichalana Prasange Sadharan Nirdeshabali, 1988, CPI(M), Midnapore District Committee, pp.9-12.

Panchayat Parichalana Prasange Nirdeshika, 1994, CPI(M), West Bengal State Committee, Calcutta, pp.7 & 10-11.

137. *Panchayat Parichalana Prasange Sadharan Nirdeshabali*, 1988, *op.cit.*, p.9.

138. *Ibid.*, p.9. *Also corroborated by Mr. H.K. Samanta, op.cit.*

139. *Interview with Mr. H.K. Samanta, op.cit.*, dated 4-8-1998.

This view is established in interactions with a sizeable number of DPC members and a representative number of *Sabhapatis* of the Panchayat Samitis in the district.

140. *Interview with Mr. H.K. Samanta, op.cit.*

141. *Interview with Dr. Ajit Narayan Bose*, the main architect of 'Planning by Villagers' of the district, dated 1-9-1995.

Also, the Proceedings of the Seminar organized by the Zilla Parishad, *op.cit.*

142. *Note:* This view is expressed by a cross-section of local leaders of Aunrai Gram Panchayat under Contai-II Block (Dist. Midnapore) in a signed statement in the preface of a document – *Grambasider Dwara Gram Parikalpana* (in Bengali), 1990 (October), District Planning Committee, Midnapore.

Also, Lieten, 1996, *op.cit.*, pp.65 & 227.

143. Sathyamurthy, T.V. 1997, *State and Nation in the Context of Social Change*, Delhi: Oxford India (Paperbacks), pp.114-15.

Mallick, Ross. 1993, *Development Policy of a Communist Government: West Bengal since 1977*, Cambridge: Cambridge University Press, pp.149-53.

144. Pranger, R.J. 1968, *The Eclipse of Citizenship*, New York : Holt, Rinchart & Winston, p.3.

145. *The Harijan*, dated 21-12-1947.

146. Valk, P.de. 1990. 'who sets the rule for decentralization? Who wants to play the game?' in Valk and Wekwete, K.H., (eds.), *Decentralizing for Participatory Planning?* U.K.: Gower Publishing Company, Aldershot, pp.266-67.

147. *Panchayati Raj Update*, 1999 (October), Vol. VI, No. 10, p. 5.

148. Recommendations of the *State Finance Commission*, 1995, West Bengal, Chapter-VI.

149. Hadden, Susan G. 1980, 'Controlled Decentralization and Policy Implementation: The Case of Rural Electrification in Rajasthan', in Merilee S. Grindle (ed.), *Politics and Policy Implementation in the Third World*, New Jersey: Princeton University Press, pp.172-73.

150. Gow, David D. and Van Sant, Jerry. 1981, *Beyond the Rhetoric of Rural Development Participation: How can it be done?*, Washington DC : Development Alternatives, Inc. p.5.
151. Hirsch, Z. Werner. 1970, *The Economics of State and Local Government*, New York: McGraw Hill Book Company, p.127.
152. Mukarji, Nirmal. 1985, 'The Future of District Governance' in *Administrative Arrangements for Rural Development*, Hyderabad: National Institute of Rural Development, pp. 197-204.
———, 1996, 'Decentralization below the State Level: Need for a New System of Governance' in Kuldeep Mathur (ed.), *Development Policy and Administration*, New Delhi: Sage Publications, pp. 271-78.
153. Report of the *Working Group on District Planning*, 1984, *op.cit.*, Vol. I, p.43, par.5.11.
154. Sundaram, K.V. 1990, 'Determining the Sectoral Matrix for Integrated Development' in R.P. Misra (ed.), *District Planning -- A Handbook*, New Delhi : Concept Publishing Company, p.177.
155. Sukthankar, D.M. and Sundarm, P.S.A. 1987, *India Country Paper*, Manila : Asian Development Bank, pp.418-19.
156. Dror, Yehezkel. 1968, *Public Policy-Making Re-examined*, Sanfrancisco: Chandler, pp.8-9.
157. Ghosh, Arun. 1992, *Planning in India – The Challenge for the Nineties*, New Delhi: Sage Publications, p. 40.

8

CONCLUSIONS

The present study has been undertaken with a view to examining the administrative aspects of decentralized planning and highlighting the issues involved in the process of district planning. The study is the result of both macro and micro surveys with the help of desk research as well as field investigation carried out in the concrete situation of a district. In this chapter, an attempt is made to sum up the major findings and the choices in policy formulations for actualising decentralized district planning in an effective manner.

Planning in India commenced with a centralist thrust towards national development in the background of a federal system of government. With the passage of years, the process has settled on decentralized district planning through experimentation in search of an appropriate level. Though the Seventh Plan emphasised the introduction of decentralization in planning with people's participation, the planning process was conceived merely as an administrative device and a delivery system for implementation of programmes.

The Constitutional Amendments (1992) have clinched the issue and accelerated the process of further decentralization based on local popular participation. While most of the states have decided to decentralize the process up to the district level, a few have come down even below the district, though the intra-state planning exercise is seldom made public or outlined in an articulated manner. The Working Groups, set up in 1977 and 1984, found little effective decentralization in most of the states. Only a few states have experimented with devolution of some responsibilities for implementation of plans to the local level bodies. In most cases, district planning turned out to be a mere aggregation of sectoral schemes at the district level. The experiments carried out in West Bengal since the middle of the eighties constitute a model in itself in decentralized planning which may claim superiority over others due to its distinctiveness and concrete achievements.

Developed on the foundations of land reforms and revitalised panchayats, and backed by people-oriented measures, decentralized planning was initiated in West Bengal as an alternative model of development. Almost all the districts soon took the initiative to carve out an additional tier of planning below the state level in which people's participation was considered axiomatic. The experiments in decentralized district planning, launched in the state with the commencement of the Seventh Plan, represent a story of both success and failure. Prior to that, from 1978 onwards, the State Government was delegating gradually the responsibilities of implementation of poverty alleviation programmes and other small schemes to the panchayats which were conceived then as agencies of the State Government, and as a delivery system to manage the target group oriented schemes. These limited objectives were realised to a large extent. With the introduction of decentralized district planning, a new methodology has been introduced by the government. According to the methodology, as already discussed in Chapter 3, the plan budget of the State Government is divided into two parts, one for the State Sector Schemes and the other for the District Sector Schemes, on the basis of twin norms: location of the schemes or projects and the coverage of benefits extended by such schemes. The initial confusion relating to the inclusion of a scheme in a particular sector is removed through the introduction of the 'White Book', in which district sector or state sector schemes are classified separately. The State Government issued a 'Guideline' in 1985, constituting the planning organizations at the district and the blocks. At the district level, a two-tier machinery comprising the District Planning and Coordination Council (DPCC) and the District Planning Committee (DPC) was formed.

It is also revealed from the study that the State Government has introduced the provision for disaggregation of the plan budget for devolution of funds to the districts through sectoral allocations. Subsequently, a separate budget head, District Plan Schemes Fund (DPF), has been identified. Allotments of funds under the DPF are placed at the disposal of District Planning Committee. Under this methodology, the allotments of the district under sectoral allocations are brought to the notice of the DPC and a certain portion of the allocations is dovetailed to the blocks. Moreover, to strengthen the resource mobilization at the district level, a scheme of decentralized resource mobilization has been introduced and a state-district collaborative programme is designed for mobilization of additional resources. The first five years of the introduction of decentralized planning comprised the period of initiation when a lot of experience was gathered. Later on, the planning machinery was revamped with the creation of a Standing Committee of the DPCC, an Urban Development Sub-Committee and separate Working Groups.

Examined from the viewpoint of development, rural West Bengal has made a tremendous progress. After pursuing the alternative development strategy, the spectre of dry and lean seasons has disappeared from rural Bengal and now there is no surplus labour in the districts to migrate to the streets in Kolkata. Apparently not so much revolutionary but reformist, the West Bengal experiment of decentralized planning has achieved what is still lacking in other states excepting Kerala. The curve of agricultural production in the state has shown appreciable upward trends and the process of decentralization in decision-making has been strengthened. Millions of citizens have been periodically electing their representatives to the three tiers of the panchayats without interruption since 1978. In conformity with the requirements of Constitutional Amendments (1992), the West Bengal Panchayat Act has been amended and the District Planning Committee Act has been passed. Subsequently District Planning Committee Rules have been framed and the District Planning Committees have been constituted. Taken together, all these measures have strengthened the process of decentralized planning in the state, which has entered the stage of 'limited decentralization' in the meantime.

Now the investigation is concentrated on the methodology of decentralized planning in the district of Midnapore which is the area of the study. Following the policy decision of the State

Government, the district authorities took the lead in 1985 by introducing *Village Based District Planning* in which the district plan was designed on the felt needs and priorities of the people at the villages. Simultaneously, the process of *Planning by the Villagers* themselves was introduced on an experimental basis in a limited number of villages where Village Planning Committees were formed. Each of the committees was provided with a modest amount of fund with which they prepared their own plans corresponding to their requirements and availability of resources. The methodology adopted in this district in 1985 for decentralized planning was quite different from that of the state and also from the all-India pattern. The methodology developed by the State Government considered the blocks as the ground units of decentralized planning where the block plans were formulated by incorporating the 'need statements' prepared by the Gram Panchayats. However, the State Government has recently revised the planning methodology in which Gram Panchayat Plans are formulated on the basis of priority plans of the villages.

The methodology of decentralized planning adopted in the district was thus village-based. The Seventh, Eighth and Ninth Plans of the district were modelled and implemented according to the methodology in which the priority plan outlined in the villages and action plans prepared at the Gram Panchayats were integrated into the block plans. The block plans were then incorporated in the district plan that was formulated by accommodating the district sector schemes and municipality-specific schemes. The district plan thus formulated was used to be sent to the state for integration with the state plan and the total plan of the country as well. Though it could not be actualised in its entirety, it created a wave of interests throughout the district, which ultimately resulted in a people's movement in the initial years. The present methodology, followed in the district considers the *Gram Sansads* in the rural areas and the *wards* in the municipalities as the micro units of planning which brightens the scope of active participation of the people. But the methodology is not all comprehensive. From the study it appears that the process of preparation of perspective plan for longer period of time, which was followed during the Seventh Plan, has been discontinued since the Eighth Plan due to lack of definite policy and absence of certainty in flow of funds to the district and below. Absence of perspective plans weakens the system of linkages between the long-run perspectives and the immediate objectives. However, it appears that the design for planning in the district is methodologically well conceived in other respects. It includes not only the methodological issues of planning but also the requirements and modalities involved at the stages prior to the formulation of plans. A comprehensive and detailed procedure for surveys and data collection, time schedule required for different phases, flow chart in planning process, identification and classification of sectors and the division of task boundaries at the relevant levels constitute the essential elements of the methodology followed in the district. Formats for preparation of plan are also included in the methodology, which contain components like physical and financial review, outlay matrix and scheme-wise distribution of individual departments including expected flow of funds, and physical targets of the district.

These are the positive aspects of the methodology. The study also identifies certain inadequacies as well. It is evident that the district and block plans have become simple collation of departmental schemes without exhibiting any focus on the core areas of development. Hence the plan document becomes a monotonous repetition of the same projects and schemes. Integration of the district plan with the total programmes of the district is an important aspect of decentralized planning. Convergence demands innovative ideas, collaborative exercise and flexibility in decision-making. Schematic allocation provides little scope for innovation and flexibility in implementation and makes the plan document a mere list of schemes and projects having little integration in the absence of such convergence.

The central focus of the study is the administrative infrastructure of district planning. Hence, the arrangement of machinery for planning at different levels, starting from the national level and resting with the Gram Panchayat levels, is reviewed from structural as well as operational viewpoints.It appears from the study that the planning organizations at the state level and above are in existence for a pretty long time and there is nothing innovative in it.

While coming to the sub-state level, we can see two models in the state, one created in 1985 and continued till the formation of the District Planning Committees in 1995 and the other now exists in the district. It is seen from the examination that the organizations established in the eighties at the district level were structured on the lines suggested by the government and there was no major deviation. There were, however, some informal organizations at different levels of the district created by the political leadership, which were extra-statutory. The District Planning Committee, constituted in the eighties, acted as an umbrella organization for planning at the district level. Apart from formulating the district plan, it had to coordinate, monitor and supervise the formulation and implementation of lower level plans taking into account the local needs, priorities and availability of resources. But subsequently the District Planning Committee, not to speak of the DPCC, became a deliberative body meeting irregularly to take broad policy decisions in most cases. The administrative supports, provided by the District Planning Cell, were minimum; the cell itself was ill equipped and without an effective establishment. Naturally, most of the planning functions were carried out by a Working Group created by the DPC, and looked after by the Zilla Parishad and its Standing Committees.

During the Eighth Plan, attempts were made to gear up the functions of the DPC and accordingly, the district level planning machinery was strengthened through the creation of separate Working Groups, each dealing with a specific subject, and the Urban Planning Sub-Committee. Moreover, a Standing Committee of the DPCC was formed as the core committee of the DPC to ensure coordination, evaluation and review of planning activities in the district. The situation at the block level was deplorable. At the block level, a two-tier planning machinery, quite analogous to the district system, was constituted. Though the State Government did not provide any scheme for creation of Block Planning Coordination Committees (BPCC), the district authorities decided to constitute the BPCC at the block level from the beginning. The BPCC was an advisory body and the planning functions were actually performed by the Block Planning Committees (BPC) which were comparatively smaller in composition. Still today there is no separate establishment for planning at the block level and the planning activities are organized by a small group under the overall supervision and guidance of the Panchayat Samiti. There was no planning organization below the block and in the municipalities. The DPC took little interest in municipal planning until the creation of Urban Planning Sub-Committee. Thus municipal planning, and gram panchayat planning were the exclusive domain of the municipalities and panchayats respectively. It is thus revealed from the investigation that the planning machinery, created previously in the district was sketchy, though representative in composition but inadequate in functioning.

We find in the study that the organizational arrangements in the districts have undergone vast changes after the 74th Constitution Amendment Act and the DPC Act passed by the state. The erstwhile DPCC now ceases to exist and the District Planning Committee is designed to be a broad and democratic body achieving a happy blending of 'local autonomy, administrative capability and planning expertise' in its composition. However, the major thrust in the composition is clearly on representativeness. The District Planning Committee consolidates the panchayat and municipal plans and prepares the draft development plan of the district with the help of a number of sub-committees, now twelve in number, created by it. The sub-committees have replaced the working groups of the earlier era. These sub-committees consist of the members representing both the local bodies and the sectoral departments, and thus the present combination ensures effectiveness, cooperation and linkages at the operational levels. The sub-committees assisted by the ill-equipped and unorganized District Planning Cell and by the district development department occasionally, review, coordinate, monitor and evaluate the formulation and implementation of the sectoral plans and ensure their convergence with the panchayat and municipal plans and the district plan. Of the sub-committees, the District Planning and Coordination Sub-Committee is the most important and it has taken over all the powers and functions of the erstwhile Standing Committee of the DPCC. From the investigation it is also clear that a functional differentiation has been worked out by the DPC to avoid possible overlapping and incongruity in the functioning between the Sub-Committees of the DPC and the Standing Committees of the Zilla Parishad. Under the existing arrangement, the functions of the Standing Committees are confined to the planning activities of the three tiers of the Panchayati Raj Institutions, while the Sub-Committees take care of the sectoral plans. The present DPC is thus an improvement upon the previous one. Previously, the members of Parliament and the State Legislature were not represented in the DPC; they were included in the DPCC but now they have found their role in the development and planning activities of the district through their representatives in the DPC.

It is further revealed that the State Act is indifferent to the creation of planning machinery below the district level but the district authorities have retained the Block Level Planning Committees with only minor modifications in their composition. The Block Planning Committees are now widened in composition and sharpened in functions with the active involvement of the Panchayat Samitis, though they depend on the same establishment. At the Gram Panchayat level, there is no standing committee for planning but the guideline prepared by the DPC provides for a mechanism in the name of Panchayat Planning Committee that meets once in a year to approve the draft plan of the Gram Panchayat. In the methodology of district planning in Midnapore, the *Gram Sansad* plans constitute the basis on which the entire planning hierarchy is developed but there is no planning organization at the *Gram Sansad* level save and except a fluid structure visualised in the *Iswar Chandra Jana Chetana Kendras*, the centres established for organizing continuing education programmes in the district. It may also be noted here that there are no separate planning organizations in the urban areas of the district. The municipalities themselves are the planning bodies and they formulate their plans on the basis of priority plans supposed to be prepared by the ward committees. But in reality, there is no attempt for preparation of plans at the ward level. Likewise, the panchayats formulate and implement their own plans, which are integrated with the block plans and district plan subsequently, through a methodological network developed by the DPC. Moreover, the special purpose and area development bodies help the District Planning Committee in the formulation and implementation of district plan through preparation of their respective action plans and implementation of the projects and schemes. Among the different tiers of the Panchayat Raj Institutions, the Zilla Parishad acts as the main organization in the development and planning activities of the district. It has a well equipped establishment which provides necessary administrative assistance for organizing effective supervision and timely monitoring of the planning operations at various levels.

Thus from the study we find the existence of a variety of interacting and well designed planning organizations consisting of people's representatives, bureaucracy and experts in the sphere of planning. Through the District Planning Committee and its sub-committees, the expertise of the departmental officers and the perceptions of the elected representatives are brought together for the formulation of an integrated plan of the district as a whole. Again, the integration and coordination of the planning activities at the area levels are also worked out and actualised through these bodies.

The study has also highlighted the state of actual implementation of decentralized planning that took place in the district during the Seventh and the Eighth Five-year Plans. We find two identifiable but integrated parts in the implementation process. The first part relates to the planning for implementation and the second to actual implementation. The study gives a total picture of the operations followed in the implementation of plans and the perspectives that prevailed during the period under consideration. It has been stated in Chapter 3 that both the subjective and objective conditions were conducive to the successful introduction and implementation of decentralized district planning in the state and, for that matter, in the district. For successful implementation of decentralized planning in the district, the district authorities initiated a campaign throughout the district to popularise decentralized planning and to familiarise the people with the processes of decentralized planning. It is revealed that the campaign was not so well designed as was the 'People's campaign for Ninth Plan' in Kerala. But the campaign aroused a sense of interest and awareness among the people, which ultimately gave it a shape of mass movement in the district. As a result, the task of data collection and raising of planning cadres at the pre-planning stage became easier. But lack of organizational infrastructure and failure in realising the essence of village based decentralized planning left the process of data collection incomplete. It is also found in course of investigation that the attempt to prepare village plan, the foundation of the decentralized district planning, did not materialise during the successive five-year plans.

The scope for flexibility in decision-making even at the stage of implementation is an essential characteristic feature of decentralized planning. At least two instances of modifications in the priorities in course of execution of district plan have been traced through the investigation. These modifications were necessitated by a variety of reasons mostly beyond the control of the DPC. However, in terms of output, both these modifications resulted in cent per cent achievement and even the targets were exceeded in some cases. At present there exists a time frame uniformly applicable throughout the state which is prepared by the government. Thus we see that implementation of planning provides scope for learning which helps the DPC in its future course of action. At the same time decentralized planning is problematic in itself due to the involvement of a number of variables as well as agencies, which cause delays and dilemmas. We find through the investigation that in the instant situation, both the formulation and implementation were delayed due to a variety of reasons which compelled the District Planning Committee to modify its existing time schedule and prepare a new one in 1994. The modified time schedule helped the DPC to overcome the problems in the succeeding years.

The study has demonstrated that whatever the flow of funds, the implementation of the projects and schemes are done at the appropriate levels in the way in which the plans are formulated. Funds are allotted to the executing agencies and the schemes are implemented according to the availability of funds. It is revealed that the small village level projects without involving much technical exercise are executed by the Gram Panchayats while the larger schemes are left to the Panchayat Samitis for execution. Bigger schemes are considered to be the exclusive domain of the Zilla Parishad. In some cases, the Zilla Parishad entrusts the responsibilities of execution to the Panchayat Samitis and the Gram Panchayats. In such cases, the Zilla Parishad or the Panchayat Samiti constitutes beneficiary committees at the relevant levels for supervision and monitoring of the projects. The sectoral schemes and projects are executed by the government departments after receipt of departmental funds. The monitoring and review of such projects and schemes are undertaken by the Sub-Committees of DPC. Moreover, the Zilla Parishad and the Panchayat Samitis, with the help of their respective Standing Committees, review the progress and provide guidance, whenever necessary.

The municipal plans are executed by the municipalities under the supervision of the District Planning Committee and the District Urban Development Agency. But the scope of such supervision is limited and weak. The Zilla Parishad, Panchayat Samitis and Gram Panchayats execute their projects which are usually formulated by them. The Zilla Parishad publishes an annual action plan each year indicating therein the schemes and projects to be executed at different tiers of the Panchayati Raj Institutions. The action plans include the cost estimates, location, expected time for completion etc. The sectorai projects are executed by the departments through the contractors under their own supervision, while the projects under the panchayats are executed by the panchayats themselves with the help of beneficiary committees. To ensure regular flow of credits from the financial institutions located within the district, review of progress in implementation of credit plans is quarterly undertaken by the Zilla Parishad with the help of District Level Coordination Committee. It is also revealed from the study that the rural development programmes comprising the Centrally Sponsored Schemes constitute a major sector in the district plan. In case of this sector, flow of fund is both regular and satisfactory and hence the implementation is smooth and the achievement is nearly cent per cent in terms of creation of assets and employment opportunities. The implementation of these schemes, as revealed from the study, has also consolidated the relationship between the bureaucrats and the political functionaries, besides strengthening the role and administrative capabilities of the democratic institutions in development and planning.

In the backdrop of the foregoing findings, the study has highlighted a number of issues together with some constraints in the actualisation of district planning. The first and the most vital of the issues in this context is the people's participation in planning. A brief review of the literature as well as the planning and plan related documents establishes the importance of people's participation as the most valuable element in decentralized planning. Under the existing arrangement, popular participation is sought to be ensured in two ways: indirect and direct. It is revealed that the scope of indirect participation is wider. After the Constitutional Amendments, people's participation in decentralized planning has been institutionalised and the scope of such participation in the district as well as in the state has been further strengthened. The people take part at every stage of planning through their representatives. But the scope of direct participation is rather limited. Neither the State Panchayat Act nor the DPC Act provides scope for direct participation of the people in the process of formulation, execution, supervision and evaluation of plan projects. The methodology of district planning in Midnapore, however, makes room for such participation in a limited way. But the constraint arises from the irregular meetings of the *Gram Sansad*. Moreover poor attendance at such meetings render the body ineffective. Again, the study also confirms similar experiences gained in Kerala during the 'People's Campaign'. Even when the meetings are well attended, these turn out to be the venue of placing general demands in most cases. In spite of a good number of instances of people's participation in different programmes of the district, organized political mobilization, and establishment of literacy centres at the *Gram Sansads* and *Wards*, the state of people's participation in planning is not encouraging, though there are of course a few exceptions.

The question of resource mobilization is another vital issue. Decentralized planning demands a sound resource base at the relevant levels, the first step being resource mobilization by the local bodies themselves. But the situation is highly deplorable and the planning depends on the flow of funds from the state, which is yet to be stabilised. There are no uniform or well-accepted principles for devolution of funds from the state to the lower levels. The recommendations of the State Finance Commission have been partially implemented. The District Planning Committee does not have any prior idea about the exact flow of funds from the state. It is a fact that over all these years more than fifty per cent of the plan budget has devolved to the district or below. But it is revealed at the same time that most of the funds devolved is meant for the departments which formulate and implement the sectoral plans more or less independently. Whatever the basis of such allocations, the District Planning Committee has very little control in this regard. The scope of inter-sectoral adjustments or re-adjustments by the DPC is not permissible.

The inflexibility found in shifting the allocations from one sector to another or a sub-sector is sought to be minimised through the introduction of District Plan Schemes Fund (DPF) by the government. But, as the study shows, the flow of fund through the DPF has been neither regular nor substantial in the last fifteen years. However, the situation has improved considerably during the Ninth Plan period. A major constraint in resource mobilization has emerged from the fact that in most cases, funds released to the district under DPF are tied to the specific schemes or sectors which reduces the decentralized planning exercise to a mere ritual.

Decentralized district planning depends on adequate linkage and integration, both vertical and horizontal, at all the levels. The DPC is visualised as an 'umbrella organization' nesting the plans originating from departments, panchayats, municipalities and other agencies. The Panchayati Raj Institutions ensure organizational linkages. The functional linkages are established through the Sub-Committees of the DPC and the Standing Committees of the Zilla Parishad. Thus integration and coordination take place at the district level. The methodology adopted in the district also provides for such linkages at the block level through the BPCC and BPC. But it is doubtful if such devolution in administration could be actualised in the context of indifferent attitude of the government and insular looking attitude of the line departments. Again, there is no scope for development of a common framework for decentralized planning and interactions among the functionaries of the different District Planning Committees. There is no organization at the state level that may deal with the inter-district problems through mutual discussions. It is further revealed from the study that the factors of horizontal and vertical coordination among the district and block level functionaries could not be fully reconciled. Lack of such coordination has left a negative impact on the decentralized planning process as a whole.

Related to the above, as the study brings out, there is the problem of poor and ill-equipped machinery for planning at the district. The District Planning Cell, which acts as the secretariat of the DPC, is poor in strength and weak in capability. The planning activities of the district are looked after by this cell with occasional assistance from the development department of the district on *ad hoc* basis. However, there exist a good number of organizations at the district level like the DRDA and DUDA, which have less functions in the present circumstances. But their services are not directly placed under the DPC.

The District Planning Cell was created in 1985 with four personnel. In the meantime, the functions of the DPC have multiplied but the establishment has remained static. The planning cell has been identified by the Working Group on District Planning as the most vital organization for planning. There is no separate wing for planning at the levels of the Panchayat Samitis and Gram Panchayats. The administrative infrastructure of the Panchayat Samitis and the Gram Panchayats, in spite of recent improvements at the Gram Panchayat level, is too meagre to meet their normal requirements. Again there is a major constraint at the micro level. The DPC has identified the *Gram Sansad* as the lowest unit of planning. But there is no organization or body which might organize the functioning of the *Gram Sansad*. In fact *Gram Sansads* are large bodies without heads.

From the study it appears that the government departments have been co-operating with the DPC and the local bodies on a more or less regular basis over a number of years. But the problem arises not from their opposition but from their indifference. It is revealed that the field functionaries and line personnel do not take adequate interest in decentralization of authority and prefer to shift their responsibilities to the panchayats.

The study also points out other constraints in the exercise of decentralized planning in the district. The constraints relate to delay in formulation and implementation of plans, insufficient and unreliable data base, communication gap between the departments and the District Planning Committee, absence of scope for interactions between the DPC and lower level bodies in determining the goals, objectives and strategies of the district plan and lack of interest among the political parties and groups. But it is evident that these constraints are of less magnitude. The issues like popular participation, flow of funds and devolution of decision-making power pose greater challenges to the success of decentralized planning.

In addition to these, the study also attempts a few suggestive policy prescriptions for the successful implementation of decentralized district planning in future. The policy prescriptions include major suggestions like the establishment of village committees, strengthening of planning machinery at the district and creation of planning organizations at the municipalities and the levels below the district, arrangement for mobilization of local resources and regular flow of untied funds, more financial devolution and placing of services of district level developmental personnel under the DPC.

Thus the study reveals that the process of decentralized district planning is a continuous process, a movement, which cannot be expected to reach total success within a short span of time by means of a one-shot effort. State Government has recently recast the methodology of decentralized district planning to make it more elaborate and effective from the viewpoint of actual implementation. Such modifications and additions are also included in the present study. The applicability and effectiveness of the revised methodology cannot be judged at this moment but the methodology seeks to plug the loopholes identified during the Eighth and the Ninth Five-Year Plans. Through the exercises so far, a modicum of self-confidence has been achieved and the on-going practices strengthen the belief that a concrete and total shape could be given gradually to the concept of *planning from below* against the traditional bias of *planning from above*.

APPENDICES

APPENDIX-I

REPORT OF THE WORKING GROUP ON DISTRICT PLANNING (VOLUME–1)

CHAPTER 1

CONCLUSIONS & RECOMMENDATIONS

1. To make decentralised planning a success, it has to be backed up by sound practices. The capabilities for decentralised planning have to be assiduously built up, the right procedures and suitable structures have to be evolved and necessary technical and administrative changes, including attitudinal changes have to be brought about among the bureaucrats and the politicians. The various initiatives and improvisations necessary should be introduced cautiously and "in steps", providing adequate time for assimilating them, thus paving the way for learning through experience at every stage and making necessary modifications in the process as we go along. *(Para 3.4)*

2. For decentralised planning to make headway, institutional mechanisms have to be made more broad-based with the active involvement of local representatives and endowed with a greater degree of autonomy in local decision-making. Simultaneously, several administrative and financial delegations as well as other measures have to be systematically worked out. *(Para 3.8)*

Concept of District Planning

3. The concept of district planning adopted by the working group is akin to the concept of integrated area planning. *(Para 3.11)*

4. At the State level, suitable decisions have to be taken about an appropriate inter-dependency mix and proper function sharing between the State and District levels taking into account the planning and other capabilities available at the grassroots level. *(Para 3.14)*

5. The totality of all planning activities at the level of District which is a sub-system would vest with a single District Planning body who would determine the priorities and allocate funds accordingly among the various development sectors. *(Para 3.15)*

6. The district plan should take into account the regional affinities and should be informed by a regional perspective. It will also be necessary to recognise the sub-regions within the district. *[Paras 3.19(1) & 3.19(2)]*

7. The Panchayati Raj Institutions and other local government institutions should play crucial role in the district planning process. Ultimately district planning will have to be taken over by these bodies. Therefore, it would be necessary to strengthen them right from now onwards, so that they could play their legitimate role in the district planning process in course of time. *[Paras 3.19(3), 5.22, 5.23, 5.32]*

8. Though, each district plan must be specific to its own agro-climatic and socio-economic conditions, it must reflect the following basic objectives of the national plan.

(i) Increasing production;
(ii) Reducing unemployment; and
(iii) Alleviating poverty. *(Paras 3.20 & 3.24)*

9. With the devolution of more planning functions to the district level the technical planning machinery (both the quality and quantity) will need to be augmented. *(Para 4.26)*

9A. It is recommended that the Planning Commission should have a fresh look at the question of staffing the District Planning Cell in the light of this report and suggest a more realistic staffing pattern avoiding duplication of staff between planning cell and line departments. *(Para 4.27)*

10. In order to improve upon the system of choosing the right schemes among the numerous suggestions made by several agencies, groups and individuals, the States could consider the

scrutiny of these proposals by a committee of experts before they are placed before the District Planning Body. *(Para 4.30)*

11. Raising the levels of persons lower down the administrative hierarchy is one of the basic necessities and this could be tackled by inducting some high calibre technical staff into the district planning machinery, and frequently organising training and refresher courses for the lower staff on a regular and continuing basis. *(Para 4.40)*

12. Evaluation should be undertaken by an independent agency, and not by the District Planning body. It could be done at the State's level or by any independent agency. Evaluation should not be confined to a project/scheme but the planning act as such should be evaluated on an annual basis. *(Paras 4.46 &10.11)*

Prerequisites for District Planning

13. The essential prerequisites for decentralised district planning will include, apart from political commitment, defining the scope and content of a district plan, some measures for the disaggregation of allocations, delegations of administrative and financial powers, evolution of new patterns of administrative behaviour, a reorientation of attitudes and relationships, building up of a capabilities and instruments of control, establishment of participatory structures and umbrella mechanisms, and continuous training and retraining of personnel. *(Para 5.2)*

14. The Working Group strongly recommends that there should be no bar for incurring some essential maintenance expenditure from plan funds to revive and rehabilitate some languishing investments. *(Para 5.3)*

15. The Working Group commends the adoption of a twofold classification of schemes into district level and state-level schemes by the States. *(Para 5.4)*

Disaggregation of Outlays

16. In the allocation of funds between the state and the districts, the guiding principle should be that while local priorities must receive importance in the district plan, they should not be at the cost of overriding national and state priorities. Keeping this in view the disaggregation of plan funds from the State to District level may be done by providing for major State Sector schemes and then derive the District Sector outlay as residuary of this. Alternatively provide for all the District Sector programmes in the first instance and treat State Sector as residuary. Perhaps the exercise could be conducted from both ends to reconcile the figures. However the proportion thus arrived at should not be made the basis for making future allocations, as this would leave little or no scope for the districts to take up new schemes. Therefore, any proportion arrived at by a State should not be continued on a permanent basis, but should be constantly watched in a dynamic context and revised. The revision may be carried out say every five years.

(Paras 4.12 & 5.8)

17. The Working Group recommends that the divisible plan outlays may be distributed among the districts on the basis of three elements, viz., population, area and level of development. Each state may work out its own criteria for giving weightage for allocation of outlays on account of level of development.

(Para 5.10)

18. Vesting the district planning body with all powers to divide the sectoral allocations in the district is an ideal goal, which can be reached only at some distant point of time. In the meantime some special steps must be taken to give some scope to the district planning body to undertake a few local development programmes on its own to meet local aspirations and requirements. This could be done by making a discretionary allocation to the district planning body. *(Para 5.11)*

19. In its allocation formula for the transfer of Plan funds for the district level, Gujarat has set aside a small proportion (5%) as

incentive grants to match efforts made at the district level for additional mobilisation of local resources in kind and/or money. The Working Group commends this approach for emulation by other States. *(Para 5.12)*

20. So far as the relatively underdeveloped districts in a State are concerned, their cause would be adequately served by giving proper weightage to the various criteria of backwardness in the allocation formula, rather than by treating them on a separate footing. *(Paras 5.14 & 6.40)*

21. The reduction of intra-district imbalances should be the aim in the allocation of district resources among the blocks. States should evolve their own methods for this purpose. In districts, where special problems are met within some blocks, some special dispensation may become necessary. *(Para 5.15)*

Organisational Framework

22. The institutional framework for District Planning should be a social instrument of decision making which would be a happy blend of local autonomy, administrative capability and planning expertise. *(Para 5.16)*

23. In District Planning bodies, the collector must play the role of the Chief Coordinator. To enable him to discharge these responsibilities properly and efficiently he must have the necessary status, power and responsibilities. He should be able to effect the necessary horizontal and vertical coordination in the planning and implementation tasks. In order to move towards this goal, the departmental functionaries must be considered as on deputation from their respective departments and posted to the District Planning bodies. In this way they will be made responsible for implementation of their respective programmes at the district level and will be held *accountable* for their performance to the District Planning bodies. This is no doubt a major structural re-organisation. But such changes are very necessary if the District Planning process is to be made effective. *(Para 5.21)*

24. As regards administrative decentralisation, the Working Group recommends that the procedure for administrative and technical sanctions should be so simplified and streamlined that none of the district level schemes be referred to state headquarters. Powers of reappropriation within minor heads of account should also be vested with the Collector. Only matters beyond the prescribed limits of sanction or reappropriation should be referred to Finance/Planning Department. In other words, the accent should be on bulk control rather than on detailed control. *(Para 5.24)*

25. It is important that district level functionaries are brought under the control of the District Collector who should be the sheet anchor of implementation of district plans. To ensure the compliance of district level departmental functionaries, their confidential reports in respect of district sector performance should be written by the District Collector, which should form part of the personal files of concerned officers. *(Para 5.25)*

26. Since the Collector's association with the developmental work is a must, it is suggested that a senior officer of the rank of Additional Collector may be provided in each district to assist the Collector and to relieve him of much of the routine responsibilities. *(Para 5.27)*

27. The size of the districts should also be made more manageable purely on administrative grounds. *(Para 5.28)*

28. The Departmental officers at the district level should not be subjected to frequent transfers. They should normally be kept in one district for a minimum period of three years. *(Para 5.28)*

29. Officers serving in remote or inaccessible districts could be paid special pay up to 35% of their salaries. Residential accommodation and other minimum facilities should also be made available in such areas. *(Para 5.28)*

30. Suitable adjustments must be made in budgetary format and Demands for Grant of the state to display district plan outlay

ɔ ensure accountability to the legislature. Within each Demand, Minor Head called 'District Sector Schemes' may be opened.

(Para 5.29)

1. An additional document called the Annual District Plan hould be placed before the legislature along with other budget apers. This document should contain district-wise information n annual plan in terms of Minor Heads and subheads. Listing of ach individual scheme and the detailed heads may be avoided.

(Para 5.29)

2. Within the framework of multi-level planning, the nctions of the District Planning Bodies should be (I) ystallisation of local needs and objectives, (II) taking stock of e natural and human endowments, (III) listing and mapping of nenities, (IV) formulation of district plans, (V) formulation of licies, programmes and priorities, (VI) coordinated implemention, and (VII) monitoring and review of the implementation of strict plans and programmes. *(Para 5.30)*

. The District Planning Body should consist of a Chairman, ember-Secretary and a reasonable number of members, say 50. ne size and composition of the District Planning Body should decided by the State Governments. *(Para 5.31)*

. In addition to the District Planning Body, it would be sirable to have a smaller Executive Body, which will be in the ture of a Steering Committee. *(Para 5.31)*

. For the District Planning Bodies statutory sanction is not cessary. These bodies may be constituted under an executive ler of the State Government as has been done in most states in country.

(Para 5.33)

. The District Planning Cell should be headed by a Chief nning Officer whose status in the district should be next only that of the District Collector/District Development Commisner. On recruitment he should be specially trained in gional/area planning methodology and techniques. *(Para 5.35)*

37. The Chief Planning Officer should be assisted by an abl team of experts drawn from various disciplines like economics statistics, agronomy, cartography, economic geography engineering, sociology, banking etc., as well as from subjec areas like agriculture, animal husbandry, horticulture and so or The actual size and composition of this team should be left to th district. *(Para 5.36*

38. There should also be a Planning Officer of BDO's rank a the block level assisted by two Research Assistants and a Typis and a messenger to help the Chief Planning Officer to coordinat the Blook Level Programmes with regard to intra-Block gaps i development and amenities. *(Para 5.37*

39. A competent unit for District Planning should b established at the state level to complement and bolster th planning capacity at the District level. *(Para 5.38*

40. There should be one single planning cadre for the stat comprising of the technical planning staff at the block, distri and state levels. *(Para 5.3*

Training

41. Those who man the District Planning Organisations shoul be given a more intensive and broadbased training in releva areas like Economics, Statistics, concepts and techniques c comprehensive, spatial, sectoral and project planning. The should also be well grounded in analytical and evaluativ techniques. *(Para 5.4*

42. At the Centre, the Department of Personnel (Trainin Wing) must come forward in a big way not merely to organi the training of trainers in the apex level institutions in th country, but also to assist the state training institutions to equ themselves for the training tasks. *(Para 5.4*

43. We recommend that the Department of Personn (Training Wing) in collaboration with the Planning Commissi

should set up a group to work out the curriculum as well as the modalities for a properly conceived training programme for district planning trainees at different levels. *(Para 5.43)*

Methodology of District Planning

44. The methodology of district planning should be simple and the district plan itself concrete, specific and practical.

(Para 6.2)

45. Following steps in sequence for the formulation of the district plans are suggested. This would in fact be the simple methodology to be adopted for district planning:

(1) Formulation of the major objectives of the district plan.
(2) Compilation of data for district planning.
(3) Bringing out the profile of the district in relation to the basic objectives.
(4) Formulating the main strategy and thrust of district planning.
(5) Analysis of the existing programmes and projects with reference to the strategy outlined.
(6) Assessment of resources for allocation to various programmes and projects.
(7) Statement of physical and financial components of the district plan.
(8) Statement of spatial dimensions of the district plan.
(9) Relationships and links between the district plan and regional and state development plans.

(Para 6.6)

46. The suggested methodology of district planning, which is normative, assumes that the districts will have the freedom to plan for the entire district sector, which may not be true for all the states at present. It is, therefore, necessary to make it clear that all the procedures outlined here would be applicable only at a stage when full-fledged district planning would be possible.

(Para 6.7)

47. The District Plan must consist of integration of development activities in primary, secondary, tertiary and infrastructure sectors so as to deal with the problem of unemployment and poverty. Full employment is both an objective of planning and also the means of reducing poverty and increasing production The district plan must essentially provide for expansion and diversification of the economy so as to reduce poverty and increase employment. *(Paras 6.10, 6.13 & 6.14)*

48. While dealing with the problem of poverty and unemployment, the district plan must focus on providing gainful employment opportunities to small and marginal farmers, agricultural labourers and artisans. *(Para 6.15)*

49. The data for district planning should be in relation to the four sectors of the economy and the various sections of the society which have been mentioned above. *(Para 6.16)*

50. Necessary minimum amount of data and information necessary for planning and decision-making at the district level should be identified and data should be collected. *(Para 6.17)*

51. It is suggested that the collection of data/information by the district planning team must cover all those areas defined as the 'District Sector', including such background information, as may be helpful in their meaningful interpretation. An illustrative list of data/information useful for district planning is shown in Annexure 6.1. *(Para 6.18)*

52. States are advised to adjust their data requirements depending on the scope to be given by them for districts planning and taking into account the analytical abilities of their planning teams. *(Para 6.19)*

53. The Group feels that regarding income and consumption levels of population and employment and unemployment, to start with, the district planning exercise may incorporate the results of NSS and IRDP Surveys as are readily available duly cross-checked with other information and refined to the extent

possible; but gradually the NSS data should be made usable by introducing the required changes in the sampling pattern.

(Para 6.21)

54. On technology and productivity, the information has to be obtained from various sources, including from some spot surveys, if necessary. In order to obtain data relating to inflows and outflows of goods and services, it would be necessary to build up regional accounts at the district level on a systematic and continuous basis. The Central Statistical Organisation should initiate this process with the active assistance of States. The Group notes that the C.S.O. had set up a Committee on Regional Accounts in 1972 and the report was given in 1976. The recommendations of this Committee should be quickly implemented. *(Para 6.22)*

55. The Working Group recommends that District-wise, estimation of 'income originating' should be attempted by all States. In the meantime, whatever information is available from various sources should be assembled and used in the planning exercise. *(Para 6.23)*

56. The database could be greatly strengthened by the utilisation of technological tools like aerial photo interpretation and remote-sensing technology. We suggest that for every district in the country, the thematic maps may be prepared.

(Para 6.24)

57. As aerial photographs will be required for an exceedingly important national task, the Defence Ministry should relax their regulations and make them available without delays. The Planning Commission should identify suitable educational and other research institutions in the country where such work could be carried out and should provide adequate funds to these institutions to undertake this work. *(Para 6.25)*

58. The data collected would then provide what we call the profile of the district and would itself suggest the strategy for development, which is particularly relevant to that district. The

district planners must have a total and comprehensive perspective of the district and a district profile would only emerge from such a comprehensive perception of the planners of the needs and potentialities of the district. *(Paras 6.26 & 6.27)*

59. When District planning becomes a full-fledged and independent operation at the district level, working out the area strategies for the district and its sub-regions will constitute the most important step and the content of the plan must be derived from these strategies. *(Para 6.28)*

60. The existing or ongoing schemes must be subjected to very close scrutiny in terms of suitability of these schemes to the specific conditions of the district; and if on scrutiny they need to be modified to suit the requirements of the district they should be suitably modified. The central or centrally sponsored schemes or even State schemes should provide for sufficient flexibility to take note of the varying local requirements and the district planners must have the freedom to suggest local modifications in the schemes on the basis of close scrutiny of how the schemes have actually worked. Also a district plan must provide for replacement of the existing schemes with new schemes or supplementing existing schemes with new schemes. *(Para 6.29)*

61. Interlinkages between various programmes and projects are extremely important though these are overlooked, with the result that individual plan schemes do not fructify in the absence of backup from supporting programmes. Indeed, successful implementation of programmes requires that all the forward and backward linkages are properly taken care of. *(Para 6.30)*

62. One of the persisting weaknesses of planning in India is the implementation gap between what is aimed at and what is accomplished. It is the specific responsibility of district planning to fill up the implementation gap. District plan should take note of various leakages that prevent the impact of plan programmes being felt. The plan programmes must contain proposals for strengthening organisation and management, which should prevent such a leakage. *(Para 6.31)*

63. At present the block may be considered as the unit area for eliminating intra-district disparities. To arrive at intra-district variations suitable indicators may be developed. *(Para 6.32)*

64. The District Planners' task would be rather focused on setting priorities among the numerous project schemes, ideas thrown up during his resource inventory and other analyses and those that emerged during his discussions with the public as to felt needs. His choice among different candidate projects has to rest on other considerations than the quantified efficiency evaluation. *(Para 6.36)*

65. The district planning should be an attempt to dovetail the various resources for different projects and schemes in an integrated manner. *(Para 6.39)*

66. While drawing up a programme for the development of specific activities, it would be desirable to look at them not as unrelated or individual items by themselves but in terms of their inter-relationship with other related, subsidiary or supplementary activities and to draw up plans for all the related activities in an integrated manner. *(Paras 6.50 & 6.51)*

67. The final plan should contain the tentative cost of each project and programme, summary of the mode of implementation, actions needed by the various agencies, the system of financial control and monitoring methods during the course of implementation and final evaluation. In the District plan, all projects and schemes should be fully reflected, with all their inter-relationships, interdependencies and comple-mentarities duly worked out. *(Para 6.55)*

68. It must be ensured that the district plan fits in the framework of the State Plan and the National Plan. The sectoral allocations as emerging from the various district plans in the States must add with the budgetary allocations made sectorise at the State level. *(Para 6.56)*

69. The draft plan drawn up as above should be placed before the District Planning Body (Board or Council, whatever be its nomenclature) and fully discussed and finalised. The district plan emerging in this manner should then be forwarded to the State Government for being dovetailed into the State Plan. *(Para 6.57)*

70. There should be a time-table for planning in the State. The District Planning Office should be given adequate time, say about 3 months to formulate the District Plan with some degree of thoroughness. The District Planning Bodies should finalise their annual plans for the ensuing year during the second half of October. *(Para 6.58)*

71. In the light of objectives set out for district planning, it could be realistic to think in terms of three kinds of District Plans in relation to different time spans. These would be:

(a) Perspective Plan- covering 10 to 15 years;
(b) Five Year Plans;
(c) Annual Plans. *(Para 6.59)*

72. A simultaneous movement in all these directions though desirable may not be feasible. The minimum expertise made available for District Planning may be initially directed towards the formulation of a medium term plan coinciding with the Seventh Five-Year Plan along with its annual breakup. In States, where the prerequisites for District Planning are already established, the annual plan exercise for the district may commence even from 1984-85 onwards. Other States, where the District Planning infrastructure and the essential prerequisites have not been established, should start providing for these from 1984-85 onwards so that District Planning could be initiated positively from the beginning of the Seventh Plan in all the States in the country. *(Para 6.60)*

73. It is recommended that the experiments made in the States of Maharashtra, Tamil Nadu, Jammu & Kashmir, Karnataka and Andhra Pradesh in respect of Perspective Planning may be carefully studied by the States desiring to embark upon district

perspective plans so that various pitfalls characterising these exercises could be avoided. *(Para 6.67)*

74. The immediate objective should be to attempt district five year plans co-terminus with the 7th Five Year Plan. These district plans should be formulated in all the districts of the country. It would be a time bound task entrusted to the district administration. The work for the Preparation of district plans, we recommend, should be immediately taken on hand because at least a period of one year would be required for the formulation of the five year district plans. *(Para 6.68)*

Manpower Planning

75. Manpower Planning and budgeting should be for the district as a whole with reference to all the activities (plan, non-plan, developmental and non-developmental) and cannot be confined only to activities included in the District Plan and implemented thereunder. *(Paras 6.42, 7.4 and 7.41)*

76. In dealing with manpower and employment problems at the district level it was recognized that those categories of manpower who were specialised and highly technical like Doctors, Engineers and Architects would be outside the purview of the district planning process except for their deployment and utilisation within the district. *(Paras 6.41 and 7.5)*

77. The large mass of unskilled manpower would be the main pre-occupation of the planning process at the district level in terms of providing employment and raising their levels of living. It is also recognised that except under special circumstances this mass of work force is not mobile and employment opportunities have, therefore, to be found for them in or near the villages where they reside. *(Para 6.43 and 7.5)*

78. In-between highly skilled and unskilled categories lies the intermediate group for occupations requiring a minimum level of education and some training. Although it is not necessary, nor perhaps desirable, to attempt to provide employment to all such

persons within the district, there must be skills and occupations, which can be wholly confined to the district both in terms of source as well as employment. Every district should be able to identify such categories and make attempts at being self-contained in respect of these by and large. *(Paras 6.41 and 7.6)*

79. To encourage employers to provide inplant training not only to their employees but also to others, the feasibility of granting concessions or assistance could be examined. *(Para 7.7)*

80. A scheme for the improvement of language among matriculates may perhaps be useful along with abolition of degree qualification for such jobs where matriculation or Higher Secondary certificates would, otherwise, be adequate. *(Para 7.7)*

81. Successful experiments have been carried out in giving special training to drop-outs at VIIIth Standard stage and enabling them to be absorbed as salaried workers or to set them up as self-employed workers. Some innovative schemes should be included in the District Plan for this purpose. *(Para 7.8)*

82. Where employment of children in occupations prohibited by law continues or where employment of children is considered otherwise hazardous or dangerous, the attempt must be to stop such employment of child labour and at the same time provide alternative employment opportunities, wherever necessary, for such displaced children. *(Para 7.10)*

83. While child labour in general should be gradually phased out, this should be done particularly carefully where they are employed to augment the family income and also where they gain skills in traditional occupations. *(Para 7.10)*

84. The district level planning process will have to take note of the need for finding employment opportunities for the physically handicapped. *(Para 7.11)*

85. It is necessary to identify low wage and/or high unemployment (chronic unemployment) areas within the district

and take appropriate investment decisions to enable such areas to come up, both in rates of wages and levels of employment. As departmental budgets may not be adequate to meet the requirements of such pockets, the need for a Free Fund from out of which suitable programmes could be financed for such areas becomes strong. Another way of directing attention to these areas will be to confine expenditure under NREP to such areas; alternatively increased allocation of funds could be made under NREP to these areas. *(Para 6.44 & 7.12)*

86. The Working Group recommends that Manpower and Employment Planning exercises should be taken up by all States in the country with whatever data and capabilities that exist. *(Para 7.15 & 7.17)*

87. The Working Group recommends that the district level Census figures may be made available without further delay. Apart from this it would be useful if the census authorities could undertake a mid-term sample census with special reference to employment and make this data available without delay up to district level. *(Para 7.19)*

88. It would be desirable to make effort to increase the size of the sample so that the NSSO is able to generate reliable district level estimates. *(Para 7.20)*

89. It is also necessary to devise measures so that results of sample surveys are available at the district level with minimum delay and, in any event, within 12 to 18 months of the completion of these surveys. *(Para 7.22)*

90. It is desirable that NSSO takes up employment surveys annually, on a regional basis; the State should then be requested to work out, making use of the State Samples, employment situation in different spheres. *(Para 7.22)*

91. Manpower planning at the district level is essentially directed to those intermediate categories of workers whose

functions lie between the level of an unskilled worker on the one hand and an engineer or a technologist or a doctor on the other. *(Para 7.26)*

92. The extent of unemployment may be estimated by one of the following methods:

(i) NSSO method suitably modified;
(ii) Family labour budget survey of sample households;
(iii) Registration method.

The demand, so identified, has to be projected for the next five years. Based on the availability of resources in the District' Block and the potential for new activities, suitable locations (growth centres) into which these jobs may go may be determined. *(Paras 7.27-7.29)*

93. All schemes operating in the block or district and directly managed by public sector authorities should be listed, categorised and summed up as on a specific date so that the benchmark information could be updated. *(Para 7.34)*

94. At the village level, it is necessary to build up information on items like housing, population, net area sown, the proportion of net area sown to net area irrigated, number of bore wells, number of handlooms, power looms, mat weaving units, artisans, the distance to various locations like railway station, bus stop, post office etc. *(Para 7.34)*

95. District Manpower and Employment Generation Councils (DMPEGC) should function as an important arm of the District planning agency and should be responsible to the latter for formulation of proposals for all employment generation activities in a district. It is necessary that the DMPEGCs are constituted as part of the District Planning Authority. *(Para 7.36)*

96. To make DMPEGC functionally effective, it should be adequately staffed with experts in different fields. The membership of the Council should also be broad-based and reflect the

pressing need for increasing employment opportunities particularly among the relatively more disadvantaged i.e. Scheduled Castes, Scheduled Tribes, Women, Physically handicapped etc. *(Para 7.36)*

97. For working out the manpower and employment policies for the district a cadre of manpower experts is required to be built up either by fresh recruitment and training or by giving intensive training to existing District Employment Officers, at selected institutions. *(Para 7.38)*

98. The exercise on the district manpower and employment plan should get initiated at least two years before the commencement of the plan period. *(Para 7.39)*

99. It is also necessary to give some training or at least orientation, to the various departmental functionaries, so that they are able to understand the context in which and the purpose for which information is sought for from them. *(Para 7.41)*

100. In an environment of increasing economic activity, it is likely that consequent on the vertical mobility in occupations by way of promotions, there is likely to result deterioration in the level of the skills all along the line. This becomes accentuated, when there is any sudden expansion of employment opportunities in projects. In such a case, it would be necessary to introduce a suitable system of upgradation of skills to maintain standards at all levels. *(Para 7.44)*

101. In respect of the large number of unskilled manpower, it is necessary that the District Manpower Planning and Employment Generation Council, in collaboration with other agencies, should work out arrangements by which, even in respect of these persons, their capabilities are increased resulting to higher productivity on the kind of jobs that they do. The tendency to import more efficient manpower from outside can also be checked if, in implementation of such programmes at the local level the practice of entrusting the work to contractors is progressively replaced and organisations like labour cooperatives

encouraged to take up these works; alternatively, the works could be executed departmentally. With reference to Scheduled Castes and Scheduled Tribes, specific steps are to be taken to develop entrepreneurial skills among the educated unemployed, so that the employment-oriented schemes are realistically covered and implemented for the benefit of these sections of our population. *(Para 7.45)*

102. It is necessary to have a look at the various legislative provisions as well as regulations that may unwittingly come as disincentives to taking up activities which are particularly employment intensive. Contrarywise specific legislative support may be needed in cases where attempts to create additional employment opportunities are thwarted by a recalcitrant minority to take up such programmmes. *(Para 7.46)*

103. The anxiety for increasing employment opportunities must take account of considerations of ecology and the need, for the protection and improvement of the environment. *(Para 7.47)*

104. Existence of established practices of inter-district and intra-district migration of working population should be taken note of in drawing up manpower and employment plans. *(Para 7.48)*

105. The District Planning authorities should have sizeable funds, which they can, in their discretion, utilise subject to broad guidelines that the State Government may issue to these authorities. The guidelines for the use of free fund should give priority for its use in providing missing links and for fulfilment of the programme of minimum needs and such items in the New 20-Point Programme as are relevant at district level. Further, it may be stipulated that free fund should be used on public works and not for liberalising existing patterns of assistance of the schemes. However, where the basic minimum needs are largely met, the funds may be used for increasing the number of beneficiaries under any existing or future scheme, but conforming to the prescribed pattern of assistance. *(Para 7.49 & 7.50)*

106. The endeavour must be to provide full employment to the total working population of the district till the end of the century. Even if this should not become possible, the endevour should certainly be to increase employment opportunities at a specified percentage during each plan period. *(Para 7.51)*

107. Within the programmes in the next ten or fifteen years, special attention will have to be given to increasing employment opportunities for women at a rate, which is much higher than the average for the district. Likewise during this period every effort should be taken to ensure a complete elimination of child labour in all these occupations which are prohibited by law or which are considered hazardous or dangerous. *(Para 7.51)*

108. A long term programme of operations relating to, say, expansion of irrigation, desilting of irrigation tanks, deepening of wells, maintenance of soil conservation works, maintenance and upgrading of roads and the like, which are labour-intensive should be drawn up and suitably incorporated in the Five Year Plans and the Annual Plans. *(Para 7.52)*

109. Projections of changes in population, as well as in the workforce, including their sex distribution, will have to be worked out and a long term plan which would take note of the increasing demands for employment drawn up. *(Para 7.53)*

110. A programme for entrepreneurial development, more particularly in the small towns in the rural areas, both among the women and the youth will have to be formulated. An important aspect of self-employment programmes can be the need for providing self-employment opportunities for part of the day particularly for women. An important element of any attempt to improve self-employment activities will be the provision of an adequate and efficient marketing arrangement for the finished/ semi-finished products. *(Para 7.54)*

111. The requirements, both in numbers as well as in categories of skilled and other manpower for any central or state level project that may be implemented in the district, will have to be

ascertained and advance action taken, wherever necessary, to make such skilled manpower available. *(Para 7.55)*

112. The long-term strategy should, in short, be not merely one of using the available manpower for implementing existing schemes and programmes but to devise such schemes and programmes as would usefully employ the manpower that is available and that would be developed. *(Para 7.57)*

Spatial Planning

113. A major task to be accomplished through the exercise of spatial planning would be to design a pattern of settlements for human activities. *(Para 7.67)*

114. Wherever the physical, social and economic characteristics of a district so require, there should be no hesitation to sub-divide it on the basis of different criteria keeping in view particularly planning obiectives. *(Para 7.69)*

115. Given the size-distribution of settlements in a district and the population and distance threshold for different functions, there will be three main categories of settlements; those which have, those which do not have but should have the function, and those which do not and need not have it. While it is the task of the planner to ensure that all settlements of the second category have the functions warranted by the accepted norms for their location, it is an equally important task for him to ensure that the last category of settlements has access to such functions. In the first category of settlements there could also be some which have the function though they may not be entitled to have them. In their case the planner will not ordinarily disturb the *status quo* unless he considers relocation desirable and feasible. *(Para 7.89)*

116. A distinction should be made between functions which are provided by the State and those provided by the private sector. *(Para 7.90)*

117. In ensuring that functional dependence is established between three categories of settlements described in para 7.89, the planner should take into consideration convenience of access in terms of time and cost burdens passed on to the users.

(Para 7.92)

118. The planner should identify *gaps* between *prevailing* and *required* levels of availability of different functions in the district (Functional gap). *(Para 7.94)*

119. The planner should also identify settlements where new or additional functions are required to be located to reduce the functional gaps. *(Para 7.95)*

120. Apart from existing functional gaps the planner should also anticipate emerging functional gaps. *(Para 7.96)*

121. If together the combined population of all settlements in the area can sustain a particular function, the real gap can be eliminated by providing the function at an appropriate location within the area. *(Para 7.97)*

122. Information relating to the explicit space preference shown by inhabitants of individual settlements in the study area with regard to their movements to avail different functions may have to be generated through field surveys for the purpose of special planning. *(Para 7.102)*

123. The use of maps in spatial planning is indispensable. The basic requirements is the latest available topographical map(s) of the Survey of India of the scale 1:50,000/1:2,50,000. The final choice of the scale of the map will depend on the area to be covered and the convenience of use. Another essential map is the revenue map of the Taluk/Sub-division showing village boundaries. *(Para 7.103)*

124. It is necessary that before the spatial planning exercise commences, the special planner acquaints himself with the objectives of the District Plan, its priorities – the norms

prescribed for different functions and the resource constraints. He should also be acquainted with the general socio-economic conditions of the district and with its relationship with other districts in the State. *[Para 7.107(i)]*

125. Another important preliminary step is the determinations of spatial units of planning which the planner will consider, that is, cluster of villages, panchayats, parts of blocks, block etc. Likewise, wherever possible spatial planning objective should be quantified and the time frame for planning be defined. *[Para 7.107 (ii)]*

126. It is desirable to collect and store data in formats which will help in quick retrieval and updating. *(Para 7.108)*

127. While the data are being collected and processed, base maps of the study area can be prepared. *(Para 7.109)*

128. After the data have been collected and processed and the base maps are ready, the spatial planner should undertake various analyses including those for planning of hierarchy of centres and service areas. *(Para 7.110-7.111)*

129. The District Plan should incorporate projections of population, of production levels and of demand for different functions in its proposals. Applying appropriate techniques, future scenarios and terminal states of important sectors should be projected and their spatial planning implications incorporated in the proposed plan. *[Para 7.112 (i)]*

130. The requirement of functions in the study area should be expressed both quantitatively and qualitatively, taking into account functions which should exist but are absent, those which are not adequately available, as also units of functions which are due for replacement because of depreciation and obsolescence. These quantitative and qualitative estimates should be expressed in specific spatial terms, that is, for individual villages, clusters of villages, service centres of different levels, etc. *[Para 7.112(ii)]*

131. The proposals of the spatial plan regarding expansion of functions in the study area should take into account the requirements of small towns such as those having Nagar Panchayats and Notified Area Committees. *[Para 7.112 (iii)]*

132. Where the spatial planner is aware that potentially good alternative proposals exist, it is desirable to indicate the range of choices rather than arbitrarily select only one of them. *[Para 7.112 (iv)]*

133. The spatial planner should be recommended *interse* priorities and phasing of implementation of his proposals. *[7.112(v)]*

134. Detailed costing of alternative proposals should be done in consultation with the concerned subject matter specialists on the district planning team. *[Para 7.112 (vi)]*

135. Assessment of the impact of the proposals on the local ecology/environment should be made for those proposals which entail major changes such as in the physiographic, hydrological, geological characteristics. *[Para 7.112(vii)]*

136. To the extent possible, the spatial planning proposals at the district, block, panchayat and village levels should be kept within existing administrative boundaries to minimise jurisdictional overlap and friction in their implementation. *[Para 7.112 (viii)]*

137. It is possible to adopt spatial planning in two graduated phases. The first stage may consist of preparation of some maps depicting present level of development blockwise and cartographic depiction of the infrastructure taking village as the unit as well as interblock comparison of the level of facilities of selected items. In the second stage, more sophisticated exercises involving determination of hierarchy of centres and service areas and working out of thresholds and norms etc. can be undertaken. *[Para 7.114-7.117]*

Integrated Planning and Coordinated Implementation

138. Integration has to be worked out carefully and consciously at the stage of plan formulation itself, i.e. at the level at which schemes are formulated, whether at district, block, village or household level. For integration at the planning stage to come about in the ideal manner the entire planning activity touching on all aspects should be undertaken by one single planning body which will prepare comprehensive plans for all activities at the district level in an objective manner. But this is a long-term goal. As we cannot erase the numerous existing structures which are now performing the planning functions for their limited areas, we have to advance towards final goal in some definite stages and sequences. We have to take note of the existing administrative set-up and the different agencies involved in various development tasks and to work out the appropriate modalities for bringing about integration during the planning stage itself. *(Paras 8.7 & 8.8)*

139. The role of the Collector in the task of coordination at the District level is very important. *(Paras 5.2 & 8.9)*

140. The District Planning Body would essentially function as an umbrella organisation nesting the plans of individual departments and agencies and integrating them into a common and consistent framework, sub-serving a central strategy formulated for the district as a whole. *(Para 8.11)*

141. It is particularly emphasised that the Central Ministries should not encourage the emergence of new agencies and all planning functions should, in future, be the responsibility of the District Planning Body. The Working Group would, therefore, like to emphasise that during the 7th Plan, efforts should be directed towards increasingly devolving the planning functions now being performed by different organisations and agencies to the DPBs so that they will ultimately emerge as the Apex Planning Bodies at the District level. *(Para 8.14)*

142 The Working Group recommends that the powers to allocate funds among the various sectoral departments and to make reappropriation within certain limits should be accorded to the District Planning bodies. *(Para 8.16)*

143. Various poverty alleviation programmes, if they are to confer anticipated benefit on a sustained basis, have to be provided with considerable external support. The concerned departments must be fixed with the responsibilities for providing such support by incorporating the same in their annual plans. Since it is important to provide the necessary inputs at the proper time, the entire exercise of planning for input and infrastructural support must be completed before April/May. *(Para 8.17)*

144. The support needed for the poverty alleviation schemes should be worked out in advance for the entire Seventh Plan period by adopting an incremental approach. *(Para 8.19)*

145. The DRDAs should not only do their internal coordination, but also learn to dialogue effectively with the District Planning Bodies, so that the present vacuum in coordination is effectively bridged. The development dialogue between DRDA and DPB could be institutionalised by providing for mutual representation in these bodies. (*Para 8.20*)

146. Projects and schemes being implemented in the district have to be coordinated both from the sectoral and locational points of view. Besides, it is also important to harmonise the projects and schemes in time, i.e. to set a coordinated time-schedule for their execution. *(Para 8.21)*

147. Integration between the District Plan and plans originating from the lower and higher levels has to be brought about through the introduction of effective development dialogue among the planning bodies at various levels. *(Para 8.22)*

148. Block level planning is necessary to ensure the development of pockets of backwardness and to bring about a more balanced development within the district. In order to ensure

integration of block plans with the district plan, the block planning should also be entrusted to District Planning Team. Besides, the district plan should also take note of the special programmes like the tribal sub-plan, for the provision of several complementarities, i.e. the input and the infrastructural facilities which are required as a back-up support to these plans.

(Para 8.23)

149. For dovetailing the district plans with the State plan the Working Group recommends the following alternatives for the States to consider:

(i) The Districts need not wait for indication about resource ceiling and can go ahead with planning on an *ad hoc* assumption of a 10% step up. They may also draw up a second short list of schemes that could be considered if more resources become available.

(ii) The State may take a decision that the District Plan component of the State Plan would be kept in tact whatever be the outcome about outlays after the discussions with the Planning Commission.

(iii) The district plan may be a composite plan for medium term, i.e. 5 years with clear annual break-up for the five years sectorwise which should be provided for in the State Plan with very little variations. There can be a second look at the provision of funds at District level as a mid-term review to correct any imbalances.

(Para 8.24)

150. In order that the District Credit Plans are realistic, the States should disaggregate the district-wise outlays and present them in State Annual Plans so that the information for the District Credit Plans would become available in November of the previous year. *(Para 8.26)*

151. The District Credit Plan should also cover the activities of the private sector and give analysis of bank-wise position of

resource deployment. Reconstitution of the District Coordination Committees and Standing Committee into Compact forums should be expedited. Besides it is necessary to ensure up-to-date land records easy availability of non-encumbrance certificates etc. *(Para 8 .27)*

Rural Urban Integration

152. The Working Group recommends that towns with a population of less than 10,000 should be treated as an integral part of the district area for purposes of overall planning and implementation of development programmes in the district. With such integration, it is also necessary to ensure that the funds provided at the state level for urban development sector are duly disaggregated on a proportional basis for meeting the cost of the urban services of urban centres thus brought into the rural framework of district plan. *(Paras 8.28 & 8.29)*

153. Benefits under programmes like IRD available to the rural poor should be extended to urban poor living in towns up to a population of 10,000. *(Para 8.30)*

154. It is necessary to tie up the potential of emerging industrial townships, mining complexes, large irrigation projects and hydel and thermal projects in the midst of rural areas with the development of rural hinterland. *(Para 8.31)*

155. Representation should be given to the urban local bodies in the District Planning Boards entrusted with the task of formulation of District Plan. *[Para 8.34(1)]*

156. Urban Local Bodies having a population of over 10,000 should be asked to prepare Annual and Five Year Plans within the framework of the State Plan. *[Para 8.34(3)]*

157. In the case of Urban area which will serve as growth centers, the linkages between the needs of these areas and plans for meeting these needs by conscious efforts taken up in the adjoining rural areas should be clearly spelt out.

[Para 8.34(4)]

People's Participation

158. Some experiments in local level planning through the local people have been made in different States. The Comprehensive Area Development Programme tried in West Bengal, Tilonia experiment in Rajasthan, Maliwada experiment in Maharashtra, the Mafatlal Group experiment (Uruli Kanchan etc.) in Maharashtra are some of the examples. A careful study of these experiments would provide useful insights on this subject. We recommend that special studies of these "Action Planning" ventures in the country should be undertaken by the Multi-Level Planning Division in the Planning Commission as part of the continuing work programme. *(Para 8.43)*

159. People's participation, to be really meaningful, should take place at every stage of planning including pre-planning, strategy setting, scheme formulation, monitoring and review and not merely at the time of plan finalisation. *(Para 8.45)*

160. Full benefit of the experience and special merits of voluntary agencies should be availed of wherever possible and desirable. *(Para 8.47)*

161. In the District Planning Bodies set up in each State, adequate representation should be provided for elected representatives, representatives of economic or occupational groups, social groups, voluntary agencies etc. as indicated in the Chapter on Pre-requisites in this report. *[Para 8.50(1)]*

162. In order to make people's participation effectives, it is necessary to organise it at every stage of planning and implementation including the stage of evaluation, monitoring and review. *[Para 8.50(2)]*

163. During the pre-planning stage, involving collection of data and conduct of surveys, the local leaders of the community, teachers, students and others, as necessary, may be associated. *[Para 8.50(3)]*

164. At the scheme formulation stage, meaningful public participation would require: (a) interaction with "people" in their village settings and with their representative organisations, (b) purposeful consultation with beneficiary groups and (c) consultation with different categories of "people" such as landless labour, tribals, scheduled castes, artisans.*[Para 8.50(4)]*

165. At the stage of formulation of strategies and determination of schemes priorities the people may be involved to assist the planning team in assessing the relative response of the people to alternative strategies. The method would be to discuss in "open forums", where representatives of various local agencies at the Block and Tahsil levels and the representatives of various interest groups could be invited to express their views.
[Paras 8.50(5)8.50(6)]

166. Certain aspects of decision-making, particularly those relating to locations of various community schemes like drinking water, school construction, feeder road construction, health centres etc. would be greatly facilitated through discussions in open assemblies in villages. *[Para 8.50(7)]*

167. Decision-making in regard to all vital planning matters may be done through the District Planning Bodies, in which elected representatives and various other interests are duly represented. *[Para 8.50(8)]*

168. Local people can be encouraged to participate in the implementation aspects of a project by (i) making contribution of resources, (ii) assisting administration and coordination efforts and (iii) enlisting themselves in programme activities for possible benefits. *[Para 8.50(9)]*

169. Involvement of people may also be secured in monitoring and evaluation of projects / programmes. *[Para 8.50(10)]*

170. People's involvement may be secured with great advantage in the running, maintenance and management of

various completed projects by constituting suitable organisations of people like Irrigation (water use) Committees etc.

[Para 8.50(11)]

171. The Working Group also recommends another aspect of public participation in local level planning by associating universities/academic institutions located in the district, for various tasks of plan formulation including collection of data, conduct of surveys, analyses of data, evaluation and review of on-going schemes etc. It is recommended that the District Planning Bodies should, in this manner, enlist all available talents and skills in the district. *[Para 8.50(12)]*

172. The Working Group recommends that public participation in centrally directed intervention strategies in rural development, should be improved by associating people's representatives in these agencies and placing the plans prepared by them before the people's organisations, like the PRI's for clearance.

[Para 8.50(13)]

173. As the scope of District Planning will have to gradually enlarge so is the scope of people's participation. For instance, to begin with, participation through representation in District Planning Bodies may be the only feasible method of inducting popular participation. In the "Stages approach" that we have visualised, this could be first stage of transition. *(Para 8.51)*

174. In the programmes like the Minimum Needs Programme, the Special Component Plan for Scheduled Castes and the plan for the tribal people, the State Governments should strive to achieve some degree of public participation by involving the target groups in the decision-making as well as in the implementation process. In States, where some "free or united funds" are provided to the District Planning Body for its discretionary spending, public participation should be encouraged in the exercise of choice of schemes and determination of their priorities. *(Para 8.52)*

175. There are various beneficiary-oriented schemes forming part of the IRD Programme, in which some States have already

used public participation method as a means to identify beneficiaries and to evaluate the success of this programme. This method could be emulated by all the States in the country.

(Para 8.53)

176. It is recommended that States should draw up their own appropriate strategies for public participation in tune with the sequence of decentralised development envisaged by them.

(Para 8.54)

177. The detailed and rigorous kind of public participation that we have advocated running, through the phases of plan programme/project formulation, implementation, monitoring and evaluation is possible only for medium term and perspective plans. So far as Annual Plans are concerned, the nature of public participation will be confined to what obtains in the District Planning Bodies in which the public will be re-presented.

(Para 8.55)

District Planning in North Eastern Region

178. The Working Group is of the view that while working out the new frame for district-level planning, it will be necessary that the special elements relating to the various constitutional and statutory obligations prevalent in different states as also the special feature of the tribal sub-plans should be in the nature of a comprehensive frame having a clear objective accommodating a variety of sub-goals. *(Para 9.9)*

179. As regards the scope and content of the District Plan, and the broad division of all plan programmes into district sector and state sector, the observations contained in the relevant chapter of this report also hold good for the North-East Region. Similarly for the distribution of divisible plan outlays among the districts, the objective mentioned, viz., population, area and level of development are also equally applicable to the North-Eastern Region. Taking into account the special peculiarities of this region, however, we recommend that as far as possible, not less than 70% of the outlay may be assigned for population, not more

than 20% for area and not less than 10% for other elements including level of backwardness. *(Para 9.10)*

180. The districts where the level of investments may be lower than their entitlements could be given a greater step up in successive annual plans compared to these districts which may be better provided. *(Para 9.11)*

181. An ideal district plan such as the one elaborated in the chapter on Planning Methodology in this report may be difficult to carry out in these states in respect of the Seventh Five Year Plan in view of the shortage of time. The preparations for making perspective plan for each district, however, should be taken in hand immediately, so that district plans can be prepared at least from the Eighth Five Year Plan. *(Para 9.12)*

182. Another aspect of district level planning is to influence the on-going programmes and to take up new programmes on a year-to-year basis, as also for the Seventh Plan period as a whole. In this case, the first disaggregated plan for the district referred to earlier should be considered at the district level and suitably adapted to the local needs. In this regard, an incremental approach could be adopted since the on-going programmes have logic of their own and changes should be effected with great care and caution. *(Para 9.13)*

183. The District Plan exercise should be started each year well ahead of the State Plan exercise so that the State Plan can be built up on the basis of the District Plans. The work on the District Plans for the following years can be started on the premise that the total outlay for the District Plan will be of the order of, say 15% over and above the current year's figure. In accordance with the incremental approach, the District authorities may prepare their plans keeping the inter-sectoral priorities, as they are. They could, however, make marginal sectoral changes up to 10%. *(Para 9.14)*

184. After the State Plans have been approved by the Planning Commission, the District Authorities may be indicated the Plan size and their plan proposals may be finally approved subject to such variations as may be necessary in different sectors on the basis of observations of the Planning Commission and discussions with the District-level Authorities and Heads of the Departments, if any. This exercise could be taken up for the year 1984-85 immediately. *(Para 9.16)*

185. An exercise for the preparation of the Seventh Five Year Plan for each district may also be taken up. The methodology for the preparation of the Seventh Five Year Plan for the district may be the same as suggested for the Annual Plan. *(Para 9.17)*

186. The Working Group suggests that the plan outlay for each district may have a 5% nucleus fund. The nucleus fund should be available to the District Planning and Executive authorities for utilisation at their discretion. Detailed guidelines should be formulated by the States for utilisation of this fund. The nucleus fund should cover schemes up to a certain financial limit, say Rs. 50,000 or less. These progrmmes should not have a large recurring component. The scheme taken up, within the nucleus fund, should normally be expected to be completed within a couple of years. *(Paras 9.18 & 9.19)*

187. The nucleus fund could also be used for the general sector programmes suitably adapted to the local needs, if necessary. The nucleus fund should not be available for subsidy programmes which should be catered in the general sectoral programmes. *(Para 9.20)*

188. The schemes covered under the nucleus fund could be of any description including those, which may normally fall in the category of non-plan activity. It could be of any description including those which may be district plan as a whole or a general scheme. It may also be used to adapt any of the on-going programmes. *(Para 9.21)*

189. It is necessary that the district plan programmes should be adequately reflected in the State budgets in a formal way. It will, however, be useful, if a budget supplement is prepared in which District level programmes in different sectors are consolidated and presented district-wise. *(Para 9.22)*

190. All District level programmes should be brought within the purview of the District Planning Authority for the purposes of planning. *(Para 9.23)*

191. We consider the block-wise investment should be aggregated and carefully reviewed although full-fledged block-level planning exercise could be taken up at a later stage, once the process of district-level planning has been stabilized. *(Para 9.25)*

192. The Integrated Tribal Development Project should be accepted as an integral part of the district level plan and, to that extent, the district plan will comprise two comprehensive plans; one for the tribal areas and the other for the non-tribal areas with mutually reinforcing elements provided in the district plan. Since our final goal is to carry planning process to the block and even a group of villages level, in the Integrated Tribal Development Project areas which already have a suitable plan frame, planning at the block level may be initiated. *(Para 9.26)*

193. The allocation for various target group programmes from the National and the State levels should give weightage to area and population as well even when the allocation is made block-wise or district-wise. *(Para 9.27)*

194. The sponsoring authorities of individual programmes should accept the district or the sub-district level comprehensive plans as the reference point for their programmes as well and should be satisfied with ensuring that adequate programmes have been built in for the appropriate target groups within the comprehensive plan and that the investment for that target group is not less than the contribution by the sponsoring authority. They should accept reporting of the overall programme including

that for the target group for the purposes of their own programme which may be of comparatively limited coverage.

(Para 9.28)

195. In those states where the districts are of bigger size, the unit for implementation could be smaller than the district as the ITDPs or a block. In Assam the sub-division is traditionally a strong unit of administration. In some other States, on the other hand, the major implementation responsibilities may continue to be at the state-level where the district technical heads may function directly under the state department heads even though the district is taken as the unit of planning. Any *ad hoc* and precipitate change in the administrative system in a hurry on a *priori* consideration just because district-level planning is being initiated must be avoided at all costs. *(Para 9.29)*

196. The Group is of the view that as large a part of developmental programmes as possible envisaged under the district level plans should be assigned to the village authorities, so that they can further consolidate their position in the changing situation and become effective units of planning and implementation in the modern system in due course. The village authorities or a group of these authorities should be provided with necessary technical support for the purpose. *(Para 9.30)*

197. The powers for according administrative, technical and financial sanction of schemes should rest with an appropriate district-level body or officials working in the district as the case may be. While most of the powers should vest with concerned departments, the residuary powers in respect of implementation of the district plans may vest in a committee of district heads of various departments with Deputy Commissioner as the Chairman. The District Planning Authority should be responsible for monitoring of implementation of programmes in the district.

(Para 9.31)

198. Keeping in view the size of the districts in the region, it may not be necessary even at a later stage to have the full-fledged technical planning unit at the district level. The Group,

therefore, suggests that a strong district level planning unit may be established at the state level in all States and Units other than Assam. In Assam, the district level-planning unit may be established at the regional level and function under the Divisional Commissioners. *(Para 9.32)*

199. The main thrust of development in each unit should determine the composition of the technical team. We recommend that the team must comprise experts in rural development planning, agriculture/horticulture/forestry, animal production/pisciculture/village industries/cooperation and a social scientist. Two other experts could be added depending upon the need of each area. The North Eastern Council may obtain services of experts in rural development planning and other fields on contract basis from other areas which could be placed at the disposal of the District Planning units in the region. *(Para 9.33)*

200. It will be necessary to take up programmes for building up manpower for the Planning Team within the region. The work of building up manpower may be taken up in right earnest in the region. A Regional Centre for Multi-level Planning may be set up under the aegis of the North Eastern Hill University.

(Paras 9.34 & 9.35)

Operationalising District Planning

201. District planning process is to be conceived as a "Stages" or "Sequence" approach. This implies that decentralised development is a continuum and different stages of it are to be crossed before reaching the final stage. This is an evolutionary process and some transitional phases in this context have to be recognised. These phases are : Stage-I will be phase of "initiation", Stage-II will be one of "Limited Decentralisation" and Stage-III would represent "Final Stage". *(Para 10.3)*

202. In this step-by-step approach even the first step must be sufficiently backed up by political and bureaucratic will as well as effective implementation measures. Also, the planning levels above (the State Planning Boards and the Central Planning

Commission) must constantly provide to the districts, technical and other assistance to stimulate and sustain this progress. *(Para 10.4)*

203. In order to operationalise the decentralised district planning concept in this manner from the Seventh Five Year Plan onwards, the State Governments should crystalise their thinking during 1984-85 and must prepare an "Approach Paper for Decentralised District Planning for the Seventh Plan for their States in which they should set out these' Action proposals". This Approach Paper will be considered by the Planning Commission during the Annual Plan discussions in its Working Group on District Planning. Later, this paper should be incorporated as a chapter into the Seventh Plan document of the State. Simultaneously the States should start taking several steps to implement the 'Action Proposals', so that implementation could proceed in a systematic manner in line with the action sequence envisaged. The District Planning Unit that we have proposed at the State level should undertake these jobs. *(Para 10.5)*

204. It is felt that the task of monitoring is better done by a smaller Committee called "Executive Committee". *(Para 10.8)*

205. It would become necessary to entrust the monitoring function specifically to one of the members of the planning team. *(Para 10.9)*

206. To look into efficient sequencing of projects/schemes at the district level during the implementation process, a separate monitoring cell in the District Planning machinery is required. A Monitoring Unit located in the State Planning Department will be its counterpart at the State level. *(Para 10.9)*

207. The use of modern cartographic methods through thematic maps portraying the development profile in a visually appealing manner is proving to be a useful aid for understanding plan progress. The States that are making a beginning to develop their monitoring mechanism at the district and the State levels are well advised to take note of these developments. *(Para 10.10)*

208. For success in decentralisation programmes it is not merely that functions, finances and powers must be deconcentrated, but also certain attitudinal, behavioural and cultural conditions conducive to decentralisation have to be built up. This 'culture of decentralisation' has to grow in strength and take deep roots in the country to successfully resist the pressures for centralisation and to sustain the march towards this goal. This is, of course, a matter of evolution through time. But action, i.e. planned and purposeful action – has to proceed much ahead of the times. *(Para 10.12).*

[***Reproduced from the report of the Working Group on District Planning, Vol. I.***
Report submitted in May 1984
Chairman: C.H. Hanumantha Rao]

APPENDIX-II

REPORT OF THE COMMITTEE TO REVIEW THE EXISTING ADMINISTRATIVE ARRANGEMENTS FOR RURAL DEVELOPMENT AND POVERTY ALLEVIATION PROGRAMMES (CAARD)

CHAPTER IX

PROPOSALS FOR FUTURE ADMINISTRATIVE SET UP

9.1 An issue about which there is broad consensus among the experts, policy makers and programme operators is that the basic unit for decentralised policy planning and programme implementation should be the district. The studied view of this Committee is that decentralisation of planning and the implementation of rural development programme at the district level will be compatible with the national objectives, regional requirements, local needs, people's aspirations and technical and administrative constraints. Therefore, a development administrative structure at the district level has to be built up which will have the dual function of planning and implementation of rural development programmes.

9.2 The district bureaucracy and its structure in this country were conceived and given shape more than a century ago with certain limited objectives. The head of the district administration has been the Collector. His principal functions were the maintenance of law and order, collection of revenue and administration of various Government regulations. However, in the post-independence period, he has been entrusted with and involved in various developmental functions. Though most of the developmental activities at the district level are carried out by the various functional/line departments, the Collector as the

Chief Executive of the district has come to assume a Central role as the coordinator of the programmes implemented in the district. Over the years, the number of departments/agencies and programmes as well as the technical content of these programmmes have significantly increased. In fact, there are more than 20 major developmental agencies/departments (a represen-tative list is in Annexure IX--A) on an average at the district-level at present. In spite of the multifarious functions which the Collector has been called upon to discharge, it must be said that the Collector has done well so far and has been able to provide coordinating leadership required for the developmental administration in the district. However, in this process certain essential maintenance functions like maintenance of land records etc., have suffered due to inadequate attention. Mixing up of law and order, land revenue administration etc., with developmental work has brought the Collector into conflict with various forces in the district and as a result, both maintenance and development administration have suffered in the process. It is not un-common to see that this has also resulted in the tenure of a Collector being shortened by quick transfers. Now that development administration has become more complex, and also the quantum of work and the need to work with people's representatives increased, it is necessary to provide leadership at a much higher level than prevalent at present. Equally, so it is necessary to insulate the Collector from other forces to enable him to take firm action in law and order matters and also discharge efficiently the maintenance and administrative functions of land revenue and land records, election matters, public distribution system etc.

9.3 Rural Development encompasses the activities of a number of departments at the State headquarters. It is needless to say that coordination and proper direction at this level is of utmost importance. This Committee recommends that a very Senior Officer of the rank of Chief Secretary designated as Development Commissioner be made in-charge of development administration at the state level. He should be an officer with outstanding managerial ability and proven track record. He should be able to give a dynamic leadership to development administration in the State. He should be the Secretary of the

State Development Council, constitution of which has been suggested elsewhere in this report.

9.4 The State Development Commissioner will have complete responsibility for planning, monitoring and concurrent evaluation of all the rural development programmes at the State Level. The major rural development departments like rural development, agriculture, animal husbandry, cooperation, rural industries etc. should be brought under his purview. The Secretaries of these departments will work directly under him. However, he should be made totally free from the routine administration at the State level which should continue to be the responsibility of the Chief Secretary. The Development Commissioner will work in close collaboration with the State Planning Board/Commission. For this purpose, his post should be functionally and structurally linked with the State Planning Board/Commission.

9.5 This Committee is of the view that development administration at the district level has to be treated as a major activity involving significant responsibilities: Hence we propose that a post of District Development Commissioner be created to look after and coordinate all the developmental activities in the district. He will be the Chief Executive of Zila Parishad in those States where the Panchayati Raj Institutions at the district level are responsible for planning and implementation of various development programmes. In those States where elected Zila Parishads are not yet established or are not in charge of planning and implementation of rural development programmes at the district level, District Development Commissioner could function as the Chairman and Chief Executive of a District Development Council as an interim arrangement until elected Zila Parishads are established; however, under such a circumstance the present set up of District Rural Development Agency (DRDA) should continue with the District Development Commissioner as Chairman until elected Zila Parishads at the district level are brought into existence to perform all the functions envisaged by the Committee.

9.6 The Office of the District Development Commissioner should be of a higher status than that of the District Collector in order to establish the primacy of development administration over house-keeping. This is essential as the District Development Commissioner will have to provide effective leadership to a district team which includes senior officers of a number of line/functional departments. Further, in the selection of such officers, care should be taken to ensure that they have the requisite understanding and appreciation of rural development problems and concern for the poor. It is suggested that an officer of at least 11 to 16 years' experience in the Indian Administrative Service should be appointed as District Development Commissioner. He should also undergo a refresher/reorientation training ranging from 3 to 6 weeks at the National Institute of Rural Development (NIRD), Hyderabad. He should have a minimum tenure of 3 years. Every officer of the Indian Administrative Service must serve as a District Development Commissioner before he becomes eligible to be promoted to the super-time scale.

9.7 Along with the establishment of the office of District Development Commissioner, significant restructuring of planning and implementation machinery at the district level should also be effected. The proliferation of development agencies and departmentalisation and fragmentation of functions at the district level should cease. The office of District Rural Development Agency specifically established for the implementation of anti-poverty programmes and other similar programmes should merge with the office of District Development Commissioner, without affecting, however, the distinct identity of the programme and its implementation and which should be supervised by a special committee of the Zila Parishad. The Project Director/Officer of the present District Rural Development Agency would work directly under the District Development Commissioner and be in charge of the anti-poverty programmes under the Special Committee of the Zila Parishad or the DRDA, as the case may be.

9.8 The practice of having deputationists to serve at the DRDA and other similar offices also should be done away with. Instead the principal technical officers at the district level of the various specialised departments along with their line formations should be part of the organisational structure of the Zila Parishad or the District Development Council headed by the Commissioner. There should be a District Administrative Officer under the District Development Commissioner to look after all administrative and personnel functions.

9.9 Along with the strengthening of District Development Administration, the Planning function at the district level should also be enhanced. There should be a clear demarcation between the planning functions at the State level and district level. The District Plan should not be simply the district segment of the State plan. The Zila Parishad or the District Development Council, which will have a Special Committee for looking after the planning function, should be properly equipped to play the decentralised planning functions to be entrusted to it. For this purpose there could also be a need for significantly enhancing the planning capabilities at the district level. A District Planning Officer of a suitable background and level will also be required.

9.10 The Special Committee of the Zila Parishad or the District Development Council for District Planning and the Special Committee or DRDA for anti-poverty Programmes will form two of the most important organs at the district level and will need to be service by an official team headed by the District Development Commissioner. The District Planning Team should consist of the principal District Officers of all the functional/line departments and other experts, with the District Planning Officer as Convener. The District Anti-Poverty programme Team should consist of the Principal District Officers of all the concerned functional/line departments, with the project directors the Convenor.

9.11 The District Development Commissioner will have to give effective leadership in planning and implementation of all the development programmes within the district. Not only that he will be the Chief Coordinator of all the programmes within the district but also he will be the main motivator for the effective implementation of all the programmes. He should ensure that the weaker sections in the rural areas are not left out in the development process and that every development programme has an effective anti-poverty orientation. Apart from coordinating the planning and implementation activities of the various departments at the district level, the District Development Commissioner has to play an important role in coordinating activities with the various agencies and institutions at the district level whose activities have a bearing on rural development. Commercial institutions, cooperatives, non-financial public sector undertakings, voluntary agencies and other non-governmental bodies are examples of such agencies/institutions.

9.12 For the effectiveness of district level plan formulation and implementation the question of introduction of district budget will have to be considered. The District Credit Plan, prepared by the lead bank now, has no organic relationship with the District Development Administration at present. The Committee suggests that the District Credit Plan should become an integral part of the district plan. Also, introduction of district budget may go a long way in achieving a measure of coordination and integration at the district level.

9.13 Apart from the District Planning Team and the District Rural Development Agency, a third important constituent of the district development body should be the office of District Finance & Accounts Officer. He will be working directly under the District Development Commissioner with a minimum complement of essential staff. He will be responsible for allocating plan funds as per criteria laid down by the Zila Parishad or the District Development Council to the sectors/programmes/schemes. He should also see that outlays are earmarked for programmes like the anti-poverty programmes, employment programmes, minimum needs programme, family welfare programme, social forestry programme and other special programmes of Central or State Governments and see that they are not diverted. The district budget should also ensure this. He should be the District Budget Officer also, under whose guidance the district budget will be prepared. He should also get the accounts for any Special programme audited by a Chartered Accountant and furnish such audit reports from year to year as may be required under the guidelines/conditions of the special programme.

9.14 The progress of district planning and decentralisation of administration in various states indicate that the States differ widely in their experience along a centralisation/decentralisation continuum. Their experiences have also crystalised over different time duration. Whereas some States have experimented with the decentralisation process for more than two decades, in some cases they are confined to a few years only and there are still others who are yet to start along the path of decentralised planning and implementation. As a consequence the decentralisation procedures and methodologies to be worked out and adopted by the different States may have to vary depending upon the local situation and competence achieved in each State, keeping one broad framework suggested by us in view.

9.15 In those States where elected Zila Parishads are in existence at the district level, all rural development programme including the schemes relating to anti-poverty programmes should be transferred to them. This will ensure participation of the elected representatives of the people in the planning of anti-poverty and other rural development programmes and make available the guidance of the local representatives in the implementation of the programmes. Their knowledge of the local situation, the needs and aspirations of the people as well as the opportunities and limitations of the local economy and the social situation would be of immense help. This will also create a sense of accountability to the people among all development functionaries. There should, however, be appropriate administrative arrangements which bring out the best from the elected representatives as well as the administrators and professional services and which provide safeguard against possibilities of deflecting from the objectives of anti-poverty programmes on account of political and other vested interests which are in conflict with the interests of the poor. There should be provision for making representatives of voluntary agencies and of the participants of the programme as associate members on the relevant special committees of the panchayati raj body constituted by proportional representation. The Committee also recommends the mayoral pattern with one-year term for the office of the Chairman of the Zila Parishad who will preside over the meetings of the Zila Parishad and its committees of which he is the chairman. The elected body and its committees should be responsible for decisions on planning, laying down policies and priorities and taking decisions within the framework of and in conformity with the guidelines prescribed by the Government of India and the State Government and review the implementation and performance. The District Development Commissioner or the Chief Executive Officer of the Zila Parishad and the team of officers and functionaries of various departments at the district, block and village levels should assist the elected bodies in the discharge of their functions, be squarely responsible for execution of the approved policies and programmes and take corrective action on the basis of reviews. While the State Heads of Departments will continue to provide technical inputs and guidance to the district level and exercise administrative control over the staff in respect of inter-district transfers and major disciplinary matters, the Committee recommends that executive powers should be vested in the District Development Commissioner (and other officers at the district to the extent necessary) for implementation of programmes and to have full administrative control on the official responsible for execution of anti-poverty and other rural development programmes, including powers of intra-district transfer and certain disciplinary action. Similar administrative arrangements should be made at the Panchayat Samiti level with the Assistant Development Commissioners having the administrative control and being responsible for execution of the programmes. Each State will have to work out suitable arrangements in this regard and delineate the role of elected representatives and the administrative agencies, so that a healthy, frictionless relationship between the two emerges.

9.16 In States where elected Zila Parishads are not inexistence, yet, there could be a District Development Council, with the President of taluk/block level panchayati raj bodies and officers at the district level as members and the District Development Commissioner as the Chairman and Chief Executive, as an interim arrangement till elected Zila Parishads are established. This can also ensure better coordination between the District Body and the State Government. In other details the arrangement would be similar to the one recommended under the Zila Parishad set-up, except that the DRDA will continue to function as now until elected Zila Parishads are brought into existence. It has also been brought to our notice that in some States where elected Zila Parishads are in existence, there is also a District Planning Committee with the Minister in charge of the district as Chairman and the Chairman of the Zila Parishad being a member along with others. However, we would prefer a system in which the district plans prepared by the Zila Parishads are moderated by a State Development Council, with the Chief Minister as the Chairman and including all Ministers and Chairmen of Zila Parishads as members and the National and State priorities and local needs and priorities are harmonised and brought within the available resources.

9.17 The District Planning and implementation has to be conceived as a single operation in which all individual sectoral activities get harmonised into a unified activity. This clearly indicates the need for horizontal coordination at the district level. This is precisely the reason for this committee to recommend the creation of a new pivotal post of District Development Commissioner. An alternative suggestion from some quarters is that the same purpose will be served by strengthening of the position of the Collector. This was also the recommendation of the Working Group on District Planning. This Committee, however, favours delinking of development administration from maintenance and regulatory administration. Development process has come of age. Reliance on Collector alone to be the leader of the District Development Team would not be feasible. He has to continue to hold the responsibilities of law and order, elections and other regulatory and maintenance administration.

In a set up where he works as the Chief Executive of an elected Zila Parishad some of these functions obviously cannot be satisfactorily discharged. However, he could always be associated wherever assistance or cooperation from maintenance of regulatory administrative agencies is required.

9.18 The District Development Commissioner's office has to become the focal point of all developmental activities in the district. In order to ensure that effective rural-urban linkages are established in the process of district development, the Chairman of the Municipalities/Urban Local Bodies/Corporations also be made members of the Zila Parishad/District Development Council. Similarly, the Chief Executive Officers of these bodies will be represented in the appropriate official district development bodies like the District Planning Team/Committee, District Rural Development Team/Agency etc.

9.19 The District level officers of the various functional/line departments will continue to handle the work relating to their respective areas. However, the schemes and programmes being implemented by them should form an integral part of the district development plan. It has also to be ensured that the departmentalism of activities do not result in artificial splitting of programmes and projects. Similarly, care should be taken to ensure that duplication of task is avoided.

9.20 Technical supervision and control over the officials of the various departments at the district level may continue to be with the concerned departments at the State and regional levels. However, these officials will be functionally and administratively under the control of the Zila Parishad/District Development Council. Also they will be held fully accountable for the implementation of their respective sectoral programmes.

9.21 The existing management information system at the district level is rather weak. Though most of the primary data/information required for planning and monitoring of the various programmes are collected by the different line/functional departments, they are not assembled and utilised at the district level at present. Most of the district officers are upward looking in communication. The existing system is designed more for record keeping rather than for monitoring and corrective actions. It is also essential that all the relevant data and information required for planning and implementation of various developmental activities in the district are collected and processed in the office of the District Development Commissioner. This will form the basic input for the work of the District Planning Team/Committee.

9.22 The major operational machinery for the implementation of district rural development plan should be the block level set up. Community Development Block as the principal administrative entity for the implementation of development programmes had taken roots in the existing hierarchy of administrative institutions in the fiftees. The Centrai role played by the Block Development Officer (BDO) in the development of the block during the community development days has to be restored. Revamping of the block machinery came for serious attention of this Committee. A number of issues have to be sorted out in this connection. What are the gaps, weaknesses and deficiencies in the existing block set up? Is the existing contingent of staff at the block level adequate enough to effectively carry out the responsibility assigned to the block under the different programmes? Should the old system of territorial village level workers (VLWs) continue or should there be both functional and territorial VLWs with appropriate supervisory staff for cluster of villages to deal with the various types of functions?

9.23 During the community development days, the technical personnel at the block level were on deputation from the various line departments. They were under dual control – in administrative matters they were to take orders from BDOs whereas on technical issues they were to follow the instructions of their superiors in the respective technical departments. During the initial years, because of the novelty and importance attached to the C.D. Block and also because of the ample plan funds available at the disposal of BDOs, the dual control arrangement did not create much of a problem for the efficient functioning of the block machinery. Gradually, however, when the block passed on to the extension stage with fewer plan schemes and when sectoral plan schemes implemented by the line departments gained importance, the position and the status of the BDO got eroded and his control over the extension personnel weakened. In a similar manner the relative importance and prestige of the gram sevaks *vis-a-vis* the other field functionaries of the various departments also got diminished. The erosion of authority of the BDO and the VLWs had serious adverse effect on the community development programme.

9.24 By the late Seventies, the Block Development Office was a significantly weakened institution. The technical officers came under the control of their respective departments. Some of them like the Veterinary Doctor was provided a higher scale of pay than that of the BDO. The T&V system, introduced for agricultural extension work, took away 40 per cent to 60 per cent of the VLWs to the Agricultural Departments. Similarly the extension officers in agriculture also became a part of the department of Agriculture. Thus, at the start of the Eighties the block was a picture of disarray.

9.25 Even during the Sixth Plan period, when in the implementation of the various rural development programmes, the BDO and other block functionaries had a very significant role to play, they could not regain their original pre-eminent position in development administration. As in the case of the district, at the block level also, though to a lesser extent, there was a proliferation of agencies and programmes over the last three decades. Along with this, the complexities and technical content of the various programmes and schemes also have increased. The BDO office which was expected to serve a limited purpose, essentially as a catalyst in the development process in the initial years is not in a position to effectively meet the demands on it now. Further, as against an annual budget of a few lakhs of rupees in the initial years of planning, at present an annual investment of over a crore of rupees is being made in a block.

9.26 For example, massive programmes like Integrated Rural Development Programme (IRDP) and National Rural Employment Programme (NREP) were introduced which were to be implemented through the block machinery. The IRD Programme is being implemented by the District Rural Development Agencies (DRDA) through the existing block machinery. The identification of the families, preparation of bankable plan for them and monitoring the implementation of the programme are basically the responsibility of block machinery. The field functionaries are also expected to play their role of liaison with banks and other organisations for mobilising credit, supply of inputs, organisation of supply & provision of inputs and marketing arrangements for outputs etc. Follow-up action of the schemes drawn up for the families at periodic intervals, ensuring supply of raw materials etc. are also the responsibility of the functionaries attached to the blocks. Apart from centrally sponsored schemes, the State Governments have a number of their own schemes to be implemented through the blocks. These relate to bio-gas, drinking water supply, housing schemes, drought relief, mid-day meals, various social security schemes, and so on. Thus, on the one hand while the block level staff got depleted, the responsibilities of the block increased manifold.

9.27 This Committee recommends that the block development office should be the sheet-anchor of the entire rural development process. For this purpose, the status of the office should be upgraded. The Chief Executive Officer of the Block/Tehsil may be designated as Assistant Development Commissioner. He should be an officer of the status of a Sub-Divisional Officer. His background, training, managerial capability and motivation should be appropriate for the task as a leader of the team which will be incharge of all development functions in the block. In the case of states which have the tradition of a strong sub-divisional set up, the states may adopt, for the present, a set-up in which the Sub-Divisional Officer/Magistrate will also be called the Assistant Development Commissioner working under the District Development Commissioner for all developmental functions and looking after the blocks in his sub-division, while the present block level set-up continues; however, these states should move towards upgrading the level of the Chief Executive of the block to the level of Assistant Development Commissioner as early as possible.

9.28 The Assistant Development Commissioner should be a dynamic young person, preferably below the age of 35 and in any case not above 40. All junior IAS officers should function as Assistant Development Commissioner, so that they can understand the problems of rural areas and of agricultural and rural development and develop sympathy for the cause of the poor. The cadre of Assistant Development Commissioners may be selected by a small committee at the state level headed by the Development Commissioner. The officers may be selected from all development departments, but mainly from the State Civil Services, Agriculture, Cooperation, Education, Social Welfare, Engineering etc. Officers should function as Assistant Development Commissioners for a minimum period of at least 3 years and if possible, for a period of 5 years. An officer of the Indian Administrative Service working as Assistant Development Commissioner should continue as such for a minimum term even if he is promoted to the senior scale. After selection they should be trained intensively for a period of 3 months in State Administrative Training Institutes. The syllabus for training and training of trainers should be undertaken by the National Institute of Rural Development.

9.29 The office of the Assistant Development Commissioner has to become the focal point of all developmental activities in the block/tehsil. The Assistant Development Commissioner will have to coordinate all the development functions within his jurisdiction and give effective leadership in planning and implementation of all development programmes. Not only that he will be the chief coordinator of all the programmes within the block/tehsil, he will also be the main motivator for the effective implementation of all the development programmes. He should ensure that the weaker and poorer sections in the rural areas are not left out in the development process and that every development programme has an effective anti-poverty orientation. In other words, he has to ensure that even the weakest and poorest are able to participate in rural development and are able to share its gains.

9.30 With the recognition of the block as the unit of planning under IRDP and provision of targets and allocation on the basis of number of blocks in the Sixth Five Year Plan, there was a spate of demand for creation of additional blocks. Certain State Governments had already created additional blocks and these could not be recognised under IRDP due to the constraint for the resources. In the Seventh Five Year Plan, the criterion for allocation of targets and funds has been changed to one of selectivity based on incidence of poverty. This will, of course, reduce to some extent the pressure on creation of more blocks with the idea of drawing more IRD funds. Since the block has now been recognised as the primary unit of planning, it is essential that the creation of blocks should not be left to pressures of vested interests and exigencies. Some uniform parameters have to be evolved to put the whole system on a sound footing. The following factors have to be taken into account :

(i) There has been sizeable increase in rural population;
(ii) The complexities and technical content of various programmes have significantly increased;
(iii) The blocks have become crucial instruments of development administration.

9.31 The Committee feels that the earlier criteria for delimitation of blocks have to be reconsidered in this revised context. It is of the view that there should be one block for every one lakh population in the plain areas and 50,000 in hilly/tribal areas. A review of the number of blocks in the country should be made from this point of view and wherever necessary it should be suitably increased. Regarding staffing at the block level, the Committee makes the following recommendations:

(i) Keeping in view the various responsibilities assigned to blocks and the need for follow-up under the various beneficiary oriented schemes, there is a need for one

VLW for every 10000 population. The norm could be 4000 to 5000 in hilly/tribal areas.

(ii) Additional posts of Extension Officers are also required to cover some new disciplines that have come up like family welfare, energy, industry, institutional finance etc. The core number of Extension Officers should be up to 10 depending on the need of the State.

(iii) There is a need to strengthen the statistical/clerical support for monitoring and accounting purpose.

(iv) There is also a need for strengthening the accounting wing at the block office.

9.32 The reorganisation of the blocks on the basis of the above parameters would mean that there will be about 6,000 blocks. The number of VLWs will be around 60,000 and an equal number of Extension Officers will also be needed. As the State finances are in poor shape, it will be necessary to provide assistance to State Governments to bring about this reorganisation. Assistance for this should be extended for a period of 10 years. Two-thirds of the additional expenditure should be met by the Government of India during the Seventh Plan period in the case of State Governments. The Government of India should bear 100 per cent of the expenditure in the case of Union Territories.

9.33 Suitable institutional arrangements for effectively linking up the offices of District Development Commissioner and the Assistant Development Commissioner and the Panchayati Raj institutions at the district and block levels may have to be worked out in each state according to their situation and requirements. Also a number of activities which have an intrinsic bearing on rural development should be directly brought under the purview of panchayati raj institutions. Agriculture including soil conservation, animal husbandry, veterinary services, rural and small scale industries, primary education, public health and primary health centres, family welfare and nutrition, rural water supply/sanitation, rural roads, social and women welfare etc. are some of them. The District Development Commissioner will have to ensure that decentralisation does not become an instrument to strengthen the hegemony of the rich and the powerful over the poor and the weak. An administrative culture which has the cause and needs of the poor at heart has to be built up. Voluntary agencies and organisations of the poor have to be encouraged, promoted and actively associated in the rural development process to help in seeing that the benefits actually accrue to the target groups.

9.34 The Committee feels that there may be need for significant restructuring of staffing at the district and block levels. There may be need for augmenting the staff at the block office as well as the number of village level workers. This could, to some extent, be achieved without augmentation of the total developmental staff in the district. This is possible by thinning the number of agencies/departments at the district level and by the transfer of surplus staff to the block level. The proposed model organisational charts for the offices of State Development Commissioner, District Development Commissioner and Assistant Development Commissioner are given as annexures to this chapter as Chart I, II and III, respectively.

9.35 The State Governments may assess the existing staffing pattern with a view to restructuring the pattern to conform to the proposed models taking into consideration the local requirements. While some existing staff like the District Planning Officer or the Project Director of DRDA at the district level would be redeployed with or without upgradation, there may be additional staff required like the District Administrative Officer and District Finance and Accounts Officer. Similarly at the Taluk/Block level, most of the staff would possibly be by redeployment. The States may work out their requirements for minimum additional staff required to conform to the general recommended pattern. The Committee recommends that 2/3rd cost of additional staff required may be met by the Government of India for the Seventh Five Year Plan. The sanctions at the Government of India level may be given by a Central Sanctioning Committee having Secretaries of the Departments of Rural Development, Agriculture, Finance and Planning Commission.

9.36 Along with the restructuring of the development administrative structure at the district level and below, major efforts will have to be made for revamping the administrative culture and attitude of the various functionaries towards the task on their hand. It is essential to ensure that the functionaries who are implementing the various rural development programmes for the benefit of the poor have perfect sympathy for the cause of the poor. Also the reward system and career prospects of the various functionaries should be linked to their performance. The performance should not be measured using narrow yardsticks like number of beneficiaries covered or financial expenditure incurred. Rather, the performance should be evaluated in terms of the end results like the improvement in the living conditions of the poor or the improvement in the physical quality of life.

9.37 In order to attract the best talent to the rural areas and to retain them there, a well-balanced package of incentives has to be provided. The implied incentives for urban postings like better infrastructural facilities and other monetary and non-monetary rewards which exist today have to be removed. The Committee proposes the following for this purpose:

(i) There should be special allowance for postings in difficult and remote rural areas;
(ii) There should be special allowance for children's education where proper schooling facilities are not available;
(iii) Government accommodation may be provided at headquarters on a priority basis to the families of employees posted in difficult and remote areas and construction of residential quarters in a phased manner should be encouraged. (iv) After a term of posting in disadvantaged areas, concerned official may be given a posting of his choice.

9.38 In order to build up a dynamic cadre of rural development functionaries, a proper career management system has to be devised. The system of promotion from the level of village level workers onwards should be based on a combination of merit and seniority. Also wherever promotion aveneues are limited, stagnation in the pay scales may be eliminated by having sufficiently broad pay scales or different grades at each level. Thus, it is possible that a village level worker may continue in the post doing the same job but getting higher grades after reasonable periods of time.

9.39 By and large the success of any programme will depend on the ability and motivation of the personnel who are involved in it. This is all the more true in the case of rural development programmes. A thorough understanding and clear appreciation of the problems of rural development as well as genuine sympathy and concern for the rural poor are prerequisites for a successful rural development functionary. A strictly beauracratic/techno-cratic, value-neutral approach to development may not be sufficient to ensure that rural poverty is eradicated. The past experience clearly indicates that such an approach will lead to an inequitable sharing of gains of development. The rural poor suffer from a number of handicaps apart from economic deprivation. Indeed, material poverty is in many cases, only a manifestation of their very weak social standing due to historical reasons. Rural Development functionaries, to be successful, will have to understand the sociological and economic reasons for rural poverty and develop a positive attitude towards the poor and their problems. We have to create a cadre of 'rural managers' committed to the cause of the poor. In other words, they should be motivated with informed idealism. The Committee feels that to a large measure, this can be achieved by appropriate training and orientation programmes.

9.40 Training/Orientation programmes for rural development functionaries at different levels have to be, necessarily, different in content, coverage and scope. Elsewhere, it was recommended that District Development Commissioners should be given refresher/reorientation training for a duration of 3 to 6 weeks at NIRD and Assistant Development Commissioners be given intensive training for a period of 3 months at the State Administrative Training Institutes. It is further suggested that Zila Parishad Chairman be given appropriate orientation training of a short duration by NIRD. The District Level Officers of the various functional/line departments involve in rural development also be given training/orientation by the State Administrative Institutes for 3 to 6 weeks depending on requirements. The State Institutes will have to organise a one year training programme for the BDOs and an orientation programme of appropriate duration for Extension Officers. Similar orientation training should be made compulsory for bank officials at different levels who are involved in rural development. The State Administrative Training Institutes will have to organise regional training centres for the training of village level workers. They may have to be given comprehensive and intensive training for duration of 2 years. The most important aspects of all such training programmes are the preparation of the appropriate course material and the deployment of the correct faculty/trainers. The Committee recommends that the State institutes should be guided and assisted in this by NIRD. The Committee also recommends that additional training facilities be created, wherever necessary and that the full cost of creation of such facilities be a charge on the Centre.

(Report submitted in December 1985 *Chairman* : G.V.K. Rao)

CHAPTER X

SUMMARY OF RECOMMENDATIONS

1. The Committee feels that the time has come to take a total view of Rural Development. It has to encompass all economic and social development activities handled by different agencies at the field level. It is not advisable any longer to limit anti-poverty programme to a few specific schemes.

2. Past experience clearly indicates that government machinery (bureaucracy) alone cannot be assigned the responsibility for achieving economic development and social justice.

3. While the objectives of removal of poverty, as laid down in the Seventh Plan, must be adhered to, local initiative must be encouraged and the detailed strategy worked out by local people. It is, therefore, essential to involve the people and their representatives effectively in drawing up programmes of rural development and their implementation.

4. Panchayati Raj Institutions have to be activised and given all the support needed so that they can become effective organisations for handling people's problems. Elections to these bodies should be held regularly.

5. It is also necessary to encourage voluntary agencies, with informed idealism, operating in rural areas, in every possible way.

6. The district should be the basic unit for policy planning and programme implementation. The Zila Parishad should, therefore, become the principal body for management of all development programmes which can be handled at that level.

7. The President of the Zila Parishad can be directly elected for a term co-terminus with the Zila Parishad, or for one year each on the Mayoral pattern. The work of the Zila Parishad should be done by a number of Sub-Committees, elected on the basis of the proportional representation so that participatory democracy could be developed and encouraged.

8. Panchayati Raj Institutions at the district level and below should be assigned important role in respect of planning, implementation and monitoring of rural development programmes.

9. Some of the planning functions at the state level may have to be transferred to the district level for effective decentralised district planning.

10. In this connection, the Committee recommends the introduction of the concept of district budget. It is desirable that it is brought into being as quickly as possible.

11. The concept of a properly prepared district plan is reiterated. The preparation of a proper plan is a pre-requisite for having a process of development which will ensure that the poor are properly taken care of. All the development departments should clearly indicate the activities which they would undertake for assisting the poor.

12. The district plan should include all the resources available both in the plan and non-plan as well as in stitutional resources.

13. It is necessary for the banking institutions including the cooperatives to ensure that the credit requirements of the rural poor are adequately met, such facilities should also cover the legitimate consumption credit requirements of the poor.

14. The process of economic development itself should be designed so as to reduce poverty. The implementation of land reforms has to be done with greater vigour so as to ultimately ensure that the land goes to the tiller.

15. Since rural development encompasses the activities of a number of departments at the state level, there is an urgent need for effective coordination and proper direction at this level.

16. The Committee recommends that a very Senior Officer of the rank of Chief Secretary designated as Development Commissioner be incharge of development administration at the state level.

17. The major Rural Development Departments like Rural Development, Agriculture, Animal Husbandry, Cooperation, Industries etc. should be directly under his purview. The Secretaries of these departments will work directly under him.

18. The Committee is of the view that development administration at the district level has to be treated as a major activity involving significant responsibilities.

19. The Committee, thereore, recommends that a post of District Development Commissioner (DDC) be created to look after and coordinate all the developmental activities in the district.

20. The DDC may be made the Chief Executive of the Zila Parishad in those states where the Panchayati Raj Institutions hold the responsibility for planning and implementation of various development programmes.

21. In those states where Zila Parishads are not in position, the DDC could function as Chairman and Chief Executive of the District Development Council.

22. The office of the DDC should be of a higher status than that of the District Collector in order to establish the primacy of the Development administration over maintenance administration.

23. The existing districts set up with weak planning machinery, multiplicity of agencies and lack of effective coordination needs revamping.

24. Along with the establishment of the office of the DDC, significant restructuring of planning and implementation machinery at the district level should also be effected.

25. The proliferation of development agencies and departmentalisation and fragmentation of functions should cease.

26. The most important consitituent of the district development office will be the District Planning Team, the District Rural Development Team and the District Finance and Accounts Officer who will be incharge of the district budget also.

27. The District Level Officers of the various functional/line departments will continue to handle the work relating to their respective areas. However, the schemes and programmes being implemented by them should form an integral part of the District Development Plan.

28. The major operational machinery for implementation of district rural development plan will be the block level set-up. For this purpose revamping of the block machinery is essential.

29. The Committee recommends that the Block Development Office should be the sheet anchor of the entire rural development process. For this purpose the status of this office should be upgraded. The Chief Executive Officer of the block/tehsil may be designated as Assistant Development Commissioner (ADC). The ADC should be an officer of the status of Sub-Divisional Officer.

30. The ADC should be a dynamic young person, preferably below the age of 35 and in any case not above 40. His background, training, managerial capability and motivation should be appropriate for the task as the leader of a team which will be incharge of all development functions in the block.

31. There is an urgent need for rationalisation/reorganisation of blocks to ensure that they become viable units for the task assigned to them.

32. On the basis of certain criteria of population, area and terrain, average size of the block may be one lakh population in the plains and 50,000 population in the hilly and difficult terrain and tribal areas.

33. On the above basis there could be about 6,000 CD blocks.

34. There is also an urgent need for rationalising the deployment of functionaries at the district level and below.

35. Considering the task to be assigned to the various levels of administrative set-up at the district level and below the State Governments may have to work out the staff requirements.

36. In some cases there may not be significant augmentation of the strength; the requirements will be met by redeployment of the staff after necessary reorientation/training.

37. Wherever additional staff requirements are involved, the State Governments may send the proposals to the Centre.

38. A Committee of Secretaries of the Departments of Planning, Expenditure, Agriculture and Rural Development will examine and approve the additional requirements on the basis of certain norms.

39. Two-thirds of the cost of additional staff should be borne by the Centre during the Seventh Five Year Plan.

40. A refresher/orientation training may be organised for the different functionaries engaged in Rural Development Programme. For this purpose, additional training facilities be created wherever necessary and the full cost thereof may be borne by the Centre.

[Report submitted in December 1985.
Chairman : Dr. G. V. K. Rao]

THE CONSTITUTION (SEVENTY-THIRD AMENDMENT) ACT, 1992

[20th April, 1993]

An Act further to amend the Constitution of India.

Be it enacted by Parliament in the Forty-third Year of the Republic of India as follows :

Short title and commencement.

1. (1) This Act may be called the Constitution (Seventy-third Amendment) Act, 1992.

   (2) It shall come into force on such date as the Central Government may, by notification in the Official Gazette, appoint.

2. After Part VIII of the Constitution, the following Part shall be inserted, namely :

Insertion of new Part IX.

PART IX
THE PANCHAYATS

Definitions.

243. In this Part, unless the context otherwise requires, –

(a) "district" means a district in a State;

(b) "Gram Sabha" means a body consisting of persons registered in the electoral rolls relating to a village comprised within the area of Panchayat at the village level;

(c) "intermediate level" means a level between the village and district levels specified by the Governor of a State by public notification to be the intermediate level for the purposes of this Part;

(d) "Panchayat" means an institution (by whatever name called) of self-government constituted under article 243B, for the rural areas;

(e) "Panchayat area" means the territorial area of a Panchayat;

(f) "population" means the population as ascertained at the last preceding census of which the relevant figures have been published;

(g) "village" means a village specified by the Governor by public notification to be a village for the purposes of this Part and includes a group of villages so specified.

Gram Sabha.

243A. A Gram Sabha may exercise such powers and perform such functions at the village level as the Legislature of a State may by law, provide.

Constitution of Panchayats.

243B. (1) There shall be constituted in every State, Panchayats at the village, intermediate and district levels in accordance with the provisions of this Part.

(2) Notwithstanding anything in clause (1), Panchayats at the intermediate level may not be constituted in a State having a population not exceeding twenty lakhs.

Composition of Panchayats.

243C. (1) Subject to the provisions of this Part, the Legislature of a State may, by law, make provisions with respect to the composition of Panchayats:

Provided that the ratio between the population of the territorial area of a Panchayat at any level and the number of seats in such Panchayat to be filled by election shall, so far as practicable, be the same throughout the State.

(2) All the seats in a Panchayat shall be filled by persons chosen by direct election from territorial constituencies in the Panchayat area; and for this purpose, each Panchayat area shall be divided into territorial constituencies in such manner that the ratio between the population of each constituency and the number of seats allotted to it shall, so far as practicable, be the same throughout the Panchayat area.

(3) The Legislature of a State may, by law, provide for the representation —

(a) of the Chairpersons of the Panchayats at the village level, in the Panchayats at the intermediate level or, in the case of a State not having Panchayats at the intermediate level, in the Panchayats at the district level;

(b) of the Chairpersons of the Panchayats at the intermediate level, in the Panchayats at the district level;

(c) of the members of the House of the People and the members of the Legislative Assembly of the State representing constituencies which comprise wholly or partly a Panchayat area at a level other than the village level, in such Panchayat;

(d) of the members of the Council of States and the members of the Legislative Council of the State, where they are registered as electors within —

(i) a Panchayat area at the intermediate level, in Panchayat at the intermediate level;

(ii) a Panchayat area at the district level, in Panchayat at the district level.

(4) The Chairperson of a Panchayat and other members of a Panchayat whether or not chosen by direct election from territorial constituencies in the Panchayat area shall have the right to vote in the meetings of the Panchayats.

(5) The Chairperson of —

(a) a Panchayat at the village level shall be elected in such manner as the Legislature of a State may, by law, provide; and

(b) a Panchayat at the intermediate level or district level shall be elected by, and from amongst, the elected members thereof.

Reservation of seats.

243D. (1) Seats shall be reserved for—

(a) the Scheduled Castes; and

(b) the Scheduled Tribes,

in every Panchayat and the number of seats so reserved shall bear, as nearly as may be, the same proportion to the total number of seats to be filled by direct election in that Panchayat as the population of the Schedu-led Castes in that Panchayat area or of the Scheduled Tribes in that Panchayat area bears to the total population of that area and such seats may be allotted by rotation to different constituencies in a Panchayat.

(2) Not less than one-third of the total number of seats reserved under clause (1) shall be reserved for women belonging to the Scheduled Castes or, as the case may be, the Scheduled Tribes.

(3) Not less than one-third (including the number of seats reserved for women belonging to the Scheduled Castes and the Scheduled Tribes) of the total number of seats to be filled by direct election in every Panchayat shall be reserved for women and such seats may be allotted by rotation to different constituencies in a Panchayat.

(4) The offices of the Chairpersons in the Panchayats at the Village or any other level shall be reserved for the Scheduled Castes, the Scheduled Tribes and women in such manner as the Legislature of a State may, by law, provide:

Provided that the number of offices of Chairpersons reserved for the Scheduled Castes and the Scheduled Tribes in the Panchayats at each level in any State shall bear, as nearly as may be, the same proportion to the total number of such offices in the Panchayats at each level as the population of the Scheduled Castes in the State or of the Scheduled Tribes in the State bears to the total population of the State:

Provided further that not less than one-third of the total number of offices of Chairpersons in the Panchayats at each level shall be reserved for women:

Provided also that the number of offices reserved under this clause shall be allotted by rotation to different Panchayats at each level.

(5) The reservation of seats under clauses (1) and (2) and the reservation of offices of Chairpersons (other than the reservation for women) under clause (4) shall cease to have effect on the expiration of the period specified in article 334.

(6) Northing in this Part shall prevent the Legislature of a State from making any provision for reservation of seats in any Panchayat or offices of Chairpersons in

the Panchayats at any level in favour of backward class of citizens.

Duration of Panchayats etc.

243E. (1) Every Panchayat, unless sooner dissolved under any law for the time being in force, shall continue for five years from the date appointed for its first meeting and no longer.

(2) No amendment of any law for the time being in force shall have the effect of causing dissolution of a Panchayat at any level, which is functioning immediately before such amendment, till the expiration of its duration specified in clause (1).

(3) An election to constitute a Panchayat shall be completed—

(a) before the expiry of its duration specified in clause (1);

(b) before the expiration of a period of six months from the date of its dissolution:

Provided that where the remainder of the period for which the dissolved Panchayat would have continued is less than six months, it shall not be necessary to hold any election under this clause for constituting the Panchayat for such period.

(4) A Panchayat constituted upon the dissolution of a Panchayat before the expirtation of its duration shall continue only for the remainder of the period for which the dissolved Panchayat would have continued under clause (1) had it not been so dissolved.

Disqualifications for membership.

243F. (1) A person shall be disqualified for being chosen as, and for being, a member of a Panchayat —

(a) he is so disqualified by or under any law for the time being in force for the purposes of elections to the Legislature of the State concerned:

Provided that no person shall be disqualified on the ground that he is less than twenty-five years of age, if he has attained the age of twenty-one years;

(b) If he is so disqualified by or under any law made by the Legislature of the State.

(2) If any question arises as to whether a member of a Panchayat has become subject to any of the disqualifications mentioned in clause (1), the question shall be referred for the decision of such authority and in such manner as the Legislature of a State may, by law, provide.

Powers, authority and responsibilities of Panchayats.

243G. Subject to the provisions of this Constitution, the Legislature of a State may, by law, endow the Panchayats with such powers and authority as may be necessary to enable them to function as institutions of self-government and such law may contain provisions for the devolution of powers and responsibilities upon Panchayats at the appropriate level, subject to such conditions as may be specified therein, with respect to—

(a) the preparation of plans for economic development and social justice;

(b) the implementation of schemes for economic development and social justice as may be entrusted to them including those in relation to the matters listed in the Eleventh Schedule.

Powers to impose taxes by, and funds of, the Panchayats.

243H. The Legislature of a State may, by law, —

(a) authorise a Panchayat to levy, collect and appropriate such taxes, duties, tolls and fees in accordance with such procedure and subject to such limits;

(b) assign to a Panchayat such taxes, duties, tolls and fees levied and collected by the State Government for such purposes and subject to such conditions and limits;

(c) provide for making such grants-in-aid to the Panchayats from the Consolidated Fund of the State; and

(d) provide for constitution of such Funds for crediting all moneys received, respectively, by or on behalf of the Panchayats and for the withdrawal of such moneys therefrom, as may be specified in the law.

Constitution of Finance Commission to review financial position.

243-I(1) The Governor of a State shall, as soon as may be within one year from the commencement of the Constitution (Seventy-third Amendment) Act, 1992, and thereafter at the expiration of every fifth year, constitute a Finance Commission to review the financial position of the Panchayats and to make recommendations to the Governor as to —

(a) the principles which should govern —

(i) the distribution between the State and the Panchayats of the net proceeds of the taxes, duties tolls and fees leviable by the State, which may be divided between them under this Part and the allocation between the Panchayats at all levels of their respective shares of such proceeds;

(ii) the determination of the taxes, duties, tolls and fees which may be assigned to, or appropriated by, the Panchayats;

(iii) the grants-in-aid to the Panchayats from the Consolidated Fund of the State;

(b) the measures needed to improve the financial position of the Panchayats;

(c) any other matter referred to the Finance Commission by the Governor in the interests of sound finance of the Panchayats.

(2) The Legislature of a State may, by law, provide for the composition of the Commission, the qualification which shall be requisite for appointment as members thereof and the manner in which they shall be selected.

(3) The Commission shall determine their procedure and shall have such powers in the performance of their functions as the Legislature of the State may, by law, confer on them.

(4) The Governor shall cause every recommendation made by the Commission under this article together with an explanatory memorandum as to the action taken thereon to be laid before the Legislature of the State.

Audit of accounts of Panchayats.

243J. The Legislature of a State may, by law, make provisions with respect to the maintenance of accounts by the Panchayats and the auditing of such accounts.

Elections to the Panchayats.

243K.(1) The superintendence, direction and control of the preparation of electoral rolls for, and the conduct of, all elections to the panchayats shall be vested in a State Election Commission consisting of a State Election Commissions to be appointed by the Governor.

(2) Subject to the provisions of any law made by the Legislature of a State, the conditions of service and tenure of office of the State Election Commissioner shall be such as the Governor may by rule determine : Provided that the State Election Commissioner shall not be removed from his office except in like manner and on the like grounds as a Judge of a High Court and the conditions of service of the State Election Commissioner shall not be varied to his disadvantage after his appointment.

(3) The Governor of a State shall, when so requested by the State Election Commission, make available to the State Election Commission such staff as may be necessary for the discharge of the functions conferred on the State Election Commission by clause (1).

(4) Subject to the provisions of this Constitution, the Legislature of a State may, by law, make provisions with respect to all matters relating to, or in connection with, elections to the Panchayats.

Application to Union territorries.

243L. The provisions of this Part shall apply to the Union territories and shall, in their aplication to a Union territory, have effects as if the references to the Governor of a State were references to the Administrator of the Union territory appointed under article 239 and references to the Legislature or the Legislative Assembly of a State were references, in relation to a Union territory having a Legislative Assembly, to that Legislative assembly:

Provided that the President may, by public notification, direct that the provision of this Part shall apply to any Union territory or part thereof subject to such exceptions and modifications as he may specify in the notification.

Part not to apply to certain areas.

243M. (1) Nothing in this Part shall apply to the Scheduled Areas referred to in clause (1), and the tribal areas referred to in clause (2), of article 244.

(2) Nothing in this Part shall apply to—

(a) The States of Nagaland, Meghalaya and Mizoram;

(b) the hill areas in the State of Manipur for which District Councils exist under any law for the time being in force.

(3) Nothing in this Part—

(a) relating to Panchayats at the district level shall apply to the hill areas of the District of Darjeeling in the State of West Bengal for which Darjeeling Gorkha Hill Council exists under any law for the time being in force ;

(b) shall be construed to affect the functions and powers of the Darjeeling Gorkha Hill Council constituted under such law.

(4) Notwithstanding anything in this Constitution,—

(a) the Legislature of a State referred to in sub-clause (a) of clause (2) may, by law, extend this Part to that State, except the areas, if any, referred to in clause (1), if the Legislative Assembly of that State passes a resolution to that effect by a majority of the total membership of that House and by a majority of not less than two-thirds of the members of that house present and voting ;

(b) Parliament may, by law, extend the provisions of this Part of the Scheduled Areas and the tribal areas referred to in clause (1) subject to such exceptions and modifications as may be specified in such law, and no such law shall be deemed to be an amendment of this Constitution for the purposes of Article 368.

Continuance of existing laws and Panchayats.

243N. Notwithstanding anything in this Part, any provision of any law relating to Panchayats in force in a State immediately before the commencement of the Constitution (Seventy-third Amendment) Act, 1992, which is inconsistent with the provisions of this Part, shall continue to be in force until amended or repealed by a competent Legislature or other competent authority or until the expiration of one year from such commencement, whichever is earlier :

Provided that all the Panchayats existing immediately before such commencement shall continue till the expiration of their duration, unless sooner dissolved by a resolution passed to that effect by Legislative Assembly of that State or, in the case of a State having a Legislative Council, by each House of the Legislature of that State.

Bar to interference by courts in electoral matters.

243O. Notwithstanding anything in this Constitution,—

(a) the validity of any law relating to the delimitation of constituencies or the allotment of seats to such constituencies made or purporting to be made under article 243K, shall not be called in question in any court;

(b) no election to any Panchayat shall be called in question except by an election petition presented to such authority and in such manner as is provided for by or under any law made by the Legislature of a State.;

Amendment of article 280.

(3) In clause (3) of article 280 of the Constitution, after sub-clause (b), the following sub-clause shall be inserted, namely:

"(bb) the measures needed to augment the Consolidated Fund of a State to supplement the resources of the Panchayats in the State on the basis of the recommendations made by the Finance Commission of the State."

Addition of Eleventh Schedule.

(4) After the Tenth Schedule to the Constitution, the following Schedule shall be added, namely—

"ELEVENTH SCHEDULE

(Article 243G)

1. Agriculture, including agricultural extension.
2. Land improvement, implementation of land reforms, land consolidation and soil conservation.
3. Minor irrigation, water management and watershed development.
4. Animal husbandry, dairying and poultry.
5. Fisheries.
6. Social forestry and farm forestry.
7. Minor forest produce.
8. Small scale industries, including food processing industries.
9. Khadi, village and cottage industries.
10. Rural housing.
11. Drinking water.
12. Fuel and fodder.
13. Roads, culverts, bridges, ferries, waterways and other means of communication.
14. Rural electrification, including distribution of electricity.
15. Non-conventional energy sources.
16. Poverty alleviation programme.
17. Education, including primary and secondary schools.
18. Technical training and vocational education.
19. Adult and non-formal education.
20. Libraries.
21. Cultural activities.
22. Markets and fairs.
23. Health and sanitation, including hospitals, primary health centres and dispensaries.
24. Family welfare.
25. Women and child development.
26. Social welfare, including welfare of the handicapped and mentally retarded.

27. Welfare of the weaker sections, and in particular, of the Scheduled Castes and the Scheduled Tribes.
28. Public distribution system.
29. Maintenance of community asset."

K. L. MOHANPURIA
Secy. to the Govt. of India.

THE CONSTITUTION (SEVENTY-FOURTH AMENDMENT) ACT, 1992

[20th April, 1993.]

An Act further to amend the Constitution of India.

Be it enacted by Parliament in the Forty-third Year of the Republic of India as follows :

Short title and commencement.

1. (1) This Act may be called the Constitution (Seventy-fourth Amendment) Act, 1992.
   (2) It shall come into force on such date as the Central Government may, by notification in the Official Gazette, appoint.

Insertion of new Part IXA.

2. After Part IX of the Constitution, the following Part shall be inserted, namely :

PART IXA
THE MUNICIPALITIES

Definitions.

243P. In this Part, unless the context otherwise requires,—

(a) "Committee" means a Committee constituted under article 243S;

(b) "district" means a district in a State;

(c) "Metropolitan area" means an area having a population of ten lakhs or more, comprised in one or more districts and consisting of two or more Municipalities or Panchayats or other contiguous areas, specified by the Governor by public notification to be a Metropolitan area for the purposes of this Part;

(d) "Municipal area" means the territorial area of a Municipality as is notified by the Governor;

(e) "Municipality" means an institution of self-government constituted under article 243Q;

(f) "Panchayat" means a Panchayat constituted under article 243B;

(g) "Population" means the population as ascertained at the last preceding census of which the relevant figures have been published.

Constitution of Municipalities.

243Q. (1) There shall be constituted in every State,—

(a) a Nagar Panchayat (by whatever name called) for a transitional area, that is to say, an area in transition from a rural area to an urban area;

(b) a Municipal Council for a smaller urban area; and

(c) a Municipal Corporation for a larger urban area, in accordance with the provisions of this Part :

Provided that a Municipality under this clause may not be constituted in such urban area or part thereof as the Governor may, having regard to the size of the area and the municipal services being provided or proposed to be provided by an industrial establishment in that area and such other factors as he may deem fit, by public notification, specify to be an industrial township.

(2) In this article, " a transitional area", "a smaller urban area" or "a larger urban area" means such area as the Governor may having regard to the population of the area, the density of the population therein, the revenue generated for local administration, the percentage of employment in non-agricultural activities, the economic importance or such other factors as he may deem fit, specify by public notification of the purposes of this part.

Composition of Municipalities.

243R. (1) Save as provided in clause (2), all the seats in a Municipality shall be filled by persons chosen by direct election form the territorial constituencies in the Municipal area and for this purpose each Municipal area shall be divided into territorial constituencies to be known as wards.

(2) The Legislature of a State may, by law, provide—

(a) for the representation in a Municipality of—

(i). persons having special knowledge or experience in Municipal administration;

(ii) the members of the House of the People and the members of the Legislative Assembly of the state representing constituencies which comprise wholly or partly the Municipal area ;

(iii) the members of the Council of States and the members of the Legislative Council of the State registered as electors within the Municipal area ;

(iv) the Chairpersons of the Committees constituted under clause (5) of article 243S:

Provided that the persons referred to in paragraph (1) shall not have the right to vote in the meetings of the Municipality;

(b) the manner of election of the Chairperson of a Municipality.

243S. (1) There shall be constituted Wards Committees, consisting of one or more wards, within the territorial area of a Municipality having a population of three lakhs or more.

(2) The Legislature of a State may, by law, make provision with respect to —

(a) the composition and the territorial area of a Ward Committee;

(b) the manner in which the seats in a Wards Committee shall be filled.

(3) A member of a Municipality representing a ward within the territorial area of the Wards Committee shall be a member of that Committee.

(4) Where a Wards Committee consists of –

(a) one ward, the member representing that ward in the Municipality; or

(b) two or more wards, one of the members representing such wards in the Municipality elected by the members of the Wards Committee, shall be Chairperson of that Committee.

(5) Nothing in this aritcle shall be deemed to prevent the Legislature of a State from making any provision for the constitution of Committees in addition to the Wards Committees.

Reservation of seats.

243T. (1) Seats shall be reserved for the Scheduled Castes and the Scheduled Tribes in every Municipality and the number of seats so reserved shall bear, as nearly as may be, the same proportion to the total number of seats to be filled by direct election in that Municipality as the population of the Scheduled Castes in the Municipal area or of the Scheduled Tribes in the Municipal area bears to the total population of that area and such seats may be allotted by rotation to different constituencies in a Municipality.

(2) Not less than one-third of the total number of seats reserved under clause (1) shall be reserved for women belonging to the Scheduled Castes or, as the case may be, the Scheduled Tribes.

(3) Not less than one-third (including the number of seats reserved for women belonging to the Scheduled Castes and the Scheduled Tribes) of the total number of seats to be filled by direct election in every Municipality shall be reserved for women and such seats may be allotted by rotation to different constituencies in a Municipality.

(4) The officers of Chairpersons in the Municipalities shall be reserved for the Scheduled Castes, the Scheduled Tribes and women in such manner as the Legislature of a State may, by law, provide.

(5) The reservation of seats under clauses (1) and (2) and the reservation of offices of Chairpersons (other than the reservation for women) under clause (4) shall cease to have effect on the expiration of the period specified in article 334.

(6) Nothing in this part shall prevent the Legislature of a State from making any provision for reservation of seats in any Municipality or offices of Chairpersons in the Municipalities in favour of backward class of citizens.

Duration of Municipalities, etc.

243U. (1) Every Municipality, unless sooner dissolved under any law for the time being in force, shall continue for five years from the date appointed for its first meeting and no longer :

Provided that a Municipality shall be given a reasonable opportunity of being heard before its dissolution.

(2) No amendment of any law for the time being in force shall have the effect of causing dissolution of a Municipality at any level, which is functioning immediately before such amendment, till the expiration of its duration specified in clause (1).

(3) An election to constitute a Municipality shall be completed,–

(a) before the expiry of its duration specified in clause (1);

(b) before the expiration of a period of six months from the date of its dissolution :

Provided that where the remainder of the period for which the dissolved Municipality would have continued is less than six months, it shall not be necessary to hold any election under this clause for constituting the Municipality for such period.

(4) A Municipality constituted upon the dissolution of a Municipality before the expiration of its duration shall continue only for the remainder of the period for which the dissolved Municipality would have continued under clause (1) had it not been so dissolved.

Disqualifications for membership.

243V. (1) A Person shall be disqualified for being chosen as, and for being, a member of a Municipality—

(a) if he is so disqualified by or under any law for the time being in force for the purposes of elections to the Legislature of the State concerned :

Provided that no person shall be disqualified on the ground that he is less than twenty-five years of age, if he has attained the age of twenty-one years;

(b) if he is so disqualified by or under any law made by the Legislature of the State.

(2) If any question arises as to whether a member of a Municipality has become subject to any of the disqualifications mentioned in clause (1), the question shall be referred for the decision of such authority and in such manner as the Legislature of a State may, by law, provide.

Powers, authority and responsibilities of Municipalities, etc.

243W. Subject to the provisions of this Constitution, the Legislature of a State may, by law, endow—

(a) the Municipalities with such powers and authority as may be necessary to enable them to function as institutions of self-government and such law may contain provisions for the devolution of powers and responsibilities upon Municipalities, subject to such conditions as may be specified therein, with respect to—

(i) the preparation of plans for economic development and social justice;

(ii) the performance of functions and the implementation of schemes as may be entrusted to them including those in relation to the matters listed in the Twelfth Schedule;

(b) the Committees with such powers and authority as may be necessary to enable them to carry out the responsibilities conferred upon them including those in relation to the matters listed in the Twelfth Schedule.

Power to impose taxes by, and Funds of, the Municipalities.

243X. The Legislature of a State may, by law,—

(a) authorise a Municipality to levy, collect and appropriate such taxes, duties, tolls and fees in accordance with such procedure and subject to such limits;

(b) assign to Municipality such taxes, duties, tolls and fees levied and collected by the State Government for such purposes and subject to such conditions and limits;

(c) provide for making such grants-in-aid to the Municipalities from the Consolidated Fund of the State; and

(d) provide for constitution of such Funds for crediting all moneys received, respectively, by or on behalf of the Municipalities and also for the withdrawal of such moneys therefrom, as may be specified in the law.

Finance Commission.

243Y. (1) The Finance Commission constituted under article 243-I shall also review the financial position of the Municipalities and make recommendations to the Governor as to—

(a) the principles which should govern—

(i) the distribution between the State and the Municipalities of the net proceeds of the taxes, duties, tolls and fees leviable by the State, which may be divided between them under this Part and the allocation between the Municipalities at all levels of their respective shares of such proceeds;

(ii) the determination of the taxes, duties, tolls and fees which may be assigned to, or appropriated by the Municipalities;

(iii) the grants-in-aid to the Municipalities from the Consolidated Fund of the State;

(b) the measures needed to improve the financial position of the Municipalities;

(c) any other matter referred to the Finance Commission by the Governor in the interests of sound finance of the Municipalities.

(2) The Governor shall cause every recommendation made by the Commission under this article together with an explanatory memorandum as to the action taken thereon to be laid before the Legislature of the State.

Audit of accounts of Municipalities.

243Z. (1) The Legislature of a State may, by law, make provisions with respect to the maintenance of accounts by the Municipalities and the auditing of such accounts.

Elections to the Municipalities.

243ZA. (1) The superintendence, direction and control of the preparation of electoral rolls for, and the conduct of, all elections to the Municipalities shall be vested in the State Election Commission referred to in article 243K.

(2) Subject to the provisions of this Constitution, the Legislature of a State may, by law, make provision with respect to all matters relating to, or in connection with, elections to the Municipalities.

Application to Union territories.

243ZB. The provisions of this Part shall apply to the Union territories and shall, in their application to a Union territory, have effect as if the references to the Governor of a State were references to the Administrator of the Union territory appointed under article 239 and references to the Legislature or the Legislative assembly of a State were references in relation to a Union territory having a Legislative assembly, to that Legislative Assembly :

Provided that the President may, by public notification, direct that the provisions of this Part shall apply to any Union territory or part thereof subject to such exceptions and modifications as he may specify in the notification.

Part not to apply to certain areas.

243ZC.(1) Nothing in this Part shall apply to the Scheduled Areas referred to in clause (1), and the tribal areas referred to in clause (2), of article 244.

(2) Nothing in this Part shall be construed to affect the functions and powers of the Darjeeling Gorkha Hill Council constituted under any law for the time being in force for the hill areas of the district of Darjeeling in the State of West Bengal.

(3) Notwithstanding anything in this Constitution, Parliament may by law, extend the provisions of this

Part to the Scheduled Areas and the tribal areas referred to in clause (1) subject to such exceptions and modifications as may be specified in such law, and no such law shall be deemed to be an amendment of this Constitution for the purposes of article 368.

Committee for district planning.

243ZD. (1) There shall be constituted in every State at the district level a District Planning Committee to consolidate the plans prepared by the Panchayats and the Municipalities in the district and to prepare a draft development plan for the district as a whole.

(2) The Legislature of a State may, by law, make provision with respect to–

(a) the composition of the District Planning Committees;

(b) the manner in which the seats in such Committees shall be filled :

Provided that not less that four-fifths of the total number of members of such committee shall be elected, by and from amongst, the elected members of the Panchayat at the district level and of the Municipalities in the district in proportion to the ratio between the population of the rural areas and of the urban areas in the district.

(c) the functions relating to district planning which may be assigned to such Committees ;

(d) the manner in which the Chairpersons of such Committees shall be chosen.

(3) Every District planning Committee shall, in preparing the draft development plan,–

(a) have regard to–

(i) matters of common interest between the Panchayats and the Municipalities including spatial planning, sharing of water and other physical and natural resources, the integrated development of infrastructure and environmental conservation ;

(ii) the extent and type of available resources whether financial or otherwise ;

(b) consult such institutions and organisations as the Governor may, by order, specify.

(4) The Chairperson of every District Planning Committee shall forward the development plan, as recommended by such Committee, to the Government of the State.

Committee for Metropolitan planning.

243ZE. (1) There shall be constituted in every Metropolitan area a Metropolitan Planning Committee to prepare a draft development plan for the Metropolitan area as a whole.

(2) The Legislature of a State may, by law, make provision with respect to—

(a) the composition of the Metropolitan Planning Committees;

(b) the manner in which the seats in such Committees shall be filled :

Provided that not less than two-thirds of the members of such Committee shall be elected by, and from amongst, the elected members of the Municipalities and Chairpersons of the Panchayats in the Metropolitan area in proportion to the ratio between the population of the Municipalities and of the Panchayats in that area;

(c) the representation in such Committees of the Government of India and the Government of the State and of organisations and institutions as may be deemed necessary for carrying out the functions assigned to such Committees;

(d) The functions relating to planning and coordination for the Metropolitan area which may be assigned to such Committees;

(e) The manner in which the Chairpersons of such Committees shall be chosen.

(3) Every Metropolitan Planning Committee shall, in preparing the draft development plan—

(a) have regard to—

(i) the plans prepared by the Municipalities and the Panchayats in the Metropolitan area;

(ii) matters of common interest between the Municipalities and the Panchayats, including co-ordinated spatial planning of the area, sharing of water and other physical and natural resources, the integrated development of infrastructure and environmental conservation;

(iii) the overall objectives and priorities set by the Government of India and the Government of the State;

(iv) the extent and nature of investments likely to be made in the Metropolitan area by agencies of the Government of India and of the Government of the State and other available resources whether financial or otherwise;

(b) consult such institutions and organisations as the Governor may, by order, specify.

(4) the Chairperson of every Metropolitan Planning Committee shall forward the development plan, as recommended by such Committee to the Government of the State.

243ZF. Notwithstanding anything in this Part, any provision of any law relating to Municipalities in force in a State immediately before the Commencement of the Constitution (Seventy-fourth Amendment) Act, 1992 which is inconsistent with the provisions of this part, shall continue to be in force until amended or repealed by a competent Legislature or other compe-tent authority or until the expiration of the one year from such commencement, whichever is earlier :

Provided that all the Municipalities existing imme-diately before such commencement shall continue till the expiration of their duration, unless sooner dissolved by a resolution passed to that effect by the Legislative Assembly of that State or, in the case of a State having a Legislative Council, by each House of the Legislature of that State.

243ZG. Not with standing anything in this Constitution,—

(a) the validity of any law relating to the delimitation of constituencies or the allotment of seats to such constituencies made or purporting to be made under article 243ZA, shall not be called in question in any court :

(b) no election to any Municipality shall be called in question except by an election petition presented to such authority and in such manner as is provided for by or under any law made by the Legislature of a State.

3. In Clause (3) of article 280 of the Constitution, sub-clause (c) shall be relettered as sub-clause (d) and before sub-clause (d) as so relettered, the following sub-clause shall be inserted, namely :—

"(c) the measures needed to augment the Consolidated Fund of a State to supplement the resources of the Municipalities in the State on the basis of the recommendations made by the Finance Commission of the State;"

4. After the Eleventh Schedule in the Constitution, the following Schedule shall be added, namely—

"TWELFTH SCHEDULE
(Article 243W)

1. Urban planning including town planning.
2. Regulation of land-use and construction of buildings.
3. Planning for economic and social development.
4. Roads and bridges.
5. Water supply for domestic, industrial and commercial purposes.
6. Public health, sanitation, conservancy and solid waste management.
7. Fire services.
8. Urban forestry, protection of the environment and promotion of ecological aspects.
9. Safeguarding the interests of weaker sections of society, including the handicapped and mentally retarded.
10. Slum improvement and upgradation.
11. Urban poverty alleviation.

12. Provision of urban amenities and facilities such as parks, gardens, playgrounds.
13. Promotion of cultural, educational and aesthetic aspects.
14. Burials and burial grounds; cremations, cremation grounds and electric crematoriums.
15. Cattle ponds; prevention of cruelty to animals.
16. Vital statistics including registration of births and deaths.
17. Public amenities including street lighting, parking lots, bus stops and public conveniences.
18. Regulation of slaughter houses and tanneries."

K. L. MOHANPURIA
Secy. to the Govt. of India.

APPENDIX– V

THE WEST BENGAL DISTRICT PLANNING COMMITTEE ACT, 1994.

[Passed by the West Bengal Legislature.]
[Assent of the Governor was first published in the Calcutta Gazette, Extraordinary, of the 3rd May, 1994.]

An Act to provide for the constitution of District Planning Committee at the district level for consolidation of the plans prepared by the Panchayats and the Municipalities in the district and preparation of draft development plan for the district as a whole.

WHEREAS it is expedient to provide for the constitution of District Planning Committee at the district level for consolidation of the plans prepared by the *Panchayats* and the Municipalities in the district and preparation of draft development plan for the district as a whole;

It is hereby enacted in the Forty-fifth Year of the Republic of India, by the Legislature of West Bengal, as follows: –

Short title, extent and commencement

1. (1) This Act may be called the West Bengal District Planning Committee Act, 1994.
   (2) It extends to the whole of West Bengal, except the areas to which the provisions of—
   (a) the Calcutta Municipal Corporation Act, 1980, or
   (b) The Darjeeling Gorkha Hill Council Act, 1988, or any Part or modification thereof, apply or may hereafter be applied.
   (3) It shall come into force on such date as the State Government may, by notification, appoint.

Definitions.

2. In this Act, unless the context otherwise requires,—
   (a) "committee" means a District Planning Committee, or Siliguri Sub-division Planning Committee, constituted under sub-section (1) of section 3;

(b) "Constitution" means the Constitution of India;

(c) "District Magistrate" includes an Additional District Magistrate, or any other Magistrate appointed by the State Government to discharge all or any of the functions of the District Magistrate under this Act;

(d) "Governor" means the Governor, appointed as such under article 155, read with article 153, of the Constitution, for the State of West Bengal;

(e) "Municipality" has the same meaning as in clause (e) of article 243P of the Constitution;

(f) "notification" means a notification published in the *Official Gazette;*

(g) "*Panchayat Samiti*" means a *Panchayat Samiti* constituted under the West Bengal Panchayat Act, 1973;

(h) "population" means the population as ascertained at the last preceding census of which the relevant figures have been published;

(i) "prescribed" means prescribed by rules made under this Act;

(j) "rural area" means an area within a Block. *Explanation.*—"Block" has the same meaning as in clause (2) of section 2 of the West Bengal *Panchayat* Act, 1973;

(k) "urban area" means an area within a Municipality;

(l) "*Zilla Parishad*" means a *Zilla Parishad*, and includes *Mahakuma Parishad* for the sub-division of Siliguri in the district of Darjeeling, constituted under the West Bengal Panchayat Act, 1973.

District Planning Committee.

3. (1) For every district the State Government shall constitute a District Planning Committee bearing the name of the district, except for the sub-division of Siliguri in the district of Darjeeling for which the State Government shall constitute a Planning Committee to be called Siliguri Sub-division Planning Committee.

(2) Subject to such rules as may be made by the State Government in this behalf, the State Government

shall, by notification, determine the number of members of a Committee including—

(a) the number of such members to be elected by, and from amongst, the elected members of the *Zilla Parishad* :

Provided that no *Sabhadhipati* of a *Zilla Parishad* shall be elected under this clause,

(b) the number of such members to be elected by, and from amongst, the elected members, by whatever name called, of all the Municipalities within the district or, in the case of the sub-division of Siliguri in the district of Darjeeling, of all the Municipalities within that sub-division :

Provided that no Chairperson of a Municipality shall be elected under this clause, and

(c) the number of such members, not exceeding one-fifth of the total number of members of the Committee, as may be appointed by the State Government under sub-section (3) :

Provided that the ratio between the number of members of a Committee and the sum total of the rural population and the urban population in district, or, in the case, of the sub-division of Siliguri, in the district Darjeeling, in that sub-division shall, so far as practicable, be the same throughout West Bengal :

Provided further that four-fifths of the total numbers of a Committee shall not exceed the total number of elected members of the *Zilla Parishad* :

Provided also that the number of members referred to in clause (a) shall bear, as nearly as may be, the same proportion to the number of members, referred to in clause (b), as the population of the rural areas bear to the population of the urban areas in the district or, in the case of the sub-division of Siliguri in the district of Darjeeling, in that sub-division.

(3) Subject to the provisions of clause (c) of sub-section (2), the State Government shall, by notification, appoint the members referred to therein, and such members shall include—

(a) the *Sabhadhipati* of the *Zilla Parishad*,
(b) the District Magistrate of the district, and
(c) such other members as the State Government may think fit to choose from amongst—
(i) the *Sabhapatis* of the *Panchayat Samitis* within the district,
(ii) the members of the House of the People and the Legislative Assembly of the State elected thereto from a constituency comprising any part of the district, not being Ministers,
(iii) the officers of the State Government or of any statutory body of corporation deemed by the State Government to have specialised knowledge,
(iv) the Chairpersons of the Municipalities within the district or, in the case of the sub-division of Siliguri in the district of Darjeeling, within that sub-division, and
(v) the economists and social and political workers of eminence.

Chairperson, Vice-Chairperson and Secretary of Committee.

4. (1) The *Sabhadhipati* of the *Zilla Parishad* shall be the Chairperson of the Committee.
(2) As soon as may be after constitution of the Committee or in the event of any vacancy, as the case may be, the members of the Committee shall select a Vice-Chairperson from amongst themselves in such manner as may be determined by the Chairperson.
(3) In the absence of the Chairperson, the Vice-Chairperson shall preside at the meeting of the Committee.
(4) The District Magistrate shall be the Secretary of the Committee and shall make available to the Committee such assistance as may be necessary for the discharge of its functions.

Election

5. (1) Subject to such rules as may be made by the State Government in this behalf and such directions as that Government may issue for the purpose, the District

Magistrate shall coordinate and supervise all work in connection with the election of members to the Committee.

(2) The District Magistrate shall appoint a Returning Officer and as many Assistant Returning Officers as may be necessary for the purpose of conducting the election of members to the Committee.

(3) The powers and functions of the Returning Officer and the Assistant Returning Officers shall be such as may be prescribed.

(4) If any dispute arises as to the validity of an election under this Act, any person entitled to vote at such election may, within thirty days after the date of the declaration of the results of such election, file a petition, calling in question such election, before the Divisional Commissioner having jurisdiction, and the order of the Divisional Commissioner in disposing of the petition shall be final.

(5) Notwithstanding anything to the contrary contained in this Act or in any other law for the time being in force, no civil court shall have any jurisdiction to entertain any petition calling in question the validity of any election under this Act.

Term of office of members of committee.

(6) A member of a committee, who is a member of–

(a) a Zilla Parishad, or
(b) a Municipality, or
(c) a Panchayat Samiti, or
(d) the House of the People, or
(e) the Lesislative Assembly of the State,

shall cease to be a member of the Committee if he ceases to be a member of–

(i) the Zilla Parishad, or
(ii) the Municipality, or
(iii) the Panchayat Samiti, or
(iv) the House of the People, or
(v) the Legislative Assembly of the State, as the case may be.

Resignation.

7. A Vice-Chairperson or a member of the Committee may, at any time, resign his office by notifying in writing his intention to do so to the Chairperson and, on such resignation being accepted, the Vice-Chairperson or the member, as the case may be, shall be deemed to have vacated his office.

Filling of casual vacancy in the place of an elected member of Committee.

8. If the office of an elected member of a Committee becomes vacant by reason of his death, resignation or otherwise, the vacancy shall be filled by election of another member in the prescribed manner.

Procedure, meeting, and records of meeting, etc. of Committee.

9. (1) The Committee shall regulate its procedure and shall, without prejudice to the generality of such power, decide as and when and in which manner, a meeting shall be held :

Provided that the Chairperson, when required by notice in writing by at least one-third of the members of the Committee to call a meeting, shall do so in ordinary manner, within one month from the date of receipt of the notice.

(2) One-third of the total number of members subject to a minimum of ten members, shall be a quorum for a meeting of the Committee : Provided that no quorum shall be necessary for an adjourned meeting.

(3) The Secretary of the Committee shall maintain records of the meeting of the Committee and shall take such actions in this behalf as the Committee may decide.

Powers and functions of Committee, constitution of sub-committees, etc.

10. (1) The Committee shall—

(a) consolidate the plans prepared by the Panchayats and the Municipalities in the district, and

(b) Prepare a draft development plan for the district as a whole.

(2) The Committee shall, in preparing the draft development plan under clause (b) of sub-section (1),

(a) have regard to—

(i) matters of common interest between the Panchayats and the Municipalities including spatial planning, sharing of water and other physical and natural resources, the integrated development of infrastructure and environmental conservation :

(ii) the extent and type of available resources, whether financial or otherwise;

(b) consult such institutions and organisations as the Governor may, by order, specify.

(3) The State Government may, by order, assign to the Committee such functions relating to district planning and coordination and monitoring of the activities of different departments of the State Government as may be deemed necessary.

(4) Subject to such rules as may, be made by the State Government in this behalf the State Government may, by notification, constitute an Urban Development Sub-Committee and such other sub-committees as may be deemed necessary for carrying out the purposes of this Act :

Provided that each such Sub-Committee shall consist of not less than seven members selected from amongst the members of the Committee or such economists, economic planners, administrators, or social and political workers of eminence, as the State Government may think fit.

(5) The Chairperson of a Committee shall forward the development plan, as recommended by such Committee, to the State Government in such manner as may be prescribed.

Power to make rules.

11. (1) The State Government may make rules for carrying out the purposes of this Act.

(2) In particular and without prejudice to the generality of the foregoing power, such rules may provide for

all or any of the matters which under any provision of this Act, are required to be prescribed or to be provided for by rules.

(3) All rules made under this Act shall be published in the Official Gazette and shall, unless some later date is appointed by the State Government, come into force on the date of such publication.

(5) All rules made under this Act shall be laid for not less than fourteen days before the State Legislature as soon as possible after they are made and shall be subject to such modification as the State Legislature may make during the session in which they are so laid

By order of the Governor,
S. MAITRA
Special Officer & Ex officio
Jt. Secy. to the Govt. of West Bengal

APPENDIX – VI

THE WEST BENGAL DISTRICT PLANNING COMMITTEE RULES, 1994.

CHAPTER – I

PRELIMINARY

1. **Short title.** –These rules may be called the West Bengal District Planning Committee Rules, 1994.

2. **Definitions**–(1) In these rules unless the context otherwise requires,–

(a) "the Act" means the West Bengal District Planning Committee Act, 1994 (West Ben. Act XX of 1994);

(b) "ballot box" includes any box, bag or other receptacle used for the insertion of ballot papers by voters;

(c) "form" means a form appended to these rules, and includes a translation thereof in Bengali;

(d) "list of voters" means the list of (i) elected members of the Zilla Parishad or (ii) elected members, by whatever name called, of the municipalities in a district as prepared by the District Magistrate under clause (a) of rule 4;

(e) "polling station", in relation to an election, means the place for taking poll of that election;

(f) "returning officer" includes any assistant returning officer when performing the function of a returning officer;

(g) "section" means a section of the Act.

(2) The expressions used in these rules and not otherwise defined shall have the same meaning as in the Act.

CHAPTER – II

CONSTITUTION OF DISTRICT PLANNING COMMITTEE

3. **Determination of number of members.** –(1) Subject to the provisions of sub-rule (2) and sub-rule (3), the State Government shall, as soon as may be within one month from the date of commencement of these rules, by notification determine the total number of members of a committee which shall be equal to the sum total of the number of constituencies, existing at the time of the notification, of the Zilla Parishad for that district and one-fourth of that number, omitting the fraction, if any:

Provided that in the event of fresh delimitation of the constituencies of a Zilla Parishad under any law for the time being in force, the State Government may, by notification, alter and modify the number of members of the Committee.

(2) When the number of constituencies, as referred to in sub-rule (1), is between forty-eight and eighty, the total number of members of the Committee shall be determined as one hundred.

(3) When the number of constituencies, as referred to in sub-rule (1), is eighty-one or more, the total number of members of the Committee shall be determined as one hundred.

(4) One-fifth of the total number of members of the Committee shall be appointed by the State Government under sub-section (3) of section 3, and the other members shall be elected under clause (a), or clause (b), of sub-section (3) of section 3 as the case may be.

Explanation.—for the purpose of calculation of one-fifth of the total number of members, the quotient shall be taken into consideration and the remainder shall be ignored.

(5) For the purpose of determination of the number of members under clause (a), and clause (b), of sub-section (2) of section 3, —

(a) the State Government shall take into consideration the population figure of the rural area and of the urban area of district in whole thousand, raising any such figure to next higher number in case of any residual figure of five hundred or more or ignoring any residual figure below five hundred, as the case may be;

(b) for the purpose of any calculation, except that for final determination of the numbers referred to in sub-section (2) of section 3, any figure up to the first place of decimal shall be taken into consideration, ignoring other places of decimal;

(c) in order to arrive at the final determination, any digit of five or higher in the first place of decimal shall be rounded off to one and added to the whole number and any digit lower than five in the first place of decimal shall be ignored.

CHAPTER – III

CONDUCT OF ELECTION (RULES 4 – 24)

■■■

CHAPTER – IV

CONSTITUTION OF SUB-COMMITTEES AND FORWARDING OF DRAFT DEVELOPMENT PLAN

5. **Constitution of Urban Development Sub-Committee.**

(1) The State Government may, by notification, constitute an Urban Development Sub-Committee and may specify, from among its members, the Chairperson and the Secretary of that Sub-Committee.

(2) The Secretary of the Sub-Committee shall conven meetings in consultation with the Chairperson maintain all records and take follow-up actions.

(3) The Sub-Committee shall meet as often as necessar and at least once in every 3 months. No quorum wil be necessary for such meeting. The Sub-Committe shall device its own procedure for functioning.

(4) Without prejudice to the general powers an functions of the Sub-Committee as respects th preparation of draft development plan for th urban areas of the district, the Sub-Committe shall—

(a) examine, co-relate and integrate plans as draw up by different municipalities of the district;

(b) deliberate upon the issues relating to periphera areas and resolution of conflicts;

(c) draw up guidelines for planning, buildin controls and aesthetics relating to the municipa lities;

(d) draw up plans for improvement of slum specially in the area of sanitation and environ ment;

(e) consider measures for environmental improve ment with special emphasis on control of wate pollution and air pollution;

(f) consider issues relating to sources of wate supply, sites of disposal of sewage, solid wast and other disposable waste,

(g) consider any other matter that may be entruste to it by the Committee.

(5) For the purpose of its deliberations, the Sub Committee may call for any record or data from an municipality or from any *Panchayat* within it jurisdiction.

(6) The Sub-Committee shall forward its recommenda tions to the Committee for consideration and inclu sion of the recommendations in draft developmer plan for the district.

26. **District Planning and Co-ordination Sub-Committee.**

(1) The State Government may, by notification, constitute a District Planning and Co-ordination Sub-Committee and may specify, from among its members, the Chairperson and the Secretary of that Sub-Committee.

(2) The Member-Secretary shall convene meetings of the Sub-Committee in consultation with the Chairperson. He shall also maintain all records of proceedings and follow-up action.

(3) The Sub-Committee shall meet as frequently as necessary and at least once in every three months. No quorum shall be necessary for its meetings.

(4) The Sub-Committee shall devise its own procedure for functioning. It shall have the authority to call for any record or data from any municipality or *Panchayat* within its jurisdiction and for any record or data relating to that district from any department of the State Government, for the purpose of the Act.

(6) The Sub-Committee shall advise and assist the Committee in the preparation of the district plan co-ordinating and consolidating the annual plans and programmes of the municipalities, *Panchayats*, other development authorities and Government departments functioning within the district planning area, shall prepare a draft development plan for a period, being the period normally of five-year term, shall generally coordinate the overall functioning of different development agencies in the implementation of the development plan for the district and, without prejudice to the generality of the above provisions, shall have functional responsibility in respect of—

(a) preparation of draft development plan of the district having regard to the matters of common interest between the *Panchayats* and the municipalities;

(b) issues relating to peripheral areas, urban agglomerations and other growth areas and resolution of conflicts;

(c) preparation of guidelines for planning, building controls and aesthetics;

(d) social planning specially for the Scheduled Castes, Scheduled Tribes and women on mobilising resources available in urban and rural areas;

(e) formulation of plans for development of integrated infrastructure like water supply schemes and disposal of sewage an solid waste which have intertwined interest in peripheral village areas and a town;

(f) overlapping functions between *Panchayats* and municipalities and resolution of conflicts;

(g) scrutiny of investment allocation on an annual basis for the *Panchayats* and municipalities within its jurisdiction;

(h) indication of the priorities to be assigned to works in the draft development plan and the phasing of the programme of development as such; and

(i) any other function as may be assigned to it by the Committee.

(6) The Sub-Committee shall forward its views and recommendations to the Committee for deliberation and further necessary action.

27. **Constitution of other Sub-Committees.**

(1) The State Government may, by one or more notifications issued at anytime, constitute as many other Sub-Committee as may be considered necessary, clearly defining the area of functions of each such Sub-Committee.

(2) The State Government may specify in the notification under sub-rule (1) the Chairperson and the Secretary of the Sub-Committee and their powers and functions.

(3) On being constituted, a Sub-Committee shall devise its own procedure for meeting and other functions and shall have authority to call for records and data relating to its area of functions from any municipality, *Panchayat* or department of the State Government.

(4) Any Sub-Committee under sub-rule (1) shall function under the general direction and supervision of the Committee and shall forward its report and recommendations to the Committee for necessary action.

28. **Forwarding of draft development plan.**

(1) As soon as may be within one month from the date when the Committee adopts the draft development plan for the district or within such date as the State Government may, by order, specify, the Chairperson of the Committee or the Secretary on his behalf, shall forward such development plan to the State Government.

(2) The State Government may, as soon as possible on receipt of the plan under sub-rule (1), in consultation with the State Planning Board and after giving the Committee an opportunity to present its plan, approve the plan with such modification as that Government deems fit.

29. **Modification of draft development plan.**

The Committee may, at any time but not more than once in every three years, revise or modify the draft development plan, and in respect of such revised or modified development plan, the provisions of rule 28 shall apply.

30. **Removal of difficulty.**

(1) The State Government may issue such general or special directions as may, in its opinion, be necessary for the purpose of giving effect to these rules, or holding any election under the Act.

(2) If any difficulty arises in giving effect to the provisions of these rules, or in holding any election, the Government, as occasion may require, may, by order, do anything which appears to be necessary for the purpose of removing the difficulty.

THE SCENARIO FROM KERALA

A NEW BEGINNING

Despite the acclaimed advantages of decentralization of planning and repeated commitments made in its favour, the planning process in India has, so far, remained a highly centralized affair. There has been very little serious effort to develop planning capabilities at lower levels. Even state plans, more often than not, are mere aggregations of departmental schemes trimmed and modified to suit the national framework and targets. It is in the above context that the newly constituted Kerala State Planning Board resolved at its very first meeting to initiate a **People's Campaign For Decentralized Planning** in order to empower the Panchayats and Municipal bodies to draw up the Ninth Plan schemes within their respective areas of responsibility. It is hoped that 35 to 40 per cent of the Ninth Plan would consist of schemes formulated and implemented from below.

The Development Crisis In Kerala :

Spurring The Need For A People's Campaign

The Campaign also assumes importance from the point of view of the existing crisis in Kerala's widely acclaimed development model. The crisis encountered by the State is widely noted and the focus of attention of relevant debates and studies has rightly been on the sustained poor growth performance of the productive sectors of the economy.

Stagnation in the production sectors — The crisis in productive sectors is manifested (i) in the virtual stagnation of the agricultural sector (ii) the deplorably lower level of productivity of important crops (iii) growing apathy among cultivators (iv) structural decay of the industrial sector dominated by the ailing traditional industries (v) rapid deterioration of the power situation and over-burdening of the fragile ecosystem.

Quality erosion in service sectors — The threats faced by other aspects of social life are also equally severe. For instance, the deterioration in the quality of services offered by crucial service sectors, such as education, public health, and transport has emerged as a major problem. In addition, the stagnation of the productive sectors has worsened the fiscal position of the State and made it incapable of making any effective intervention. The contemporary crisis has already started affecting the redistributive gains of the past and standard of living of the people.

The role of mass movements — The focus of mass movements, which made the 'Kerala model' possible, has so far been on the question of equity in distribution of wealth and income. But it is becoming increasingly evident that even the pursuit of equality cannot be sustained in the absence of economic growth. The People's Campaign for the Ninth Plan is an initiative to utilise the legacy of collective social intervention to face the contemporary challenge of development.

The People's Campaign :

A New Development Culture

The Campaign seeks to motivate and bring together the following groups of people in every locality in the preparation of the Ninth Plan. *First*, the elected representatives themselves have to be made aware of their responsibility and equipped for a new style of team work. *Secondly*, the officials have to be reoriented to shoulder the planning responsibilities under the direction of the Panchayats. *Third*, the expertise of non-officials has to be made available to the Panchayats and Municipal bodies. Unlike most villages in India, every village in Kerala has a large number of educated people, many of them with high technical and professional qualifications as well as experience. The number of retired experts is also quite large. The Campaign strives to motivate them to come out of their retirement to actively participate in local level planning. *Fourth*, the mass of people, who remain passive objects of the development process, have to be activated for the new democratic project to improve their own daily lives. And *finally*, the mass organisations of people have to be reoriented to mobilise their members for the new development initiatives.

In short, there has to be a major change in the attitude of officials, experts, elected representatives and the people at large. This is what is sought to be achieved through the people's Campaign for the Ninth Plan. By this, we hope to create the atmosphere for a new development culture, devoid of narrow party politics and rivalries on non-issues.

The Various Phases Of The Campaign

The Primary objective of the Campaign is to ensure that Panchayati Raj/Municipal bodies prepare and prioritise a shelf of integrated schemes, in a scientific and participatory manner, so that programmes for the Ninth Plan can be selected from them on a priority basis. This process of planning from below was initially divided into *five phases*. Each phase was to be preceded by a preparatory stage, the most important component of which was the training of Resource Persons (voluntary workers, officials and people's representatives) at various levels.

Identifying needs — The *First Phase* in the planning process was the identification of the needs of the people and the gaps in local development. This was sought to be achieved through discussions at *gramasabhas* in Panchayats and ward conventions in Municipalities. About 30 lakh people participated in the *Gramasabhas* and Ward Conventions specially convened during September-October.

Development Seminars — The key event of the *Second Phase* (November-December) was the organisation of Development Seminars at Panchayat and Municipal levels. At these seminars, integrated solutions for the various problems identified at the *gramasabhas*/ward conventions, were worked out. Apart from the representatives selected by *gramasabhas*, the seminars were attended by all the key officials of the area and invited experts from the locality and outside. An objective assessment of the natural and human resources and the related development problems was made through systematic secondary data collection, rapid appraisal techniques such as transit walks, semi-official reviews of ongoing programmes. This culminated in the preparation of Development Reports. These reports totalling more than one lakh printed pages in all, is a virtual compendium of local history, resources, problem analysis and development potential.

Task Forces and Projectisation — The Development Seminars at the Panchayat and Municipal levels only arrived at broad statements of solutions to various development problems. The *Third Phase* (January – March) of the Campaign sought to convert these solutions into project/scheme proposals in a format that could be included in the plan. The Task Forces formed at the Development Seminars in 13 key development areas like health, education, agriculture etc., prepared project proposals based on the Development Reports.

Panchayat/Municipal Plan Document — The *Forth Phase* (March – April) of the Campaign involves the actual formulation of the Panchayat or Municipal Plan. Now that the Ninth Plan allocations for the local bodies are clearly known, proposals and schemes are being selected from the shelf of projects that had been prepared by the Task Forces.

Kerala Development Congress — The *Fifth Phase* starts with the organisation of district and block level development seminars and integration of the local plans at the block and district levels. Plans will be drawn up for these higher tiers of Panchayats. A major state-level Congress to discuss the State's Ninth Five-Year plan and to mark the 40th anniversary of the formation of the State is to be organised by the State Planning Board in October 1997. The Congress will mark the culmination of the People's Campaign for the Ninth Plan.

Voluntary Technical Corps :

Phase VI of the People's Campaign

A recent meeting of the State Planning Board has resolved that a separate *Sixth Phase* for project appraisal be included in the People's Campaign. The main task of this phase would be to examine the technical feasibility, financial viability and social acceptability of the projects included in the plans of the local bodies. This would be done by a competent authority so that necessary technical and other sanctions may be easily obtained for the projects thus approved.

The dimensions of the tasks involved — Around 1.5 lakh projects have to be evaluated. The evaluation is not for selection or rejection but to actually correct and finalise the projects. The projects may be divided into *two categories* : (1) projects that are included in the annual plan (1997-98) (2) projects for subsequent years. The former requires thorough evaluation. Technical specifications and even designs may be made and finalised. This is expected to be completed by the beginning of May at the latest, so that the first allotment for the annual plan can be made in the month of May itself and implementation of the development activities started before the onset of the monsoon. The latter requires only a general evaluation as to technical feasibility and financial viability. This again has to be completed by June so that the Ninth Plan for the State is finalised as per the national timetable. The appraisal has to be carried out not only with respect to Gram Panchayats but also the higher tiers and Municipalities.

The Project Appraisal Team/Voluntary Technical Corps. (VTC) — It would take a team of up to fifty to sixty experts in every block and municipality during the months of April/June to complete the above tasks in a time bound manner – which would mean the need for 10,000 experts in the State as a whole. Since the team is an official body, eligibility for membership in the Project Appraisal Team would be based on specified qualifications. Members will have at least minimum experience in any development sector along with a professional or post-graduate degree. The specifications for educational qualification will be relaxed in the case of people with sufficient experience.

Database for the Voluntary Technical Corps — A comprehensive list of potential retired and non-official experts in the State is being prepared. Any expert who is willing to spend at least one day a week to render voluntary help to the Panchayats will be enrolled in the Voluntary Technical Corps (VTC).

Empowering the VTC — A district level convention has been arranged for the first week of April, at which details of the appraisal work, responsibilities as members of the expert team and other arrangements will be discussed. An orientation course will also be organised for the members in every district. Every block will be assigned a group of experts. Once the projects have been appraised, workshops will be organised at block levels to which representatives of the task forces will also be invited. Here, comments and suggestions will be discussed, corrections made and projects finalised and approved. Special consultants will be appointed for each of the development sectors.

It may be a little too early to speculate on the future of this initiative to mobilise professionals and experts for local level development. But this Phase of the Campaign will, by its very nature, have the potential to develop into a unique movement of concerned intellectuals and experts. Further, this movement may be sustained into implementation stage, even after the completion of the present Campaign.

We welcome you to the VTC — We are gratified that you are interested in knowing more about the People's Cam-paign and inclined to contribute your knowledge and skills to the success of this unique development experiment. The district level convention of the identified experts will be held during the first week of April. You shall be intimated of the date and venue of the conference at the earliest.

We look forward to working together with you.

(Reproduced from : *We Can Create A Better Tomorrow*, People's Campaign for Ninth Five Year Plan, *u.d.*, *Government of Kerala*, Kerala State Planning Board, Trivandrum.)

GUIDELINES FOR SELECTION OF BENEFICIARIES IN KERALA

Introduction : With the decentralisation of powers and functions the selection of beneficiaries in most of the schemes is the responsibility of local bodies. In the case of rural areas, the Grama Panchayat should select the beneficiaries and in urban areas the Municipalities or Municipal Corporations as the case may be. As decentralisation implies participatory development, it is imperative that people's participation is realised fully in the identification and selection of beneficiaries of various schemes. It goes without saying that when people are empowered these should be a process of self-selection based on clear criteria and norms evolved by consensus and applied in a transparent manner. There is absolutely no scope for discretion or patronage. Fare and open selection of beneficiaries is also a legal necessity as has been clarified by the Hon'ble High Court of Kerala in its judgment in OP No. 18175/1996-L dated 4th April 1997 where it has ruled that Panchayats are not selecting authorities, but only approving authorities in the case of beneficiary selection. It is the Grama Sabha which has the power to identify beneficiaries. The judgment has made it amply clear that any selection of beneficiaries has to follow a transparent procedure and any exercise of discretion or arbitrariness is tantamount to violation of not only the Kerala Panchayat Raj Act but also Article 14 of the Indian Constitution. Arbitrary selection of beneficiaries violates the right to equality which is the essence of the Indian Constitution. In keeping with the spirit of the laws and principles governing decentralisation, Government has decided to prescribe the following general guidelines for selection of beneficiaries.

A. For the three tiers of Panchayati Raj Institutions — District, Block and village.

Agency for selection :

In the case of Panchayati Raj institutions, basically the Grama Sabha will identify the beneficiaries. Since the District Panchayat and Block Planchayat cannot convene the Grama Sabha, they will get the beneficiary selected through the respective Grama

Panchayats who will carry out selection process through the Grama Sabha and give the selected list to the Block or District Panchayat for approval. This would mean that the number of beneficiaries to be selected by each Grama Panchayat would have to be determined in advance by the District and Block Panchayats. For determining this number the District and Block Panchayats have first to lay down objective criteria for dividing the target. These criteria would be related to the type of scheme. In the case of beneficiaries to be selected for schemes implemented by the Grama Panchayat, the priority list for each Ward for a particular scheme would be prepared by the Grama Sabha and selection made at the Panchayat level based on the criteria for eligibility and prioritisation. There shall not be any ward-wise targets and eligibility will be considered at the level of the Grama Panchayat keeping in view the priority list prepared by the Grama Sabha. However, Panchayat may, if necessary determine the upper ceiling of nominations to be prioritised by Grama Sabha. In no case should the total number of nominations exceed twice the target for the Grama Panchayat as a whole. From the priority list the selection has to be made based on specific criteria of prioritisation which are to be laid down in advance. Priority fixed by Grama Sabha cannot normally be changed for that area.

Procedure for selection of beneficiaries :

1. *Determination of criteria.*—In the case Centrally and State sponsored schemes, eligibility criteria prescribed by those scheme guidelines have to be followed. In the case of schemes/projects planned for by the different tiers of Panchayats, the eligibility criteria would be determined by that Panchayat as stated in the project approved by the DPC. The Panchayats at each level should also state clearly in writing the prioritisation criteria to be followed to short list eligible beneficiaries in cases where all the eligible beneficiaries cannot be considered under the scheme. While applying the prioritisation criteria the Grama Sabhas can fine tune them going into greater detail within each criterion if required.

2. *Publicity.*—The criteria both for eligibility and for prioritisation should be given widespread publicity. Publicity should be given through elected persons, resource persons of the Planning Campaign, political parties and their affiliated organisations, voluntary organisations, field staff etc. A notice clearly indicating the number of schemes, the criteria for each scheme and the number of beneficiaries to be selected should be displayed at the Panchayat office, Village office and concerned offices and other prominent places. A separate notice board has to be set up in each ward for this purpose. Pamphlets may also be printed and circulated. Press releases can also be made.
3. *Application Form.*—For all schemes application forms are to be designed in Malayalam or local language. The application form should be simple but should contain provisions for incorporating all required details needed for applying the eligibility as well as prioritisation criteria. The application form should state these criteria in its Annexure. The application form should be distributed for a fixed period preceding the Grama Sabha meeting and at the Grama Sabha. A common application form for group of similar schemes can be prepared.
4. *Verification.*—The application form should contain in it a proforma verification form. The Grama Panchayat should decide on a system of verification either through designated officers or designated sub-committee. Three types of verification are possible. Initially before the Grama Sabha, as many applications as possible should be enquired into using the arrangements made by the Panchayat. Then the applications for which verification is not complete and the applications which are received on the spot should be enquired into on the spot in the Grama Sabha by the Chairperson of the sub-group and the official nominated for this purpose by the Grama Panchayat. In case factual details are not available during the meeting of the Grama Sabha, the same arrangements made for verification earlier should continue and verify the facts. In such cases the priority

list would be prepared by the Grama Sabha subject to the verification report and this should be made amply clear in the Grama Sabha.

5. *Grama Sabha.*—Grama Sabha meetings should be called immediately thereafter. Application forms should be distributed at the beginning of the Grama Sabha also. Then the list of applicants from the applications received earlier and on the spot should be drawn up. The eligibility criteria and prioritisation criteria should be explained to the Grama Sabha. Thereafter the Grama Sabha can break up into groups for various sectors and in the sectoral groups the prioritisation of the applicants can be made. In addition to the criteria decided by the Panchayat, sub-criteria for prioritisation to match the local perceptions of eligibility can be made. All the applications should be vetted according to the criteria and the priority list prepared by consensus. If there is no rational method of discrimination then lots can be drawn if agreed to by everybody. Wherever neighbourhood groups exists, Panchayats can utilise their services for vetting the eligibility of a beneficiary.

In the case of beneficiary oriented schemes under Tribal Sub-Plan selection should not be made in the General Grama Sabha. Special Grama Sabhas consisting of all the tribal families in the ward would be called and selection made by this general body of tribal families from all the tribal settlements in the ward.

6. *Selection of beneficiaries.*—With the prioritised list from each ward, after completing verification of facts, a list based on clear criteria of prioritisation should be drawn up for the Grama Panchayat as a whole. This should be drawn up in the Grama Panchayat Committee meeting. In that special meeting the local Press and the public may be given access.

Once the Grama Panchayat finalises the list it shall publish it as a draft in the order of priority and indicating the factors which resulted in the priority rank in a tabulated form. If any objections are received on the draft list, Grama Panchayat shall consider it after further verification if required and record its views on accepting or rejecting it. Thereafter the final list shall be published. In the case of Block Panchayats and District Panchayats, Grama Panchayats shall send the final list to them with all the applications and documents related to the selection for taking the final decision. The lists submitted by the Grama Panchayats should be published as drafts by the District and Block Panchayats calling for objections if any. This should be published simultaneously in the District or Block Panchayats and the concerned Grama Panchayats. Only after clearing the objections should the list be finalised.

7. *Transparency. –All the documents like application forms, verification reports, enquiry reports and decision minutes are public documents to which everyone has access and copies of which everyone can procure. In the next Grama Sabha meeting after the selection the selected Grama Sabha list concerning that Grama Sabha may be given with adequate justification. Comments by Grama Sabha may be recorded. If it is proved later that the beneficiary or the enquiring officer or the selecting authority is responsible for an ineligible selection, such person or persons would be liable to reimburse the expenses with interest. ... (Emphasis added.)*

B. For The Municipal Bodies

In the case of Municipalities and Municipal Corporations, the procedure prescribed in the case of Panchayat Raj Institutions would *mutatis mutandis* apply. In the place of Grama Sabhas, Ward Committees would perform the function. In the urban areas the close contacts and homogeneity normally seen in rural areas may not be there. Therefore the applications for various schemes should be called in advance after giving much publicity as suggested earlier. The Ward Committees, the CDS structures and residents associations should be given advance intimation of the selection of beneficiaries. Press releases should also be invariably made.

After receipts of all the applications, a detailed verification has to be done of the facts mentioned in the application. Based on this verification report and on the eligibility and prioritisation criteria, the Ward Committees would prepare a priority list. The ceiling of nominations for each Ward Committee under each scheme must be prescribed by the municipal body. In the case of anti-poverty programmes the specific recommendations of the Area Development Societies should be obtained and placed before the Ward Committee. In the Ward Committee meeting all the eligible applicants should be called and prioritisation done in their presence based on the prioritisation criteria applying the facts revealed in the verification process. Here again all the records are deemed to be public document.

[Reproduced from :
Government of Kerala, Local Administration (P) Department, Thiruvananthapuram, G.O. (P) No. 220/97/LAD. Dated 2nd October, 1997.]

APPENDIX – IX

GENERAL GUIDELINES FOR IMPLEMENTATION OF PLAN SCHEMES BY THE LOCAL BODIES IN KERALA

GENERAL POINTS

1. As soon as the approval of the DPC has been received the Plan should be analysed by the Local Body at a specially convened meeting. Projects which can be taken up for implementation immediately have to be identified. Action has to be taken to prepare estimates and get technical sanction for the public works components.
2. The projects to be taken up using the first installment have to the listed out. Before starting implementation, the Local Body should take a resolution to that effect separately for each project containing the following details in brief.
   (i) The estimated expenditure.
   (ii) The time-table for various activities up to completion.
   (iii) The location of the scheme in cases of infrastructure creation.
   (iv) In the case of beneficiary oriented schemes the target groups, eligibility criteria, prioritisation criteria to be applied to short list the actual beneficiaries from among the eligible applicants, mode of application, mode of verification etc.
   (v) The officer or agency for implementation, the amount to be allotted to him and the conditions he has to observe before incurring expenditure, the Local Body may as it deems fit indicate items for which prior permission of the Local Body is required and items for which no prior sanction is required.
   (vi) Reporting requirements by the implementing officer/agency.
3. The selection of beneficiaries shall be as per the guidelines issued for the purpose.

4. Implementation of public works should be as per the provision of the Public Works Rules issued separately for Municipalities and Panchayats.
5. When the selection of beneficiaries is completed, beneficiary committees of all such beneficiaries should be formed. If the number is too large the beneficiary can elect a 11-member committee from among themselves. The scheme details should be explained to the beneficiary group and this committee should be actively involved in the scheme right from the initial stages up to the monitoring stages. Whenever required, short training can be arranged for the beneficiaries.
6. For purchase of assets/materials the following procedure is prescribed :
   (a) For direct purchase of materials by local bodies required for works and schemes, the existing rules of purchase will apply. If the purchase is required for an approved component of an approved project no prior sanction of any authority is required but wherever standards and specifications are prescribed, they have to be adhered to. The departmental officers will be able to inform the local bodies of such stipulations.
   (b) In the case of purchase of land, either land acquisition can be resorted to or direct purchase based on the value prescribed by the Collector.
   (c) In the case of purchase of assets/materials to be supplied to beneficiaries of schemes, direct purchases of assets and materials should be avoided by the local bodies. The local body should prescribe the standards and specifications and indicate the quality and leave the purchase to the beneficiary fixing a ceiling for the subsidy. Payment should be made to the seller of the asset after ascertaining that a *bona fide* purchase has been made by the beneficiary. However, in cases where bulk purchase is required for the reasons of economy like purchases of chicks, animal feed, planting material, manure etc., it can be procured by the local bodies from Government or

public sector agencies. If purchases are to be made from private agencies, then it can be made only by the beneficiary committee technically assisted by nominated officials and supported by a sub-committee of the local body.

7. The subsidy norms would be as prescribed, i.e. the highest level of subsidy now given for a scheme by the Government cannot be exceeded by the local body for a similar scheme. However in exceptional cases, prior permission of the DPC have to be obtained and DPC will receive suitable instructions from the Government. The DPC should not ratify the requests made after implementation if they do not conform to the guidelines. Any person or any group of persons responsible for payment of excess subsidy would be deemed to have misutilised Panchayat or Municipality funds as the case may be.

8. No Plan Schemes should be taken up which involves creation of staff involving payment out of the local body fund or the plan fund or Government funds. However, if schemes are designed in such a way that all revenues generated by the schemes or donations are channelled to an agency like PTA or Hospital Development Society, the required personnel can be employed on payment of honorarium by this committee. But such schemes should be designed to be sustainable on a long-term basis.

9. Any donations or receipts from the Plan Schemes have to be credited to the VPF accounts in the case of Grama Panchayats, to the general PD account in the case of Block and District Panchayats and to the fund where own receipts are kept in the treasury in the case of Municipalities.

10. *All documents regarding implementation of Plan Would be public documents open to any citizen for scrutiny. .... (Emphasis added.)*

[Reproduced from :
Government of Kerala, Local Administration (P) Department, Thiruvananthapuram, G.O. (P) No. 221/97/LAD. Dated 3rd October, 1997.]

BIBLIOGRAPHY

DOCUMENTS AND OFFICIAL PAPERS

The Calcutta Gazette (Extraordinary), dated 10.5.1992, Calcutta.

The Calcutta Gazette (Extraordinary), dated 22.4.1994, Calcutta.

The Calcutta Gazette (Extraordinary), dated 3.5.1994, Calcutta.

The Calcutta Gazette (Extraordinary), dated 28.9.1994, Calcutta.

The Calcutta Gazette (Extraordinary), dated 15.2.1995, Calcutta.

The Calcutta Gazette (Extraordinary), dated 30.3.1995, Calcutta.

The Calcutta Gazette (Extraordinary), dated 10.7.1996, Calcutta.

The Calcutta Gazette (Extraordinary), dated 29.7.1997, Calcutta.

Census of India (1991), Government of India, Series- 26, paper -1.

The Constitution of India.

District Planning Committee, *District Annual Plan 1985-86,* DPC, Midnapore.

________, *Revised Annual Plan 1985-86,* DPC, Midnapore.

________, *District Annual Plan 1986-87,* DPC, Midnapore.

________, *District Annual Plan 1987-88,* DPC, Midnapore.

________, *District Annual Plan 1992-93,* DPC, Midnapore.

________, *District Annual Plan 1993-94,* DPC, Midnapore.

________, *District Annual Plan 1994-95,* DPC, Midnapore.

________, *District Annual Plan 1995-96,* DPC, Midnapore.

________, *District Annual Plan 1996-97,* DPC, Midnapore.

________, *District Annual Plan 1997-98,* DPC, Midnapore.

________, *District Annual Plan 1998-99,* DPC, Midnapore.

________, *District Seventh Five Year Plan 1985-90,* District Planning Committee, Midnapore.

________, *District Eighth Five Year Plan 1990-95,* District Planning Committee, Midnapore.

________, *Revised Eighth Five Year Plan 1992-97,* District Planning Committee, Midnapore.

________, *A Prelude to Ninth Plan* (1997-2002), District Planning Committee, Midnapore.

District Planning Committee, Burdwan, (1985), *No.22 DPC,* dated 17-10-1985, District Planning Committee, Burdwan.

________ Midnapore, (1986), *No. 713 (54) Dev.*, dated 2.6.1986, District Planning Cell, Midnapore.

________, (1986), *No. 841 (54) Dev.*, dated 16.7.1986, District Planning Cell, Midnapore.

________, (1986), *No. 903 (75) Dev.*, dated 2.8.1986, District Planning Cell, Midnapore.

________, (1987), *No. 460 (19) Dev.*, dated 9.4.1987, District Planning Cell, Midnapore.

________, (1987), *No. 913 (50) Dev.*, dated 17.7.1987, District Planning Cell, Midnapore.

________, (1987), *No. 934 (50) Dev.*, dated 21.7.1987, District Planning Cell, Midnapore.

________, (1997), *No. 773 (120) Dev.*, dated 24.6.1997, District Planning Cell, Midnapore.

________, (1997), *No. 815-A/43 Dev.*, dated 6.7.1997, District Planning Cell, Midnapore.

________, (1997), *No. 913 (50) Dev.*, dated 17.7.1997, District Planning Cell, Midnapore.

Divisional Commissioner, *No. 44 LSG,* dated 9.6.1997, Burdwan Division, Burdwan.

Employment Assurance Scheme - Guidelines, (1993), Government of India, Ministry of Rural Development, New Delhi.

Employment Assurance Scheme - Annual Action Plan (1996-97), Midnapore.

The Gazette of India (Extraordinary), No. 69, dated 20.4.1993, New Delhi.

The Gazette of India (Extraordinary), No.70, dated 20.4.1993, New Delhi.

Government of India, Planning Commission (1969), *Guidelines for District Planning,* New Delhi.

Government of India, Planning Commission (1952), *First Five Year Plan,* New Delhi.

________ (1956), *Second Five Year Plan,* New Delhi.

________ (1961), *Third Five Year Plan,* New Delhi.

________ (1964), *The Planning Process,* New Delhi.

________ (1969), *Fourth Five Year Plan,* New Delhi.

________ (1974), *Approach of the Fifth Five Year Plan,* New Delhi.

________ (1976), *Fifth Five Year Plan,* New Delhi.

________ (1978), *Draft Five Year Plan,* New Delhi.

________ (1978), *Report of the Working Group on Block Level Planning,* New Delhi.

________ (1978), *Draft of the Sixth Five Year Plan,* New Delhi.

________ (1980), *Sixth Five Year Plan,* New Delhi.

________ (1984), *Report of the Working Group on District Planning,* New Delhi.

________ (1985), *Seventh Five Year Plan,* New Delhi.

________ (1988), *Induction Material,* Internal Work Study Unit, New Delhi.

________ (1990), *Towards Social Transformation: Approach to the Eighth Five Year Plan,* New Delhi.

________ (1992), *Eighth Five Year Plan,* New Delhi.

________ (1993), *Annual Report,* New Delhi.

________ (1996), *Draft Approach Paper to Ninth Five Year Plan,* New Delhi.

________ (1996), *Guidelines for the Formulation of District Plans,* New Delhi.

________, *No. PC(P) 35/WB/85-MLP,* dated 19.2.1986, Planning Commission, New Delhi.

________, *(2001), DO. No. V – 24011 / 34 / 2001 / SGRY, dated 12th October, 2001,* Department of Rural Development of Rural Development, Government of India, New Delhi :

Government of Karnataka (1988), *District Government and Decentralised Planning, (Karnataka shows the way),* Department of Rural Development and Panchayat Raj, Bangalore.

Government of Kerala, *(1996), G.O. (Ms) 10 / 96 / Plg., dated 30 July, 1996.*

________, (1996), *G.O. (Rt.)No. 350/96 Plg., dated 10 September, 1996.*

________, (1997), *G.O., (P) No. 676/97/Fin., dated 6 August, 1997,* Department of Finance (BWJ).

________, (1997),G.O. (P) No. : 220/97/LAD., dated 2 October, 1997.

Government of West Bengal, *Annual Plan 1985-86,* Development and Planning Department,. Calcutta, Vol. I & II.

________, *Annual Plan 1986-87,* Development and Planning Department, Calcutta, Vol. I & II.

________, *Annual Plan 1994-95,* Development and Planning Department, Calcutta, Vol. I & II.

________, *Annual Plan 1995-96,* Development and Planning Department, Calcutta, Vol. I & II.

________, *Annual Plan 1996-97,* Development and Planning Department, Calcutta, Vol. I & II.

________, *Annual Plan 1997-98.* Development and Planning Department, Calcutta, Vol. I & II.

________, *Seventh Five Year Plan 1985-90,* Development and Planning Department, Calcutta, Vol. I & II.

________, *Eighth Five Year Plan 1992-97.* Development and Planning Department, Calcutta, Vol. I & II.

________, Ninth Five Year Plan,1997-2002,Vol.I & II. Development and Planning Department.

________, Revised Ninth Five Year Plan,1997-2002,Vol.I & II. Development and Planning Department

________, *Tenth Five Year Plan,* West Bengal (2002 – 2007), *Vol. I, &. II,* Development and Planning Department.

Government of West Bengal (1985), *D.O. Letter of the Vice-Chairman, State Planning Board addressed to the Sabhadhipati(s) of the Zilla Parishad(s),* dated 12.3.1985.

________, (1985), *Guidelines for District Planning,* dated 12.3.1985, *State Planning Board,* Calcutta.

________, (1985), *D.O. No.1068-1082, SPB/1S-4/85,* dated 29.3.1985, *State Planning Board,* Calcutta.

________, (1985), *Resolution No. 3230/P-1S-6/85,* dated 12.5.1985, Development and Planning Department, Calcutta.

________, (1985), *No. 6299 (30)/Dev.,* dated 23.8.1985, Development and Planning Department, Calcutta.

________, (1985), *No. 6372/P/1F-8/85,* dated 28.8.1985, Development and Planning Department, Calcutta.

________, (1985), *No. 7593 (30)/P/1S-43/85,* dated 15.10.1985, Development and Planning Department, Calcutta.

________, (1985), *D.O. No. 7965 (45)/P/1S-43/85,* dated 6.11.1985, Development and Planning Department, Calcutta.

________, (1985), *No. 9191(4)/P-1S-31/85,* dated 20.11.1985, Development and Planning Department, Calcutta.

________, (1985), *D.O. No.10084(5)/P-1S-6/85,* dated 23.12.1985, Development and Planning Department, Calcutta.

________, (1985), *No. 10131/P/1E-5/85 Pt.I,* dated 24.12.1985, Development and Planning Department, Calcutta.

________, (1985), *No. 10180 (30)/P-1S-6/85,* dated 26.12.1985, Development and Planning Department, Calcutta.

________, (1986), *No. 189(30)/Dev.,* dated 8.1.1986, Development and Planning Department, Calcutta.

________, (1986), *No. 636/P/1F-8/85,* dated 28.1.1986, Development and Planning Department, Calcutta.

________, (1986), *No. 1692(16)/P-1S-16/85,* dated 10.3.1986, Development and Planning Department, Calcutta.

________, (1986), *No. 1950/DP-1F-2/86,* dated 19.3.1986, Development and Planning Department, Calcutta.

________, (1986), *No. 2237(12)/DP-2C-2/86,* dated 31.3.1986, Development and Planning Department, Calcutta.

________, (1986), *No. 2252 (31) DP-1S-39/86,* dated 1.4.1986, Development and Planning Department, Calcutta.

________, (1986), *No. 2720(45)/DP/1S-21/86,* dated 19.4.1986, Development and Planning Department, Calcutta.

________, (1986), *No. 3328(46) DP/1M-21/86,* dated 19.5.1986, Development and Planning Department, Calcutta.

________, (1989), *G.O. No.2510/DP/1F/89,* dated 15.4.1989, Development and Planning Department, Calcutta.

________, (1989), *G.O. No.5465/DP/1F-2/89,* dated 2.9.1989, Development and Planning Department, Calcutta.

________, (1989), *G.O. No.6671/DP/1F-4/89,* dated 9.11.1989, Development and Planning Department, Calcutta.

________, (1990), *G.O. No.911/DP/1F2/89,* dated 1.3.1990, Development and Planning Department, Calcutta.

________, (1990), *No. 5186/DP/1S-12/89,* dated 22.11.1990, Development and Planning Department, Calcutta.

________, (1991), *G.O. No. 453/DP/1F-4/90,* dated 7.2.1991, Development and Planning Department, Calcutta.

________, (1991), *G.O. No.1046/DP/1F-2/91,* dated 16.3.1991, Development and Planning Department, Calcutta.

________, (1991), *No. 2114(16)/DP/1S/91,* dated 21.6.1991, Development and Planning Department, Calcutta.

________, (1991), *Resolution No. 2337/20-2/90,* dated 16.7.1991, Development and Planning Department, Calcutta.

________, (1992), *No. 96/92-CS,* dated 28.2.1992, Chief Secretary, Calcutta.

________, (1992), *No. 5757(16)/RD,* dated 1.9.1992, Panchayat and Rural Development Department, Calcutta.

________, (2002), *No. 1 / PA / JS (DG) / P & R.D. / 5 M — 19 / 99* dated, 2 January, 2002, Panchayat and Rural Development Department, Kolkata.

________, (1995), *G.O. No. 110/1F-4/94,* dated 12.1.1995, Development and Planning Department, Calcutta.

________, (1995), *G.O. No. 3011/1F-4/94,* dated 30.11.1995, Development and Planning Department, Calcutta.

________, (1996), *G.O. No. 3163/DP/1F-3/94,* dated 17.10.1996, Development and Planning Department, Calcutta.

________, (1997), *G.O. No. 1193/DP/1F-3/94,* dated 14.3.1997, Development and Planning Department, Calcutta.

________, (1997), *No. 2441(17)/DP/1F-7/95,* dated 27.6.1997, Development and Planning Department, Calcutta.

________, (1997), *No. 781(34)SPB,* dated 6.8.1997, State Planning Board, Calcutta.

________, (1999), *No : 183 (18) PA / JS (D.G.) / P & R.D.* dated 1 November, Department of Panchayat and Rural Development, Kolkata

________, (2001), *GO. No. 574/PA/JS(DG)/ P & RD/O/Trg./5 M-17/2001,* dated, 9 November, Kolkata.

________, *(2002), G.O.No. 785/DP/O/DP/2M-03/2002*, dated 8 March, 2002, Department of Development and Planning, Kolkata.

________, *(2002),* No. *786/DP/O/DP/2M-3/2002*, dated 8 March, 2002, Department of Development and Planning, Kolkata.

Government of West Bengal (1978), *Left Front Government and Some Aspects of Activities in Rural Areas : A Study by an Observer,* Department of Information and Culture, Calcutta.

________, (1982), *Panchayats in West Bengal, 1978-79 to 1980-81 : A Review,* Department of Panchayat and Community Development, Calcutta.

________, (1981), *Rural Development Planning under the Left Front Government in West Bengal,* Department of Information and Culture, Calcutta.

________, (1981), *The Working of Panchayat System in West Bengal*, Department of Panchayat and Community Development, Calcutta.

________, (1984), *Left Front Government and Land Reforms*, Calcutta.

________, (1985), *Guidelines for District Planning*, State Planning Board, Calcutta, March 12.

________, (1986), *Left Front Government in West Bengal - Nine Years*, Department of Information and Culture, Calcutta.

________, (1992), *District Statistical Handbook 1991-92*, Bureau of Applied Economics and Statistics, Calcutta.

________, State Institute of Panchayat and Rural Develop-ment, Government of West Bengal.

________, (1995), *West Bengal Statistical Report - 1994-95*, Calcutta.

________, (1997), *Panchayati Raj,* March-April, Calcutta.

________, (1998), *District Statistical Handbook 1996-97*, Bureau of Applied Economics and Statistics, Calcutta.

Gram Bhittik Block Parikalpanar Paddhati-O-Proyoger Ruparekha, Midnapore, 1989.

Gram Bhittik Zella Parikalpanar Paddhatigata Ruparekha, Midnapore, 1985.

Gram Panchayat Parichalanar Nirdeshika, Left Front Committee, Calcutta, 1983.

Gram Sambandhiya Tathyabali, Government of West Bengal, Department of Panchayat and Community Development, Calcutta, 1981.

Jawahar Rozgar Yojana - Prakalpa Rupayaner Nirdeshabali, Midnapore Zilla Parishad, 1989.

Jawahar Rozgar Yojana - District Annual Plan 1989-1990.

Jawahar Rozgar Yojana - Functional Guidelines, Government of West Bengal, Rural Development Department, 1993.

Jawahar Rojgar Yojana - Mannual, Government of India, Department of Rural Development, New Delhi, 1994.

Jawahar Rozgar Yojana - District Annual Action Plan 1996-1997.

The Karnataka Panchayat Raj Act, Government of Karnataka, 1993, Bangalore.

Kayekti Agradhikar Kshetra, Bikendribhuta Parikalpana-O-Medinipur Zella, 1994.

The Madhya Pradesh Panchayati Raj Adhiniyam, 1993, Bhopal.

Medinipur Zellar Grambhittik Parikalpana Ruparekha-O-Unnayaner Pratichhabi, District Planning Committee, 1996.

Medinipur Zellar Janaganer Kachhe Abedan, Zilla Parishad, Midnapore, 1985.

An Outline of Methodology of Village-Based Decentralized Planning, District Planning Committee, 1985.

O'Malley, L.S.S. (1911), *Bengal District Gazetteers,* Government of West Bengal, Calcutta (First Reprint, 1995).

Panchayat Parichalana Prasange Sadharan Nirdeshabali, CPI(M) Midnapore District Committee, 1988.

Panchayat Parichalana Prasange Nirdeshika, CPI(M) West Bengal State Committee, 1994.

Panchayati Raj, Government of West Bengal, Department of Information and Culture, March-April, 1997, Calcutta.

Parikalpana Paddhati, Samay Suchi abong Talika Puraner Niyamabali, Zilla Parishad, Midnapore, 1985.

Proceedings of the National Workshop on Administrative Arrangements for Rural Development, National Institute of Rural Development, Hyderabad, 1985.

Proceedings of the meeting of the Working Group of the DPC, District Planning Committee, Midnapore, dated 8.1.1987.

Proceedings of the meeting of the Working Group (PWD) of the DPC, District Planning Committee, Midnapore, dated 8.1.1987.

Proceedings of the meeting of the Working Group (Monitoring) of the DPC, District Planning Committee, Midnapore, dated 8.1.1987.

Proceedings of the meeting of the DPCC, Midnapore, dated 9.1.1987.

Proceedings of the District Level Seminar on Alternative Strategy of Planning, Zilla Parishad, Midnapore, dated 19.6.1987.

Proceedings of the meeting of the Working Group (Fishery) of the DPC, District Planning Committee, Midnapore, dated 26.6.1987.

Proceedings of the meeting of the Instructors for Village Level Planning Cadres, District Planning Committee, Midnapore, dated 2.7.1987.

Proceedings of the meeting of the Working Group (PHE) of the DPC, District Planning Committee, Midnapore, dated 17.8.1987.

Proceedings of the meeting of the Working Group (Agriculture) of the DPC, District Planning Committee, Midnapore, dated 15.7.1987.

Proceedings of the meeting of the Working Group (Roads and PWD) of the DPC, District Planning Committee, Midnapore, dated 24.8.1987.

Proceedings of the meeting of the DPCC, Midnapore, dated 17.5.1988.

Proceedings of the meeting of the DPCC, Midnapore, dated 17.8.1991.

Proceedings of the meeting of the Standing Committee of the DPCC, Midnapore, dated 8.4.1992.

Proceedings of the meeting of the DPCC, Midnapore, dated 20.7.1992.

Proceedings of the meeting of the District Planning Committee, dated 21.7.1992.

Proceedings of the Annual General Meeting of the District Urban Development Agency, Midnapore, dated 11.7.1996.

Proceedings of the meeting of the District Planning Committee, dated 19.9.1996.

Proceedings of the meetings of Sub-Committees of the District Planning Committee, dated 10.3.1997.

Proceedings of the meeting of the Special Area Development Sub-Committee of the DPC, dated 11.3.1997.

Proceedings of the Seminar on Land Use Planning, District Development Department, Midnapore, dated 21.7.1997.

Proceedings of the Annual General Meeting of the District Urban Development Agency, Midnapore, dated 28.7.1997.

Proceedings of the meeting of the District Planning Committee, Midnapore, dated 20.8.1997.

Proceedings of the meeting of the District Vigilance and Monitoring Committee, Midnapore, dated 27.8.1997.

Programme of the CPI(M), Seventh Congress, Communist Party of India (Marxist), Calcutta, 1964.

Recommendations of the *Expert Group on District Planning at LBS Academy of Administration*, dated 11-13 June, 1990.

Recommendations of the *State Finance Commission*, Government of West Bengal, Calcutta, 1995.

Records of the Department of Development and Planning, 1998-99, 1999-2000, 2000-01, Government of West Bengal.

Records of the *District Planning Committee*, Midnapore, 1987-88.

Records of the *District Planning Committee*, Midnapore, 1990-98.

Records of the *District Planning Committee*, District Planning Cell, Midnapore, 1995-1998.

Records of the *District Panchayat Office*, Midnapore, 1988, 1993 and 1998.

Records of the *District Rural Development Agency*, Midnapore, 1988, 1989, 1992, 1995, 1996 and 1997.

Records of the *District Urban Development Agency*, Midnapore, 1995, 1996, 1997 and 1998.

Report of the *Team for the Study of Community Projects and National Extension Service* (1957), Committee on Plan Projects, New Delhi, 3 Vols.

Reports of the *Administrative Reforms Commission* (1966), Government of India, Department of Administrative Reforms, New Delhi.

Report of the *Task Force on Agrarian Relations* (1973), Government of India, Planning Commission, New Delhi.

Report of the *National Commission on Agriculture* (1976), Part XIV, New Delhi.

Report of the *Working Group on Block Level Planning* (1978), Government of India, Planning Commission, New Delhi, Vol. I & II.

Report of the *Department of Rural Development* (1979), Government of India, New Delhi.

Report of the *Commission on Power* (1980), Government of India, New Delhi.

Report of the *National Committee on the Development of Backward Areas (NCDBA)* (1981), Government of India, New Delhi.

Report of the *Working Group on District Planning* (1984), Government of India, Planning Commission, New Delhi, Vol. I & II.

Report of the *Committee to Review the Existing Administrative Arrangements for Rural Development and Poverty Alleviation Programmes* (1985), Government of India, Ministry of Agriculture, New Delhi.

Report of the *Commission on Centre-State Relations* (1988), New Delhi, Part I & II.

Report on the *Evaluation of Total Literacy Campaign* (1992), District LIM Cell, Midnapore.

Report of the *Annual General Meeting of Keshpur Gram Panchayat (No.10)*, dated 24.2.1995.

Report of the *Evaluation of Post-Literacy Programmes,* District LIM Cell, Midnapore, 1995.

Report of the *Sabhapati of Bhagwanpur I Panchayat Samiti,* dated 20.8.1997.

Rural Development Centre (1986), *The Rural People of Midnapore District,* RDC, I.I.T., Kharagpur.

United Nations Development Programme (1993), *Human Development Report,* Oxford University Press, Delhi.

Village Based planning and Development, 2001, Government of West Bengal, Department of Panchayat and Rural Development, Kolkata.

The West Bengal Zamindari Abolition Act, 1953.

The West Bengal Land Reforms Act, 1955.

The West Bengal Panchayat Act, 1973.

The West Bengal Panchayat (Amendment) Act, 1978.

The West Bengal Panchayat (Amendment) Act, 1983.

The West Bengal Panchayat (Amendment) Act, 1984.

The West Bengal Panchayat (Amendment) Act, 1988.

The West Bengal Panchayat (Amendment) Act, 1992.

The West Bengal Panchayat (Amendment) Act, 1993.

The West Bengal Panchayat (Amendment) Act, 1994.

The West Bengal District Planning Committee Act, 1994.

The West Bengal Municipality Act, 1994.

The West Bengal District Planning Committee Rules, 1994.
The West Bengal Panchayat (Amendment) Act, 1995.
The West Bengal Panchayat (Amendment) Act, 1997.

BOOKS AND ARTICLES

Agarwal, P.P. (1957), 'The Planning Commission', *The Indian Journal of Public Administration,* Vol. XIX (3), July-September.

Arora, Hari C. (1991), 'Decentralized Planning', *Indian Journal of Public Administration,* Vol. 37(2), April-June.

Arora, Ramesh K. and Hooja, Rakesh (eds., 1994), *Administration and Rural Development: Indian and Comparative Perspectives,* Arihant Publishing House, New Delhi.

Aziz, Abdul. (1993), *Decentralized Planning – The Karnataka Experience,* Sage Publications, New Delhi.

Bagchi, Amiya Kumar (ed., 1988), *Economy, Polity and Society: Essays in the Political Economy of Indian Planning*, OUP, Calcutta.

____________, (1998), 'Studies on the Economy of West Bengal since Independence', *Economic and Political Weekly,* Vol.33 (47 & 48), December.

Bandyopadhyay, N. (1988), 'The Story of Land Reforms in Indian Planning' in Amiya Kumar Bagchi (ed.), *Economy, Society and Polity*, OUP, Calcutta.

Banerjee, Sarmila and Roy, Samik. (1998), 'On Construction of District Development Index in West Bengal', *Economic and Political Weekly,* Vol.33 (47 & 48), December.

Bardhan, P. (1984), *The Political Economy of Development in India,* OUP, Delhi.

Baruah, Sanjib. (1990), '*The End of the Road in Land Reforms – Limits to Redistribution in West Bengal*', Development and Change, Vol.21.

Benninger, Christopher C. (1991), 'District Planning Methods and Techniques: An Overview' in Yugandhar and Mukherjee (ed.) *Reading in Decentralized Planning* Vol.1, Concept Publishing Company, New Delhi.

Bettelheim, Charles (1961), *Some Basic Planning Problems*, Asia Publishing House, Bombay.

Bhaduri, A. and Rahaman, M.D. (eds., 1982), *Studies in Rural Participation*, Oxford and IBH Publishing Company, Delhi.

Bhalla, G.S. and Singh, G. (1997), 'Recent Development in Indian Agriculture – A State Level Analysis', *Economic and Political Weekly*, March 29.

Bhargava, B.S. and Sasmal, Avinash (1998), 'Institutional Mechanism for Decentralised Planning', *Kurukshetra*, Vol.XLVI (7), April.

Bhat, L.S. and Others (1976), *Micro-Level Planning*, K.S. Publishers, New Delhi.

Bhattacharya, K.N. (1963), *Indian Plans: A Generalist Approach*, Asia Publishing House, Calcutta.

Bhattacharyya, Tarundeb. (1979), *Medinipur*, Firma K.L.M. Pvt. Ltd., Calcutta.

Bhaumik, Swapan. (1991), 'Bharater Panchayat Babasthyar Ruparekha-O-Bartaman Paschimbanger Abhijnata' in *Samaj Samiksha*, Indian School of Social Sciences, Calcutta, Vol. 5(4).

Binniger, Aneeta. (1990), 'Micro-Level Planning for Development: A Brief Outline' in Yugandhar and Mukherjee (eds.), *Readings in Decentralised Planning*, Concept Publishing Company, New Delhi.

Byres, Terence J. (1994), 'State, Class and Development Planning in India' in T.J. Byres (ed.), *The State and Development Planning in India*, OUP, Oxford.

Byres, T.J. (ed.) (1994), *The State and Development Planning in India*, OUP, Oxford.

Cemea, Michael M. (ed.) (1985), *Putting People First: Sociological Variables in Rural Development Projects*, Oxford University Press, New York.

Chakravarty, Sukhamoy. (1969), *Capital and Development Planning*, M.I.T., Cambridge.

Chakravarty, Sukhamoy. (1987), *Development Planning*, Clarendon Press, Oxford.

Chanda, Ashok. (1958), *Indian Administration*, George Allen and Unwin, London.

Chandran, T.R. (1995), 'Karnataka', in George Mathew (ed.), *Status of Panchayati Raj in the States of India,* Concept Publishing Company, New Delhi.

Chathukulam, Jos and Thomas, Jose T. (1997), 'Power to the people: People's campaign for Ninth Plan in Kerala', *Kurukshetra,* June.

Chatterjee, Partha. (1994), 'Development Planning and the Indian State' in T.J. Byres (ed.), *The State of Development Planning in India,* OUP, Oxford.

Chatterjee, B. and Ghosh, D.K. (2001), In *Search of A District Development Index,* State Institute of Panchayats and Rural Development, West Bengal.

Chattopadhyay, Manabendu, *et al.* (eds.) (1996), *Planning and Economic Policy in India,* Sage Publications, New Delhi.

Chaturvedi, T.N. (1988), *Politics, Bureaucracy and Development: Some Issues,* Uppal Publishing House, New Delhi.

Cohen, John and Upholf, Norman. (1978), *Rural Development Participation,* AID, Washington, D.C.

Curtis, Donald. (1991), *Beyond Government-Organizations for Common Benefit,* Macmillan, London.

Dandavate, Madhu. (1997), 'Ethics of Planning and Plan Implementation in India', *Indian Journal of Public Administration,* Vol. XLIII (4).

Dandekar, V.M. (1992), 'Forty Years After Independence' in Jalan (ed.), *The Indian Economy: Problems and Prospects,* Viking, New Delhi.

Dantwala *et. al*. (eds.) (1986), *Asian Seminar on Rural Development,* Oxford & IBH, New Delhi.

Dash, Binode Sankar (ed.) (1989), *Medinapur: Itihas-O-Sanskritir Bibartan,* Vol.1, Sahityaloka, Calcutta.

Desai, P.B. (1979), *Planning in India,* Vikas Publishing House, New Delhi.

Dasgupta, Atis. (1998), Seminar paper presented to the State Level *Seminar on 'Decentralization: Devolution and Participation'*, organised by the State Planning Board, Calcutta on 20-22 November.

Dasgupta, Sailen. (1983), *Gram Panchayat Parichalanar Nirdeshika*, Left Front Committee, Calcutta.

Datta, Amlan. (1973), *Perspective of Economic Development*, Macmillan, New Delhi.

Datta, Bhabatosh. (1963), *Essays on Plan Economics: A Commentary on Indian Managing Experience*, World Press, Calcutta.

Datt, R. and Sundharam, K.P.M. (1995), *Indian Economy*, S. Chand, New Delhi.

David, C. Korten. (1984), 'People Centred Development : Toward a Framework,' in Korten and Rudiklaus (eds.) (1984), *People Centred Development : Contribution Toward Theory and Planning Framework*, Kumarian Press, Connecticut.

Degaonkar, C.K. (1990), *District Planning and Economic Development*, Pointer Publications, Jaipur.

Dobb, Maurice. (1951), *Some Aspects of Economic Development*, University of Delhi, Delhi.

Dreze, Jean and Sen, Amartya. (2002), *India : Development and Participation*, Oxford University Press, New Delhi.

Dror, Yehezkel. (1968), *Public Policy-Making Re-examined*, Chandler, Sanfrancisco.

Dubashi, P.R. (1966), 'Decentralisation, Planning and Public Administration', *Indian Journal of Public Administration*, Vol.12(1), January-March.

Dubashi, P.R. (1984), 'The Federal Principle in Indian Polity', in R.S. Rajput and D.R. Meghe (ed.), *Panchayati Raj in India*, Deep & Deep Publications, New Delhi.

Fagence, Michael (1977), *Citizens' Participation in Planning*, Paragon Press, Oxford.

Frankel, F.R. (1971), *India's Green Revolution: Economic Gains and Political Costs*, Oxford University Press, Bombay.

________, (1978), *India's Political Economy, 1947-77*, Oxford University Press, London.

Gadgil, D.R. (1965), *Planning and Economic Policy in India*, Asia Publishing House, Poona.

________, (1966), *R.R. Kale Memorial Lecture*, Asia Publishing House, Bombay.

________, (1967), 'Planning without a Policy Frame', *Economic and Political Weekly*, Vol. 2 (3 & 4).

Gent, John Echeverri. (1993), *The State and the poor: Public Policy and Political Development in India and the United States*, California University Press, Berkeley.

George, Mathew. (1994), *Status of Panchayati Raj in the States of India*, Concept Publishing Company, New Delhi.

Ghosh, Arun. (1988), 'Decentralized Planning: West Bengal Experiment', *Economic and Political Weekly*, March 26.

________, (1985), Decentralized Planning, paper presented at a Seminar, Indian Institute of Public Administration, West Bengal Regional Branch, *Newsletter*, July-September.

________, (1989), 'Lessons for the Future', *Seminar*, No.360, New Delhi.

________, (1989), *West Bengal Landscape*, K.P. Bagchi & Company, Calcutta.

________, (1992), *Planning in India – the Challenge for the Nineties*, Sage Publications, New Delhi.

Gow, David D. and Jerry, Van. Sant. (1981), *Beyond the Rhetoric of Rural Development Participation: How can it be done?* Development Alternative Inc., Washington.

Grindle, Merilee. (1980), 'Policy Content and Context in Implementation' in Grindle (ed.), *Politics and Policy Implementation in the Third World*, Princeton University Press, New Jersey.

Gulati, I.S. (1986), 'Decentralised Planning Loopholes that Remain', *Economic and Political Weekly*, Vol.21 (32), August 9.

Hadden, Susan. G. (1980), 'Controlled Decentralization and Policy Implementation : The Case of Rural Electrification in Rajasthan', in Merilee S. Grindle (ed.), *Politics and Policy Implementation in the Third World*, Princeton University Press, New Jersey.

Handa, K.L. (1984), 'Planning and Budgeting in India: Concept and Practice', *Indian Journal of Public Administration*, Vol. 30 (3), July-September.

Hadinius, Axel. (ed.) (1997), *Democracy's Victory and Crisis*, Cambridge University Press, U.K.

Hanson, A.H. (1966), *The Process of Planning: A Study of India's Five Year Plan, 1950-1964*, OUP, London.

Hegde, Ramkrishna. (1992), 'Seminar' Paper reproduced in *Nation*, Vol. 3 (26), October 16.

Heller, Patrick. (1996), 'Social Capital as a Product of Class Mobilisation and State Intervention : Industrial Workers in Kerala, India', *World Development*, Vol.24, No.6.

Hirsch, Z. Werner. (1970), *The Economics of State and Local Government*, McGraw Hill Book Company, New York.

Hirway, Indira. (1986), *Abolition of Poverty in India*, Vikas Publishing House, New Delhi.

Hooja, Rakesh. (1994), 'Decentralized Planning and the Hanumantha Rao Report', in Asha Kaushik (ed.), *Democratic Concerns: The Indian Experience: Essays in Honour of Professor Iqbal Narain*, Vol.II, Jaipur.

________, and Mathur, P.C. (!991), *District and Decentralized Planning*, Rawat Publications, Jaipur.

Inamdar, N.R. (1992), *Development Administration in India*, Rawat Publications, Jaipur.

________, and Kshire, V.K. (1986), *District Planning in India*, Oxford & IBH Publishing Co., New Delhi.

The *Indian Journal of Public Administration* (1984), Special Number on Planning Systems, Vol. 30 (3), July-September.

Isaac, T.M. Thomas and Hiralal, K.N. (1997), 'Planning for Decentralized Planning in Kerala', *Economic and Political Weekly*, January 4-11.

________, Thomas Issac, T.M. (2000), 'The Story of People's Plan', *Panchayati Raj Update*, September.

Iwasaki, T. *et al.* (eds.) (1992), *Development Strategies for the 21st Century*, Institute of Development Economics, Tokyo.

Iyer, K. Gopal (1989-90), *The Findings of the Empirical Study on Land Reforms in India*, (Summary Report), Land Reforms Unit, L.B.S. National Academy of Administration, Mussoorie.

Jain, Anil Kumar. (1986), *Economic Planning in India*, Ashis Publishing House, New Delhi.

Jain, L.C. *et al.* (1985), *Grass without Roots: Rural Development under Government Auspices*, Sage Publications, New Delhi.

Jain, R.B. (1984), 'Planning in the Third World,' *Indian Journal of Public Administration*, Vol. 30(3).

Jalan, Bimal. (1992), *The Indian Economy: Problems and Prospects*, Viking, New Delhi.

Jana, Anil Kumar. (1993), *Quit India Movement in Bengal*, Indian Publishers Distributors, New Delhi.

________, (1998), 'Participatory Governance: In Search of An Effective Model for Rural India' in Anil Kumar Jana (ed.), *Indian Politics at the Crossroad*, Commonwealth Publishers, New Delhi.

Jha, D.N. (1988), 'Regional Disparities have widened', in V.S. Mahajan (ed.), *Studies in Indian Planning*, Deep and Deep Publications, New Delhi.

Johnston, B.F. and Clark, W.C. (1982), *Redesigning Rural Development: A Strategic Perspective*, John Hopkins University Press, Baltimore.

Joshi, B.M. (1989), 'Evaluation and Practice of Decentralized Planning in India', *The Indian Journal of Public Administration*, January-March.

Kabra, Kamal Narayan. (1978), *Planning Process in a District*, IIPA, New Delhi.

________, (1984), 'Planning of Plan Implementation', *Indian Journal of Public Administration*, Vol.30 (3).

________, (1989), 'Centre-State Relations and Purposive Decentralized Planning', *Mainstream*, Vol. 27(40), July.

________, (1997), *Development Planning in India*, Sage Publications, New Delhi.

Kamat, A.R. (1974), 'D.R. Gadgil: The Last Phase', *Economic and Political Weekly*, Vol.9 (26).

Kaplan, A. (1973), 'On the Strategy of Social Planning', *Policy Sciences*, Vol.4(1).

Khan, Rasheeduddin. (1992), *Federal India: A Design for Change*, Vikash Publishing House, New Delhi.

Khanna, S.K. and Malhotra, S.L. (1997), *Integrated Rural Development*, Abhinav, New Delhi.

Kohli, Atul. (1987), *The State and Poverty in India*, Orient Longman, Bombay.

________, (1995), *Democracy and Discontent*, Cambridge University Press, U.K.

Korten, David C. (1980), 'Community Organization and Rural Development: A Learning Process Approach' *Public Administration Review*, Vol.40 (5), September-October.

Kothari, Rajni. (1999), 'Isses in Decentralised Governance' in Jha, S.N. and Mathur, P.C. (eds.), *Decentralization and Local Politics,* Sage, New Delhi.

Krishnamachari, V.T. (1962), *Fundamentals of Planning in India,* Orient Longman, Bombay.

Kshire, V.K. (1991), 'Legislative Behaviour and the Reversal of Democratic Decentralization in Maharashtra' in Rakesh Hooja and P.C. Mathur (eds.), *District and Decentralized Planning,* Rawat Publications, Jaipur.

Kurien, C.T. (1968), 'Planning in India: A Theoretical Critique', *Economic and Political Weekly,* Vol. 3(4).

________, (1978), *Poverty Planning and Social Transformation,* Allied Publishers, New Delhi.

Lange, O. (1960), *Essays on Economic Planning,* Asia Publishing House, Bombay.

Leelakumari, P. (1997), *Functioning of Gram Sabhas through 73rd Amendment,* Seminar paper, Institute of Social Sciences, New Delhi, October 21.

Lieten, G.K. (1992), *Continuity and Change in Rural West Bengal,* Sage Publications, New Delhi.

________, (1996), *Development, Devolution and Democracy,* Sage Publications, New Delhi.

Maddick, Henry (1963), *Democracy, Decentralization and Development,* Asia Publishing Company, Bombay.

Maheswari, S.R. (1972), *The Administrative Reforms Commission,* Lakshmi Narain Agarwal, Agra.

________ (1985), *Rural Development in India,* Sage Publications, New Delhi.

Mallick, Ross. (1993), *Development Policy of a Communist Government: West Bengal since1977,* Cambridge University Press, Cambridge.

Marcus, Franda. (1979), *India's Rural Development,* Indiana University Press, USA.

Mathur, Kuldeep. (ed.) (1996), *Development Policy and Administration,* Sage Publications, New Delhi.

Meenakshisundaram, S.S. (1994), *Decentralization in Developing Countries,* Concept Publishing Company, New Delhi.

Mehta, Asok. (1955), *Who Owns India?* Popular Book Depot, Hyderabad.

Minhas, B.S. (1974), *Planning and the Poor,* S. Chand & Company, New Delhi.

Misra, Baidyanath. (1972), *Capitalism, Socialism and Planning,* Oxford & IBH Publishing Co., New Delhi.

Misra, R.P. (1969), *Regional Planning – Concepts Techniques,* Concept Publishing Company, New Delhi.

________ , (ed., 1990), *District Planning – A Handbook,* Concept Publishing Company, New Delhi.

Misra, R.P. (1991), 'On the task of District Planning, in B.N. Yugandhar and A. Mukharjee (eds.), *Reading in Decentralized Planning,* Vol. I, Concept Publishing Company, New Delhi.

________ , (1992), 'Regional Development Planning: Search for Bearings' in R.P. Misra (ed.), *Regional Planning* (revised edition), Concept Publishing Company, New Delhi.

Misra, R.P. and Sundaram, K.V. (1980), *Multi-Level Planning and Integrated Development,* Heritage Publishers, New Delhi.

Mishra, S.N. (1981), *Rural Development and Panchayati Raj,* Concept Publishing Company, New Delhi.

Misra, R.P. and Sundaram, K.V. (1988), *Regional Development,* Heritage Publications, New Delhi.

Mishra, Suryakanta. (1999), *Shreni Dristibhanghite Panchayat,* Calcutta : National Book Agency, p. 103.

Mishra, Sweta (1997), 'Decentralized Planning: Retrospect and Prospect', *Kurukshetra,* June.

Mozoomdar, A. (1996), 'The Rise and Decline of Development Planning in India', in Kuldeep Mathur (ed.), *Development Policy and Administration,* Sage Publications, New Delhi.

Mukarji, Nirmal. (1996), 'Decentralization below the State Level: Need for a 'New System of Governance' in Kuldeep Mathur (ed.), *Development Policy and Administration,* Sage Publications, New Delhi.

________, (1985), 'The Future of District Governance' in *Administrative Arrangements for Rural Development,* National Institute of Rural Development, Hyderabad.

________, (1993), 'Plan from below: Time for Decentralized Governance', *Statesman,* 29 February.

Mukherjee, Amitava. (1992), *Methodology and Database for Decentralized Planning,* Vol. III, Part-A, Part-B & Part-C, Heritage Publishers, New Delhi.

_______, (1990), *Researches in Decentralization,* Heritage Publishers, New Delhi.

Mukhopadhyay, Asok. (1995), *Seminar Paper,* Seminar organized by the Institute of Social Sciences, New Delhi in Calcutta on November 24-25.

Mundle, Sudipta. (1997), *District Planning in India,* Indian Institute of Public Administration, New Delhi.

Myrdal, Gunnar. (1968), *Asian Drama: An Inquiry into Poverty of Nations,* The Penguin Press, London.

Nair, K.R.G. (1982), *Regional Experience in a Development Economy,* Wiley Eastern Limited, New Delhi.

Namboodiripad, E.M.S. (1996), 'A Kerala Experiment: Planning from the Below and Above', *Frontline*, October.

________, (1996), 'From Land Reforms to People's Planning', *People's Democracy,* September 21.

Nanjudappa, D.N. (1991), 'Concepts, Approaches and Techniques of Decentralized Planning' in B.N. Yugandhar and Amitava Mukherjee (ed.), *Readings in Decentralized Planning,* Concept Publishing Company, New Delhi, Vol. I.

Nayyar, Deepak. (1998), 'Economic Development and Political Democracy - Interaction of Economics and Politics in Independent India' *Economic & Political Weekly,* Vol.33, No.49, December.

Pal, Mahi. (1996), 'Participatory Planning, Decentralized Government and the Kerala Panchayat Act', *Seminar Paper,* Institute of Social Sciences, New Delhi, December 9-11.

Palanidurai, K.V. (1993), in Rakesh Hooja and B.Y. Rajes (ed.), *Decentralized Planning in Multi-Level Framework,* Rawat Publications, Jaipur.

Panchyati Raj Update (1997 & 1998), Institute of Social Sciences, New Delhi.

Paranjape, H.K. (1964), *The Planning Commission: A Descriptive Account,* Indian Institute of Public Administration, New Delhi.

Parikh, K. (1986), 'Planning Without Policy', in S. Guhan and M. Shroff (ed.), *Essays on Economic Process and Welfare*, Orient Longman, Madras.

Parkar, R.S. (1972), 'Planning and Politics' in Parker and P.N. Troy (eds.), *The Politics of Urban Growth*, ANU Press, Canberra.

Patel, Himmat (1991), 'Decentralized District Planning in Gujarat' in Rakesh Hooja and P.C. Mathur (eds.), *District Planning*, Rawat Publishers, Jaipur.

Potter, David C. (1986), *India's Political Administrators 1919-83*, Clarendon Press, Oxford.

Pranger, R.J. (1968), *The Eclipse of Citizenship*, Holt, Rinehart & Winston, New York.

Prasad, C.S., 'District Planning: An Approach to Decentralized Planning', *The Administrator*, Vol. 36, July-September 1991.

Prasad, Kamta. (1988), *Planning at the Grassroots*, Sterling Publishers, New Delhi.

Raj, K.N. (1965), *Indian Economic Growth: Performance and Prospects*, Allied Publishers, Bombay.

Rajan M.A.S. (1990), 'District Plans, Monitoring and the Poor – An Administrators Viewpoint', *Indian Journal of Public Administration*, Vol.31 (2), April-June.

Ranga Rao, S.P. (1997), 'Decentralized Planning – the Emerging Scenario', *Kurukshetra*, Vol. XLV(9).

Rao Hanumantha, C.H. (1989), 'Decentralized Planning: An Overview of Experiences and Prospects', *Economic and Political Weekly*, Vol.24 (8).

Rao, V.M. (1988), '*Decentralized Planning: Priority Economic Issues*, Conference Volume, India Economic Association, Calcutta.

Rogaly, B., Harriss - White, B. and Bose, Sugata. (eds.) (1999), *SONAR BANGLA ? Agriculture growth and Agrarian Change in West Bengal and Bangladesh*, Sage, New Delhi.

Roy, Ajit. (1965), *Planning in India : Achievements and Problems*, National Publishers, Calcutta.

Roy, Prodipto and Patil, B. (1977), *Manual for Block Level Planning*, The Macmillan Company, Delhi.

Rudolph, L. and S. Rudolph. (1977), In *Pursuit of Lakshmi: The Poltical Economy of the Indian State*, Chicago University Press, Chicago.

Rudra, Ashok. (1974), *Proceedings of the Inter-regional Seminar on Organization and Administration of Development Planning Agencies*, Vol. I, United Nations, New York.

________, (1975), *Indian Plan Models*, Allied Publishers, Bombay.

Ruud, Arild Engelsen. (1999) 'From untouchable to Communist : Wealth, Power and Status among supporters of the Communist Party (Marxist) in Rural West Bengal', in Rogaly, B., Harriss - White, B. and Bose, Sugata. (eds.) (1999), *Sonar Bangla Agriculture growth and Agrarian Change in West Bengal and Bangladesh*, Sage, New Delhi

Saha, Anamitra and Swaminathan, Madhura. (1994), 'Agricultural Growth in West Bengal in the 1980's', *Economic and Political Weekly*, March 26.

Samaj Jijnasa. (1996), Vidyasagar Centre for Social Sciences, *Inaugural Number*, Midnapore.

Sanyal, Manoj Kumar *et al.* (1998), 'Transitional Change and Output Growth in West Bengal Agriculture – End of Impasse', *Economic and Political Weekly*, Vol. 33 (47 & 48), December 4.

Sarkar, B. *et al.* (1989), *The Myth of Planned Development*, Indian Academy of Social Sciences, New Delhi.

Sarkar, Bikram (1991), 'Decentralized District Planning : West Bengal Scenario' in Rakesh Hooja and P.C. Mathur (eds.), *District and Decentralized Planning*, Rawat Publications, Jaipur.

Sarkar, Goutam K. (1995), *Agriculture and Rural Transformation in India*, OUP, Delhi.

Sarup, Anand and Brahme, Sulabha. (1990), *Planning for the Millions*, Wiley Eastern Limited, New Delhi.

Sathyamurthy, T.V. (1997), *State and Nation in the Context of Social Change*, Oxford India, Paperbacks, New Delhi.

________, (1985), *India Since Independence Centre - State Relations: The Case of Kerala*, Vol.I, Ajanta Publications, New Delhi.

Sengupta, Ramprasad. (1996), 'Planning Institutions and Technical Change: 'A Review of Development Planning in India', in Manabendu Chattopadhyay, *et al. Planning and Economic Policy in India,* Sage Publications, New Delhi.

Sharma, P.N. (1991), 'Decentralized District and Sub-District Planning : Shorting out the Basic Issues' in B.N. Yugandhar and Amitava Mukherjee (eds.), *Readings in Decentralized Planning,* Concept Publishing Comppany, New Delhi.

Sheela Varghese and Rejimon, P.M. (2001), 'People's Campaign for Decentralised Planning : An Assessment', *Mainstream.*

Simon, H.A. (1957), *Administrative Behaviour,* The Free Press, New York.

Sinha, Arun. (1990), 'Decentralized District Planning : The Indian Experience' in R.P. Misra (ed.), *District Planning : A Handbook,* Concept Publishing Company, New Delhi.

Somsekhara, N.S. (1985), *State Planning in India : Techniques, Procedures and Management,* Himalaya Publishing House, New Delhi, Vol.II.

Sridharan, L. (1990), 'Coordination in Development Administration', *Indian Journal of Public Administration,* Vol.36(2), April-June.

Srivastava, K.B. (1990), 'Management of Rural Development in India : The Case of Decentralized Planning', *Journal of Rural Development,* Vol.9(2), March.

Sukthankar, D.M. and Sundaram, P.S.A. (1987), *India Country Paper,* Asian Development Bank, Manila.

Sundaram, K.V. (1989), 'Multi-level Planning: Concepts, Principles and some Aspects of its application of Sectoral Planning' in Sundaram, Ramesh and Tiwari (eds.), *Regional Planning and Development,* Heritage Publishers, New Delhi, Vol.I.

Sundaram, K.V. (1990), 'Determining the Sectoral Matrix for Integrated Development' in R.P. Misra (ed.), *District Planning – A Handbook,* Concept Publishing Company, New Delhi.

________, (1997), *Decentralized Multi-level Planning,* Concept Publishing Company, New Delhi.

Thaha, M. (1991), 'Database for Decentralized Planning' in B.N. Yugandhar and Amitava Mukherjee (eds.), *Readings in*

Decentralized Planning, Concept Publishing Company, New Delhi.

Thavaraj, M.J.K. (1984), 'Decentralized, Planning and People's Participation, *Mainstream*, April 14.

________, (1994), 'Politics of Planning', *Indian Journal of Public Administration*, Vol.30(3), July-September.

Tiwary, K.N. (1970), 'Planning at the State and District Level', *Indian Journal of Public Administration*, Vol.15(4), October-December.

Turner, Mark and Hulme, David. (1997), *Governance, Administration & Development Making the State Work*, Macmillan Press, London.

Uphoff, N.T. (1979), *Feasibility and Application of Rural Development Participation*, Cornell University Press, U.K.

Valk, P. De and Wekwete, K.H. (eds.) (1990), *Decentralizing for Participatory Planning?* Aldershot, U.S.A.

Webster, Neil. (1992), *Panchayati Raj in the Decentralization of Development Planning in West Bengal*, K.P. Bagchi & Co., Calcutta.

________, (1992), '*Panchayati Raj in West Bengal : Popular Participation for the People or the Party? Develop-ment and Change*, Sage Publications, New Delhi, Vol.23(4).

________ , (1999), 'Institutions, Actors and Strategies in West Bengal's Rural Development — A Study on Irrigation', in Rogaly, B., Harriss - White, B., and Bose, Sugata. (eds.) (1999), *Sonar Bangla? Agricultural Growth and Agrarian Change in West Bengal and Bangladesh, Sage, New Delhi* .

Wekwete, K.H. (1990), 'Constraints to Planning for Socialism in Zimbabwe' in P.De. Valk and K.H. Wekwete (eds.) *Decentralizing for Participatory Planning?* Aldershot, U.S.A.

Westergaard, Kristen. (1987), 'Marxist Government and People's Participation : The Case of West Bengal' *Journal of Social Studies*, Bangladesh, No.38.

Yugandhar, B.N. and Mukherjee, Amitava. (1991), *Readings in Decentralized Planning*, Vol. I & II, Heritage Publishers, New Delhi.

PERIODICALS AND NEWAPAPERS

Administrator.
Economic And Political Weekly.
Indian Journal of Public Administration.
Journal of Rural Development.
Journal of Indian Political Science Association.
Kurukshetra.
Mainstream.
Nagarlok.
Panchayati Raj Update.
West Bengal Political Science Review.
World Development.
The Ananda Bazar Patrika.
The Asian Age.
The Chhapa Khabar (Local Daily).
The Ganashakti.
The Harijan.
The Hindustan Times,
The Biplabi Sabyasachi (Local Daily).
The Statesman.
The Telegraph.
The Tribune.

INDEX